M000247962

FontFont is the type library published by
FSI FontShop International, Berlin.

Made with FontFont
Type for independent minds

edited by

Jan Middendorp

Erik Spiekermann

BIS Publishers

© 2006
FontShop International, BIS Publishers and the authors

Concept   Jan Middendorp, Erik Spiekermann
Design   UDN | United Designers Network
Layout   Susanna Dulkinys, Jan Middendorp, Erik Spiekermann
Cover   Strange Attractors
Typefaces   FF Meta Headline, FF Meta and most other FontFonts
Translations   Jan Middendorp
Proofreading   Charles Clawson, Emily Smith

Publisher   BIS Publishers
                     Herengracht 370–372
                     1016 CH Amsterdam
                     Postbus 323
                     1000 AH Amsterdam
                     The Netherlands
                     T +31 (0)20 524 7560
                     F +31 (0)20 524 7557
                     bis@bispublishers.nl
                     www.bispublishers.nl

In cooperation with FSI FontShop International
                     Bergmannstraße 102
                     10961 Berlin
                     Germany
                     T +49 (0)30 693 7022
                     F +49 (0)30 692 8443
                     www.fontfont.com

ISBN-10: 90-6369-129-7
ISBN-13: 978-90-6369-129-5

All rights reserved.
No part of this publication may be reproduced
or transmitted in any form or by any means,
electronic or mechanical, including photocopy,
recording or any information storage and
retrieval system, without permission in writing
from the copyright owners.

Printed in Singapore

To all type designers,
everywhere,
but above all to those
who trusted us to publish their work
and who, collectively,
have made this the coolest
type library I know.

Erik Spiekermann

To the memory of
Evert Bloemsma (1958–2005),
colleague, critic, and friend.

Jan Middendorp

| 18 | | 120 | | 150 | |

① **Thinking FontFont**

② **Talking FontFont**

③ **Making FontFont**

Contents

Foreword

✎ Erik Spiekermann   set in FF Meta Pro
                (with Discretionary Ligatures switched on)

HOW DO YOU celebrate fifteen years of FontFonts? Give away free fonts? Organise a party? Publish a book?

Well, we wouldn't be designers if the idea of a book wouldn't have been the most appealing. Little did we know what we had got ourselves in for: we not only thought we could do this easily, but also quickly and on time. Not to mention within the budget. A familiar plight to us designers, and yet we keep thinking it can be done. We also know that we could (and perhaps should) have spent even more time on getting files in order, checking line-breaks, making sure all our spreads and chokes were correct and hundreds of PMS colours would print as 4c.

Fifteen years ago we had no idea that one day we could fill a 352-page book with showings of FontFonts. In fact, we're not exactly certain when the library was officially launched. Jan Middendorp writes in his introduction on the following pages that Neville and myself 'created' a new library of digital type. While, normally, I hate the c-word, we certainly didn't plan very much, relying on our intuition instead.

There was no budget, no timetable, no business plan – not a spreadsheet in sight. We just knew all these great designers who now had the tools to do their own type, while we had the tool for distributing them through FontShop. We also knew that we were not the only designers who were ready for alternatives to Helvetica, Times and even Garamond.

All the early FontFont designers were practising graphic designers, not full-time type designers, and they all *used* type every day. We didn't have to do market research to find out what we needed. Our claim 'a library from designers for designers' was simply stating a fact.

Meanwhile, more than fifteen years later, I have 3524 FontFonts activated in my font library, and that may not be the latest number. While I'm quoting numbers: this book contains 540 illustrations, counted as links in my InDesign folders. Those include most specimen pages only as *one* illustration, so the real number of individual images that show off our typefaces must be in the thousands.

The work that friends and colleagues have put into the specimen pages and the articles is tremendous – it is incredible that we got all this work just by asking for it. I see it as proof of the fact that the FontFont library still reflects what we designers want and require.

One thing needs pointing out about the articles:

Jan collected the material from many sources, and most of the articles were written years ago. We did not do any major editing of content, so they may occasionally mention facts that have been superseded by time and, sometimes, reality.

The people who 'officially' produced this book are all credited properly on the previous pages. The many other contributors are mentioned in the final section, from page 348, in alphabetical order. We all share an emotional approach to type: for us, it is more than a tool to do our work with. We *love* type, and we think that this book shows our affection and enthusiasm for all things typographical.

The mistakes are all my fault.

Jan Middendorp   set in FF Meta Pro

When the FontFont type library was founded in 1990, it provided a meaningful alternative to what was then available to graphic designers.
Over time, FontFont has grown to become one of the most influential players in the type world; it is now a large library among several others. But some of the initial pioneering spirit has remained intact.

A very young Just van Rossum with the first Random Fonts.

The first Font-Font brochures, smaller than a cigarette pack, by Erik Spieker-mann.

THE LATE 1980s were an era of unprecedented changes in the world of typography. A new technology – desktop publishing – had recently been introduced and quickly gained popularity. More and more designers and pre-press studios began offering in-position typesetting on a Macintosh computer using Aldus (later Adobe) PageMaker software. In a mere five or six years the scene was to change dramatically, in terms of distribution and technology as well as design. Those design and printing companies that still relied on conventional typesetting, paying specialized firms by the centimetre for slips of text, soon found out that continuing to do so was bad for business; the most forward-looking among them had already begun buying PostScript fonts for their own use. Soon a font would cost about as much, or as little, as a few sheets of set text had cost before.

The type business, however, was slow in catching up. Throughout the 1980s the main players in the typographic world had been a handful of manufacturers who had struggled their way through the quick transition from photographic to digital technologies: Monotype, Linotype, Berthold, Hell. All these firms were still developing digital stand-alone typesetting systems which used dedicated font technologies; specialized type production firms such as ITC, URW and Bitstream provided fonts that were customized for each machine. After the advent of Adobe PostScript (a digital page description language developed to streamline the exchange between computers and printing devices), type manufacturers began converting their fonts to the new system. Few, however, realized that the new technology involved new dimensions and a different relationship with customers – and therefore a different mentality. Although the actual production cost of a single copy of a font went down to the price of a diskette, companies continued packaging and marketing their typefaces as if they were still major investments. Yet the quality of the ty   pe did not always justify such presumption. A lot of the typefaces in the catalogues had been handed down from the metal era to phototypesetting to digital systems to PostScript, losing part of their character and integrity with each conversion. The new technologies called for new typefaces, but most type foundries reacted conservatively, even arrogantly, to proposals from younger designers.

Type designers were among the first to realize it was time for a change. Two of the first firms specializing in digital type design and production, Bitstream and Emigre, had been founded by designers. In the Netherlands, young type designers began organizing themselves in order to exchange information about type production and juridical matters. Then, in 1990, a big change happened. In March of that year Adobe Systems decided to release the specifications of its PostScript Type 1 font format (which had been proprietary software up to then), hoping to turn it into a worldwide standard. This opened up possibilities for every designer to make fonts with simple, affordable font design software.

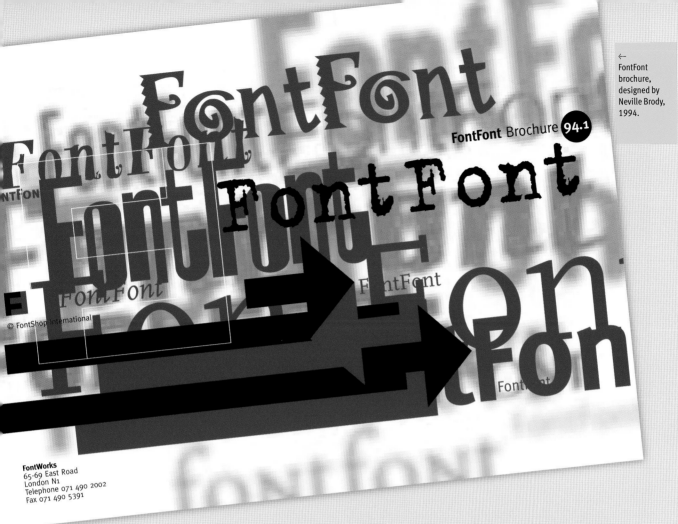

FontFont Brochure **94.1**

© FontShop International

FontWorks
65-69 East Road
London N1
Telephone 071 490 2002
Fax 071 490 5391

FontFont
brochure,
designed by
Neville Brody,
1994.

Never before had type designers had the freedom, the autonomy and the control they were to have from that moment onwards.

FontShop: from distribution to production

The year 1990 was also when designers Erik Spiekermann (Berlin) and Neville Brody (London) created a new library of digital type: FontFont, to be distributed through Spiekermann's firm FontShop, which up to then had limited itself to distributing fonts from other foundries. A separate company, FontShop International (FSI) was founded to act as font publisher.

Erik Spiekermann was one of the very few typographic designers in Germany who operated internationally. He had founded MetaDesign, a Berlin corporate design company that would soon establish offices in London and San Francisco. He had designed typefaces for Berthold AG in Germany and occasionally worked as typographic consultant for Adobe, a Silicon Valley software company that had its own type program. He was also well informed about the activities of recently founded American companies such as Bitstream – the first type foundry specialized in digital type – and Emigre Graphics in California. Every time Spiekermann crossed the Atlantic he carried a shopping list from typographer friends in Europe, instructing him as to which new digital typefaces to buy

(they came on floppy disks and diskettes at the time, of course). Most of these emerging type collections did not have a European distributor. It was his wife, Joan Spiekermann Sargent, who suggested to Erik that by stepping into that niche, the type shopping expeditions could be replaced by a real business. So in 1989, the Spiekermanns founded FontShop, Europe's first distributor of type produced for desktop computers; as the slogan went, their activities were performed 'by designers, for designers'.

Graphic designer Neville Brody, one of Spiekermann's London friends, was at the height of his success in the late 1980s, having been the subject of a major exhibition at the Victoria and Albert Museum and of a successful monograph (*The graphic language of Neville Brody* by Jon Wozencroft, the world's best selling design book). Brody had drawn dozens of alphabets, notably as art director for *The Face* magazine, and had published a few fonts at a major foundry. However, he had not been pleased with the limited control he had over his work and was eager to find new opportunities.

The type library which Brody and Spiekermann envisaged was to have its own design-oriented philosophy; it would be curated and marketed in a way that was distinctly different from what other companies were doing.

When FontFont made its first appearance, it created somewhat of a splash in the type world, and was inevitably scorned by traditional vendors. The collection was in fact like no other. It had some points in common with Emigre – mainly in that it was a library of new fonts by, largely, young designers – but its scope and ambitions were different. While the Emigre library essentially represented the cutting-edge view of two people, Zuzana Licko and Rudy Vanderlans, FontFont was multiform right from the start. It set out to provide type in many different styles and for many purposes: the historically inspired alongside the contemporary; experimental and unorthodox 'fun fonts' alongside business-like and pragmatic text faces. And unlike most other libraries, FontFont seldom, if ever, published re-releases of fonts that had been previously available for other technologies.

Unreleased fonts

The FontFont type library was off to a flying start, releasing dozens of remarkable families during its first years. With hindsight, it is amazing how things fell into place within such a brief timespan. Intuition, passion, attitude and serendipity – rather than a carefully calculated master plan – were major factors contributing to FontFont's early expansion.

Both Spiekermann and Brody had unreleased typefaces from the 1980s waiting in the wings; Brody had several hand-drawn alphabets that could be expanded into complete fonts. Among the early FontFonts based on this work were FF Typeface Four, Six and Seven, iconic faces of the early 1990s, and the FF Tyson/Tokyo series. FF Blur, the first typeface by Brody that explored the specific aesthetics of digital typography, became even more successful. And then there was Spiekermann's FF Meta. Named after Spiekermann's design firm MetaDesign, the font was based on a typeface that Spiekermann had drawn in the mid-1980s for the Deutsche Bundespost – although it had never been adopted by the client. While Brody's faces represented the trendy, display-oriented side of the FontFont library, FF Meta epitomized the pragmatic, conventional-yet-modern aspect. Meta became an instant classic and has remained the best selling FontFont to date.

↑
Just van Rossum and Erik van Blokland were in Berlin when the Wall came down, November 1989.

⟶
FF Dolores by Tobias Frere-Jones, 1991, one of the first FontFont releases,

↘
The original FontFont logo by Neville Brody. It was later changed to yellow and black.

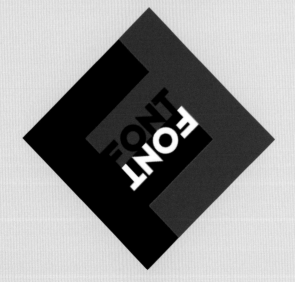

12

Parallel to FontFont, Neville Brody developed another project with co-editors Jon Wozencroft and John Critchley. FUSE, published by FSI, took the idea of innovation in typography one step further, to a place where functionality was not an issue any more. FUSE was a series of experimental typefaces and posters; each issue was conceived around a theme, which was contributed to by a host of type designers and graphic designers, many of whom did not have a direct relationship to the FontFont library.

International connections

One of the factors which made possible the rapid growth and diversification of the FontFont library was Brody's and Spiekermann's international, informal network of design professionals. Spiekermann has many business relationships and friendships in international typographic circles – notably in the Association International Typographique (ATypI). Moreover, his company MetaDesign had become a fast-growing studio which attracted some of the best young typographic talents from Germany and abroad. Brody was well-placed to convince some of the best talents in British typography to step on board. Among the other people who contributed to Font-Font's internationalization was Ed Cleary, a Toronto-based Brit who was one of the main players in the Canadian type world, ran FontShop Canada and made important contributions to the early editions of FSI's FontBook, until his untimely death in 1995. Cleary brought unorthodox Toronto designers such as Paul Sych and Barbara Klunder into the FontFont library. Other North American contacts included the founders of Boston's Font Bureau, David Berlow and Roger Black; Black got involved in the creation of an Italian branch of the FontShop network and Berlow was, among other things, a collaborator on the digitization of Brody's alphabets. Berlow also introduced Tobias Frere-Jones, who published his very first typeface as a FontFont – the lively, charming FF Dolores.

A key contribution to FontFont's early growth was made by a group of young Dutch designers, many of whom studied at the Royal Academy of Arts (KABK) in The Hague. The typographer-craftsman-type historian Gerrit Noordzij had established an influential type programme here. Spiekermann hired The Hague graduates Just van Rossum, Erik van Blokland, and later Luc(as) de Groot, as assistants for his corporate type projects at MetaDesign. It was the time when Spiekermann postulated, half-jokingly, that 'every design studio in Germany needs its Dutchman.'

A type project by Van Rossum and Van Blokland (who called themselves LettError, or LetTerror, depending on the mood) kick-started the type library. While working at MetaDesign in 1989, they began experimenting with the PostScript Type 3 technology in order to spice up digital type design. They wanted to bring back the liveliness of metal type by introducing a random function into digital typography. The result was Beowolf, 'the world's first randomfont', equipped with a built-in algorithm that unpredictably modifies the outlines of each character while sending it to the printing device. Whereas the Dutch twosome saw it as pure experiment

Record sleeve by Neville Brody, featuring his own Typeface 6.

– and found the results rather ugly – their colleagues at Meta-Design were enthusiastic about Beowolf's graphic possibilities. Spiekermann decided to publish the font, even before the idea of the FontFont collection had materialized. Initially Beowolf was not thought of as the start of a new collection; instead, it served to draw attention to FontShop as a smart, trend-conscious distribution firm.

Once the FontFont library was up and running, the Dutch connection made sure there was a fast growing offer of high-quality typefaces in a wide range of genres. Apart from the designers from The Hague – initially the LettError duo and Peter Verheul, later Luc(as) de Groot and Albert-Jan Pool – there were three designers trained at the Arnhem Academy who contributed some of the most striking text faces of the era: Martin Majoor's FF Scala, Fred Smeijers's FF Quadraat, and Evert Bloemsma's FF Balance. One of Holland's most outspoken and iconoclast graphic designers was also recruited by FontFont: Max Kisman, a pioneer of computer-aided graphic design, contributed fonts originally created for magazines such as *Language Technology*, the forerunner of *Wired*.

Kisman and LettError, especially, used their digital tools to break new ground. Kisman's Fudoni was one of the very first cut-and-paste type hybrids; LettError experimented with self-changing type but also made a series of 'found fonts' such as FF Trixie (a typewriter font), FF Hands (digitized handwriting) and FF InstantTypes, based on toy stamp letters and the like. Many of these 'novelty fonts' now seem part of a short-lived fashion, but at the time they were genuinely original. No one had done it before and many would imitate them, so that, with hindsight, each of these fonts heralded a new genre.

Local contacts

MetaDesign Berlin, having developed into Germany's most prominent hothouse of corporate design, attracted many talented designers in the early to mid-1990s; several of them designed typefaces, either within the firm or after hours, which were welcomed to the FontFont catalogue. One such MetaDesigner was Italian-born Alessio Leonardi, who later joined xplicit in Frankfurt and went on to start his own company.

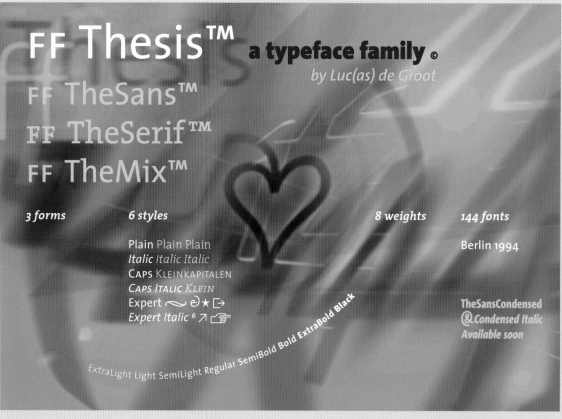

1994: First
showing of
FF Thesis;
with 144
weights the
largest type
family at the
time.

FF Thesis™ a typeface family ©

by Luc(as) de Groot

FF TheSans™
FF TheSerif™
FF TheMix™

3 forms

6 styles

Plain Plain Plain
Italic Italic Italic
Caps Kleinkapitalen
Caps Italic Klein
Expert
Expert Italic 6

8 weights

144 fonts

Berlin 1994

TheSansCondensed
@Condensed Italic
Available soon

ExtraLight Light SemiLight Regular SemiBold Bold ExtraBold Black

---

Better known for his hilarious cartoons than for the serious corporate design which he is also capable of doing, Leonardi contributed a large number of entertaining hand-drawn and computer-processed fonts to the library. Another early contributor of unorthodox fonts was Fabian Rottke, designer of FF Ekktor and a number of Dirty Faces, and now a senior designer at Spiekermann's firm United Designers Network. Berlin-born Martin Wenzel was not at MetaDesign directly but worked in the same building: in the early 1990s he was a young typesetter at the Meta-affiliated CitySatz. As a neighbour of FSI and MetaDesign, Wenzel had little trouble finding a publisher for his well-made early display fonts, such as FF Marten and FF Rekord. After having met Meta's Dutch designers, who had all graduated from the KABK in The Hague, Wenzel decided to travel to the Netherlands and study there in order to learn how to design a real text font. Years later the result was published as FF Profile, a sans serif made for legibility.

In the mid-1990s, Dutchman Luc(as) de Groot was Meta's type director. He drew corporate typefaces for Volkswagen and other Meta clients. In the evening hours and weekends he worked on what became the Thesis family, consisting of three sub-families (TheSans, TheSerif and TheMix) and eight weights – 176 fonts in all. Large families with different styles had been published before (e.g. Rotis), but never in such a consistent manner and in such a wide range of weights, including small caps and different sorts of numerals for each variety. At the time of publication in 1994 it was the largest ditigal font family ever. Five years later De Groot decided to start distributing his own fonts, withdrawing his designs from the FontFont library.

Italian Albert Pinggera came to Berlin to become De Groot's assistant at Meta Design. He was commissioned to redesign Letter Gothic as part of FSI's program of revamped 'industrial' sans-serifs. He then decided to take up studying advanced type design at the KABK in The Hague, after which he designed a much more personal typeface, the beautiful FF Strada.

Erik Spiekermann, MetaDesign's founder, has always relied on help from more patient designers for finishing and producing his typefaces. In the mid-1990s, Ole Schäfer became his main accomplice. Some of the Spiekermann FontFonts – parts of the FF Meta family, FF Govan, FF Info – were co-designed by Schäfer, who set up shop for himself a few years ago.

Today, Spiekermann works with a transatlantic assistant: American Christian Schwartz, who spent three months as an in-house type designer at MetaDesign Berlin in 1999. Schwartz, a freelance type designer, has worked with Spiekermann on FF Unit and FF Bau as well as the corporate typefaces for the German Railways and Bosch. Hamburg-born Johannes Erler briefly worked at MetaDesign before founding his own company, Factor Design. He designed two packages of pictograms, FF Care Pack and FF Dingbats, of which the latter has become one of the library's long sellers. Among the other former MetaDesigners who contributed to the library are Henning Krause (Magda Clean, with Berlin designer Critzler) and Jürgen Huber, who was type director at MetaDesign and made FF Ginger and FF Plus.

artwork by Gordon Protz

FF
Providence

AIRCRAFT

FF Providence by Guy Jeffrey Nelson, 1994.

Stealth, part of FUSE Classics, by Malcolm Garrett, 1991.

FF Angie by Jean-François Porchez, 1995.

FF Aircraft, part of the FF Bastille Display package, by Albert Boton, 2002.

ANGIE,

WHEN WILL those **clouds** all *disappear*?

The British and French connections

Neville Brody's London contacts also yielded a number of highly original FontFont designers. John Critchley was a co-editor of Brody's FUSE series and went on to become head of MTV's print design department. He collaborated with illustrator Darren Raven on the delightful and smart FF Bokka and digitized the handwriting of many children for FF Child's Play. Swiss-born Cornel Windlin was an assistant of Brody's and later became his successor as art director of *The Face*. Working both individually and with his long-time typographic partner, Stephan Müller, Windlin designed a number of Font-Fonts based on 'found' alphabets originally made for specific technologies. Rian Hughes, another prominent designer on the London scene, published about half a dozen families as part of the FontFont library before founding his own company Device Fonts. Many of his fonts recall the unmistakable style of his famous vector illustrations. One British designer who established a long-time relationship with FSI is David Crow of Manchester. He participated in the fuse series and put forward his original ideas on signs and typographic signifiers as a lecturer at the fuse conferences organized by FSI. He designed only one FontFont – FF Beadmap, made with artist Ian Wright – but has made an important contribution to the quality of the library as a member of its Type Board.

There has been a French Connection as well. FF Angie, published in 1995, was one of the first text faces to come out of a new wave in French type design. Its maker was Jean-François Porchez, who went on to become one of the most outspoken representatives of the French type world and quickly established his successful 'Typofonderie Porchez.' He is now the chairman of the typographers' association ATypI. It

was through Porchez that FSI came into contact with a prolific young voice in French type design: Xavier Dupré, who had worked as type director of a Paris packaging design agency but had also researched renaissance writing with one of the grand old men of French type design, Ladislas Mandel. In less than five years Dupré published seven families in the FontFont library – from tasty display faces such as FF Tartine Script to highly original text faces like FF Absara and FF Megano.

Dupré's older colleague Albert Boton has been at it a little longer. His type designing career, although he did not publish his first FontFont until 2002, spans five decades: in 1957 he worked under Adrian Frutiger on Univers and later designed such classics as Eras and Elan. Boton, born in 1932, has now retired from his day job at an advertising agency but has been immensely prolific since. In a few years time he produced six families of text and display faces, all published as FontFonts. Pierre di Sciullo, finally, is a special case within the French type world. He is a graphic designer, writer, organiser and editor; each of his typefaces is a philosophical statement and/or thing to play with rather than a neutral tool. To the FontFont library he contributed FF Minimum, a series of alphabets based on a grid of squares; but it's the witty variants, from 'ceiling' (Plafond) and 'floor' (Sol) to 'drunk' (Ivre), which make the family such fun.

Stylistic exercises

If the substance of the FontFont library lies in its innovative yet practical text typefaces, from the ubiquitous, straight-faced FF Meta to the poetic, vulnerable FF Maiola, part of its unity lies in the broad range of experiments and exercises it has accomodated over the years. There is probably no other type

FontFont Library

http://www.fontfont.de

846
typographic
geometric
amorphous
ironic
historic
intelligent
handwritten
destructive fonts &
pi + symbols

5/96

collection that has so many 'firsts' – and made so many contributions to the ongoing discussion about the forms and functions of digital type.

Di Sciullo's Minimum is just one example; there have been other highly personal, one-off experiments. FF Disturbance by Jeremy Tankard is a take on the 'universal' alphabet with no separate upper- and lowercase. What was once the Holy Grail of Modernist typography became a stylish, clasically inspired postmodern exercise in Tankard's hands. The package FUSE Classics brought together some of the more usable typefaces that came out of the FUSE project. Moonbase Alpha is a space-age modular alphabet by Cornel Windlin. Malcolm Garrett, a central figure in British

graphic design, made FF Stealth: a minimalist geometric alphabet set in a mosaic of squares. Phil Baines, a typographer as well as researcher and author, examined the outer limits of legibility in his FUSE font CanYouReadMe?. By the time it was re-released as a FontFont, it had already been used effectively by many graphic designers – and so its name was changed to the affirmative FF YouCan(ReadMe). Pierre di Sciullo's FF ScratchedOut is a damaged variety of FF Minimum that tests the reader's ability (and willingness) to decode bitmap patterns and put the letters back together again.

Many tendencies and techniques in 1990s type design were pioneered by FontFont designers. Layered fonts such as FF Kipp, FF Identification and FF Advert Rough were made to create multicoloured typographic constructions. FF Dot Matrix, Screen Matrix and other bitmap fonts allowed designers to project the anti-aesthetics of electronic displays onto the printed page. FF Childs Play, FF Providence, FF Dolores, FF Priska and many others explored the allure of the hand-drawn and the hand-written in an informal and personal way that had hardly been practised before. The Dirty Faces packages, edited by Brody, were Font-Font's contribution to grunge typography, as were such diverse and individualist inventions as FF Double Dutch and the FF Steel family. Equally individualist were many of the 'alphabets' of symbols, drawings and dingbats which provided the not-so-talented-draughtsmen within the graphic design world with bags of tricks to spice up their work.

Although FontFont was never about reviving older typefaces, a number of fonts in the collection were actually based on historical alphabets – either printing types or hand-written ones found in manuscripts. Manfred Klein and Jürgen Brinckmann's FF Scribe Type series were painstakingly distilled from these ancient examples.

Type classification

As the collection grew, repeated attempts were made to classify its wide range of typefaces in a way that would make sense to the user while throwing into relief the unorthodox aspects of the library. Type classification has become an increasingly problematic exercise as the freedom of designers has grown and the number of possible variants on the letterform exploded.

Older classification systems are deeply rooted in the past and strongly biased towards serifed book types. To the present-day user, to define the difference between early and late Venetian styles is definitely less essential than to have a basic understanding of the differences between, say, FF Meta and FF Scala Sans; and this is where traditional systems fail. In display type, the situation is even more serious. Since 1990 there has been a new trend about every two years, each bringing with it several new sub-categories which might be given names that might sound something like Forward-Moving Extended Semi-Geometric Mostly-Sans Faux-Italic (FF Blocker and

↑
FiFFteen, the exhibition featuring 15 years of FontFonts; curator Jan Middendorp, designed by UDN. FUSE section curated by Neville Brody/Research Studios
←····
Banners designed, programmed and random-generated by Erik van Blokland.

FF Overdose could fall into this category, a sub-genre of 'Techno'). All these 'unusual' letterforms are now mostly dumped into a group called 'Other'.

FSI – that is, Spiekermann with marketing manager/writer Jürgen Siebert – came up with totally new categories for unusual faces: the 1996 FontFont catalogue offered no less than seven classes of display fonts, several of which were given names that were new to the type world: 'ironic', 'amorphous', 'intelligent', 'destructive' (in a way, more like a classification of designers' intentions than of forms). On the other hand, the text typefaces that in traditional systems are so carefully categorized, were simply grouped under 'Typographic'.

To some extent, this has helped to draw attention to the 'otherness' of contemporary digital type. In subsequent catalogues the number of categories was drastically reduced, but some of the novel and somewhat ambiguous terms remained. What began as a kind of in-joke, or tongue-in-cheek pseudo-typology, became the basis of something simpler and presumably more usable — but is certainly not yet definitive. And of course it shouldn't be, in a field which is continuously moving and developing. It is amazing how a discpline such as type design, which must necessarily limit itself to creating minimal (and if not minimal, then audacious) variations of a given code, can still reinvent itself continuously. The recent publication of such a novel invention as Evert Bloemsma's FF Legato – which invests sans-serif forms with new legibility qualitities – suggests that the end is not in sight. There will always be room for new thoughts in type.

An exhibition and a book

In late 2004, FontShop International first presented a travelling exhibition titled 'FiFFteen: 15 years of type for independent minds'. The exhibition, celebrating the FontFont type library as well as the experimental FUSE project, premiered in London in November and subsequently travelled to Manchester, Berlin, New York and Helsinki, where it was shown during the annual ATypI conference. In early 2006, stops were made in The Hague (where Erik Spiekermann was celebrated as winner of the prestigious Gerrit Noordzij prize) and Antwerp. Later that year, the exhibition went to Bologna, Barcelona, Valencia and Goa (!).

We never had any hope of finishing a full-size catalogue in time for the exhibition. Instead, we took our time to collect existing material and commission pages from writers and designers. Making a book about FontFont was an ideal occasion to dig up (and edit) some interesting writing that had previously been published in printed and online magazines or as part of limited-edition books. It also enabled us to ask a host of eminent designers – FontFont designers as well as typographers from several parts of the world – to contribute words and images. The diversity of what they have come up with is staggering. The result is a unique collection of type specimens and visual essays that is as rich and multi-layered as the FontFont collection itself.

Many thanks to you all. ⊕

Post Mortem, pre-Meta. **Erik Spiekermann**

Is Best really Better? **Erik van Blokland and Just van Rossum**

LettError. **Emily King**

Type, Geometry, Construction. **Jan Middendorp**

Max Kisman. **Emily King**

FF Quadraat: Legibility, versatility, flamboyance. **Fred Smeijers**

Infographics.
Erik Spiekermann

The Nexus
Principle.
Martin Majoor

| 20 | 24 | 28 | 34 | 44 | 50 | 54 | 58 |

Thinking FontFont
An anthology of essays and type critiques

Post Mortem, pre-Meta:
or how I once designed a typeface for Europe's biggest company

Erik Spiekermann
1985

set in FF Meta Pro

In 1991 *Meta Bleifrei**, the corporate typeface of Erik Spiekermann's company MetaDesign, became FF Meta. The first sans-serif intended for corporate communication within the FontFont collection, it soon became the library's best selling type family.
Before becoming *Meta Bleifrei*, the font had been something else: the PT typeface.
The following article, written at a time when the PT typeface was still buried in a drawer, describes the pre-history of FF Meta.

* lead-free

NAME, LOGO, COLOUR and typeface – these are the basic elements of any corporate design system. Once the first three of these elements have been defined or, indeed, designed, the fourth hardly ever presents a problem. In Germany, the fourth element has got to be Helvetica. And if it isn't Helvetica, Univers just might be allowed. If a company wants to look more traditional and considers a serif face, one usually chooses Times New Roman.

When Sedley Place Design in Berlin was commissioned to develop a corporate identity for the West German Post Office – Deutsche Bundespost – it became clear right from the start that this time Helvetica did not fit the bill: being used by too many other companies because of its 'neutral' appearance, it would fail to distinguish the Bundespost on this very basic level.

One of the reasons so many companies have chosen Helvetica as their corporate typeface is that it is perhaps the most widely available typeface today. This availability has, however, been achieved at the expense of recognizability. There are so many weights, versions, legal and illegal adaptations and so many other almost identical typefaces, that in specifying simply 'Helvetica' one ends up with a range of 'almost right' and 'not quite right' solutions. The result is visual chaos instead of one typeface serving as the common denominator of all corporate communications.

Since Helvetica first appeared in the late fifties, the typesetting and printing industries have been subject to a series of technical changes, if not revolutions. Poor Helvetica was never intended for use in very small sizes, set on low-resolution CRT-setters and printed on rough, recycled papers. It was also never meant as a space-saving typeface for listings, tables or telephone books. Condensing it electronically to fit a given space also doesn't help much to enhance the original design, which was made to give a generous and even appearance.

Faced with all these arguments – and considering the fact that today it is possible to go straight from fairly rough artwork into digitisation via the Ikarus software, thus saving enormous time and cost – the Bundespost gave Sedley Place Design the go-ahead for the development of an exclusive type design based on the necessities of its corporate design program.

Original diskette for in-house use of the Meta-Design corporate typeface, 1991.

Hamburg
Hamburg
Hamburg
Hamburg

burg
burg

B D H

a b c d e g h i l

m n o p r s t u

1 4 5

Deutsche Bundespost

Dorothea geht mit Hammer und Degen
Dorothea geht mit Hammer und Degen

Dorothea geht mit Hammer und Degen
Dorothea geht mit Hammer und Degen

Dorothea geht mit Hammer und Degen
Dorothea geht mit Hammer und Degen

Dorothea geht mit Hammer und Degen
Dorothea geht mit Hammer und Degen

Sketches for the Bundespost typeface PT55 by Erik Spiekermann at Sedley Place Design's Berlin office, 1985.

The brief

A typeface for Europe's biggest employer (with more than 500,000 employees) has to do more than look pretty. It has to work pretty hard. Rather than going for attractive novelty, we decided that it needed to be:

- very legible, particularly in small sizes and with the special requirement of facilitating the finding of names and figures;
- used for reading extensive amounts of copy;
- neutral, not fashionable, trendy or nostalgic;
- identical on all typesetting systems;
- available from all typesetters in the country at very short notice and at reasonable cost;
- economical in its application, i.e., space-saving;
- designed in clearly distinguishable weights;
- distinct and unmistakable;
- technically up-to-date.

Practical circumstances

When one designs type, particular problems present themselves when the typeface is meant for printing under difficult circumstances, such as: rough, thin or otherwise problematic paper stock; the coarse resolution of high-speed type-setting systems; uneven inking; extremely small type sizes; minimum line feed to save space; and finally, as in listings of all sorts, the occurrence of line after line of similar word shapes. These adverse conditions can be counteracted only by technical and aesthetic manipulations during the design process. Pretty shapes viewed at large sizes are thus less important than the fact that individual characters must work well within words and fulfil their purpose within the constraints of that particular brief. Specially designed faces such as Matthew Carter's Bell Centennial, developed for telephone books, show that solutions can be found for such clearly defined problems.

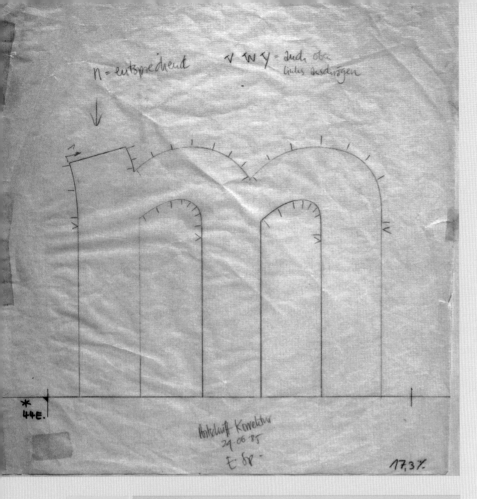

"Artwork" –
Drawing of a
character from
the PT typeface
for digitization
using the
Ikarus system.

--->

Postcard-size
forms, before
and after:
below shows
a redesigned
form, set in the
new typeface
for comparison.

The concept

In order to define the typeface's task, instead of relying on individual inspiration by gifted artists, we analysed six families of faces to see what they have in common and how far one can deviate one way or the other.

After having measured various proportions such as x-height, stroke thickness to cap height, average width, dimensions of ascenders, descenders and figures as well as having looked at critical shapes – letters which are easily mistaken for each other and the relationship between white space and black shape, etc. – we had a clear view of what our typeface should look like:

- ● it had to be a sans-serif typeface – to go for anything else would have been too much of a culture shock for a rather conservative client;
- ● we needed a narrow typeface, but not a condensed version of an existing design;
- ● the main strokes had to be thick enough to withstand printing on rough paper, but at the same time light enough to give an even appearance with enough space between letters to distinguish individual characters;
- ● characters needed to be individual enough to avoid mix-up with similar characters, but not over-designed;
- ● capital letters had to mark the beginning of new words (in German, all proper nouns start with capital letters) but not stick out obtrusively when used as caps only;
- ● x-height had to be relatively large without being conspicuously large;
- ● figures needed to be clearly differentiated from each other as well as somewhat smaller than the caps, so that groups of figures would not stand out too much from the surrounding text;
- ● curves, indentations, flares and open joins were to counteract bad definition, over-inking and optical illusions, especially in small sizes;
- ● tension between smooth outer shapes and somewhat squared-off counters was to increase clarity and legibility;
- ● counters and negative shapes were to be given special consideration.

Having a family of three weights (regular, regular italic and bold) would provide enough diversity for the Bundespost's needs. The regular and bold weights had to be drawn by hand, and after digitization, the data could be used to interpolate the italic, which would then need small adjustments.

For signage systems, architectural lettering, vehicles and large headline sizes, a special medium weight would have to be made. This display weight would be free from the constraints dictated by use in very small sizes; it could be less articulated in its individual characters. Instead, it would have to be legible in large sizes and from a distance. This version, too, could initially be developed as an interpolation between regular and bold and then adapted to its specific purpose. Once the data would be available on the Ikarus system, one could even consider a slightly more condensed and exaggerated version for setting telephone books with specifically adapted weights and figures.

Special signs such as pictograms, symbols, signs, the Bundespost logo, etc., could be included in a font for typesetting, thus eliminating the necessity for photo-reproduction and paste-up work. It would eventually be feasible to use the design as the basis for an exclusive typewriter face for daisywheel machines.

The result

Once a font for typesetting was available, the forms Sedley Place had re-designed were all set in the new typeface, as were some publications. This was all done without any major corrections to the original design, which would, of course, be needed eventually.

Through talks with all the relevant manufacturers of typesetting equipment it was guaranteed that the typeface would simultaneously become available on all systems. As the Bundespost had paid for the design work, the fonts could be sold at a considerable discount, thus allowing even the smallest typesetting firm to invest in the new typeface.

The Minister of Telecommunications himself had expressed interest in the typeface. The Bundespost publicity department, which had asked Sedley Place to go ahead with the project, wanted it implemented, and it had received favourable feedback from the academic world. The Bundespost administration, however, decided not to go ahead with the introduction of the exclusive corporate typeface because it would 'cause unrest'.

Instead, it was decided that all the known Helveticas were to continue to be used as the Deutsche Bundespost's house typeface.

So go back to the beginning and start reading again.

Hairlineto**Black**

Book Condensed Book **Headline Condensed** Headline Compressed

Twenty years after its inception, the FF Meta family has been extended to include eight weights and two widths, as well as a special headline version.

Although the German postal service never used the typeface that eventually became FF Meta, Spiekermann did get a chance to use it on a postage stamp design when he received a commission from the Dutch Post in 1992.

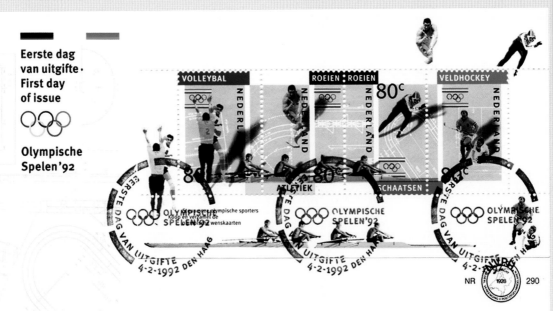

✎ Erik van Blokland and Just van Rossum   set in FF Beo Sans Soft
1991

The full version of this article was originally published in Emigre magazine issue 18.
When republishing it on the LettError website, Erik van Blokland wrote: 'Reading it back after all those years makes me cringe at the language. Lots of big words, and we even mention Gutenberg! Unforgivable. But the point is still there.'
For this book, the article was edited down, and Gutenberg was thrown out. The point remained intact, as did some big words. With thanks to Emigre.

Developments in typesetting, typeface design and printing have always been aimed at the improvement of 'quality'. Compared to printing techniques as they existed in the early 15th century we have indeed come a long way. We can digitally output the most perfectly drawn typefaces onto film or plate in resolutions of up to 5000 lines per inch. We can print in offset, in perfect registration, on the smoothest papers and finish it off with layers of varnish, all at a speed that our 15th century forefathers would find baffling. However, the technical quality of the printed product and the resolution of the type are not necessarily what makes for good design or clear communication. Often, perfection is absolutely boring.

In reply to this development, we decided to create a typeface that would add a liveliness to the page that has long been lost. While the developers of digital type usually strive for perfect outlines and fast rendering, our typeface was to have a high-resolution distortion of its digital outlines, with lengthy rasterizing times to boot.

The unsmooth and slow versus the slick and quick.

Random technology

It has always taken a while for people to realize the potential of a new technology. Today's fonts work the way they do because they are still created in a metal type kind of way. Their design is based upon the process of punchcutting, which creates a matrix from which an infinite number of identical copies of each letter can be made. The usage of type is still based upon the proverbial typecases that were divided into different compartments, each for a different letter. When a certain letter is needed, it is put in line with the others to make words and sentences. Today the typecase is replaced by a font and a keyboard.

Through our experience with traditional typesetting methods, we have come to expect that the individual letterforms of a particular typeface should always look the same. However, there is no technical reason for making a digital letter the same every time it is printed. It is possible to calculate every point and every curve differently each time the letter is generated by slightly moving the points that define a character in various 'random' directions. We discovered that the PostScript technology allows for the creation of fonts featuring these characteristics; the result was Beowolf, the first 'RandomFont' typeface.

Random technology, which is what we call the programming that is involved, is about letting the rasterizer behave randomly within the boundaries of legibility. Instead of recreating a fixed outline or bitmap, the RandomFont redefines its outlines every time they are called for. Thus, each character will be different each time it is printed. All the points that define the outline of any character will be nudged in a random direction. The distance moved depends on the parameters. For instance, Beowolf 21 has a little deviation, Beowolf 22 has a noticable wrinkle and Beowolf 23 is definitely mad.

⇢
Postcard promotion released by FontShop in 1990.

⇢ ⇢
Active interference with the shape of the letters by moving points around.

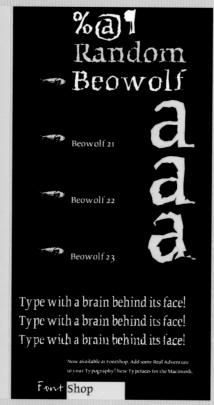

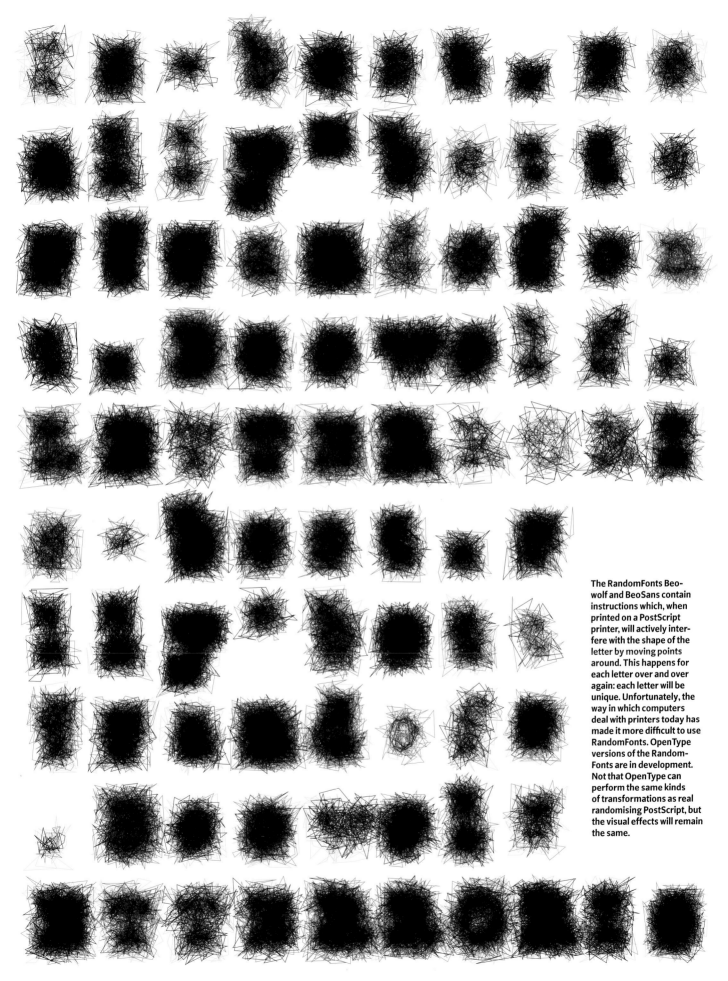

The RandomFonts Beowolf and BeoSans contain instructions which, when printed on a PostScript printer, will actively interfere with the shape of the letter by moving points around. This happens for each letter over and over again: each letter will be unique. Unfortunately, the way in which computers deal with printers today has made it more difficult to use RandomFonts. OpenType versions of the RandomFonts are in development. Not that OpenType can perform the same kinds of transformations as real randomising PostScript, but the visual effects will remain the same.

Eric Gill:
Letters are things, not pictures of things.

LettError:
Letters are programs, not pictures of things.

Random Font Beowolf: every single letter different, all the time.

What is interesting about this typeface is that the deviations in the individual letterforms create an overall unity, while the liveliness of the page that we were after is accomplished. We also discovered an interesting side effect when creating color separations for four color printing. Since the printer (Linotronic in this case) generates different outlines each time it prints a particular letter, the color separation will result in four different non-matching films. The resulting letterform in print will be outlined in bright colors.

Type as programs
While working on Randomfont we became aware that if we treated typefaces as computer data instead of fixed letterforms, we could create some very bizarre systems. One idea was to connect a font file to a self-copying mechanism to create a virus font. A self distributing typeface: a great way for young and ambitious type designers to get their typefaces known and used. No type manufacturer would be able to compete with that kind of immediate proliferation.

We could change typographic awareness of computer users around the world by creating a font virus that would transform every Helvetica into something much more desirable – the Postmodern typographer's revenge. Or we could hand out our fonts at conferences and meetings, but after a while the files would turn sour just like milk. A perfectly good font would deteriorate over

time, slowly turning into a Beowolf-like face. A great way to scare people into buying a legitimate copy.

We could create letters that wear out through frequent use, combined with a feature that uses up certain often used letters. You want real letterpress quality? You can get it! How about a font that adds typos? Link a number of typos to a particular time of the day and simulate an erratic (human) typesetter, or a font that does not work overtime.

Dynamic typography, random design
If we put more data into our typefaces we can have some very intelligent fonts. Some applications could be quite practical. For instance the data could include the information to create automatic inktraps that would switch on or off automatically, or as specified by the user, depending on the size of the type or printing technique used. A font would modify its outline when it is to be printed in offset, or shown on TV or screened on wood, or whatever. Or a typeface could research weather data, in particular the amount of direct sunlight on the spot where it will be printed, and modify itself to the best possible contrast.

The idea of Randomfont can be applied elsewhere too. Why should a letterhead always be the same? It can be slightly different each day. If you print your correspondence or invoices on a

El rito demoniaco

The demonic rhythm begins with an initiating baptism. Now in the immersion, some female hands rise from the very waters stirred by Faust, someone was waiting for him in t

Fausto.firm

Faust signs his commit

El ritu demoniac comença amb un bateig iniciàtic. Ja en la

Faust firma el seu lliurar

El rito demoniaco empieza con un bautismo iniciático. Ya en la inmersión, unas manos femeninas surgen de las propias aguas removidas por Fausto, alguien le esperaba en la bañera. Fausto firma con sangre su entrega.

The demonic rhythm begins with an initiating baptism. Now in the immersion, some female hands rise from the very waters stirred by Faust, someone was waiting for him in the bath. Faust signs his commitment with blood.

El ritu demoníac comença amb un bateig iniciàtic. Ja en la immersió, unes mans femenines sorgeixen de les mateixes aigües remogudes per Faust, algú l'esperava a la banyera. Faust firma el seu lliurament amb sang.

sang　　sangre　blood

PostScript printer, you can have a random logo: a logo that changes itself, moves around the page or tells something interesting about your company, the person you are writing or the nature of the letter. The dynamic logo can be much more informative than its fixed alternative.

For years graphic designers, especially those who subscribe to the ideas and philosophies of Swiss design or modernism, have argued that logos and typefaces should appear consistent to establish recognition. We don't think that this is necessary. Creating a random logo for a company does not necessarily decrease recognisability. Recognition does not come from simple repetition of the same form but is the result of a much more intelligent mental process. When you hear somebody's voice on the phone and he or she has a cold, you can still recognise who is talking. We can recognise handwriting and even decipher how quickly a note was written and sometimes pick up on the state of mind the person was in when writing the note. Randomness and change can add new dimensions to printwork.

The constant improvements in type and typography may have led to technical perfection, but a lot of vitality was lost. We believe that the computer, although considered by many to be cold and impersonal, can bring back some of these lost qualities. Randomfont is our contribution to this idea. ⊕

↑
Double page spread from the program book of the theatre performance 'Faust' by La Fura dels Baus from Barcelona. The design studio Typerware used FF Beowolf because it simultaneously evokes the roughness of the Middle Ages and the sophistication of digital technology – much like the show itself.

←
When printing FF Beowolf, every character looks different.

↖ ↖
Postscript version of Beowolf showing the four random outlines in CMYK.

LettError:
Motivated by curiosity

Emily King
1995

set in FF Advert

Widely considered craftsmen rather than artists, typeface designers traditionally inhabited the most cloistered of environments. Since the mid-80s, however, they have had to come to terms with the outside world as new technology has equipped a generation of relatively unskilled type users, facilitating a proliferation of new font designs. While many designers and typographers are still reeling from the shock of the new, Erik van Blokland and Just van Rossum, a pair of young designers collectively known as LettError, have set out to take technology to its limits. Rather than simply adapting to change, they are waiting impatiently for computers to catch up with their ideas.

Ever-changing fonts

Beowolf, the first LettError typeface to be commercially released, is still their best known. Originally called Random Font, its starting point was the designers' understanding that PostScript fonts are sets of mathematical instructions, rather than physical forms. When letters are stored as coded outline information, they need not necessarily take the same form each time they are printed: if a random element is introduced, the same set of instructions can produce a variety of different letterforms. Beowolf is available in different degrees of randomness: Beowolf 23, for instance, is a great deal more irregular and jagged than Beowolf 21. While no two instances of a character ever come out the same, the letters of the Beowolf typeface are instantly recognisable as part of the same family.

While Beowolf and many of the subsequent fonts have broken with current typographic convention, LettError view the standardisation of letterforms that resulted from mechanical typesetting not

The original LettError booklet (reproduced at almost full size) which was presented to the members of the international typographers' association ATypI during the 1989 conference in London.

as typographic perfection, but merely as a phase in a much longer history of written communication. Erik van Blokland explains, 'For a short while, maybe 300 years, there was a system that implied that letters had to be the same. A mechanical system of producing type meant that there was one master form and you made copies of that; it was all very logical. That is why all the 'A's are the same and all of the 'B's are the same. We have grown up expecting that to happen, but it is the result of a mechanical process, not for any reason of understanding or legibility.'

Van Blokland recalls that Beowolf found its name almost by chance. Suggested by a friend, the title seemed suitable because of its gothic feel, but it also referred to more than simply the style of the face. The manuscript held in the British Museum of the Anglo-Saxon poem Beowulf was probably made by scribes in the year 1000. It is thought the poem reached its first literary form late in the eighth century, but existed in any number of oral forms for centuries before that. The surviving version of the text, which is considered as the origin of English literature, was simply one of many. Just as the poem Beowulf resists traditional modes of literary criticism because it cannot be treated as a unique, fixed document, so the typeface escapes conventional typographic judgements. Discussions about the finer points of spacing and ligature are irrelevant when each letter is of uncertain form.

New areas

Broader questions of legibility do still apply; Beowolf remains a recognisable alphabet when printed as part of a continuous text. In this respect, LettError's enthusiasm for the new is tempered by an understanding of tradition. Both studied at the Royal Academy of Fine Arts in The Hague under Gerrit Noordzij, whose teaching is based on the idea that handwriting is the origin of all typographic communication. LettError see their designs as continuing the traditions of written communication that pre-date printing, recognising that established type designs have taken their forms from handwritten script. LettError's 'handwritten' fonts display these ideas most literally. Van Blokland and van Rossum each wrote out the alphabet then scanned and digitised the letters on a computer. Marketed as Justlefthand and Erikrighthand, these fonts became the first of many which allowed people to indulge in the irony of typing a letter in a handwritten script. Since then, having your handwriting digitised has become a service widely offered to computer users. While the value of this exercise might be debated — just what kind of layer of meaning are you adding to your typed communications by using this kind of font? — LettError's pioneering work in this area has opened up whole new areas in type design. Subsequently LettError have pursued explorations along these lines with a range

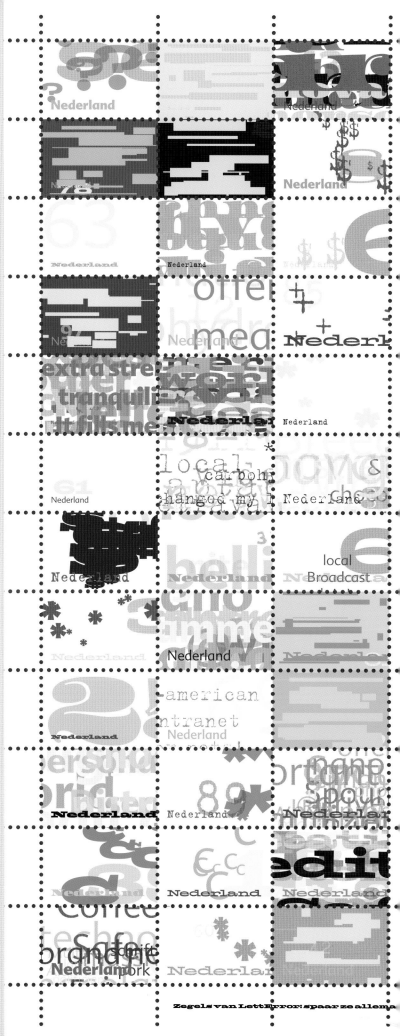

Zegels van LettError: spaar ze allema

Episode #1 **THE ANCIENT** *slightly shorter, but still quite* **History** of **ff Hands**

as recalled by Erik, 15 years later.

In 1990 Erik was in New York and Just was in Berlin. The early days of digital design.

This takes place at the premises of the 'Cable Guide', Erik only spent a couple of days there.

Nothing to do, really.

Just was in Berlin at Meta Design actually getting all sorts of stuff done.

METADESIGN

Pots dam mer platz!

21" Sony — Apple Mac Ci

The third party in this story is a precursor to email, a machine known as "fax". It scans a document on one end, whistles the information through a phone line to a similar device which would then print the page at the same time. Mostly free if you called from work.

Hello!

BEEEP BEEEP mup mup mup mup

Hoi Erik, remember those handwriting fonts we promised to Joan?—I'm designing the catalog, so it's time to draw.

I've tried a couple..

Just outlines his plan for a thick and a thin face, to be executed in the 'The Hague' handwriting which the two picked up while studying at the academy.

⊕Lefthanded Just draws with a thin fineliner.

Erik looks for a fat marker and his trusty PostScript Language Reference Manual, and writes out all the letters. They planned to include smallcaps and non-lining figures for typographic refined applications. Just and Erik set to work.

Righthanded Erik draws with a fat marker.

Postkrit

⊕Now who would take a PostScript book to New York. Makes you think, doesn't it.

ABCDEFGHIJKLM NOPQRSTUVWX abcdefghijkl mnopqrstuvwx yz012345 !@#$% ()[]{}/ ??§¶···· œ?®†¥ Fat! aß

This way, real world shapes could be put into fonts and used in typography with relative ease. Shortly after Erik faxed his letters to Just in Berlin, Just faxed back writing "Look, now I can write like you!" Further editing and finishing was needed before they could be sold.

Scanner

Photo Shop — Streamline — Font ographer

The digitisation process used a couple of new tools: a scanner, the first releases of PhotoShop, and Streamline, Illustrator to Fontographer. All of this seems old fashioned by now. But it was exciting then.

ABCDEFGHIJKLM NOPQRSTUVWX abcdefghijklmno pqrstuvwxyz012345 !@#$%^&*({}/€∞fi§¶··· £¢?§¶€œ?® ¥^"ø?˚aß

Thin

Every now and then a version is spotted in which some glyphs have been changed by a designer. Sometimes counters are opened up, in other cases the light is made a bit heavier. In case you're planning something like that: just give us a call please.

The typefaces were expected to disappear after a while but surprisingly folks kept coming back for more. In the mean time a lot of other "rough" handwriting fonts have been designed by others. Yet ErikRightHand and JustLeftHand remain quite different from the rest. A couple of small regrets though. ErikRightHand's lower case i has a very thick, slanted dot which gets mistaken for an acute quite often. And some of the counters are too small, but cleaning it up now would be a mistake. Many handwriting fonts get too pretty because the shapes are regularised too much. Hands are just fine!

Right! Thick *Left! Thin!*

LEFT! RIGHT

Greeting cards, baby care products and many magazines for families, women, kids: all o'them have Hands somewhere. We apologise.

```
Triumph 'Durabel'
Triumph Werke Nürnberg A.G. Nürnberg

Trixiefont
abcdefghijklmnopqrstuvwxyz
ABCDEFGHIJKLMNOPQRSTUVWXYZ
1234567890 "ᴅᴍ%&()_$/:+ß;=` ´üÜöÖäÄ,.-?!'
nnnnnnnnnnnnnnnnnnnnnnnnnnnnnnnnnnnnnnnnnnnnnn
a b c d e f g h i j k l m m n o p q r s t u v w x y z
A B C D E F G H I J K L M N O P Q R S T U V W X Y Z
a b c d e f g h i j k l m n o p q r s t u v w x y z
1 2v3 4 5 6 7 8 9 0      1 2 3 4 5 6 7 8 9 0
ß ü ö ä ` ´ ´ - ' " . , ? ! ; : / _ ( ) % & § + =
Ü Ö Ä Ü Ö Ä Ü Ö Ä Ü ö ä Ü ö ä
. , - ; : ( _ ) & - " ' ? ! = + / 9 § 3 ᴅᴍ ᴅᴍ % ß ß ` ´

Trixiefont halfvet
a b c d e f g h i j k l m n o p q r s t u v w x y z
A B C D E F G H I J K L M M N O P Q R S T U V W X Y Z
1 2 3 4 5 6 7 8 9 0 0    . , - ; : ? ! ' " ( ) ø / /
ᴅᴍ % & _ § / ß = + ` ´ ´ ü ö ä ü ü  Ü Ö Ä
aaaaaa eeeeee iiiii ooooo uuuuu ccc nnnn yyyyy
AAAAAA EEEEEE IIIII OOOOO UUUUU CCC NNNN YYYYY
```

called Instant Types: rather than returning to the handwritten form, they have created fonts by scanning and digitising a variety of existing letterforms. Trixie, the original Instant Type, was taken directly from a typewriter that belonged to a woman whose name was… Trixie (Beatrix in full). Trixie and other fonts based on found letterforms, such as Confidential and Dynamoe, have become widely used, almost invariably as a very literal way to convey urgency or spontaneity. While accepting that some fonts tend to dictate use, van Blokland and van Rossum do not subscribe to the strict divisions that have been made between text and display faces. They argue that every typeface has both an image and a text factor, and could be used for either purpose, illustrating this argument with a graph. Image factor, the extent to which the viewer is drawn to the type, is plotted against text factor, the font's legibility. While this has the appearance of a scientific process, van Blokland admits that the way they plot a typeface is actually subjective and arbitrary. LettError are not seeking absolutes through their type designs.

↑
The original Trixie typewriter with the typed character set for scanning. LettError archive.

←—
Transavia, a Dutch airline, used Advert for its livery. Identity by Tel Design.

Although they subscribe to the current typographic orthodoxy — the easiest typeface to read is the one you read most often, the catchphrase of the Californian type magazine Emigre — van Blokland shows a healthy respect for typographic nicety. Convention or not, he feels Trixie makes a poor text face because 'it is dirty, has some disadvantages in the spacing and some of the shapes are a bit unclear.' While acknowledging that technology has made experimentation with typographic abstraction viable, he feels that this kind of experimentation is not part of LettError's project. 'If you are making typefaces now, then you are making them for people who need type to communicate ideas to other people.'

Like many of their more forward-looking colleagues, LettError have designed fonts for the type magazine FUSE, which is supplied on five posters and a disk. Some involved with the magazine claim to be engaged in a project of revolutionising visual language, although what is meant by this is often not entirely clear. Jon Wozencroft, the editor of FUSE, has drawn an analogy between the recent developments in type design

GEGARANDEERD DE MEEST
VERSPILLENDE & INEFFICIËNTE

LETTERS
TER WERELD

Met ENORME BALKEN van schreveN.
{& de leesbaarheid zit in de schreef — dat weet iedereen}
++++++++++ DAAROM EXTRA LEESBAAR! ++++++++++

Font • Font

ZAPATA
LettErroR © FF Zapata™

Onverantwoordelijk
VEEL PAPIER
Andere Letters Verbleken Bij Het Zien Van Het Zwart van Zapata!
MEER INKT! MEER TONER!

"Moet alles er hetzelfde uitzien? — NEE

ONZIN

Neem dan ook niet altijd dezelfde Lettertjes! — WEES NIET BANG
Het ZWITSERS rationalisme heeft LANG GENOEG geregeerd!
Negeer de BEVELEN van het MODERNISME! ≡ KIES JE EIGEN FONTS!

Gebruik? ECHTE? Schreven Voor? ECHTE?

TYPO
GRAFIE

& Dan Niet Van Die Zuinige
MAGERE SCHREEFLOZE DINGETJES!
"Vreselijk Saai & Ouderwets!"
Daarom Stevige Letters Met Mooie Rondingen Van:

[LettError Sinds 1989]

PAS OP
ECHTE LETTERS ZIJN SOMS HEEL ERG
GEVAAARLIJK
< — >
Maar — als je ze goed behandelt zullen ze je altijd trouw blijven!

De SCHREVEN van ZAPATA zijn — RECHT —, in plaats van — PUNTIG —
Daarom MINDER kans op VERWONDINGEN!

FF Zapata Is Een Overzichtelijke Familie Van Slechts 5 {vijf} Gewichten!
1: Light ✳ 2: Regular ✳ 3: Medium ✳ 4: Bold ✳ 5: Black
"Geen Overvolle FONTMENU's? Daarom Geen Moeilijke Keuzes? Minder Te Onthouden"
Geen Dilemma Tussen Cursief & Kleinkapitaal! — DIT IS MEER DAN

GENOEG

¡VIVA ZAPATA!
Stel uw DRUKKER wel op de hoogte in verband met de EXTRA INKT.
[METEEN BESTELLEN]

— and typesetting technology — and the invention of photography. According to Wozencroft, just as photography made the reproduction of reality easy and obliged painters to do something more interesting instead, desktop publishing has enabled even mere clerks to set a competent piece of type, allowing the professionals the freedom to roam new creative territory. This comparison is ripe for criticism: it adopts a discredited view of the relationship between painting and photography; it assumes that the task of the typesetter before the advent of desktop publishing was absurdly limited; it requires a belief that many issues in type design and typography have been conclusively resolved, and so on. Most irritatingly, some designers use this argument as justification to adopt the title of artist, as if by doing so they were scaling the dizzy heights of a supposed cultural hierarchy.

The fact that many of LettError's inventions are not immediately marketable, are motivated by curiosity rather than commerce and would not appear to have a lot to do with the majority of day-to-day printed communication, might prompt some to suggest that they have similar aspirations. But LettError make no such grand claims for their work. As usual, they take a disarmingly common-sense approach, suggesting that artists and designers have very different motives. They do not predict any revolutions, arguing that the development of type is closely linked to the slow development of language.

At a recent conference organised by FUSE, LettError went against the grain by boycotting the terms 'multimedia,' 'cyber' and 'Internet,' but still applaud the magazine for providing a forum for the systematic exploration of type.

Technology and experiment

LettError's technological skill and enthusiasm mean that their inventions are often several leaps away from the marketplace. Their new BitPull fonts are bitmapped typefaces, which allow control of the individual pixels. BitPull does to typefaces what 'pitbulls do with little children.' Although the BitPull idea is three years old, the fonts are not yet on sale. Called a 'typetoy' by LettError, it is more of a system than a typeface. The faces work with an application written by Just van Rossum, but it is in a far from distributable form: it has no interface and you can only click on certain buttons otherwise it crashes. The latest product to see release is Kosmik, which includes a random element but abides by certain rules: each letter is selected from three alternative forms, ensuring that no three characters in a row are ever exactly alike. LettError call Kosmik a 'Flipperfont,' and believe such fonts are especially appropriate for use on screen. By using a different letterform on each consecutive frame, the letters can be made to jiggle — instantly reminding those of us brought up on British TV of the wavering forms of Rhubarb and Custard.

LettError's experimentation with random fonts was prompted by a desire to take full advantage of PostScript technology. Historically, designers aiming to exploit technological innovation have done so under the banner of function: when typographers earlier this century proposed abandoning the uppercase, they argued it would lead to more effective use of contemporary typesetting machinery. LettError would not claim that their typefaces are efficient in that sense: an article set in Beowolf for Emigre magazine took an hour and a half to print. LettError's objective is 'to use the technology for what it is worth.' They point out that a laser printer is a very large and expensive machine capable of responding to complex sets of instructions, so why, when you ask for an 'A,' should it print the same form each time?

You might have to wait three quarters of an hour for your page of Beowolf to emerge, but at least the printer is doing something instead of just sitting around. ⊕

© Copyright Frieze 2004

FF Kosmik OT
Autoffflippperr*
0123456789012345 6789
Plain & **Bold** ¶ ✈ 🌐
✱In OpenType Savvy Applications
Liveliness, Onomatopaea
MACOS+WIN, SCREEN+PRINT
OpenTypeFontFont

←---
Specimen for FF Kosmic, with built-in Autoflipper, an application that picks a different version of each letter when more than one of each are used in the same word.

←--- ←---
Poster designed by Erik van Blokland, showing FF Zapata.

GEOMETRY LITERALLY MEANS: MEASURING, OR QUANTIFYING, THE EARTH. MEASURING IS A STEP TOWARDS KNOWLEDGE AND, HOPEFULLY, towards GETTING A GRASP ON THE STUFF THAT SURROUNDS US.

Originally invented by the Egyptians and Babylonians as a set of principles and calculations needed for astronomy and construction, geometry was developed into a sophisticated science by the ancient Greeks. Since then geometric concepts have evolved to include a high level of complexity and abstraction.

Meanwhile, in typography what we mean when we talk about 'geometric typefaces' is often not so sophisticated at all. In our little world, any design that has been constructed using the ruler and the compass – or the digital equivalents of these tools – is referred to as geometric. Triangle, square, circle – these are the elementary building blocks for a whole category of letterforms which has been born and reborn three times in the course of the twentieth century.

Adrian Frutiger wrote that it may be assumed that Man has an innate sensibility to geometry. All over the earth archeologists have found signs based on the primary shapes (to triangle-square-circle, Frutiger added the arrow and the cross). When it comes to language notation, however, most early systems were based on figurative forms – such as the famous oxen's head (aleph) of the Phoenecians, from which our capital A was derived. It took many centuries for those two aspects of human sign-making – figuration and abstraction – to merge into what has become our alphabet.

Geometric letterforms, as geometry itself, reached their first high point in Greece. Inscriptions from the 4th and 5th centuries BC – the age of Plato – show letterforms based on almost perfect squares, triangles and circles. The stoichedon style of inscriptions from that period has monolinear letters organized in a perfect grid, aligned vertically as well as horizontally – 'monospaced' – with no word spaces. Not until the 20th century would page layout be so cool and modular again.

The alphabet of the Roman empire – the capitalis monumentalis – followed the same construction principles, adding a smart rhythm of alternating narrow and wide letters, as well as a marked contrast between thick and thin strokes and prominent serifs. These were the letterforms that would guide the design of capitals to the present day.

Caught in a square

During the Renaissance, artists, printers and inventors began to pay close attention to letterforms. In the hands of writers and punch cutters, the category that we call 'roman' had more or less found its definitive appearance, in which the ever-monumental capitals had become the flag-bearers heading platoons of more

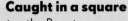

colourful and messier lower-case forms. This pair of two contrasting alphabets showed many traces of the various techniques used to make letters. The serif is possibly a remnant of the brush stroke with which a character was painted on the marble before being carved; the contrast between thinner and thicker strokes suggests a trace of the flat brush or the broad-nibbed pen as well as the forward movement of the writing hand.

Obsessed with rationalism, the scholars and scientists of the 15th and 16th centuries found it hard to live with that

of principles derived from it, became their ally. In Russia, Malevich peeled off layer after layer of figuration to reach the core of his visual language: the black square. In the Netherlands Piet Mondriaan and Theo van Doesburg liberated the painting from its representative function, reducing it to a composition of coloured squares and triangles. Even the circle was deemed too frivolous for their purposes.

Van Doesburg and other artists and architects set out to invent a kind of graphic design that was compatible with this vision of 'New Imaging' (Nieuwe Beelding, a term

<--- <--- Albrecht Dürer, construction of a capital 'A' (1525).

<--- Herbert Bayer's Universal Alphabet, 1926.

<--- <--- Geometric Greek alphabet, 4th century B.C.

much arbitrariness, especially in an architectural context where planning was crucial. They set out to redefine letterforms in rational, geometric terms. They placed a square around each capital letter and linked its proportions to a grid of horizontal, vertical, diagonal and circular guides. The letterform was drilled into behaving like a predictable, reproducible and 'harmonic' construction. The same was done for the textura ('gothic'), which by then had already been developed into a very modular and repetitive system. Lowercase romans were harder to tame; the totally rational alphabet was still a far-away ideal.

Yet step-by-step, the appearance of printing type was disconnected from its origin, the hand-written word. In late 17th century Paris, Louis XIV commissioned the development of the 'Romain du Roi.'Its alphabets were drawn on a grid of 2304 squares – the first printing type completely designed before being cut. Of course, the punch cutter's handwork still made sure that the breach with the past was not as radical as the designs on paper seemed to envisage; yet the King's Roman was a crucial step towards a less intuitive text type. A hundred years later, Didot and Bodoni took the printed alphabet one step further towards an artificial construction, preparing it for the industrial age.

The new image
In the early twentieth century the faith in rationality and efficiency entered a new dimension. The leading figures of the international avant-garde – the Constructivists in Russia, De Stijl in the Netherlands, Bauhaus in Germany – aspired to simplicity and purity, to an art that was to be objective and universal. Geometry, or a rather crude set

coined by Mondriaan). It is easy to see why professional typographers did not feel a calling to lead the way here. For many decades – one might say to this day – typographers have instead remained the custodians of tradition, viewing type as a modest piece of equipment with virtually unchangeable basic shapes allowing for carefully crafted variations at most. The artist-designers of the new age wanted exactly the opposite: they aimed to liberate the letterform from its leaden past. To them the shape of letters was a set of conventions like any other, a tradition to break free from or even destroy. Down with decoration! Down with elegance and coquetry! Down with the visual language of the Middle Ages and the Renaissance!

Ruler and compass
Many Modernist designers simply discovered alternative typographic tools in their printer's typecases: they turned to existing 'grotesques' – late 19th-century, plain-looking sans serifs – which fit the new age and the industrial processes in which these artists had become interested, better than the baroque or classicist romans. Others constructed elaborate straight-lined letters using the brass rules with which the typesetter usually makes borders and lines. As early as 1900, however, there were also artists who drew their own experimental alphabets. More often than not, these alphabets were based on circles and squares. This was partly done for ideological reasons – all means of communication had to be elementary and simple to the point of being impersonal. Yet at the same time it was a very practical thing to do. The ruler and compass can be helpful expedients to an artist or architect who embarks

on a type design project free of any relevant knowledge or skills, as long as he can convince himself that those are the instruments par excellence to draw letters with. Traditional typographers were horrified by this approach, and by the 'decline of legibility' that it resulted in. Yet it was precisely their lack of traditional knowledge that made it possible for the new school of letter-makers to explore untrodden terrains in typography – allowing both their supporters and their opponents to get a taste of the possibilities as well as the limitations of the new idiom. Furthermore, as long as the use of geometric alphabets remained limited to headlines, titles and logos, their readability was usually more than sufficient.

Square typography in Russia and the Netherlands

Towards 1920, each avant-garde movement had its own typographic experiments. In 1919 Theo van Doesburg drew an alphabet based on squares. He designed quite a lot of printed matter with it, taking liberties with his geometry in an undogmatic approach. The squares could be stretched at will into vertical or horizontal rectangles so as to freely regulate the length of words. During the same period Vilmos Huszár, a Hungarian living in Holland, drew logotypes and vignettes composed of squares and rectangles. His best-known design is the masthead of the early issues of De Stijl magazine, edited by Van Doesburg, which began publication in 1917. In Russia, the revolutionary regime produced a radical form of 'government art': graphic and three-dimensional design at the service of Bolshevist propaganda. Between 1922 and 1929 the constructivist artist Aleksandr Rodchenko, often in collaboration with the poet Vladimir Mayakovski, designed dozens of posters and book covers for which Rodchenko developed elementary letterforms made with straight lines only – other artists, such as the Stenberg brothers, gratefully made use of these ideas.

In Italy, Marinetti's Futurists had little interest in the geometric principles that were doing so well in northern Europe. What the Futurists aimed to represent in their paintings, sculptures, theatre and printed matter, was speed, noise, surprise, even violence; this called for a more dynamic and less rigid visual language. But the Italian Futurists did at times come up with constructions that seemed to have taken clues from the international tendency towards geometrically constructed, minimalist signs. For instance, Fortunato Depero designed an exhibition pavilion in 1926 almost completely built with rectangular letterforms.

The Bauhaus and Futura

The most influential typographic innovation came from the country with the most complex typographic tradition: Germany. Gothic typefaces were standard (this category is also called 'broken script' because when writing, the pen is lifted from the page before each new stroke, thus making the writing a process of strokes and interruptions). German grammar requiring each noun to be written with a capital letter made the overall page image even heavier.

One of the principal innovative forces in changing the typographic tradition in Germany was the Bauhaus, a college of art and design founded in Weimar in 1919 and relocated to Dessau in 1925. The painter Wassily Kandinsky, who joined the Bauhaus staff in 1922, helped radicalize the school's theoretical foundations by putting forward (in a 1923 essay) the three basic shapes of geometry as 'an elementary sentence in the language of vision' and assigning to each shape its 'natural' colour: yellow for the triangle, red for the square and blue for the circle.

Hungarian-born Bauhaus teacher Moholy-Nagy, who had not been trained as a typographer, wrote an essay in which he advocated 'absolute clarity in all typographic work.' He wanted a standard alphabet in which there would be no dichotomy between uppercase and lowercase. Other Bauhaus teachers shared his dream of a 'universal' alphabet with no capitals, and used geometry to build one. Herbert Bayer designed such an alphabet in 1925: a set of characters constructed using parts of circles and straight lines which in spite of its lack of contrast was still legible. Bayer's alphabet is one of the first serious attempts to bring geometry closer to typography. In that same year, Josef Albers drew his Stencil alphabet: a typeface consisting of uppercase as well as lowercase, built from quarter circles, squares and triangles. In 1929 the young Austrian Jan Tschichold designed a universal alphabet made of elementary forms; although subtler than Bayer's, it certainly wasn't more usable.

Jan Tschichold summarized the new insights regarding the design of printed matter in a 1928 essay that has become a classic: *The New Typography*. The man who appointed Tschichold as a teacher at the Munich graphic college would enter history as the maker of the typeface that bridged the gap between the New Typography and the traditional world of typographers and printers. It was Paul Renner who designed Futura between 1924 and 1927.

The early drawings for Futura drastically departed from the conventional shapes of text type. Renner's alphabet was closely related to the formal research of De Stijl and the Bauhaus designers. He was convinced that the

ABCDEFGHIJKLMNOP QRSTUVWXYZÄÖÜÆŒÇ abcdefghijklmnopqrſstuvw xyzäöüch ck ff fi fl ffl ffi ſſ ß æ œ ç 1234567890 &.,-:;·!?('«»§†*

Auf besonderen Wunsch liefern wir auch nachstehende Figuren

a g m n ä & 1 2 3 4 5 6 7 8 9 0

ABCDEFGHIJKLMNO PQRSTUVWXYZÄÖÜ abcdefghijklmnopqrſst uvwxyzäöüch ck ff fi fl ffl ffi ſſ ß 1234567890 &.,-:;·!?'(*†«»§ 1234567890

←← ←
Theo van Doesburg, cover design for his own book *Klassiek, barok, modern*, Antwerp 1920

←
First specimen for Futura, showing alternate sorts for some characters. Bauersche Gießerei, Frankfurt 1927.

Post-war functionalism and the new technologies

The Second World War was followed by a period of cultural restoration, during which graphic design in many parts of Europe was characterized by a predilection for the painterly, the personal and the hand-crafted. It was only in Switzerland (which had been neutral during the war) that the pre-1940 experiments regarding form and function had developed into a consistent, professional design method; in many other countries it would take more than 10 years until functionalist research was resumed.

The case of the Netherlands may serve as an example. In the early 1960s a new generation of designers, heavily influenced by the Swiss school, set out to develop a Dutch variant of the new functionalism. In the typographic realm, a handful of designers who were part of the Amsterdam firm Total Design presented pioneering work. Both Wim Crouwel and Benno Wissing liked using 'no-nonsense' sans serifs such as Akzidenz Grotesk and Univers.

essence of contemporary design was what he called its 'timeless' aspects. The most direct way to attain timelessness, according to Renner, was to use primary geometric shapes as the basic principle. He explained: 'The artistic worth of simplification does not lie in a mysterious magical power emanating from the circle, triangle and square; instead the artist simply designs so that the consistent variation, the logical differentiation from these highest categories is apparent, because we only understand such forms.'

All characters of the original Futura were constructed using partial circles, rectangles and triangles, and some lowercase letters looked very unusual indeed. Futura subsequently evolved into a less radical typeface during a lengthy collaboration between Renner and the Bauer typefoundry in Frankfurt, although for a long time during the process the matter of the geometric **a, g, m, r** and **n** seems to have remained undecided. The foundry finally opted for the more conventional form (although for some years the more radical versions could be supplied at special request) and Renner expressed some regret at this.

Yet in his 1939 treatise *Die Kunst der Typografie*, he wrote that it might have been a bad idea to deny the forward dynamic of **m, n** and **r** based on handwriting, and replace them by static forms: 'it seems that the forms of **m, n** and **r**, which press to the right, are indispensable in all European script.' (Translation of the Renner quotes from Christopher Burke, *Paul Renner: The Art of Typography*, Hyphen Press, 1998.)

Their colleague Jurriaan Schrofer was known for his elaborate typographic constructions; he created his own letterforms using ruler and compass. In 1987 Schrofer wrote: 'What is the minimum number of basic elements with which one can create a language of forms? ... A personal test: an alphabet with only two given shapes: a square and a quarter circle to be used in four positions. The resulting image is reminiscent of the alphabets developed during the 1920s and 1930s.'

Wim Crouwel also designed letterforms using geometric elements, including his famous typeface, New Alphabet (1967). Meant as a speculative 'machine type' for the new typesetting techniques, New Alphabet was a series of revolutionary (and at times unrecognizable) letterforms based on a simple grid consisting solely of vertical and horizontal lines with sheared corners. Crouwel's hand-drawn lettering for posters and art catalogues was not as radical as that, but it was invariably constructed from geometric elements.

Schrofer and Crouwel – and many of their contemporaries – showed that with these elementary building blocks it was possible to make letterforms that were not only cool and simple but, when needed, also legible. At the same time these forms were easily recognizable, could be reproduced without difficulty and executed efficiently by draughtsmen. As Schrofer wrote, with characteristic lucidity and irony: 'Functionality and usefulness are other words for laziness and repetitiveness.'

Geometry in the digital age

As Schrofer suggests, there is something ambiguous about using geometry to draw letters. It can be cool and suggest tension; it can (amazingly) still be a means of achieving some kind of 'contemporary' or 'futurist' feel. But it also can turn type design into a modular and repetitive exercise.

For decades, home-made typography or lettering was characterized by a certain sloppiness or roughness that was part of its appeal. With the advent of the personal computer, it has become easier to draw straight lines and perfect circles than to do something more personal. Copying, lining up and combining elementary shapes is a piece of cake. The first years of desktop type design – and in individual cases the first steps in many a type designing career – are characterized by a strong reliance on simple, elementary forms. But as with any technology, talent, fantasy and discipline are needed to take it beyond the elementary possibilities of its default functions. Some fine examples can be found within the FontFont library – one of the few places in the early 1990s where a desire to invent new forms of type was coupled with a strong sense of quality. Geometrically inspired FontFonts have added new possibilities to the typographer's palette. Not only have they established a connection to the achievements of the pre-1940 avant-garde, these typefaces can also be seen as antidotes to the mass of shapeless, nostalgic or deliberately chaotic display faces that have been unleashed since the early 1990s.

Brody before and after the Mac

Londoner Neville Brody was one of the first typographers of his generation who rediscovered the power of simplicity. At a time when postmodernism – with its tongue-in-cheek references to kitsch, classicism and trashy street culture – was about to reach its high point, Brody drew inspiration from pre-war avant-garde design and began drawing letterforms reminiscent of the 1920s and 30s – he has cited Futurism and Rodchenko as important sources of inspiration.

Throughout the 1980s Brody hand-drew numerous logos, titles and alphabets for packaging, posters and magazines. One of his most outstanding achievements was the art direction and design of *The Face* magazine. Initially, the designers used rubbed down type from Letraset transfer sheets, which enabled them to use several typefaces within one headline, or digital typesetting, which made it possible to modify the type. However, Brody soon began noticing his style being imitated and realized something more personal was called for. 'It was easy to find the typefaces that we were using, and to modify them in the way that we were. ... I wanted to produce something that others would find difficult to mimic. The second point was that I wanted to start working with my hands again. We xeroxed the typeface, and then stuck the letters together on a line, which meant that there was

even more control than before. During my last year with The Face, this culminated in every single headline being hand-drawn for its specific use.' (Brody quotes from Jon Wozencroft, *The Graphic Language of Neville Brody*, Thames and Hudson, 1988)

All Brody's letterforms were based on geometric shapes, but he managed to attain a remarkable sophistication with these simple means. As he told Jon Wozencroft: 'I've always tried to work to the best of my abilities, and within my limitations – I wouldn't know how to draw Baskerville, for example. What I was trying to point out was that people shouldn't feel limited to the range of typefaces made available to them by typesetters.'

In 1984–1986, Brody designed several complete alphabets for use in The Face headlines. They were numbered rather than named: Typeface One, Two, etc.

In the late 1980s and early 1990s many of Brody's alphabets were digitised. While his first published fonts Industria (based on Typeface Two) and Insignia where brought out elsewhere, after 1990 – the year in which Brody and Erik Spiekermann founded the FontFont type library – all his typefaces were released by FontShop.

Brody's early FontFonts were digital versions of the hand-drawn alphabets and headlines he had made during the previous decade. The person who helped Brody complete and digitise his fonts was David Berlow, founder of the Font Bureau in Boston. Berlow produced digital versions of fonts such as FF Typeface 4, 6 & 7 and FF Gothic. The Dome/World/Tokyo series was the result of an interesting collaboration. Brody had designed a poster for the boxing match between heavyweight champion Mike Tyson and Tony Tubbs, which took place in the Tokyo Dome in March 1988. Brody showed Berlow the poster, for which he had drawn single words using a different type of lettering in each line; the idea was to create a complete font based on each style. After scrutinizing the poster, the analytic Berlow remarked that in most lines two or three slightly different construction principles has been used. Consequently, not only did each of the lines in the poster become a font (named after the words they had been used for: FF Tyson, FF World, FF Dome), each of those fonts also had two or three variants, based on Berlow's critical analysis of Brody's lettering.

At the time of his first book, published in 1988, Brody was still wary of using the computer as a creative tool – 'instant design' he called it; a few years later he had become one the pioneers of digital typography. Around 1990, Brody began exploring the possibilities of designing type directly on the computer; this resulted in typefaces such as FF Blur, FF Harlem and FF Autotrace, fonts in which specific features of the Mac, such as blurring and the cut-and-paste functions, were used to create and edit letterforms.

TYSON

TONY TUBBS

WORLD HEAVYWEIGHT CHAMPIONSHIP

FIGHT

TOKYO

DOME

FontFont geometrics: variations on a theme

As noted above, geometric construction is a recurring theme in the FontFont library. This certainly does not imply that all designers who make use of it have similar motives. To some the simplification of letterforms is a philosophical exercise, to others it is a shortcut to creating one's own typographic tools.

Brody, Kisman and Sych have designed rather idiosyncratic letterforms using basic geometric shapes; FF Motter Festival uses a similar approach. The typeface was drawn by Othmar Motter from Austria, an ITC, Berthold and Letraset veteran and the designer of such quintessential 1970s fonts as Motter Femina and Motter Ombra. In his work he has alternated luscious, outrageous letterforms

Dig Dog Hip

Your ®Brand NAME here™

OCR-F 1234
OCR-F 5678
OCR-F 9012

euphemismatch

When working on magazine design in the early 1980s, Dutchman Max Kisman had very practical reasons for simplifying the alphabet: his letters originated – pre-Mac and, in his case, also pre-Amiga – as shapes that were hand-cut out of red ulano film. So straight lines came in handy and also lent a particular character to the typography. In the early 1990s, Kisman began processing his earlier experiments into digital fonts. FF Scratch was one of the fonts derived for his hand-cut headline alphabets. FF Rosetta was based on a headline font originally drawn (on the computer) for the magazine *Language Technology* which Kisman art directed and which morphed into *Wired* when its founding editor, Louis Rossetto, moved back from Amsterdam to the States. While producing these fonts on the Mac, Kisman started exploring completely different possibilities of the computer as well. One of the results was FF Jacque, which was directly 'hand-drawn' on the screen.

Both Brody and Kisman have drawn inspiration from music, designing posters, magazines and packaging and, in Kisman's case, playing in a band. Paul Sych from Toronto studied graphic design and jazz simultaneously, and was a professional musician before opening his own studio, Faith. Each of his FontFonts Dig, Dog and Hip has one basic vertical shape for most letters – oval, rectangle or parallelogram – which are transected by strong horizontals, which give them a certain aggressiveness. FF Dog is described by Sych as 'my interpretation of early Old English manuscript text. I used the sharpness of Old English and combined it with a compressed gothic font.'

with stern geometry. FF Motter Festival, which marked his return to type design after a long break, has a bit of both: a constructed typeface with highly personal forms. According to its designer, Motter Festival 'was born of the desire to forge an alliance of a universally legible serif face with the rhythm and elegance of a gothic.' The result is a striking design with a particular interchange of pointed and rounded endings. Motter Festival comes in three weights: Light, Book and Bold.

Paris-based designer Albert Boton, whose career in type spans almost five decades, has worked in a broad range of styles, suiting the needs of his many corporate clients. The Boton typefaces published as FontFonts in recent years reflect this versatility. They include a family of sans and serif for optimum legibility (FF Page), an Art Nouveau-style alphabet (FF Elegie), a typeface in the 'Didone' category (FF Cellini) and a book face based on classic Roman capitals (FF Tibere). Hand-drawing is at the basis of most of these letterforms; but none are based on pure construction. Boton's FF Bastille series of display faces, however, does show a geometric approach. Boton drew dozens of display alphabets when working at the Paris design company Carré Noir; FF Bastille Display is closely connected to that period. Its members FF District and FF Aircraft are striking, squarish designs with clear-cut shapes; District was later extended into a four-weight family. FF Studio uses mainly straight lines to build a spartan, open alphabet, although its 'O's and 'Q' are perfectly circular. The most peculiar family member is FF

Zan. With its black, simplified forms and little round holes for counters, it is reminiscent of some of the more experimental faces of the Art Deco period, such as Indépendant from the Brussels Plantin foundry (ca. 1930).

Rian Hughes was a pioneer. Hughes, who is also an illustrator and a fervent fan of science fiction comics, has designed dozens of font families, many of which reflect his personal, retro-futurist style of drawing. He began publishing his alphabets as FontFonts in 1993; a few years later he started his own foundry, Device Fonts. Both FF Outlander and FF Identification are based on simple construction;

←--- ←--- ←---
Wordsets by
Gordon Protz
for FF Dig, Dog, Hip:
FF Trademarker
and FF Localizer.
Jürgen Siebert
made the
unofficial
German
car plates.

←---
FF Zan on furniture.

←---
Poster by
Rian Hughes for
FF Identification.

Yesterday's tomorrows

During the 1960s and 1970s, many artists and designers were fascinated with technological progress; no endeavour represented that progress more spectacularly than space travel. The conquest of outer space opened up a new relationship between man and machines, and a wholly new perspective of the earth (both of which were brilliantly visualized in Kubrick's 2001: A Space Oddyssey). From Wim Crouwel's New Alphabet to the NASA logo itself, typography tried to somehow find ways to express the new age and design typefaces that machines might like; geometric construction seemed to be an indispensable tool to achieve this.

What was futurism then has now become 'retro-futurism': 1970s-style geometric lettering was rediscovered in the 1990s and, used more or less ironically, became a constant factor in techno design. It tied in nicely with the revival of 1970s fashion and colour schemes, and it had the advantage of being modular and easy to combine with wallpaper motives or abstract illustration.

Quite a few typefaces issued in the FontFont library during the nineties speak to us in a robot-like, synthetic voice. Some refer to 1970s techno-futurism, others move away from its chilliness and use the objective elements of circles and lines to create their own tongue-in-cheek science-fiction idiom. Others again have 'sampled' contemporary machine typography, translating elemental alphabets into complex font families.

both are subtly ironic in their use of technological references. Outlander is the kind of typeface one could find in the lettering of a spaceship. Hughes wrote a hilarious description which refers, in a deliberately obscure way, to some kind of sci-fi narrative and, in passing, parodies the jargon of type descriptions: 'The four basic weights (Light, Medium, Bold, Black) are stringently applied across the ten sub-sectors that comprise the main organisation and are covered in detail in Paragraphs 3544-3998 of the TCI Design for Exploitation CD-ROM.' Hughes's FF Identification is a sophisticated set of letters and shapes, which can be layered to build a multicoloured sign system. There is the suggestion of a code loaded with meaning, but unless the user finds a particularly smart use for it, its signs and pointers are empty containers. Among Hughes's other FontFonts is FF Knobcheese, a typeface that combines the informality of hand-lettering with the geometry of circular counters, to lively and charming effect.

The Berlin artist and VJ who goes by the name of Critzler has also produced several typefaces that are clean and technological in form, yet subtly ironic. A former sign-painter in East Germany, Critzler has managed to combine the clarity of geometric elements with amorphous lettershapes in FF Localizer, and its 'Localizer Clones,' among which is the ingenious FF Chemo. FF Trademarker was conceived as a kind of updated version of 1972's Serpentine – a typeface rediscovered by the techno movement. Cleaner and simpler than its model, FF Trademarker is meant for creating logo-like headlines – hence the name.

Elke Herrnberger's FF Yokkmokk also uses elementary shapes for construction, but the result is completely different from any of the above-mentioned display fonts. Her font was designed as part of a student project based on the FUSE series: experimental type design where legibility is not necessarily an issue. FF Yokkmokk (and its inline companion, Yakkmakk) can be read, though with some difficulty.

tables, luggage tags and check-in systems, glorified in FF Airport. With FF Backstage, the twosome paid a tribute to yet another kind of utilitarian (and constructed) type: the stencil alphabets made for the lettering on industrial buildings (including the Chernobyl reactor) and transport containers.

Based on the same idea as Lineto's Matrix fonts, three German designers called Ignaszak, Kister and Scheuerhorst

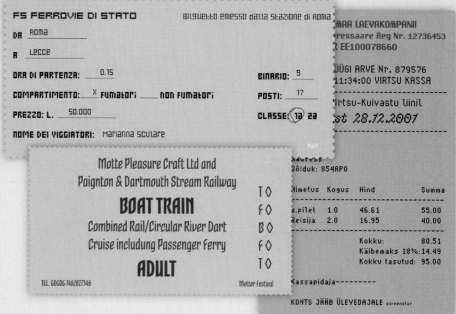

Its monolinear shapes, all based on circle segments and straight lines, playfully creep across the page, like electric circuits, or the writing of some robot race; the impression is highly technological and festive at the same time.

Machine aesthetics

In the course of the 1980s graphic designers began getting interested in alphabets that had an 'undesigned' look or seemed to have escaped from some machine's digital system. OCR, DIN and Letter Gothic, made for industrial and office purposes, were welcomed into the realm of 'serious' graphic design. Ever since, the interest in typographic 'machine language' has been growing – to compensate, as it were, for the increasing attention paid to typographic minutiae by more traditionally inclined typographers. The FontFont library has accommodated a large number of fonts that are direct translations of alphabets designed by engineers for particular high-tech uses. Considering these origins, it's logical that most of these fonts are made of basic circular and rectangular shapes.

Stephan 'Pronto' Müller and Cornel Windlin – collaborating as Lineto – were among the first to discover the charm of electronic display alphabets. FF Dot Matrix and Screen Matrix are rooted in 'the everyday banality of the techno dream world: state of the art typography, available at your TESCO check-out till, ready-made by your bus ticket vending machine, flashed at you in a seedy travel agent's office, screaming at you by an out-of-date needle printer.'One step up, it's the slightly more glamorous appeal of electronic time

made FF Call – an extended suite of alphabets based on different brands of mobile phone. In some ways the quintessential type family of the year 2000.

Office machines have inspired a large number of FontFonts. After Erik van Blokland had made FF Trixie, the first dirty typewriter font, Cornel Windlin soon followed suit with FF Magda – a more geometric, 1970s typewriter face. Much later, Henning Krause and Critzler, drastically laundered Magda and made FF Magda Clean.

Like Magda, FF HardCase by the Berlin-based Russian mathematician Dmitri Lavrow refers to the last generation of hand-operated typewriters; it even has mono-spacing, which Magda doesn't. But while Magda is a digital reworking of an existing model, HardCase is pure fantasy, combining perfectly clean shapes with unexpected typographic niceties and lively details.

The same can be said of FF Typestar by Steffen Sauerteig of eBoy, one of the most sophisticated typewriter-inspired fonts of the library – typographically refined, yet essentially geometric. Most of the other FontFonts that have come out of the eBoy's studio are somehow related to their work as image-makers for print and screen. EBoy are specialized in pixel-based illustration and have designed a family of compatible 'pixelated' fonts, FF eBoy, as well as a series of low-resolution digital characters, FF Peecol. Other eBoy fonts that somehow refer to low-resolution screen technology are FF ReadOut and FF Jigger by Sauerteig, and FF SubVario/Sub Mono by Kai Vermehr.

The most exotic font in this category of machine type comes all the way from Korea. Hyun Cho and Min Choi from Seoul had a look at the transmission verification reports spit out by fax machines and created FF Tronic, a font family made entirely of perpendicular and diagonal lines; the italics are wonderfully quirky.

Straight lines

Some extreme typographic experiments from the 1910s and

Considering a career in architecture?

1 555 WIL MONT

Julia Sysmäläinen faked these tickets, using FF Readout, FF eBoy, FF Motter Festival and FF Screenstar.

Cassette-catalogue for the Frischluft exhibition, Duisburg 1987, designed by Gábor Bódy with the original Yokkmokk typeface.

FF Hardcase (FontCard made by Dmitri Lavrow).

FF Call (poster by Mark van Bronkhorst).

1920s did away with two out of three of the basic geometric shapes: designers like Rodchenko and Van Doesburg used only straight lines, trying to avoid diagonals as well. Taking clues from their iconoclast thinking, designers in the 1990s have made ample use of the possibilities of the Mac to create their own minimalist, straight-lined alphabets. Here, again, Neville Brody led the way. FF Pop is a monoline typeface based on a rectangular grid; most of its diagonals are merely suggested by the oblique inner terminals of strokes.

In 1993, French designer Pierre di Sciullo published FF Minimum; the large family of grid-based fonts was something of a milestone. There is probably no other typeface of its kind that is equally experimental and entertaining at the same time – and still utterly usable, as di Sciullo himself has shown in his impressive design of the signage of the Centre National de Danse in Pantin. FF Minimum's basic forms are rigorous and rigid – a truly modernist exercise. The variations, however, take this initial idea into every possible direction, making the family into an undogmatic, eclectic series of fonts that dance, hang down from the ceiling, lie flat on the floor, wait for a companion or indulge in drinking. Di Sciullo, the philosopher of French typography, has created the Minimum as a kind of visual essay on transformation. The 17-style retail version contains only a part of his many variations; others remain reserved for the designer's own exclusive use.

Donald Beekman of Amsterdam, like so many type designers, is also a musician – in his case, a professional

bass and guitar player. Many of his FontFonts are based on headlines and logos he originally drew for music techno-style posters and packaging. FF Beekman is an exception. It was based on Beekman's research into simplified lettering that makes using of straight lines only – from Van Doesburg's alphabet to crude self-made lettering on shop signs across Europe. Beekman created three weights based on an extended square; their simplicity allows for extreme deformation. FF Beekman is probably the only FontFont whose creator encourages digital scaling to make condensed, compressed or extended variants.

Mitigated geometry

Although geometric construction is a useful expedient for creating new forms and researching extreme typographic solutions, it is not the best tool for creating legible type. In the past, engineers have constructed letterforms for signage and for the industry using the ruler and the compass; using these typefaces in print today can be a means of creating a specific style, but the reader may not be happy with it.

The FontFont library has made an important contribution in 'mitigating' the geometry of certain constructed typefaces from the past. Albert-Jan Pool took DIN Mittelschrift and DIN Engschrift, the standard types of German industry, and adapted their somewhat clumsy curves to more sophisticated typographic criteria. The operation resulted in one of the best selling families of the FontFont library. Pool did the same with OCR B, making it into a small but usable family, OCR F. The Italian Albert Pinggera who, like Pool, studied at the Royal Academy in The Hague, was commissioned to make a more refined version of Letter Gothic. The stories of FF DIN and FF Letter Gothic can be read elsewhere in this book. ⊕

The fonts of Max Kisman
Crafting cultural identity

Emily King
1999

set in FF Meta Pro and FF Jacque Fat

Unlike most Dutch designers who contributed to the FontFont library in its early years, Max Kisman was never concerned with book typography or text fonts. His attitude is radical rather than functionalist. During his 30-year career as a graphic designer, he has established himself as one of Holland's most independent graphic communicators. Although his view of typography has affinities with that of FontFont co-founder Neville Brody, there are also remarkable differences.

Thus writes Emily King in a chapter from her thesis on contemporary typography, reprinted here in book form for the first time.

BORN IN GRONINGEN in 1953, Max Kisman was educated at Amsterdam's Rietveld Academy in the mid 1970s. He remembers it as a period of student radicalism, 'Those were the days of student revolt and other activities like squatting. It was a crisis, so there were a lot of reasons for students to be involved and that had an influence on the way of thinking about design and educating designers. We saw this very clear relation between society and education.' [1]

Amongst Kisman's teachers at the Academy was Jan van Toorn, veteran of the debate with Wim Crouwel and inspirer of the politically active design group Wild Plakken. While Kisman has claimed never to have been highly politicised himself, he has argued that such an environment left him with a strong sense of social responsibility, 'As a designer or an art student you should be aware of your responsibilities and the consequences of everything that you do.'

Emerging from this environment left Kisman with an antipathy toward working within 'the commercial field.' Maintaining that stance throughout his career, Kisman's work has been primarily for non-mainstream magazines, cultural institutions and, more recently, a subscriber-sponsored arts-based TV station.

Alongside Jan van Toorn, Kisman studied at the Rietveld Academy under Gerard Unger. Although at that time Unger was employed by Hell as a type designer, he did not offer formal teaching on the subject or encourage students to concentrate upon type design in any depth. The tools with which to create fonts remained inaccessible at that time and subsequently type design was still viewed as the field of specialists. On leaving art school in 1977, Kisman set up as a freelance graphic designer and a few years later, in the early 1980s, he became the designer of a small, independent music magazine *Vinyl*. This Amsterdam-based publication was set up very much as a response to the innovative British magazine, *The Face*. Responding to Neville Brody's radical designs for that magazine, Kisman began to experiment by creating new headline typefaces for each issue.

Pre-digital type

Like Brody, Kisman began designing alphabets well before the advent of desktop font creation software. Crafting designs using basic means, for example by hand using stencils, or manipulating existing alphabets using optical systems, lenses and copy paper, Kisman created a host of new typographic styles for the magazine. This ingenuity notwithstanding, Kisman was quick to pick up the technology to produce digital typefaces when it did emerge in the mid-1980s. He acquired a very basic home computer in 1984, and a couple of years later invested in one of the very first Macintoshes, a MacPlus. Like Zuzana Licko at Emigre in Berkeley, California,

Nouveau Salon des Cent
Exposition Internationale d'Affiches
Hommage à Toulouse-Lautrec

Paradiso Amsterdam *donderdag 21, vrijdag 22 en zaterdag 23 februari 1991*

Donderdag 21 Februari: Annette Peacock, Terminal Cheese Cake, Cop Shoot Cop, Pain Teens. Vrijdag 22 Februari:
Simon Turner, Mark Springer, The Cranes, Gagar Radai, Caspar Brötzmann. Zaterdag 23 Februari: Surkus,
Psychic Warriors Ov Gaia, Jackofficers, The Orb. Entree F12,50 & lidmaatschap per avond. Passepartout F25,
& lidmaatschap. Voorverkoop AUB VVV Nwe Muziekhandel Plaatwerk Get Records Boudisque RaF

Posters by
Max Kisman

Kisman constructed his first digital alphabets from the very basic bitmaps that were available on the Mac, long before the widespread accessibility of the PostScript format.

In spite of Kisman's speed in exploiting the type design possibilities of desktop digital technology, he has claimed that the focus of his interests never lay with the design of type. Rather, he has insisted that his concern lay with the significance of technological change within the broader field of communication. Not viewing himself as a type designer, Kisman would probably never have completed any of his alphabets were it not for the encouragement of Erik Spiekermann of FontShop who hoped to release certain designs under the FontFont label.

In the first group of Max Kisman's designs to be distributed as FontFonts was FF Network, a PostScript version of a former bitmap font. Like designs by Zuzana Licko, which arose from identical technological circumstances, such as Oakland, Network's awkward blocky forms began to assume a retro appeal only a few years after their design. The other typefaces within the original group of Kisman FontFonts are less basic. But in spite of a relative formal sophistication, these fonts – FF Scratch, FF Cutout and FF Vortex, all published by FontShop – still appear firmly rooted in the era in which they were first conceived. With their geometric construction, apparently influenced by certain strands of early modern type design, and their jarring forms they immediately bring to mind the pages of the magazines for which they were designed. Discussing these kinds of angular styles, the critic Rick Poynor noted that 'fate has overtaken the angular post-constructivist type design of Neville Brody, Zuzana Licko and Max Kisman.' Poynor described a process by which typefaces, once 'fresh, unexpected, precisely attuned to the moment,' get used increasingly often in less and less appropriate contexts and end up looking 'irredeemably passé.'[2]

Brody: affinities and disparities

Addressing the fonts of Max Kisman, the most obvious point of comparison, in terms both of formal semblance and of the similarity of the circumstances in which they were created, are the designs of Neville Brody. The influence of Brody's work for *The Face* on Kisman's designs for *Vinyl* is apparent, and as such both are firmly embedded in the youth-generated fashion of the early to mid-1980s. But dig a little deeper and disparities between the work of these two designers begin to appear. Expanding upon his innovative designs for *The Face*, Brody has suggested that they were wrought from 'frustration' with the limits of his education and a desire to avoid falling into the 'trap' of tradition.[3] This language smacks of that of the more nihilistic strains of early twentieth-century modernism. Kisman, on the other hand, has justified his design work from the early 1980s in a more positive manner. For Kisman typeface design is about 'identity', and by creating a host of new faces in the early 1980s he was catering to a youth culture in which identity was becoming increasingly 'pluriform'. Kisman has argued that 'designers represent groups' and are able to make a positive contribution in the crafting of 'cultural identity'.

In an article about *The Face*, the cultural critic Dick Hebdige argued that the magazine sought to 'liberate the signifier from the constraints imposed upon it by the "rationalist" theology of representation.'[4] The implication of this argument is that *The Face* amounted to no more than a procession of meaninglessly fashionable imagery, according to Hebdige, a 'ceaseless procession of simulcra.' From Brody's own words, and from Hebdige's analysis, it is possible to form a view of the designer as an iconoclast, crafting fashionable imagery out of the ruins of meaning. But while Brody danced upon the 'fissure' between signifier and signified, Kisman saw himself as being an active creator of cultural signification.

Curiosity versus nihilism

The differences between Brody and Kisman's approaches to design could be seen to be emerging from more deeply embedded cultural contrasts. Britain in the early 1980s was in the throes of the first Thatcherite recession. In the immediate post-punk period, some young people, for example those termed the New Romantics, developed increasingly extravagant and theatrical styles that appeared to be deliberately divorced from the misery of many of their immediate circumstances. The Netherlands shared Britain's recession and also much of its fashion, but possibly the prevailing culture of the country prevented the nihilism that was apparent in Britain at the time from ever completely taking hold. While Kisman has viewed the early 1980s as a time when 'people were discovering themselves' and, as a result, coming together in tribes to exert more effectively their new found identities,[11] in Britain, youthful fashions were more likely to be interpreted as a celebration of lack of meaning. Discussing the style of Boy George, an icon of the early 1980s British pop scene, the music critic David Rimmer argued, 'It's like an everyman culture where all those symbols are used together and each one contradicts the other. Used together they can't have meaning because they represent different things.'[5] Far from witnessing the creation of a coherent youth tribe, Rimmer believed he was looking upon the disintegration of the very possibility of such a thing.

Moving on from *The Face* to design the men's magazine *Arena* in 1987, Neville Brody turned his back upon his pioneering typographic palette and embraced more conventional styles. Referring to the widespread imitation of the design with which he had become associated, Brody claimed that 'With the choice of Helvetica, I'm simply saying "STOP".'[6] For Brody, the innovative visual language of The Face was justified for only as long as it maintained its position at the very point of the spearhead of fashion. Not so concerned with being at the vanguard, Kisman has appeared to believe that his designs for *Vinyl* served a broader societal role.

Kisman and Emigre

As well as the work of Brody, as Poynor pointed out, another comparison that suggests itself to the work of Max Kisman is the type design used on the pages of the Californian magazine *Emigre*. In the fifteenth issue of that magazine, published

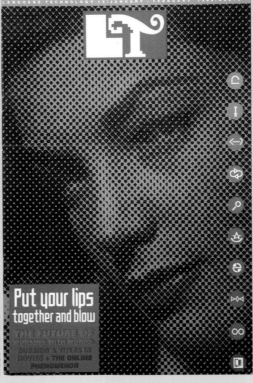

↑
Capital alphabet
cut from Ulano
masking film;
this later became
FF Scratch.

←···
Magazine covers
designed by Kisman
in the 1980s.
The typeface used
for LT (right) later
became FF Rosetta.

FF Kisman

Cutout

Vortex

Scratch

Scratch Outline

FF Fudoni

Fudoni One

Fudoni Two

Fudoni Three

FF Rosetta

Rosetta Regular

Rosetta Italic

Rosetta Bold

Rosetta Bold Italic

FF Jacque

Jacque Slim

Jacque Regular

Jacque Fat

in 1990, *Emigre* addressed the design of Kisman, having become aware of his work through the experimental type journal *TYP/ Typografisch Papier*. Kisman had shared the responsibility of editing/designing this magazine, the purpose of which was to explore the relationship between technology and communication, as part of a collective team since the late 1980s. The editors of *Emigre* claimed that for them becoming aware of the journal was 'instrumental in confirming [their] beliefs that there exist alternative opinions about type and that [their] own ideas concerning this topic were not entirely alien.'[7]

Kisman's font designs do not look out of place within *Emigre*, and the speculation regarding the relative nature of legibility that occurs within the articles of *TYP* is similar to much of that within *Emigre*. But in issue 15 of the magazine, where Kisman's typefaces are placed alongside contributions from Jeffrey Keedy and Barry Deck, important differences between Kisman's school of experimental design and those which were thriving in the United Sates in the late 1980s and early 1990s do become apparent. These differences are explored in an article published in the same issue of *Emigre* by Ellen Lupton and Jay Abbott Miller.

Under the title 'Structuralism and Typography,' Lupton and Miller defined and explored various stages in the development of type design. Arriving at the late 1980s, they classified the designs of Max Kisman and also those of *Emigre's* co-editor Zuzana Licko as neo-modernist: the criteria for this term being a defamiliarisation of the alphabet; a turn 'to technology for their aesthetic cues;' and a self-definition 'against the pop mainstream'. In contrast, they called the designs of Barry Deck and Jeffrey Keedy post-structuralist: a mode of practice characterized by a rejection of 'master codes'; a loss of 'faith in renewal'; and a 'figurative and narrative character that is distinct from ...hermetic abstraction'.[8] Lupton and Miller's distinction emphasized the optimism and the sense of responsibility that informed the work of the Dutch designer, in comparison to the more theoretically sophisticated gloom of many of his American counterparts.

Lupton and Miller's categorisation of the early output of Slovak ex-patriot Licko alongside the work of Kisman does seem appropriate. However, through the 1990s, while Kisman remained concerned with the technological cutting edge, Licko's work became more and more bound up with the culturally-embedded nature of typography. Licko's 1996 design Mrs Eaves, an exploration of Baskerville, amounts to an attempt to reconcile technological innovation with the deeply ingrained character typographic convention. Investing a great deal in the traditional letterform, it is possible that Zuzana Licko would estimate a longer survival rate for the written word than the '50 years' that Kisman has ventured. In contrast to the techno-futurist work of her early career, Licko has displayed more of what has been called a 'narrative' sensibility in her type design.[9]

Humanist concern

Kisman's interest in technological innovation led him to become art director for the magazine *Language and Technology* in 1987. A forerunner to the American magazine *Wired*, this publication claimed 'computer-aided communication' as its field of expertise.[10] *Language and Technology* offered Kisman an important outlet for his techno-centred design style. But although, over the course of his

ontwerp: 1991 Max Kisman

**30 jaar
Amnesty
International**

career, Kisman has become more preoccupied with technology, his interest has always been overlaid with a guiding humanist concern. Unlike the present editorial team of *Wired*, who can be accused of having become obsessed with gadgetry while giving little or no thought to social or cultural consequences, Kisman has remained attune to these kinds of issues, arguing, 'It is important to be involved in societal developments, you have to be motivated, take a position and be responsible for that position '.

Kisman's optimistic yet humanist stance toward technological innovation can also be contrasted with that of the editorial team of FUSE, another publication that has addressed various techno-concerns. Kisman contributed the font Linear Konstrukt to the second issue of the publication, an issue claiming 'Runes' as its theme. The editorial of the magazine, with its emphasis upon the 'mystical' and the 'spiritual', [11] pursued an argument that was to become well-trodden within FUSE – that technology was in fact returning us all to the threatening wilds of pre-history. Not fully in keeping with the tone of the editorial, Kisman's typeface was an exploration of the possibility of combining geometrical reduction with a style-driven brand of multi-cultural awareness. In fact derived from the roman alphabet, the characters of Linear Konstrukt resemble those of various non-European cultures, the result being a font that is more suggestive than practical.

Although the stance might appear naive to certain of his colleagues, Max Kisman has continued to believe that technology can be a force for positive social change. He has argued that the technologies that have emerged around type design have made a contribution of broader significance, 'Programs like Fontographer are giving groups, through the designers who represent them, a cultural identity. So you have a pluriform society – all these identities.'

Aware that his position contrasts with that of many of his American or English counterparts, Kisman has identified his guiding concern for issues of social responsibility as 'particularly Dutch'. In the landscape of post-1987 type design, the work of Kisman can be strongly related to that of other designers who have pursued fashionably driven or technologically informed courses. But in spite of the similarities between his own work and that of various international designers, Kisman does seem correct in the assertion he has been informed by a set of attitudes and codes that are specific to the culture around design in the Netherlands. ⊕

Notes
1. Max Kisman quotes from an interview held on 26 May, 1995
2. Rick Poynor, 'American Gothic,' *Eye* 6/1992, p.64–67
3. Jon Wozencroft, *The Graphic Language of Neville Brody*, London 1988, p.18
4. Dick Hebdige, *Hiding in the Light*, London 1988, p.163
5. Dave Rimmer, *Like Punk Never Happened*, London 1985, p.58
6. Wozencroft 1988, p. 38
7. 'Do You Read Me? (Special Type Issue),' *Emigre* No.15, 1990
8. ibid.
9. Lupton, Ellen, 1996, *Mixing Messages*, London 1996, p.57
10. 'Max Kisman,' *Aldus Magazine*, April/June 1994, p.30
11. FUSE 2, 1991

FF Quadraat:
Legibility, versatility, flamboyance

Fred Smeijers
2000

set in FF Quadraat Sans and Head

FF Quadraat, designed by Fred Smeijers, was named after the Arnhem design group Quadraat, of which Smeijers was a founding partner in 1991.
What started out as a small family of serifed Romans steadily grew to become one of the FontFont library's most versatile families of text and display faces.

ALTHOUGH ALWAYS A digital typeface, FF Quadraat is based on hand-made forms. It has qualities that are rooted in sixteenth-century type; in fact it is FontFont's only Garamond-style old face. Developments since its initial release encouraged the designer to expand the design to meet a very wide range of requirements. First the seriffed fonts were expanded with full expert sets. A matching sans serif family was added. Further additions are a Cyrillic and some strong display versions. This makes FF Quadraat a rarity among traditional seriffed designs. The initial roman and italic styles provide a str ong character that is maintained throughout the whole family. FF Quadraat is proof of its designer's view that in tradition lies the future.

FF Quadraat was first released at the end of 1992 and it consisted then of the following styles: Roman, Bold, Italic and Small Caps. At first there was no Bold Italic: at that time I was making this typeface to satisfy my immediate typographic needs and Small Caps were a higher priority than Bold Italic.

Contrast: not too much

The FF Quadraat design did not come out of the blue. There were some strong starting requirements. The general character had to be definitely traditional – it had to be a proper text face – and at the same time it had to have a certain contemporary atmosphere. It had to be as economical with space as Times Roman, but without the rather high contrast between the thick and thin strokes of Times. Too much contrast is often the reason that many typefaces look too thin in text sizes and are simply irritating to read in substantial passages of text. In the long run, a little too bold is better than a little too thin. Plantin has less contrast than FF Quadraat, and this is more pleasing to the eye, but its general character tends towards the static and clumsy. The new design had to be more flamboyant but not at the cost of legibility. For example the lowercase roman letters were given a little optical slant to the right. It is a detail that I think is helpful in reading long texts. Manuscript letters often show this feature. Although its effect is not open to any scientific proof, it is simply more pleasing to the eye. My intentions here can be seen when the three typefaces are printed at the same x-height.

Italics cut in wood

FF Quadraat Italic is quite a different kind of letter than the roman or minuscule forms. Here, too, it is traditional. The first typographic italics were cut separately from romans. Aldus Manutius, the Italian renaissance printer who is seen as the introducer of italic fonts, printed whole books in italic type. This custom did not last long and soon italic had to take second place to roman. FF Quadraat Italic is based on renaissance examples cut in wood. This was less exact a reproduction technique than the copper-engraving that was used later. The influence of a coarser material (wood), and probably also the use of less delicate cutting tools than the very refined graver, left its traces on the shapes of the letters. In those prints, the italic letters written delicately with a goose-quill by writing masters such as Arrighi or Vespasiano were translated literally into cut-out shapes. FF Quadraat Italic is based on these simple cut-out shapes, and this gives an italic which serves well enough as a companion to the roman. In larger sizes its character is both strong and elegant. This may be why FF Quadraat Italic soon began to be used on its own, as a display letter. The slant of the italic is only 7 degrees: normally a Garamond italic has a slant of around 12 degrees. This is also a feature of the writing examples rather than of typographic sources. At the same time FF Quadraat Italic is rather narrow and thus has an entirely different rhythm than the roman. All this ensures – paradoxically – that it is different enough to serve as a companion to the roman.

Three years after the first release, the FF Quadraat roman and italic fonts were expanded with expert sets; and a Bold Italic was also added.

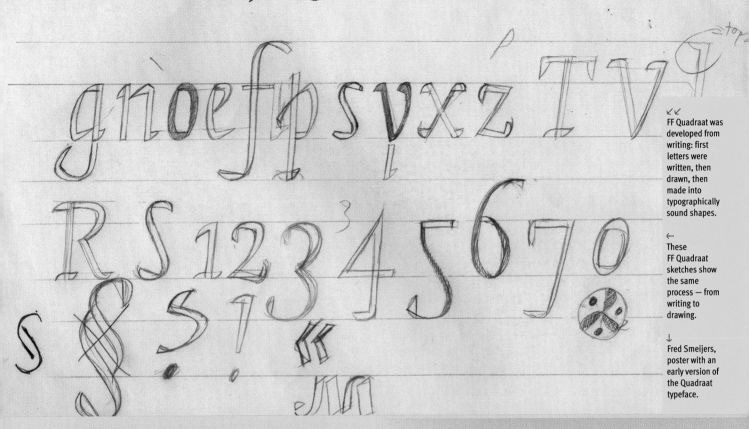

FF Quadraat was developed from writing: first letters were written, then drawn, then made into typographically sound shapes.

←
These FF Quadraat sketches show the same process — from writing to drawing.

↓
Fred Smeijers, poster with an early version of the Quadraat typeface.

Quadraat Sans

In 1997 the FF Quadraat family was expanded with a sans serif version. People thought it was not possible to design a matching sans serif for FF Quadraat. These people were mainly graphic designers who began to say they needed a matching sans. At first I told them that there were enough sans serif designs available that could be used with FF Quadraat; for example Gill Sans or FF Balance. Even Helvetica is suitable if you need a strong contrast. From a traditionalist type designer's point of view, type mixture is a graphic designer's choice. But for some graphic designers today, mixing type designs seems to be too much hassle, and I was challenged by friends to at least make an attempt. So I did, and before long FF Quadraat Sans was born.

Matching sans serif and seriffed designs may be part of a small Dutch tradition. In the 1930s Jan van Krimpen was the first type designer to make such an attempt, with his Romulus typeface. In the digital age he has been followed by Martin Majoor (FF Scala) and Lucas de Groot (FF Thesis), and FF Quadraat takes its place in this line. FF Quadraat Sans follows the character of its seriffed model, resulting in a humanist sans suitable for setting longer texts. Since the seriffed typeface has a strong character, the sans has a specific flavour too. It is not just humanist but very humanist, and quite a character among the sanses. Unlike seriffed typefaces, sans serifs naturally allow variations of weight and width, and FF Quadraat Sans was soon accompanied by an elegant condensed version.

Display versions

The thought of adding some display versions started with a commission for a book cover design. I used FF Quadraat Italic and despite its strong character I was not entirely satisfied. The design proportions were based on text sizes and I was tempted to change these proportions so that they would stand out more in the cover design. To be honest, I enjoyed exaggerating my own design so that it was more suitable for use in large sizes. Making type designs suitable for display use is fun; it seems as if you have to think in the opposite direction to that of designing for text sizes. The display versions are very suitable for the few words that have to draw attention, as on posters, magazine or book covers, logos and even packaging. So in 1998 FF Quadraat was expanded with four display versions. FF Quadraat Sans Display Semibold and FF Quadraat Sans Display Black are based on the Sans. FF Quadraat Display Italic and FF Quadraat Display Bold Italic are based on the seriffed italic.

Latest additions

The FF Quadraat family's newest members make it one of the few typeface designs that can be used for almost any typographic problem. The main branch of the family remains the seriffed version, suitable for books and other extended texts. But these days, a lovely roman with an italic – and nothing more – is something for connoisseurs only. Now even the general graphic designer does not belong to that group. A typeface is in fact a humble tool, something to be used every day and on a large scale. To meet present demands, a type family has to be big, with members that excel in their own definite and special ways. This, and the challenge of blending additions into the 'Quadraat character,' were the main reasons for these extra members.

FF Quadraat Headliners

The headliners are different from the display versions of FF Quadraat in short they are less strong in character. While the FF Quadraat display fonts really stand out, the headliners are like the 'display versions' that were provided with metal typefaces for larger sizes. In all those situations where you need to use large sizes frequently – in a magazine, for example, but also in advertising – the combination of display and headliner can be a very useful one.

FF Quadraat Monospaced

A monospaced is simply a typeface whose characters have a single width. The monospaced look is associated with the world of business correspondence, and thus has a degree of formality missing from handwriting. This is true in reading sizes. However many typographic fonts come onto the market, the monospaced will have a firm place in our ordinary use of letters, and the fact that we no longer use typewriters is hardly an argument. So, it is not surprising that the monospaced is now even gaining ground as part of the typographic palette. Its off-beat character can be very pleasing.

So FF Quadraat is not just a type family made up of the usual visual variations of weight and width. It is also an attempt to make a typeface with variations that relate to common typographic and social customs. ☕

Scripts & lettering done by 'd'n Rooije Snijer', a local market-

You know Quadraat, the roman with the tasty flesh, **now try QUADRAAT SANS!** New flavour!

bully, available as fonts soon. Be careful designers, BULLY fonts are **not** amateur proof!'!

BE SMART
first: BUY
then: USE
Quadraat Sans
the sans with the lovely figures!

Tip of the week! Have guts, use simple black & white!

Shop till you drop

National Galleries of Scotland Shops mailing list

We can keep you up to date about events, sales and special offers. Be first to receive details of new Christmas cards and exclusive National Galleries merchandise. Please fill in your details overleaf, and either hand it in at any of our shops or post it to us.

National Gallery The Mound
Portrait Gallery Queen Street
Gallery of Modern Art Belford Road
Dean Gallery Belford Road

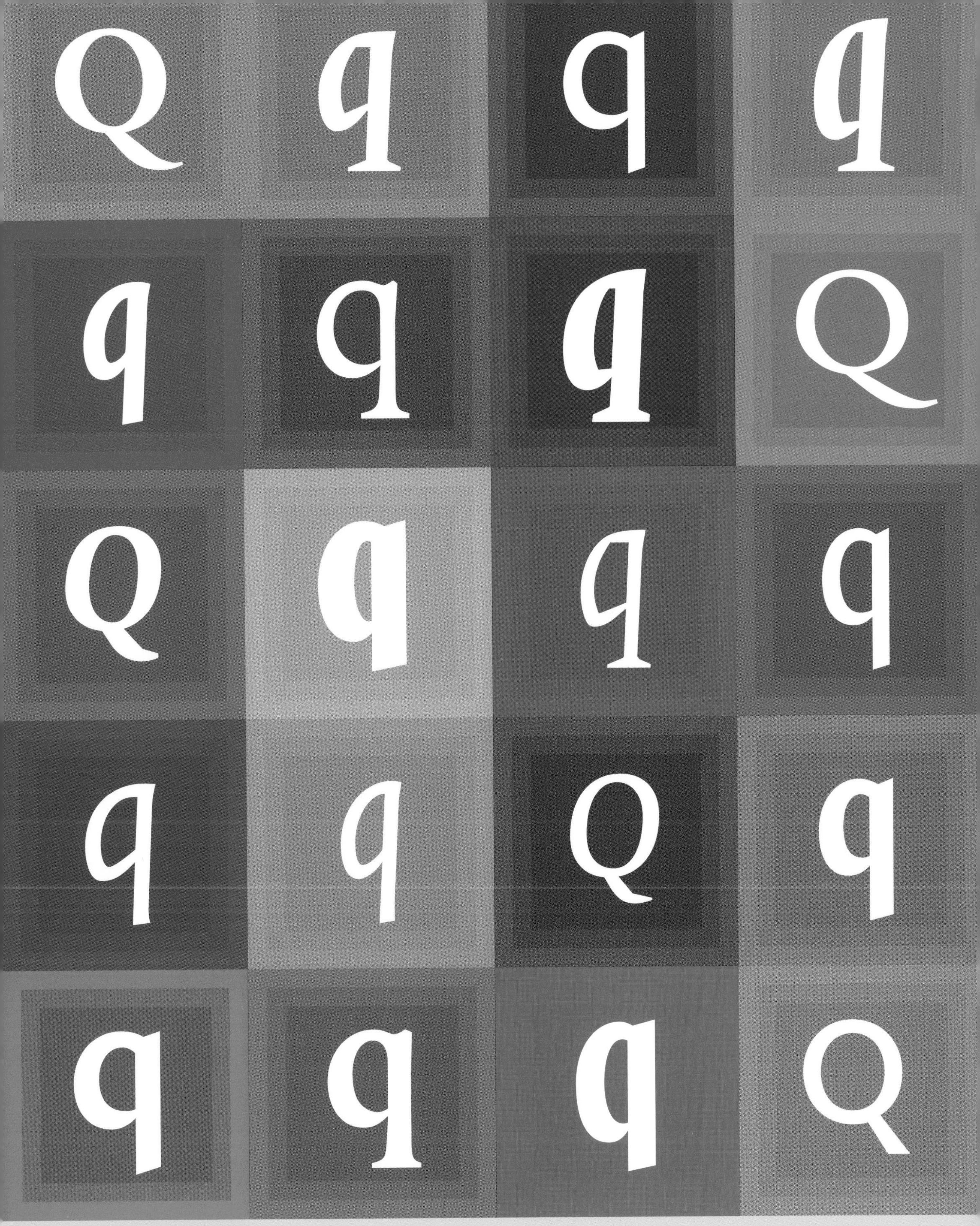

CAPS BOLD
SANS CONDENSED BOLD ITALIC
CAPS BOLD ITALIC
SANS ITALIC
SANS BOLD

BOLD ITALIC
REGULAR
DISPLAY SANS BLACK
SANS CONDENSED ITALIC
BOLD

SANS REGULAR
DISPLAY BOLD ITALIC
ITALIC
CAPS ITALIC
DISPLAY SANS MEDIUM

DISPLAY ITALIC
CAPS
SANS CONDENSED REGULAR
SANS CONDENSED BOLD
SANS CAPS

FF QUADRAAT: SERIF · SANS · CONDENSED · DISPLAY

Erik Spiekermann
1996

set in FF Info Text and Info Display

Its name speaks volumes: FF Info was designed to convey information from the writer to the reader in a way that is as independent as possible from typographic trends or reproduction technologies. The form of the characters follows their function – that, in a manner of speaking, is their duty. Yet every typeface must be visually up-to-date, even if it shuns trendiness and fashionable features. To express the Zeitgeist while maintaining a unique personality and still remain, to some extent, objective – this is what constitutes the basis of any relevant type design.

This face had originally been designed in 1986 as Fidia, to be used on pharmaceutical labels for an Italian company. They lost interest halfway through production, but it had become obvious (once again) that type made for very small sizes would be well suited for large sizes, e. g. signage. I gave the old data to Albert Pinggera, who made it into the first version of FF Info Display.

FIDIA 55 NORMAL
abcdefghijklmnopqrstuvwxyz
ABCDEFGHIJKLMNOPQRSTUVWXYZ
äöüß1234567890
(.,-;:!?"/)

FIDIA 75 BOLD
abcdefghijklmnopqrstuvwxyz
ABCDEFGHIJKLMNOPQRSTUVWXYZ
äöüß1234567890
(.,-;:!?"/)

FIDIA SERIF
abcdefghijklmnopqrstuvwxyz
ABCDEFGHIJKLMNOPQRSTUVWXYZ
äöüß1234567890
(.,-;:!?"/)

Made for signage

The earliest designs of FF Info, a typeface which in spite of its neutral outlook does not give an impression of technical coldness, were made to be used in signage – for instance in traffic, at railway stations and in public buildings. In most of these cases the problem lies mainly in the limited space available. The Info typeface therefore had to be narrow without giving an impression of being cramped. Many orientation systems, such as the one in Munich airport, use Univers Condensed for lack of alternatives. It allows large quantities of text to be accommodated in a limited space but is not easy to read because the crushed letterforms are very similar to each other. The condensed version of Frutiger is considerably more legible but runs too wide for such purposes.

FF Info's x-height is fairly large without being dominant. The tension between its round outlines and slightly rectangular counters makes for clarity and, simultaneously, for vivacity – an important prerequisite to motivate the reader. Subtly flared and rounded strokes and open joints compensate for the fuzziness and optical illusions that happen when reading text under poor conditions. The uppercase characters are large enough to articulate the beginnings of words, while discreet enough not to stand out from the body text when used as initials or in all-caps acronyms.

FF Info runs ca. 15 percent narrower than most current text faces, even while the character spacing was deliberately kept open and somewhat loose. All-too-tight spacing is a common flaw in signage systems. One of our main concerns was to accommodate the limited space with agreeable letterspacing; another, to create letterforms that would be easy to distinguish from each other. It is a known fact that when reading signs we don't perceive continuous texts but decipher the single characters of a message that is often imposed upon us unexpectedly. Every character should be clearly separated from the next, and especially the numerals must be easily differentiated from each other. Four of the most easily confused forms in signage are: the lowercase 'i' and 'l,' uppercase 'I' and the number '1'. Therefore, the display version of FF Info's lowercase 'i' has a small top serif, the lowercase 'l' is bent towards the right at the bottom, and the capital 'I' is characterized by top and bottom serifs. This description may sound kind of cryptic, as you are now reading the text version of FF Info, which lacks most of these features, but we'll get back to this later.

Bureaucratic heritage

The differentiating characteristics described were also used in ITC Officina, for which I made the earliest drawings in the late 1980s – the same period in which FF Info and FF Meta were first conceived. All these traits originally stem from typewriter faces, in which the broad serifs serve to widen the narrow letters 'i', 'l', 'I' and the number '1' in order to accommodate them in the mono-spaced system without causing gaps in the text.

i

Airline

Fluggesellschaft Airline

Aer Lingus
Aeroflot
Aero Lloyd**
Air Alfa
Air Berlin
Air Canada
Air Europa
Air France
Air Malta
Bulgarian

i
YP
LFA
AB
AC
AEA
AF
KM
UK
VIM
YRG
AZ
TZ
IQ
QS

Düsseldorf International

FF Info was first used
for signage and a
Corporate Design
Programme for
Düsseldorf International
airport in 1996.

Because of the wide diffusion of typewriters and the massive presence of office correspondence, we have gotten used to these peculiarities; as a result of our bureaucratic heritage they are somehow associated with a certain urgency that when used in signage, is just as welcome as formal distinctiveness. We usually read signs while in motion, and often from sharp angles, so that characters are distorted. On backlit signs the radiation of the light makes straight angles appear rounded.

From the outset, FF Info was conceived as a typeface with rounded strokes, resulting in characters that aren't as heavily distorted when back-lit as those with sharp angles. Cynics may remark that sharpness cannot be lost where the letters have none. However, it must be realized that, from the outset, the construction of the FF Info characters was conceived to foster legibility and distinctiveness without relying on sharp details.

White type on a dark background, as often used in signage, is more powerful than black type on a light background because of the glowing effect. This effect is even more obvious when used in backlit signage. We carefully balanced the steps between the subsequent weights of FF Info – Regular, Book, Medium, Semibold and Bold – so that the subtle increase allows users to compensate for backlighting and/or negative type. The weight steps were established using Luc(as) de Groot's 'Interpolation Theory', a formula for calculating subsequent weights which he used to develop his eight-weight Thesis family – originally a FontFont. It is based on the assumption that our eyes do not register the increase of stroke weights in a linear way but exponentially, whereby the contrast values of, say, Light and Extra Light should be less far apart than those of the Black and Extra Black weights of the same family. In practical terms, this means that when using FF Info, the Regular weight has precisely the same optical strength when used as light type on a dark background as the Book weight will have as black type on a white background. On backlit signs, on the other hand, black type on light background will seem thinner – a perfect occasion for using FF Info's Semibold weight.

As a bonus for those who actually use FF Info for developing a signage system, the typeface offers an easily accessible range of arrows in all directions and in each of the weights.

Text version

The text version of FF Info lacks some of the mentioned features of the display version. As my colleague Ole Schäfer and I were studying laser prints of the new typeface meant for use at large sizes, we found that it did not look bad at all at 10 point and even smaller. This confirmed a thesis I have always defended,

namely that specific technical constraints that influence the construction of a typeface also foster its usability under difficult circumstances of a different nature.

FF Meta, for instance, was developed for use at very small point sizes, on low-quality stock and with bad printing techniques. Nowadays, it is also successfully used for headlines as well as signage systems, although at those large sizes certain effects may occur which remain hidden at 6 point. Perhaps it is precisely these unusual visual aspects that define its aesthetic appeal and were conducive to its success.

When I designed ITC Officina back in 1988, it was meant for office communication, as an optimized typewriter font to be used on laser printers. This requirement resulted in a certain simplicity which makes it look good on the screen as well; now ITC Officina is one of the most widely used typefaces for the design of multimedia and online publications.

Keeping in mind the multiple functionality of typefaces originally conceived for a particular use, we decided to include an optimized text version in the FF Info family. The spacing of FF Info Text was designed to be slightly looser, the way it should be for text sizes. As we register complete words rather than single letters when reading, the need to clearly distinguish between similar characters such as 'i', 'I', 'l' and '1' becomes less urgent; therefore the serifs incorporated in the display version were no longer necessary. The lowercase 'g', which in FF Info Display has an open tail (g), was given the typical double-storied shape it also has in most seriffed romans. The text version contained small caps and oldstyle figures and, some time after the release of the original family, italics.

The two sub-families – FF Info Display and FF Info Text – are so closely related that they match and mix perfectly. The stroke weights of both versions are identical. However, as their respective letterspacing values are different it may be necessary to fine-tune these values using the tracking possibilities of today's page layout software.

The design of a typeface family consisting of many fonts and containing thousands of signs represents a huge amount of work, which I would not have been able to do on my own. Albert Pinggera – who also digitised Letter Gothic for the FontFont series and later designed FF Strada – undertook the work of processing my old sketches and original data from the 1980s. The honing of many characters and the completion of the character sets was done by Ole Schäfer, who worked as a typographer at MetaDesign at the time. Ole also developed the text version of FF Info and added the small caps and oldstyle figures, as well as the Italic and, later, FF Info Office.

In other words, the development of FF Info is typical of the function-driven collaborative process which I have favoured over the years. ☻

Illiheig

Illiheig

Illiheig

Illiheig

Illiheig

Illiheig

Illiheig

Illiheig

Illiheig

Illiheig

Illiheig

Illiheig

The first negative box is set in the lightest weight, Regular. The second word, black on white, appears lighter, although set in the same weight. The third word is set in the next heavier weight, Book, and now appears as heavy as the first word.
Below that, all the weights of FF Info Display and Text are shown. They all share the same width.

Informations- und Leitsystem Flughafen Düsseldorf

Piktogramme sind ein wichtiger Bestandteil des Informations- und Leitsystemes. Wer den deutschen oder englischen Text nicht verstehen kann, weil er die Sprache nicht spricht, orientiert sich an den Symbolen.

Unbewußt werden die Zeichen von allen benutzt, weil sie eine viel schnellere Orientierung erlauben als der erklärende Text. Die meisten Piktogramme sind international gleich und von vielen Menschen bereits gelernt.

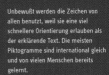

Wozu die vielen Symbole, die inhaltlich gar nicht neu und schon aus anderen Umgebungen bekannt sind?

In einem gut funktionierenden und gestalteten System beziehen sich alle Elemente auch formal aufeinander. Dies gilt für ein Info- und Leitsystem genauso wie für Architektur oder Kleidung. Deshalb wurden die Piktogramme stilistisch mit der Info in eine Beziehung gebracht, die den Betrachter optisch einen einheitlichen Eindruck vermittelt.

Bereits bekannte Zeichen erleichtern die Benutzung dabei erheblich.

Durch Verwendung von Farben als Codierung für Inhalte bekommen die Piktogramme im Informations- und Leitsystem eine „dritte Dimension". Der Benutzer bemerkt die Unterschiede und erlernt die Bedeutung der Farben unbewußt. Die Symbole stehen auf verschiedenfarbigen Fonds. Jede dieser Farben beschreibt eine Hierarchie im System. Grün steht für Verkehr, grau für Service und gelb als Signalfarben für besondere Aufmerksamkeiten.

Durch die quadratischen Flächen unter den Piktogrammen bekommt der Benutzer eine zusätzliche Information. Sie sind entweder weiß oder gelb, mit Ausnahme von Sonderzeichen, wie z.B. Polizei oder Erste Hilfe. Gelb steht für das Ziel, entweder als Bestätigung oder bei Pfeilen für die Bewegungsrichtung. Ein weißes Piktogramm ist nach dieser Logik immer mit einem gelben kombiniert.

The Nexus principle
A type design

Martin Majoor
2002–2005

set in FF Nexus Sans and Serif

About 20 years ago Martin Majoor graduated from the Academy of Fine Arts with a serif type design called Serré. It was never released; but in hindsight, Majoor realised it had provided the preliminary groundwork for his later typefaces. Subsequently he designed four major type families – Scala, Telefont, Seria and Nexus – adding new features with each new project.
Yet, in all those years Majoor's ideas and principles about type design did not fundamentally change.
The following article, a personal retrospective, is an updated and extended version of 'My type design philosophy,' published in 2002 in *tipoGráfica*, Buenos Aires, Argentina.

The headache of mixing type

It is my conviction that you cannot be a good type designer if you are not a book typographer. I am not talking about display types but about text types. A type designer must know how type works in a piece of text; he must know what happens with type on different sorts of paper; he must know how a typeface behaves with different printing techniques.

As a book designer I have worked on several complex books in which more than one typeface were needed in order to clarify things in the text. It is often quite useful to mix a sans with a serif typeface, but the problem is always which ones to choose. It is common to mix Times New Roman and Helvetica simply because both these fonts are available in the computer. It is not even the worst possible combination one can think of. Using sans serifs such as News Gothic, Gill Sans or Futura as text type is definitely acceptable, but with which serif faces can they be combined? Unfortunately, numerous combinations end up being used with no sense of style or knowledge of history. From an aesthetic point of view, combinations such as Garamond/Univers or Bodoni/Gill Sans produce a severe headache, and it is only in advertising (where a headache can be useful) that these combinations are possible. It became clear to me that the best solution for complex text was to use a combination of a serif and a sans that share a common ground. But which combination of serif and sans could meet this criterion?

TWO LINES ENGLISH EGYPTIAN.

W CASLON JUNR   LETTERFOUNDER

ACCIDENZ-GROTESK
EINE UMFANGREICHE SCHRIFTEN-FAMILIE FÜR MERKANTILE UND PRIVATE DRUCKSACHEN

Die einfache Grotesk hat sich unter den Schriften des Buchdruckers einen hervorragenden Platz errungen. Aber nicht nur für Druckwerke. Überall da, wo für das lebendige Wort ein monumentaler Ausdruck gefordert wird, stellt auch die Grotesk sich zur Wahl. Ihre Ruhe und Klarheit, die strenge Einfachheit ihres Aufbaues befähigen sie zur Wiedergabe jeder ernsten, gehaltenen Darlegung. Man sollte meinen, daß in diesen scheinbar nüchternen, nur auf den Zweck bedachten Formen zu wenig Anreiz läge, um die hohe Stellung der Grotesk im Schriftenschatze besonders des Buchdruckers zu halten. Aber liegt nicht gerade in diesen einfachen Konstruktionen, wenn sie wie bei der Accidenz-Grotesk von Meisterhand geschaffen wurden, mehr Schönheit, als in der Ausgestaltung mancher Kunstschrift? Kann die Formung einer durchdachten Eisenkonstruktion nicht auch zur Bewunderung hinreißen?

The origin of the sans

Before the mixing of serif and sans in text can be explained, the origins of sans serif typefaces should be clarified, as it is only for about the last hundred years that they have been in use. Officially, the very first sans serif typeface used in print was published around 1816 by the English typefoundry of William Caslon IV. This display face contained only capitals, and it is not clear where the rather clumsy forms originated. As a design, this sans serif typeface has little value.

Akzidenz Grotesk, published in 1898 by the German Berthold typefoundry in Berlin, is much more interesting. This sans serif immediately became a great success and was soon imitated by several typefoundries. Like all sans serifs of the time, Akzidenz Grotesk was meant to be used as a display face (the German word *Akzidenzschrift* means display face or jobbing type), however as it also included a lowercase it was suitable for text. But what was the basis for Akzidenz Grotesk? The first printing types date from the 15th century and consisted of serif typefaces that imitated handwriting. When the sans serif typefaces appeared in the 19th century they could be based on only the serif typefaces that were in use at that time. Most of the Akzidenz

acfs

Grotesk weights were probably cut by experienced but anonymous punchcutters at Berthold and other foundries rather than by individual type designers. This means the punchcutters had to have a general idea of serifless forms, and they could probably derive these ideas from only the then popular classic typefaces such as Walbaum or Didot. This can be seen clearly upon superimposing Walbaum and Akzidenz Grotesk characters. The ground form, or skeleton, of both typefaces is identical. Yet these classic typefaces were far from good examples on which to base a sans serif. In Walbaum the thin tail ends in characters such as the 'c' and in numbers such as '2' and '5' which were elegant, but when these thin parts were simply made thicker, the result was a sans serif typeface with almost 'closed' forms. Because Akzidenz Grotesk derives itself from Walbaum, the two are an acceptable combination.

In 1917 Edward Johnston designed a typeface for the London Underground. The capitals were clearly based on Caslon Old Face, but the lowercase was a result of the calligraphic skills of Edward Johnston. It was the first time a sans serif was not based on an existing serif typeface but on handwriting with a broad-nibbed pen.

Eric Gill, an extraordinary type designer by all standards, started his career cutting letters in stone. When he began designing printing types, he knew by heart what a serif typeface should look like. He designed Gill Sans in 1928, and although this is a sans serif, he used his experience as a letter-cutter of serif letterforms. While he may not have realised it, he based his Gill Sans on the serif typefaces in his head. Mixing Gill Sans with his seriffed Joanna (1930) results in a typographically harmonious page. Joanna is a sort of Gill Sans Avec! Had Eric Gill planned Joanna and Gill Sans as one family he would have been the first in history to design a family of serif and sans.

In 1928 Paul Renner designed his Futura. This sans serif typeface was not based on the watered down classic letterforms on which Akzidenz Grotesk was based; instead he started his drawings from scratch. It

25 santa cruz
25 santa cruz

Edward Johnston's
LONDON TRANSPORT
alphabet

Gill Sans

Gill Sans Avec

FUTURA Figuren-Verzeichnis

ABCDEFGHIJKLMNO
PQRSTUVWXYZÄÖÜ
abcdefghijklmnopqrſst
uvwxyzäöüch ck ff fi fl ff ſi ſl ß
mager 1234567890 &.,-:;·!?'(*†«»§
Auf Wunsch liefern wir Mediäval-Ziffern 1234567890

ABCDEFGHIJKLMNO
PQRSTUVWXYZÄÖÜ
abcdefghijklmnopqrſst
uvwxyzäöüch ck ff fi fl ff ſi ſl ß
halbfett 1234567890 &.,-:;·!?'(*†«»§
Auf Wunsch liefern wir Mediäval-Ziffern 1234567890

ABCDEFGHIJKLMNO
PQRSTUVWXYZÄÖÜ
abcdefghijklmnopq
rſstuvwxyzäöüch ck
ff fi fl ff ſi ſl ß
1234567890
fett &.,-:;·!?'(*†«»§

←--- ←---
3 Display face published around 1816 by the typefoundry of William Caslon IV.

Akzidenz Grotesk, published in 1898 by the Berthold type foundry.

↑
Akzidenz Grotesk and Walbaum superimposed upon each other.

The thin tail ends in Walbaum.

The London Transport alphabet by Edward Johnston.

Gill Sans and Joanna.

←---
Futura specimen.

256 Buenos Aires <small>Akzidenz Grotesk</small>
256 Buenos Aires <small>Helvetica</small>
256 Buenos Aires <small>Univers</small>
256 Buenos Aires <small>Arial</small>

ABCDEFGR
<small>Helvetica Arial</small>

abcdefgr123

agf ≠ agf

21 variations sur un thème unique

←·· ←··
A comparison between Akzidenz Grotesk, Helvetica, Univers and Arial.

Arial compared to Helvetica.

The original Frutiger (1977) with a slanted roman, and Frutiger Next (2000) with a semi-real italic.

←··
The original Univers specimen from 1954 with an example of its system of weights and widths.

↙
Akzidenz Grotesk Italic as it could have looked (interpretation by Martin Majoor).

would seem that Futura was influenced by the ideas of the Bauhaus movement and constructivism as its letterforms look very much constructed, even though they aren't at all. Instead, Renner based his Futura on classic principles, like roman inscriptional capitals. This was one of the reasons for its success; it is a very well balanced text typeface, yet it has the aura of the then popular Bauhaus movement.

Around 1957 Helvetica, Folio, Univers and numerous lookalikes were published as a sort of reaction to pre-war geometric faces such as Futura. These typefaces were all based on the old Akzidenz Grotesk, and in no time they became extremely popular. Basing one sans serif on another is rather cheap, so it is not unusual that these typefaces had hardly any new features compared to Akzidenz Grotesk. Pretending to be better than Akzidenz Grotesk, these sans serifs were actually bereft of the character and charming clumsiness of Akzidenz Grotesk. Rock bottom was reached in 1982 when Arial was published, an almost one-to-one copy of Helvetica; it was the ultimate plagiarism of plagiarism.

Of all the Akzidenz Grotesk imitations, Univers (designed by Adrian Frutiger) had one strong feature that was new in type design: it was made up of an almost scientific system of 21 weights and widths that could be mixed perfectly. It was an answer to the jungle of different sans serif faces that lacked a clear system of weights and widths. Univers was completely redrawn a few years ago and now has more than 60 versions.

a ≠ a   g ≠ g   k ≠ k   z ≠ z
a → a   g → g   k → k   z → z

Akzidenz grotesk italic (original)

Akzidenz grotesk italic (interpretation)

Unfortunately this has not been an improvement; there are now too many superfluous versions, the justification is too tight and the italic that was already too slanted has been slanted even more. Redesigning an old successful typeface is something a type designer should maybe never consider.

The italic form of the sans-serif

The italic in Akzidenz Grotesk is nothing more than a slanted version of the roman, but why was the italic not based on a real italic? A real italic has a different form principle than the roman, and it seems not so difficult to make an Akzidenz Grotesk italic that is based on, let's say, Walbaum italic. It is possible that with the huge competition among different typefoundries, the 19th century punchcutters were under great pressure to produce quickly and therefore had to imitate others. A real italic version was probably too much work or too difficult to make, while a slanted roman was relatively easy to copy from the roman. The strange thing is that this slanted roman became a sort of standard for sans italics, even until today. With a few exceptions all sans serif italics are slanted romans. Even the great type designer Adrian Frutiger made slanted romans with his sans serif designs. It was only recently, when his Frutiger typeface (1977) was redrawn in 2000, now with a semi-real italic instead of a slanted roman, that he acknowledged that a real italic makes a better contrast with the roman.

Typefaces such as Futura have slanted romans too, but in this case it is much more understandable as there was no real old serif model on which to base the italic. Futura looks like a constructed typeface that borrows its forms from geometric squares and circles, giving it a truly original type sensibility. A more interesting italic is that of Gill Sans. It is the first among the sans serifs that has true italic characteristics. His first sketches for the italic show some very calligraphic features.

ff fi fl ffi ffl á è ĭ ø û
Ç Ł ļ Ø W ñ
Ho Ho **Ho Ho**

grote zaal - 20.15 uur - *De Nieuwe Serie / i.s.m. NOS Radio*

Schönberg Ensemble *goes Latin America*

Reinbert de Leeuw, *dirigent*
Claron McFadden, *sopraan*

Milhaud/Schönberger Saudades do Brasil
Villa-Lobos Choros nr. 7
Villa-Lobos Bachianas Brasileiras nrs. 5 & 6
Revueltas Planos; Homenaje a Federico García Lorca; Toccata

Zie pagina 3 • ƒ 20,- / 65 + ƒ 17,50 / CJP ƒ 15,- / coupons geldig

an an an

Drawings for Romulus by Jan van Krimpen.

An early example of the use of Scala, designed by Jan Willem den Hartog.

Romulus and Romulus Sans enlarged and overlayed.

Designing and mixing serif and sans

In my opinion, mixing serif with sans only makes sense when the serif and the sans typefaces are both derived from the same foundation, or even from the same skeleton. It sounds simple: take a serif design, cut off the serifs, lower the contrast, and there you have a sans serif. But of course there is more to it than that.

The first conscious attempt to design a sans based on a serif typeface was undertaken by the Dutch type designer Jan van Krimpen. In the early 1930s he designed Romulus and Romulus Sans to be part of a big family. Superimposing the serif upon the sans shows how literally Van Krimpen based them on each other. Romulus Sans was cut in four weights but unfortunately it remained at an experimental stage and was never released.

Scala and Scala Sans. Two typefaces, one form principle

I started designing Scala in 1987. At that time I was one of two graphic designers at the Vredenburg Music Centre in Utrecht, a large concert hall that programmed more concerts than any other hall in the Netherlands. We worked on one of the first models of Apple Macintosh, using PageMaker 1.0, with only 16 typefaces to choose from. I was typographically educated with lowercase numbers (also known as old style figures), small caps and ligatures, none of which were available in these 16 PostScript-fonts. The concert programmes, booklets and posters contained very diverse information, such as composers, titles, conductors, orchestras, soloists, time, date and venue. In order design this information effectively, we needed lowercase numbers, small caps and ligatures. And so it happened that Jan Willem den Hartog, the leader of the graphic design studio, asked me to design a typeface especially for Vredenburg. The result was Scala, named after the Teatro alla Scala, the concert hall in Milan.

The form principle of Scala was definitely influenced by humanist typefaces such as Bembo, and by typefaces from the mid-18th century French typographer Piere Simon Fournier. But I wanted Scala to have low contrast and strong serifs, as I had experienced that most PostScript-fonts were too thin. The italic was more or less based on the work of the 16th century Italian writing masters like Arrighi, although to a large extent the details were closely related to the roman. During the design process of the Scala family one thing was obvious to me: I wanted the lowercase numbers to be included in the normal fonts, and not in a separate Old Style Figures (OSF) font. This was against the rather illogical tradition of putting the table figures in the normal font.

Scala Sans was literally derived from Scala. Using a black marker and some correction fluid, I changed the serif characters into sans. The result was that Scala Sans became 'humanistic' in appearance. Until then this had rarely been seen in sans serifs, the only notable exceptions being London Underground, Gill Sans, Romulus Sans and Syntax (1968, Hans Eduard Meyer). The Syntax roman is truly one of the most beautiful sans serifs ever, but unfortunately the accompanying italic was a slanted roman. It was probably too early for Meyer to free himself from the generally accepted ideas of how the sans of an italic should look like.

After I had designed the lowercase numbers for the sans serif, I discovered that until that time lowercase numbers had not been seen in sans serif typefaces – Eric Gill never made them for his Gill Sans (although in the 1990s they were added by Monotype). Strangely enough, Renner was the only one who designed them for his Futura, although they are seldom used.

The Scala Sans italic follows the forms of its serif counter-part quite literally. There are italic small caps, ligatures and lowercase numbers, making Scala the first family with all these features in both a serif design and a sans design, and in both roman and italic.

→→
The method of changing Scala
with serifs into Scala Sans.

→→ →→
Syntax roman and italic.
Lowercase numbers in
Futura and Gill Sans.

↘
Skeletons of the roman and
italic versions of the Scala
and Scala Sans typefaces.

↘ ↘
An overview of Scala and
Scala Sans.

↘ ↘ ↘
The essential features in
Scala: lowercase numbers,
small caps and ligatures.
↓
Type specimen
of Scala Sans, concept by
Martin Majoor, design by
Jaap van Triest,
FontShop 1993.

ABCDEFGHIJKLMNOPQRST
abcdefghijklmnopqrstuvwxyz
ABCDEFGHIJKLMNOPQRST
abcdefghijklmnopqrstuvwxyz
1234567890 Futura
1234567890 Gill Sans

When I was designing Scala and Scala Sans my motto became: 'two typefaces, one form principle.' This can be demonstrated by isolating the common skeleton of the roman and the italic. I exercised great freedom in executing my ideas regarding serif and sans thanks to the possibilities of new digital design technologies. And since I did not work for a typefoundry, there was no time pressure and the music centre trusted me completely. Under these circumstances I was able to think very freely about the concept of serif and sans. Many of the generally accepted ideas did not seem logical to me; as an independent designer I was luckily not obliged to follow them.

Scala was released in 1990 by FontShop International as its first serious text face, but it was only when Scala Sans was issued three years later that the family became extremely popular. In 1997 I augmented Scala with other weights such as light, black and condensed. I also designed a set of four display versions called Scala Jewels. The use of a serif typeface and an accompanying sans resulted in a very happy combination for graphic designers around the world.

nnn ppp

Scala *Scala Italic* **Scala Bold** *Scala Bold Italic*
ABCDEFGHIJKLMNOPQRSTUVWXYZ
abcdefghijklmnopqrstuvwxyz
ABCDEFGHIJKLMNOPQRSTUVWXYZ
1234567890 & .,:;-?!''* 1234567890

Scala Sans *Scala Sans Italic* **Scala Sans Bold** *Scala Sans Bold Italic*
ABCDEFGHIJKLMNOPQRSTUVWXYZ
abcdefghijklmnopqrstuvwxyz
ABCDEFGHIJKLMNOPQRSTUVWXYZ
1234567890 & .,:;-?!''* 1234567890

Scala Regular
lowercase numbers 1234567890
SMALL CAPS & ligatures ff fi fj fl ffi ffl

Scala Sans Regular
lowercase numbers 1234567890
SMALL CAPS & ligatures ff fi fj fl ffi ffl

Scala Italic
lowercase numbers 1234567890
SMALL CAPS & ligatures ff fi fj fl ffi ffl

Scala Sans Italic
lowercase numbers 1234567890
SMALL CAPS & ligatures ff fi fj fl ffi ffl

Telefont List **Telefont List Bold** *Telefont List Italic*

ABCDEFGHIJKLMNOPQRSTUVWXYZ
abcdefghijklmnopqrstuvwxyz
1234567890 & .,:;-?!''*

Telefont Text **Telefont Text Bold** *Telefont Text Italic*

ABCDEFGHIJKLMNOPQRSTUVWXYZ
abcdefghijklmnopqrstuvwxyz
ABCDEFGHIJKLMNOPQRSTUVWXYZ
1234567890 & .,:;-?!''* 1234567890

Arnhem (026)

Majoor M
Weg langs Klim en Dal 2 6813 GH ____ 443 00 49
typografisch ontwerper
Major A P Hanzestraat 126
6826 MP _____ 06 - 19 44 08 95
mobiele telefoon
Mak L Emmastraat 67/A 6828 HD _____ 445 65 03
Mak P
Jacob Cremerstraat 43 6821 DB _____ 351 70 27
Makaaij H F M
Bertha von Suttnerstraat 21 6836 KL   327 27 31
Makel R G W
St. Caeciliapad 5 6815 GM _____ 364 99 97

Makelaar Actief Makelaars Lid NVM
Steenstraat 9/A 6828 CA _____ **446 44 90**
fax_____ > 446 57 35
Oranjesingel 30
6511 NV NIJMEGEN_____ (024) 324 49 77
fax _____ > (024) 360 76 05

An overview of Telefont List and Telefont Text.

A detail from the Dutch telephone book.

Telefont. An in-between sans

In 1993 I designed Telefont List and Telefont Text for the Dutch national telephone book. The typeface I had in mind was a sans serif, yet I did not resort to using a serif typeface as the basis for the sans. I was able to use the experience I had gained in designing the Scala family however, compared to my work on Scala Sans, I had to think in a much more restricted way. Telefont List (which I designed first) was to be used in a small size on cheap paper; it had to take up as little space as possible, and it had to be much more readable than the worn-out Univers that PTT (Post, Telefonie, Telegrafie) had been previously using. Simultaneously I was thinking about the typographic redesign of the phone book itself. This proved to be a great advantage as I could now fine-tune the typeface as a result of the changes I made in the four-column grid and, what is more, I could adjust the page layout after I had made changes in the typeface. It is a rare situation but an ideal situation for a type designer. In any case my experience as a book designer came in handy.

Telefont List is a real workhorse, to be used in the automatically generated phone book listings, while Telefont Text was designed for the custom-made introductory pages, using many more typographic refinements such as small caps and lowercase numbers. I was wont to put it as follows: 'The most-used typeface has the least possibilities; the least-used typeface has the most possibilities.'

Telefont List and Telefont Text have been used exclusively for the Dutch phone book since 1994, but it is not inconceivable that they will be released in the near future. However I am not planning a Telefont Serif, as I do not believe in deriving a serif design from a sans.

Seria and Seria Sans. A literary typeface

I made the first sketches for Seria on the train from Berlin to Warsaw in the summer of 1996, using some table napkins from the dining car. Designing Seria was born out of dissatisfaction with the use of Scala in a literary context. As a book designer I could not use Scala for poetry and other works of literature, as I found the ascenders and descenders, too short for this purpose. I thought of making a version of Scala with longer ascenders and descenders, but then realised I wanted to change more than just a few details. I decided that Scala is Scala and if I wanted to make changes I would have to make a new typeface with long ascenders and descenders (I had no intention of making the most economical or space-saving typeface).

I soon found myself working on a completely new typeface. The individual characters of the Seria family have a lot of subtle details and unconventional curves that can best be seen in a large size. In small sizes, while one cannot see these details, one can maybe 'feel' them. The rather edgy curves make Seria 'wittingly irregular', a principle that was used by W. A. Dwiggins, the American type designer, and also by my Dutch colleague Bram de Does. It comes from the belief that a certain degree of irregularity leads to better legibility. The upward italic has become a major feature of Seria.

The need to augment Seria with a sans serif version was obvious to me from the start. Again using a black marker and some correction fluid, I changed the seriffed characters into sans. Making it stand out as a sans serif, Seria Sans kept the long ascenders and descenders as its seriffed partner. The strength of Seria Sans also lies in the consistent derivation from Seria, obviously noticeable in its italic and bold italic forms.

In 1999, a year before finishing Seria, I was asked by Tadeusz Wielecki, composer and director of the Warsaw Autumn Festival in Poland, to do the graphic design for

→
The English and
Polish book
covers for the
programme
book for
Warsaw Autumn
Festival. Nexus
Sans and Nexus
Mix typefaces.

↓
The original
'napkin' sketch
for Seria.

↘
Skeletons of
the roman and
italic versions of
the Nexus Serif,
Nexus Sans and
Nexus Mix type-
faces.

↗↗
Some examples
of Nexus Italic
Swash.

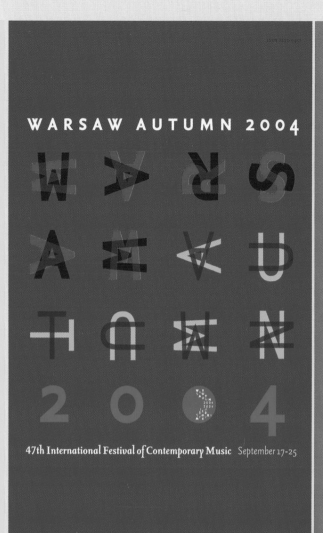

WARSAW AUTUMN 2004

47th International Festival of Contemporary Music   September 17-25

WARSZAWSKA JESIEŃ 2004

47. Międzynarodowy Festiwal Muzyki Współczesnej   17-25 września

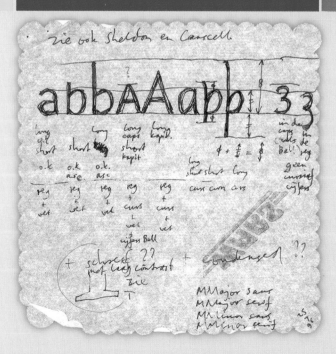

his music festival. Not only could I design the posters, the leaflet and the CDs, but I was also interested in redesigning the inside typography of the rather amateurishly designed programme books. I became the type designer and book typographer at the same time, and it was the perfect chance for me to use and to test the newly designed Seria and Seria Sans. The result was typography so clear that we have not changed it in over 6 years.

Serif–Sans–Mix. The nexus principle

At the time Scala and Seria were designed, my motto had been 'two typefaces, one form principle': the serif version and the sans version coming from the same source, or better the sans being derived from the serif. One doesn't need a lot of imagination to think about a third version, a slab serif derived from the sans by simply adding thick serifs to the sans characters. My initial type design philosophy of 'two typefaces, one form principle' is simply changed into 'three typefaces, one form principle.'

I call this the 'nexus principle', nexus being the Latin word for connection. And from 2002 to 2004 I designed Nexus, a family of three 'connected' typefaces including a serif, a sans- serif and a slab serif version. I still believe that the serif should come first, then the sans serif, and finally the slab.

Nexus started as an alternative Seria with shorter ascenders and descenders, but the design quickly became it's own typeface with additional changes in the proportions and details, including a redrawn italic. The result was a workhorse typeface similar to Scala, with added features like small caps in all weights, four different sorts of numbers, ligatures etc.

In addition, I designed two sets of swash capitals, two sets of swash lowercase endings, and a corporate mono-spaced font in four weights. When the Nexus family (Nexus Serif, Nexus Sans, Nexus Mix, and Nexus Typewriter) was released in 2004, it was one of FontShop's first OpenType font families. The addition of the word 'Mix' in the name 'Nexus Mix' is a result of my idea that a slab serif is really a mixture between a sans and a serif.

The situation now

When I started with type design in 1983 I produced only a single serif typeface. It has taken me twenty years to get where I am now, with my latest typeface consisting of three complete versions.

In a way, the last 15 years have been revolutionary for sans serif typefaces. As more and more type designers become aware of the origins of sans serifs, sans serif designs become full partners alongside serif designs. Maybe the next 15 years will bring a revolution for slab serifs, and in the future it might even be possible that the 'nexus principle' expands into a fourth or fifth dimension. Time will tell. ⊕

Koninklijke Bibliotheek DEN HAAG
Dead Poets Society
The Amsterdam Baroque Orchestra
FontShop International
Warsaw Autumm Festival

Nexus Typewriter Regular
Nexus Typewriter Italic
Nexus Typewriter Bold
Nexus Typewriter BoldItalic

MWImwi

Nexus Serif
Nexus Sans
Nexus Mix

Akzidenz Grotesk™ is a trademark of Berthold Types Limited. The 'interpretation' shown on page 60 is a speculation based on historical sources and has no direct relationship to the digital typeface currently marketed under this trademark.

FF DIN is based on DIN Mittelschrift, the standard typeface developed in the 1930s as part of the Deutsche Industrie Norm, and is still used for road signage in many countries. Engineers, not type designers, developed DIN Mittelschrift; purely a product of geometric construction, it lacked typographic sophistication. Yet, since the late 1980s, there has been an increasing interest in these industrial 'non-designed' letterforms. The digital version of DIN Mittelschrift has been used for display purposes, but its clumsy curves make it unsuitable for setting text. Albert-Jan Pool's FF DIN solved this problem by successfully combining the cool, industrial look of the DIN Schriften with a sophisticated view on legibility and word formation. Like Font Bureau's Interstate, FF DIN has become a fetish among contemporary graphic designers.

'DIN, the *Deutsche Industrie Norm* (German Industrial Standard) is the magic word for everything that can be measured in Germany, including the official German typeface, appropriately called DIN Mittelschrift. Ever since it became available in digital form, this typeface has been picked up by many graphic designers who like it for its lean, geometric lines.' Thus Erik Spiekermann explained the success of DIN Mittelschrift in his book *Stop Stealing Sheep*, first issued in 1993. In 1994 Spiekermann suggested to Albert-Jan Pool, a Hamburg-based type designer from the Netherlands, to completely redesign the DIN Mittelschrift, and have it released by FontShop International.

In Germany, typography in the public environment has been dominated by two typefaces defined by the German Industrial Standard DIN 1451; DIN Mittelschrift and its condensed companion, DIN Engschrift. These alphabets are commonly known as *Autobahn* typefaces because they have been used on German traffic signs for decades.

Industrial archaeology

One of the very few historical references found in the archives of the DIN Institute in Berlin is this quote from *Normschriften* (Standard Typefaces), a DIN publication from 1936. 'To supply a typeface that can be executed using a grid, ... the long-used typeface of the *Deutsche Reichsbahn* was chosen.' During World War II, the archives were bombed twice; as a result little documentation on the origin of the design of the DIN Mittelschrift remains.

Fortunately, the history of almost everything connected with the German railways has been researched at length. Not only steam engines and timetables have their collectors, admirers and specialists – almost any kind of object does, even signposts and owner plates.

The first German corporate typeface?

In 1905, the Royal Prussian Railways (KPEV, Königliche Preußische Eisenbahn) defined a new master drawing for its lettering. Its original purpose was to unify the descriptions on freight cars; soon it was adapted for all sorts of lettering including the names of railway stations on platforms. It thus became one of the first corporate typefaces in Germany.

In 1920 the foundation of the Weimar Republic enforced the process of the unification of the patchwork of German states into a single German state and was followed by a merger of all state railways into the *Deutsche Reichsbahn*. The master drawings of the Prussian Railways became the reference for most railway lettering. When counting from the 1905 KPEV master drawing, the DIN typeface celebrated its 100th anniversary in 2005.

FSI promotional postcard from 1995 by Jürgen Siebert, using FF DIN.

German motorway signage using DIN Mittelschrift

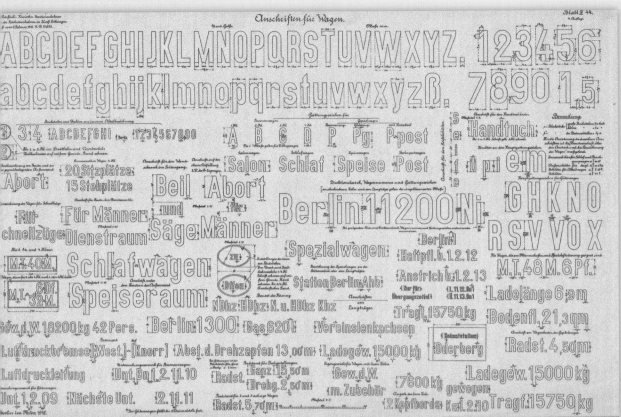

Anschriften für Wagen.

Master drawing of the Prussian Railways from 1912, similar to the version of 1905. This is the model for DIN Engschrift.

KPEV standard typeface for the owner plate of the steam engines built for the Deutsche Reichsbahn by AEG.

Older KPEV master drawings, like these from 1883 and 1897, document the variety of typefaces in use rather than a set standard.

Since 1920, steam engines have had identical owner plates. After World War II, Reichsbahn was changed to Bundesbahn.

'Deutsche Bundesbahn' survived until new DB logos were introduced in 1951 and 1955. The logo from 1951 uses DIN Breitschrift.

A Reichsbahn steam engine was mainly a number. Obviously for reasons of legibility, the figures of the KPEV master drawing are of regular width while the typeface itself is condensed.

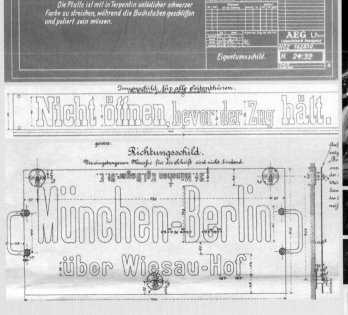

© Photograph by Axel Zwingenberger.

MEJSTER PREJSE

MŪSJK JM LEbEN dĒR VÖLKER AM 2. JŪLJ
20 ŪhR dJRJGJERT JM OPERNhAUS
WARSᗺAUS bERŪhMTER dJRJGENT WERKE
POLNJSᗺER MEJSTER PREJSE 1–5Mk.

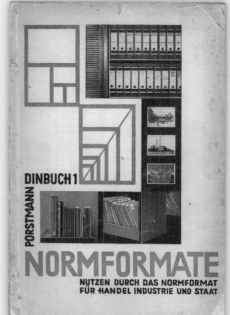

⟵⟵ Left: Kurt Schwitters' Systemschrift (example from 1927). Obviously, the 'M,' 'e' and 'o,' as well as the figures show a close resemblance to DIN, and the 'A' calls to mind certain designs by Herbert Bayer.

⟵ DINbuch 1 on standard paper sizes by Walter Porstmann from 1930, the first in a series of books on DIN Standards. The lettering closely relates to DIN Engschrift. As the political situation changed, DIN abandoned the 'Bauhaus style.' DIN, Berlin © Beuth Verlag.

⟶ Early (condensed) version of Bayer's Universal typeface from 1924/1925.

Comparison of KPEV/Reichsbahn characters (1905) and a Bauhaus logotype by Joost Schmidt (1929). The grid is identical to that of DIN Engschrift.

FF DIN - a child of its time

During the Dessau Period of the Bauhaus (1923-1932), type characters were drawn with a ruler and compass on coarse grids. In doing so, Herbert Bayer and Joost Schmidt, who were responsible for the typography courses, became exponents of the so-called Constructivist style of lettering. A comparison of the KPEV typeface/DIN Engschrift and Schmidt's designs shows a remarkable resemblance. Although there were no direct connections between Bauhaus and DIN as far as type design is concerned, it is very likely that the railway lettering was well known at the Bauhaus. The proposal that the KPEV/Reichsbahn lettering would become a part of DIN 1451 had been published in 1924 and had been discussed by several printers and graphic magazines.

Constructing a standard

Walter Porstmann, who conceived the DIN standards for paper sizes, held lectures at the Bauhaus in 1924–25, in which he promoted *kleinschreibung* (the use of lowercase letters only) as well as his visions on a new phonetic and universal alphabet. Such a reformed alphabet should be economical, legible and easier to read, and would therefore be of great help in globalizing communication. Both DIN and the Bauhaus proposed standardisation on the basis of plain solutions. With his typeface Universal, developed from 1925 to 1930, Herbert Bayer concentrated on a constructed alphabet with lowercase letters only. Both he and Joost Schmidt propagated the 'single alphabet' in various publications.

New typography, new alphabet?

Porstmann's ideas on alphabet reform also inspired designers outside the Bauhaus, such as Kurt Schwitters and Jan Tschichold. Both developed 'optophonetical' type designs in which the letterforms should visually resemble the sounds connected to them. Both Schwitters and Tschichold were members of the *Ring neuer Werbegestalter*, a circle of graphic designers advocating constructivism. Kurt Schwitters in particular based his alphabets on forms showing a remarkable resemblance to those of the DIN typefaces. Walter Dexel, also a Ring member, designed a similar style of lettering.

Architectural standards ...

Another interesting link between Bauhaus and DIN is the architect Ernst Neufert. Like Joost Schmidt he was a Bauhaus student from the early days in Weimar, and both attended Gropius' classes. Later Neufert managed Gropius' architecture studio (1925-1929). In this period Gropius designed the *Konsumgebäude* in Dessau-Törten. The lettering is almost identical with DIN Mittelschrift, which had been published as a preliminary design in 1926. Since 1926 Neufert had been working on what later became his *Bauentwurfslehre*. While 'Building Design Instructions' would be a literal translation of this term, the English translation of his book was titled *Architects' Data*. The *Deutsche Normenausschuß* (German Standard Committee) supported the book's publication and contributed a foreword to the first printing in 1936. In this work Neufert propagated standardization. Many of his guidelines refer to DIN standards; his proposals for a standardized layout of architectural drawings naturally use DIN alphabets. By 1944, over 100,000 copies had been sold; most German architects used Neufert's *Bauentwurfslehre*. It is internationally recognized as a standard work still today, and has been translated into 17 languages.

With hindsight, the idea of basing a standard typeface on geometric forms may seem questionable. It has to be realised, though, that Constructivism was a major cultural force during this period, which certainly influenced the conception of this typeface.

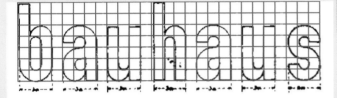

—›
Gropius'
'Konsum-
gebäude'
from 1928.
Whether the
typeface is
DIN currently
remains specu-
lative. Bauhaus
Archive, Berlin.
© VG Bild-
Kunst, Bonn,

—›—›
Cinema poster.
Design and
lettering by Jan
Tschichold
(Munich, 1927),
author of
'The New Typog-
raphy.'

—›
Poster for an ex-
hibition. Design
and lettering by
Herbert Bayer
(Dessau, 1927).
Bauhaus
Archive, Berlin.
© VG Bild-
Kunst, Bonn.

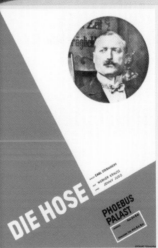

As President of the DIN Committee of Drawings, Siemens Engineer Ludwig Goller (1884-1964) was responsible for the development of the typeface designs of DIN 1451.
© DIN, Berlin

A Lufthansa Focke-Wulf Fw 200 with DIN markings.
Archiv der Lufthansa AG.

Engraving pattern for the Siemens-Halske monogram from 1899 (right) and for DIN 1451 from 1987 (left).

Setting a standard

In the young Republic of Weimar (1919–1933), unification and standardization soon became important themes. Originally founded to coordinate the specifications of war industry products, the *Normenausschuß der Deutsche Industrie* (Committee for German Industry Standards, uniting AEG, Bosch, Siemens and others) turned the idea of standardization into reality. Originally intended to help post-World War I Germany back on its feet again, standardization was envisaged to become one of the main ingredients of the quality and success of German products. As early as 1917, committee meetings were held where the standardization of lettering on technical drawings was discussed. Type expert Soennecken advised on the design of DIN 16, the first standard concerning letterforms.

Construction and objectivity

Among the first committee members was the engineer Ludwig Goller. From 1920 onwards he worked for the Siemens & Halske Company. They must have appreciated his work tremendously, as Goller's newly drawn DIN Mittelschrift became the model for the new Siemens logotype in 1936. In the 1936 brochure on DIN 1451, Goller, who was responsible for the development of DIN 1451, can be found acting as a true 'Dean of DIN '. In it, he wrote: 'For the typefaces of the future neither tools nor fashion will be decisive.' This has remained a guideline throughout the development of DIN alphabets, from the earliest work on DIN 1451 (ca. 1924) until the most recent versions of 1985. Identical characters were to be drawn with all kinds of tools, varying from drawing pens and engraving tools to compass and rulers. All strokes should share the same heartline. Depending on the tool, stroke ends could be rounded or angular. Great care was taken that all letters be designed in such a way that they could be drawn with a continuous stroke width. Here, DIN 1451 partly coincides with the aforementioned DIN 16, which had been released in 1919. A striking point to be mentioned is that the concept of continuous stroke width is a constraint that positions the DIN typefaces outside of the world of 'real' type design. The principle of continuous stroke width is con-

tradictory to the principles of traditional typography, where it is assumed that only varying stroke weight will enable optimal word-images. This is why most traditional typographers have rejected the DIN typefaces, or at least refuse to take them seriously.

DIN 1451 on its way up

Goller's 1936 brochure on DIN 1451 illustrates the standardization of DIN typefaces for traffic signs, road signs, street names, house numbers and license plates. DIN 284 even defined DIN 1451 as a standard for the border stones of the German Reich.

By 'Temporary Order Nr 10' from 1938, DIN 1451 was to be used for all road signs along the new 'Reichsautobahnen' (state motorways). The *Autobahn* typeface was born. In September 1939 the DIN Standards practically acquired the status of a law, as an official regulation was proclaimed in which the use of DIN standards could be dictated by administrative order. In 1941 Hitler officially prohibited the use of the Fraktur (Broken Scripts); the various types of Antiqua (serif and sans-serif Roman) were now officially favoured. Although DIN 1451 was 'introduced' in most occupied countries – a poorly designed Cyrillic version being published in 1943, shortly after the fall of Stalingrad – the DIN Institute carefully kept itself out of political issues. They even managed to stay out of the *Reichskulturkammer*, a body that controlled all cultural utterances, by disguising the publishing of DIN literature as trade activities. Since the 1930s DIN 1451 had been used on all military objects, including tanks, aeroplanes and even bomb shelters. Fortunately, no traces have been found of DIN typefaces being used for Nazi propaganda. Usually it was Futura that had to play this ungrateful role. Once civil aviation got off the ground, Junker planes and the Lufthansa company helped DIN on its way up.

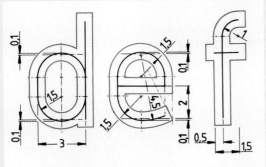

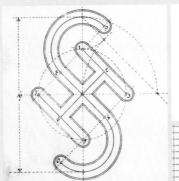

M

Mit Hilfe des gleichen Hilfsnetzes können auch „Eng- und Breitschriften" geschrieben werden.

abcdABC2 abcdAB2

DIN 1451 Beiblatt 3	Normschriften Engschrift Mittelschrift Breitschrift mit Hilfsnetz gemalt Hilfsnetz für Malschablonen Beispiele

Fette Engschrift

abcdefghijklmnopqrstuvwxl

yzßäöü&.,-:;!?") 1234567890

ÄÖÜABCDEFGHIJKLMNOPQRST

UVWXYZ

Fette Mittelschrift

abcdefghijklmnopqrs

tuvwxyzßäöü&.,-:;!?")

1234567890ÄÖÜABC

DEFGHIJKLMNOPQR

↑↑
Siemens Logo of 1936 by
Hans Domizlaff, one of the first
German brand consultants.
The characters relate to DIN 1451,
which allowed a 'pointed M' as an
alternative design. DIN 1451 was
released in 1936.

↑
The condensed (eng) and
extended (breit) versions of DIN
were created using the same grid.
This diagram is from DIN 17, the
1940 standard for lettering with
drawing pens.

←
Correction sheet from 1931.
DIN, Berlin © Beuth Verlag.

←·· ←··
Lettering rulers with DIN
typefaces were officially the
standard for quite a long time.
An attempt to apply them as an
ISO-Standard failed.
In 1976 it was decided to
supersede them by Isonorm 3098.
Most devices stayed in use until
the late 1980s when architectural
drawings were mostly done on
computers.

Being used for all traffic signs along the Autobahn as one of the significant exponents of the German Wirtschaftswunder (the post-war phenomenon of explosive economic growth), DIN Mittelschrift made part of the visual expression of that era.

---➔
Reference drawing from the Guidelines for Measurement and Design of Road Signs, issued in 1957 by the German Ministry of Traffic.

A growing number of agencies seem to recognize the suitability of DIN typefaces for car advertising.
Detail from an advertisement for Toyota, the Netherlands. Typeface: FF DIN.

↘↘
"I think electricity is yellow"; branding for a German utility.

Abb. 7: Vorweaweiser an einem Autobahnkreuz

By 'Temporary Order Nr 10' from 1938, DIN 1451 was declared for use on all road signs along the new *Reichsautobahnen* (state motorways); it has been used for this purpose to this day. The DIN type design was especially updated for motorway signage around 1981.

Together with Stefan Rögener of AdFinder, one of the largest advertising archives worldwide, Albert-Jan Pool analysed the use of typefaces in car advertisements in the USA, Great Britain and Germany in 1995. Unlike other product groups (such as cosmetics, where the same team detected an overwhelming preference for Optima), a specific typeface for car ads could not be brought to light. However, since its release FF DIN is constantly gaining popularity within this category, closely followed by older digital versions of DIN. ⊕

„Also ich glaube, Strom ist gelb."

Gelb.

Gut.

Günstig.

Yello Strom

aoneli

█ DIN
▢ FF DIN

abfjklnorsty

DIN Engschrift
Ludwig Goller 1926

abfjklnorsty

DIN Engschrift
Redesign 1981

abfjklnorsty

FF Din Condensed
Albert-Jan Pool 1995

Light	*Italic*	Condensed
Regular	*Italic*	Condensed
Medium	*Italic*	**Condensed**
Bold	*Italic*	**Condensed**
Black	*Italic*	**Condensed**

ij;:123456CG€ Regular

ij;:123456CG€ Alternate

FF DIN – Ingredients of a successful recipe

When comparing FF DIN regular (this column) to DIN Mittelschrift (below) within body text, typographic differences become visible. DIN Mittelschrift is far too heavy to suit the reading eye. Its continuous stroke width causes a spotty image. The condensed version, DIN Engschrift, stands out. The weight scheme for FF DIN was conceived in such a way that a new and lighter 'regular' version would fit in. Italic, bold and condensed weights allow for all levels of typographic emphasis.

FF DIN regular

DIN Mittelschrift

When comparing DIN 1451 Mittelschrift (this column) to FF DIN regular (above) within body text, typographic differences become visible. DIN Mittelschrift is far too heavy to suit the reading eye. Its continuous stroke width causes a spotty image. The condensed version, DIN Engschrift, stands out. The weight scheme for FF DIN was conceived in such a way that a new and lighter 'regular' version would fit in. Italic, bold and condensed weights allow for all levels of typographic emphasis.

Comparison of DIN (solid) and FF DIN (outline). In FF DIN the horizontals were designed 10% thinner, abandoning the principle of continuous stroke weight. The curves were also designed more fluidly.

For FF DIN the principle of continuous stroke width was abandoned. The weight of the horizontal strokes has been reduced. Curves, as well as their transitions into straight lines, were designed in a more fluent way.

Both FF DIN and FF DIN Condensed have five weights.

FF DIN Alternate is a typographically more refined version with round dots, oldstyle figures and a one-storey italic 'a.' The recent FF DIN OpenType Pro version also has a more legible @ (at) glyph.

The roman weights of FF DIN are available in Central European, Baltic, Turkish and OpenType Pro character sets.

Signage for Centre Pompidou in Paris by Intégral Ruedi Baur et Associés, 2000.

Exhibition panel for the Dutch national archive. Logo and corporate design by UNA Designers Amsterdam 2002.

Three major type families by Danish designers were released in the FontFont series since 2000: FF Signa, FF Max and FF Olsen. Although their designers, Ole Søndergaard and Morten Rostgaard Olsen, belong to different generations, they share certain typographic sensibilities. These may be traced back to a Danish 'national style' of type and lettering design.

FROM THE EARLIEST days of printing, the history of letter-forms and type production has been an international one. Many of the earliest romans were cut by German and French printers working in Italy; the French style of Claude Garamond was adapted to Dutch thriftiness by the Flemish punchcutter Vandenkeere and later rationalized by Miklós Kis from Transylvania, working in Amsterdam; and through-out the 19th and 20th centuries, experiments with new forms and techniques rapidly travelled from one European country to another and across the Atlantic. Yet in spite of the seemingly universal character of typography, there still exist national and regional type cultures to this day. Some, like the Dutch tradition of pragmatic book faces or the English style with its reference to stone carving, are obvious and well known. Others, like the Czech and Slovak taste for individualist and unorthodox forms, are still in the process of being discovered and defined.

One European type design tradition that was little known abroad until recently is the Danish school. In fact, the Danish type families in the FontFont series – FF Signa by Ole Søndergaard, FF Olsen and FF Max by Morten Rostgaard Olsen – were among the first Danish text faces ever published in an international collection. Their designers belong to two distinctly different generations. Ole Søndergaard, now in his late sixties, was part of a group of Danish designers that made its mark in the 1970s and 1980s; his earlier logos and alphabets in clear-cut functionalist style were all hand-rendered. Morten Rostgaard Olsen is much younger and learned to use the computer in art school; in fact, one of his first jobs in type design was digital production work for Søndergaard. Both, however, are representatives of the same unique regional style in type design.

Unclassifiable

Released in 2000, FF Signa is radically different from most sans-serif text typefaces introduced during the 1990s. It does not belong to the category of 'humanist sans-serif'; nor can it be classed with the 'grotesques' based on 19th-century models. Its forms are basic and simple, showing minimal details. Yet its proportions are classical, and the underlying geometry has been subtly adjusted in order to create letterforms which are at once interesting and harmonious, making for pleasant reading even at very small sizes. Originally designed for signage – hence the name – FF Signa is now a family with three widths, including italics and small caps for all weights,

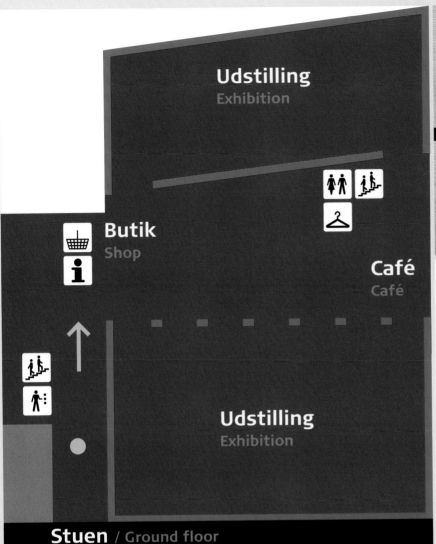

Udstilling
Exhibition

Butik
Shop

Café
Café

Udstilling
Exhibition

Stuen / Ground floor

ID prisen 1965 - 1999
The ID Prize 1965 - 1999

MEDbetydningsfuld hilsen
DESIGNating greetings

Garderobe, Toiletter
Cloakroom, Toilets

Lørdag   *mayland*

16

SEPTEMBER

Uge 37   195 / 170   7.22 ☼ 20.16   **2006**

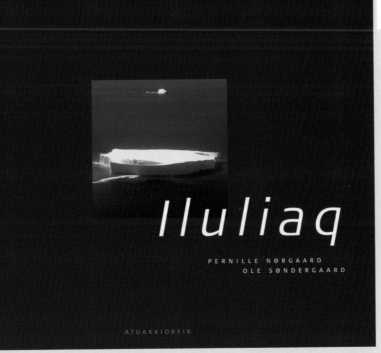

ISBJERGE ICEBERGS

Iluliaq

PERNILLE NØRGAARD
OLE SØNDERGAARD

ATUAKKIORFIK

Kolding Bibliotek

Work designed
by Ole
Søndergaard
with FF Signa.

←
Signage
and ground
plan for the
Danish Design
Institute in
Copenhagen.

↙
Calendar
for Macover

↙ ↙
Cover for Iluliaq,
a self-published
book with
texts and
photographs
by Søndergaard
and his wife
Pernille
Nørgaard.

↓
Logo for the
Kolding City
Library

and several types of figures. A correspondence version, containing specially designed bitmap fonts for better on-screen reading, was introduced in 2002. The typeface has developed into a versatile family which can be used for corporate identities, brochures, magazines, communication, books and on-screen publications. The designer's goal with Signa was to make a typeface as universal and versatile as some of the best known modern sans-serifs – types like Helvetica, Univers, and Frutiger – while bringing a fresh, contemporary aesthetic to the genre. It is safe to say that FF Signa lives up to this ambition.

Signa's roots

Despite its user-friendliness, Signa has a slightly unfamiliar feel to it: a sturdy character that is notice-able without being distracting. This trait can be traced back to the Danish lettering tradition.

Signa's origin is utterly different from that of the calligraphically inspired text types from Germany or the Netherlands. Rather than boasting a storied history of fine book printing, Denmark's typographic community proudly points to a different sort of heritage: architects and craftsmen who excelled in handmade lettering, both on buildings and on the page. This tradition is still very alive.

Born in 1937, Signa's designer Ole Søndergaard was one of the first Danish typographers to take this tradition of craftsmanship and architectural lettering into the realm of contemporary corporate design. Before entering the Copenhagen Royal Academy, he worked as a signpainter in London's Soho district. At the Academy, his mentor Gunnar Billmann Petersen

taught him, as Søndergaard puts it, 'the secrets of the graphic form'. In 1962, while still at the Academy, he was invited by Petersen to do the letter carving for a monument to Knud Rasmussen, explorer of the Arctic world. The rugged typeface Søndergaard designed especially for carving in the monument's coarse granite was inspired by the lettering styles developed by famous predecessors such as Knud V. Engelhardt, Claus Achton Friis and Petersen himself. On this occasion Søndergaard's father, a well-known sculptor, initiated his son in the art of stonecarving.

During the '60s Søndergaard worked as a graphic designer at an architecture studio. In 1973 he estab-lished his own design firm, which quickly became one of Denmark's leading studios for corporate design. Søndergaard designed corporate identities and sign-posting systems for some of the country's largest banks, industries and government organisations. In 1985 Søndergaard co-founded Eleven Danes, a group of graphic, industrial and interior designers, and an influential force in the Danish design world for ten years. His small design studio is located in a back street of Helsingør, a short train ride from Copenha-gen; called Elsinore in English, it's the harbor town that was the home of Hamlet's mythical castle.

The Signa project: Danish style

In the mid-1990s Søndergaard decided it was time to make his mark in digital type design. Using his experience in signage and lettering, he drew the extensive family that later became FF Signa. At an early stage Signa was implemented in a prestigious corporate identity project: it became the face of the Danish Design Centre. When the new DDC building was inaugurated in early 2000, Signa (then still unpublished) was used for the signage system; it has also become the standard text face for the DDC's publications. More recently, the Toronto writer Joe Clark chose FF Signa for a book about internet sites for the visually impaired (Building Accessible Web-sites), precisely for its clarity and openness. In 2002, the complete FF Signa family received the most prestigious design award in its country of origin: the Danish Design Prize.

Although FF Signa is not modelled on any existing printing typeface and is strikingly original, several Danish fonts developed around the same time show similar sensibilities. Of these recent typefaces, the most conspicuous one to any type enthusiast travelling to Denmark is the corporate alphabet developed around 2000 by the Copenhagen design firm Kontrapunkt for the Danish Railways. It, too, has a certain ruggedness about it, despite the smooth, low-contrast shapes. Its most extraordinary character is the lowercase 'g', with its angular, open tail, quite similar, in fact, to the same letter in FF Signa. It is no

↑
Ole Søndergaard, sketches for FF Signa.

⤑
The typeface that was de-signed by the Copenhagen studio Kontrapunkt as part of the Danish Rail-ways' corporate identity has similar characteristics to FF Signa, including an oddly shaped 'g'.

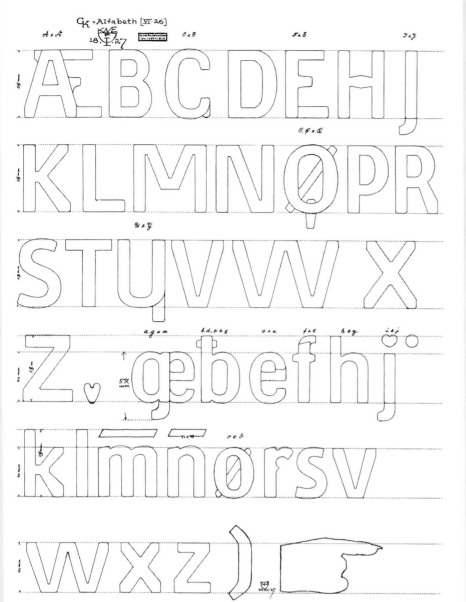

Anemonevej

Optaget

KDAK DANSK AUTOMOBILKLUB & FORENEDE DANSKE MOTOREJERE
AUTO GIVAGT

KDAK DANSK AUTOMOBILKLUB & FORENEDE DANSKE MOTOREJERE

Lettering projects for public transport and street signage designed by the architect Knud V. Engelhardt in the 1910s and 1920s.

↓

Lettering by Claus Acton Friis.

↙ ↙

In 1962, Ole Søndergaard designed the carved lettering for a momument to explorer Knud Rasmussen. (See also the large **R** on page 74)

RSA
ENC
▶D

RASM
PCÆY
1924E

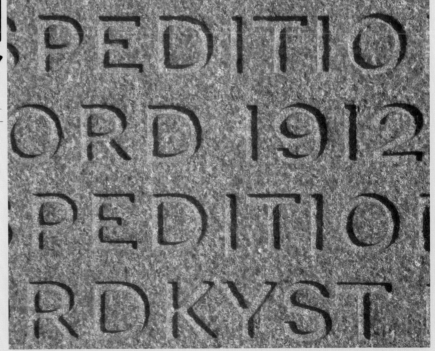

coincidence, then, that the Kontrapunt designers have also cited the lettering work of Engelhardt and Achton Friis as sources of inspiration.

Some four years after it was first published, FF Signa was given a somewhat surprising companion. Signa Serif is not, as could be expected, a slab-serif that continues the low-contrast, high-performance theme of the sans-serif original. Instead, Søndergaard drew a high-contrast roman with the vertical stress typical of the classicist style. Combined with the unusual, wide Signa structure and remarkable details such as the asymmetric serifs on the 'k', 'm', 'v' and certain capitals, this has resulted in an unorthodox text face with limited possibilities of use, but a highly original text image.

FF Signa Correspondence

FF Signa Correspondence is a sub-family of four Signa fonts: regular, italic, bold, bold italic. All are especially redesigned for use in the office environment. For convenient on-screen reading and use in correspondence, its spacing is slightly wider than that of the original Signa. Signa Correspondence is a TrueType set designed especially for PC users, with a range of bitmap screen fonts to make every single character appear as clearly as possible on the screen. These bitmaps were created with a new program, BitFonter, developed in the US by FontLab. It allows the designer to construct, within the limitations of the screen's pixel grid, screen characters with a minimum of lumps and irregularities, and embeds them in TrueType fonts. FF Signa Correspondence was thoroughly tested and compared to Arial and Verdana, which have long set the standard for high quality on-screen performance. Using the BitFonter bitmaps, Signa's screen appearance rivals that of hand-hinted TrueType fonts.

Morten Olsen's modernism

Morten Rostgaard Olsen is of a much younger generation than Søndergaard – more than 25 years his junior.

FF Signa Condensed + *Italic*

Light Book **Bold** Black
*Light Book **Bold Black***

FF Signa Normal + *Italic*

Light Book **Bold** Black
*Light Book **Bold Black***

FF Signa Extended + *Italic*

Light **Book Bold** Black
*Light Book **Bold Black***

1234567890
1234567890   TF ('COLUMN')

FF Signa Serif + *Italic*

Light Book Semibold **Bold** Black
*Light Book Semibold **Bold Black***

1235647890
1235647890   SC
1235647890   TF

The outlines of FF Signa Normal Black and FF Signa Serif Bold superimposed at the same point size. The difference in contrast is striking; Signa Serif also has a slightly lower x-height.

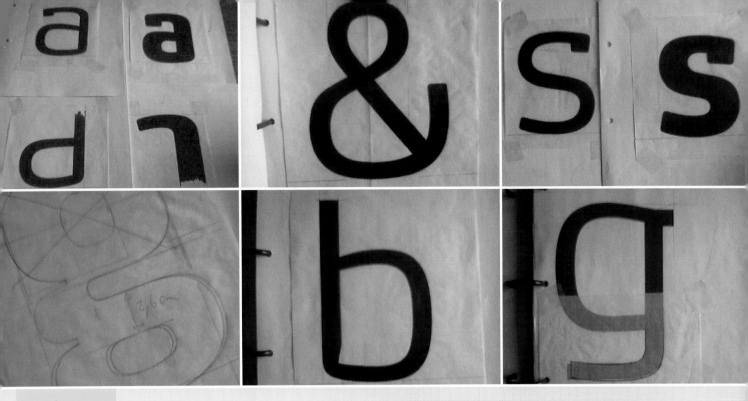

Drawings for FF Max.
Although Morten
Rostgaard Olsen is a
computer-savvy designer,
he does not shy away from
pencil and paper:
many of his letterforms
were first drawn by hand.

FF Max + *Italic*

Light   Regular   Book   **Semibold**
Bold   Extra Bold   Black
Light   Regular   Book   Semibold
Bold   Extra Bold   Black

FF Max Demiserif + *Italic*

Light   Regular   Book   **Semibold**
Bold   Extra Bold   Black
Regular   Book   Semibold
Bold   Extra Bold   Black

1234567890
1234567890   LF
1234567890   TF

So far, he has published two typefaces, both large families of text faces: FF Olsen and FF Max. He has also designed a number of custom fonts for business clients, a corporate design tool for which there is a growing interest in Denmark. Olsen graduated from The Danish School of Art and Design (Danmarks Designskole, Copenhagen) in 1999. Among his teachers was Finn Simonsen, an 'old-school' modernist like Søndergaard, who introduced Olsen to a functional approach in information design and signage programmes. In recent years, Olsen himself has been teaching at the same school, as well as the Royal Danish Academy of Fine Arts. 'So now,' he notes laconically, 'some of the students inspire me sometimes...'

Having been attracted to letterforms since childhood, he naturally gravitated towards type design. Although Olsen has clearly taken cues from the Danish lettering tradition, he is also an admirer of Dutch type design, as well as the Dutch-Finnish type studio Underware, of which FontFont designer Sami Kortemäki is a co-founder. However, he says, 'I try to make my own things, without looking around too much.'

Sans and semi-serif
Of Morten Rostgaard Olsen's two FontFont families, FF Max (2003) has the most outspoken Danish features. Characters such as 'k/K', 'M', 'v/V' and 'w/W' are fairly wide, and sport the horizontal 'bridges' that are so typical of much architectural and commercial lettering in Denmark. Although Olsen has chosen to give FF Max a conventional two-storey 'g' instead of the picturesque bended, open-ended tail referred to above, the overall look

of the lower-case is immediately identifiable as being nordic: low-contrast, open, sturdy, non-literary, squarish. According to its designer, FF Max was based on Aldo Novarese's Eurostyle (1960). However, where Novarese's landmark design is almost rigidly geometric, combining rectangular proportions with rounded angles, FF Max is more complex and subtle: it has a pronounced tension between the rounded outside corners and the angled inside joins. In terms of cultural history one could say that Eurostyle's pure modernism has been infected with postmodernist details that refer to typographic tradition. This is all the more clear in the serif version, which is, in fact, a semi-serif. Here, the basic forms of FF Max Sans have been adorned with minute top left serifs or slightly bent verticals – but not more so than in a sans-serif like FF Meta – and, at bottom right, script-like strokes bending off to the right. Thus, while in most multi-style families the serif version is the more bookish variant, FF Max Serif is rather like a 'Max Informal'.

In its country of origin, FF Max has immediately been recognized as a typographic expression of the Danish soul: it has been adopted as a corporate typeface by several organisations, including the country's largest trade union 3F, and the Konservative party. In 2006, FF Max was upgraded to an OpenType version, adding Central European characters.

Morten Olsen's predilection for hybrid forms also shows in FF Olsen, his first published type family. Here, it is the italic that has the structure of a semi-serif. The roman is almost a slab-serif, with firm, tapered serif – not unlike those of Gerard Unger's Swift – and is virtually indestructible, even in small sizes and on bad quality paper. Even before FontShop published it, the Danish Ministry of Education adopted FF Olsen as its corporate typeface.

Although FF Signa, FF Olsen and FF Max are very different type families, they have several qualities in common. They consist of clear-cut functional, yet original, letterforms combining a modernist attitude with a humanist approach. In that sense, their designers are part of the same Danish design tradition that gave us Poul Henningsen lamps, or Jacobsen and Panton chairs. ⊕

---→ ---→
Title page from the Danish issue of the FontShop Benelux magazine *Druk* (2001), designed by the author of this article.
The Werner Panton chair seems to follow the same logic as the FF Signa lower-case 'g'.

FF Olsen + *Italic*

Light Regular **Bold**
Light *Regular* ***Bold***
1234567890
1234567890 LF
1234567890 TF

+
Druk 009 goes
Dansk
+

Kulturordfører
GRUPPEVÆRELSE

Logo

Symbol

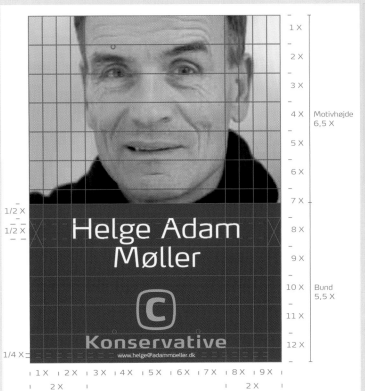

FF Max was recently selected as corporate typeface of the Danish Konservative party. Illustrations from the guidelines and from a brochure concept.

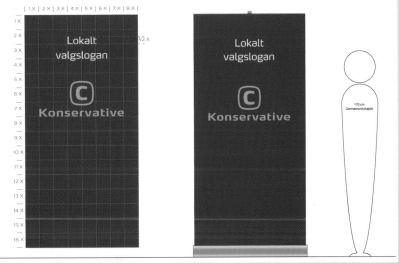

Mod til at skabe sammenhæng
mellem familie og karriere

· Vi vil investere 2 mia. kr. i bedre daginstitutioner
· Vi vil sænke den årlige forældrebetaling til daginstitutionerne
  med 4.000-8.000 kr. pr. barn
· Vi vil forhøje børnechecken med 2.000 kr. årligt for barn mellem 0-3 år
· Vi vil sænke indkomstskatten, så det bedre kan betale sig at arbejde
· Vi vil gøre det lettere at starte virksomhed
· Vi vil nedsætte afgiften på miljøvenlige biler

Evert Bloemsma
Reinventing type design

Jan Middendorp
2004

set in FF Legato

This article was completed on the occasion of the release of FF Legato, Evert Bloemsma's fourth FontFont family and, as it turned out, his last typeface to be completed before his untimely death in April, 2005. Like his earlier typefaces, FF Legato began as a personal investigation. Bloemsma aimed to design a sans-serif that would owe its inner cohesion to the diagonal contrast typical of renaissance romans – and at the same time to steer clear of the all-too-familiar model of the 'humanist sans' based on writing with the broad-nibbed pen. Bloemsma was never a traditionalist; like all his typefaces, FF Legato was an attempt to reinvent type design itself.

EVERT BLOEMSMA STRIVES to design typefaces that befit our times. He is convinced that type, like buildings or automobiles, is an expression of contemporary thinking. He therefore has little affinity with the traditionalism that often prevails in the design of today's text faces. Contrary to many of his Dutch colleagues, he prefers not to seek inspiration in handwriting, let alone indulge in creating revivals of typefaces of the past.

'Think of how Mr. Plantin must have heated his house. Imagine how Francesco Griffo must have lit his working table while cutting the Bembo type. Did these circumstances influence the expression of their work? Of course they did! Compare it to how we heat and light our rooms today: you push a button and it's done. We live in a completely different world. However hard a contemporary designer may try to comply with traditional construction principles, he will not be able to make a truly classical typeface; he will at best succeed in making a typeface that looks like a classical design. The difference will at any time be palpable; and there's a severe risk of being trapped in some kind of kitsch.'

FF Balance: reversing conventions

FF Balance, the first typeface that Evert Bloemsma completed, took these principles to the extreme. During his studies at the Royal Academy of Arnhem he had been fascinated by what is often referred to as 'Swiss typography' – the approach to graphic design which has been labeled 'functionalist'. For the project *Opvattingen over typografie* ('Opinions on typography', a box of publications issued by the Arnhem Academy in 1984) he conducted an extensive interview with Wim Crouwel, the best-known representative of the Dutch branch of functionalism. Given Bloemsma's interest in modernist typography, it followed that his first typeface was to be a sans-serif: his opinion at the time was that there was no place for serifs in the era of new technologies.

Yet the typefaces nearest his heart were not Univers and Helvetica, those impeccably cold Swiss faces, which functionalist designers had

nt, daß Gebäude, Möbel und
ine breite Basis und eine
oziiert uns, daß die Dinge fest
rgen zu machen brauchen,
Iruck von Standfestigkeit hat
eutung bekommen, er
dität, Würde und
rund zu finden, daß auch die
der Schwerkraft zu unter-
stabenformen ihren Dienst
hwere' so eingebürgert, daß
stellen können.
ichtsverhältnisse genau
rdenden Buchstabenformen
d zugänglich erscheinen.
en sind unterhalb der
esers durchgeführt: man

Équilibre inversé

Dans notre rapport quotidien avec le mobilier, l'architecture et tout ce qui remplit l'espace, nous sommes habitués au fait de reconnaître une base large avec un haut étroit, qualités qui garrantisent la stabilité de l'objet. Or cette suggestion d'un état inébranlable de stabilité, a acquis avec le temps une signification plus large. Elle évoque aussi pour nous d'autres qualités telles que la solidité, la noblesse, la monumentalité. Comme si, les lettres aussi, pouvaient subir les lois de la pesanteur. Dans la typographie, cette lourdeur est si généralisée qu'on ne connaît pratiquement rien d'autre.

Dans le FF Balance, ces proportions sont inversées: les formes groississent vers le haut ce qui lui attribue une lisibilité accrûe et une grande clarté visuelle. La perception de cet accès direct à l'image n'est pas conscient. Tout comme dans les équilibres conventionnels, l'idée est *sentie* sans être vue.

regular c. 9 / 12,5

nd im Industriedesign sind schon öfter Maßverhältnisse
rinzipien radikal verändert und umgestoßen worden.
Sie beispielsweise beim japanischen Kleinbus auf das
ionen von Fahrer, Vordersitzen und Motor zueinander
h zwischen den Vordersitzen). Im Vergleich dazu ein Auto
rhunderts.

Dans l'architecture et le dessin industriel les équilibres et les structures en place ont souvent été renversés.
Comparez par exemple la position de l'automobiliste par rapport à la roue avant et le moteur dans le minibus japonais, dans cette voiture du début du siècle.

light c. 6,5 / 8

Une ligne a *toujours la même longueur* quelle que soit la graisse de la LETTRE.

Une ligne a *toujours la même longueur* quelle que soit la graisse de la LETTRE.

Une ligne a *toujours la même longueur* quelle que soit la graisse de la LETTRE.

Une ligne a *toujours la même longueur* quelle que soit la graisse de la LETTRE.

embraced emphatically. In spite of his fascination with rational thinking, Bloemsma had a penchant for the non-conformist, the Latin, the elusive. He admired, for instance, the typefaces of Roger Excoffon, the quintessential French type designer. He was intrigued by Excoffon's Antique Olive, a type which still enjoys popularity in latin countries, in spite of – or perhaps because of – its eccentricity. In his FF Balance, Bloemsma adopted the two unusual features that defined Antique Olive's peculiarity. It was given an 'inverted stress', where the horizontals are heavier than the verticals; and it is top-heavy, i.e. subtly sturdier at the top than at the base.

It is typical of Bloemsma that he took so much trouble to rationalize and justify his intuitive predilection for such unusual proportions. 'Experience has taught us that bodies that are heavier at the bottom than at the top stand firmer on the ground and fall over less easily. Therefore, perhaps, these proportions give a sense of safety, security and continuity. Proportional relations like these can be found in most printing types of past centuries. But is this idea really applicable to type? Aren't letters simply printed on paper? They are not affected by gravity, are they? There is

no functional reason for the classic proportions of letterforms. In fact, recognizability and readability largely depend on the top half of most characters. So perhaps enhancing this half can have a positive effect on readability.' The objective of improved readability is also used to explain FF Balance's other unusual feature: the stressing of the horizontals. This 'inverted contrast' leads the eye along the lines of text and thus attempts to compensate for the absence of serifs, which have a similar function.

Even though Balance has been designed with the reader in mind, it is nevertheless a typeface with unorthodox shapes. This is not necessarily problematic, and it makes the typeface an interesting alternative to Univers or Frutiger. It is clearly part of the same modern tradition, but it is more idiosyncratic and contemporary.

Bloemsma tried in vain to sell the first versions of Balance to a number of well-known international foundries: Berthold, Linotype, Purup, Monotype, ITC (several of which, as he subtly pointed out in a lecture, have now folded or been taken over). In 1986 he was provided the opportunity to digitize the font using the Ikarus system developed at URW in Hamburg, although they were not interested in publishing the font. Finally, in 1992, the PostScript

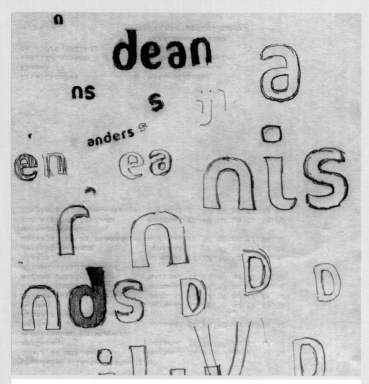

anders biologie erna cadeau
niveau enthousiast brede
basis folkloristisch

anders biologie erna cadeau
niveau enthousiast brede
basis folkloristisch

anders biologie erna cadeau niveau
enthousiast brede basis folkloristisch

anders biologie erna cadeau niveau
enthousiast brede basis folkloristisch

Sketches and proofs illustrating the painstaking design process

version of Balance was completed and that same year it was published as part of the FontFont library. FF Balance – a well-equipped family with four weights, small caps and two sets of figures – was not an immediate success. Designers were not easily convinced of its usability until they saw it applied in an interesting way. Since its publication, however, interest has steadily risen as some remarkable books employing the typeface have appeared both in Europe and North America.

Cocon: extremely sans

Bloemsma's second typeface, FF Cocon (1998), like FF Balance, questions conventional principles of type forms. It tackles an aspect that is part and parcel of the tradition of type design, so much so that it is hardly noticed any more: the origin of letterforms in writing. 'Type designers should beware of unthinkingly adapting and repeating accepted conventions,' wrote Bloemsma. 'Typography is full of traditions, and is therefore a field full of designer pitfalls. Before getting to work, you must be aware of all those conventions passed down to us, otherwise you won't succeed in adding something substantial.'

In the first sketches for Cocon the designer made an attempt at erasing every trace of handwriting. He observed that even an 'autonomous' typeface such as Helvetica contains many references to writing in its stems and terminals. It was more complicated than expected to eliminate these elements and yet retain a convincing, natural-looking result. Bloemsma's experiment with a letterform with completely straight terminals turned out unsuccessfully. Finally, he let a calligraphic element in through the backdoor: the terminals of the stems and extenders were given an elegant asymmetrical rounding, creating the suggestion that the characters were drawn with a round brush. These ingenious curves seem to have a practical function as well: they propel the eye forward from left to right, an effect similar to that of FF Balance's unconventional stress.

When writing about Cocon, Bloemsma has described it as a 'serious typeface', apparently referring to the many hours of experimentation that went into the design, as well as the wide spectrum of possible uses. In large sizes, Cocon is a display face with beautiful details, while in small sizes it remains surprisingly readable. In spite of its claims to seriousness, Cocon is a family of seductive, voluptuous fonts. Since its release it has been used for a multitude of purposes, from architectural books and design catalogues to the packaging of Durex condoms. The British National Lottery, too, chose FF Cocon as its corporate font.

Photos by Evert Bloemsma.

↑
Photos taken by
Evert Bloemsma of
FF Cocon in use:
toiletry packaging of the
Dutch drugsore chain DA;
a sign at AH supermarkets
(the Netherlands)
announcing that payments
will be 'rounded off' at
5 Eurocents;
packaging of Durex
condoms;
a Danone poster in
Germany.

---→
Development of FF Avance.
In an initial design phase,
the asymmetric serifs
caused the characters to
optically 'fall over' to the
left (top).
This was amended by
introducing subtle curves
into the verticals (center
and bottom).

uni

uni

uni

Some years after its release, Cocon was expanded with an italic – which the original version oddly lacked – and a compressed variation.

Avance: ever forward

Observing how others used his FF Balance as a book typeface for long texts, Bloemsma became curious about alternative possibilities to facilitate the reading process. It had to be possible to think of other means to guide the eye, using easily recognizable elements. At first he refused to believe that the result could be a serifed typeface – serifs being synonymous to tradition and convention. However, as Bloemsma had previously experienced while designing FF Cocon, there is much that escapes the designer's rational planning. 'In our trade,' he wrote, 'tradition works as an inescapable magnet. It's no use trying to deny the significance of conventions. What counts is how smartly and creatively one incorporates these traditions in one's designs.'

And so Avance was allowed to grow serifs. The serif makes for a more regular and steadier text image, and leads the eye along the line. The text may look more agreeable than is in the case with sans-serif because serifs allow for a larger variety of shapes. Moreover, the use of serifs results in visual dynamism: reading is moving.

In order to avoid the traps of convention, the designer made a list of results to be avoided: the serifs were not allowed to be characterized by symmetry and static monumentality, or to assume the role of ornament or decoration. As in his earlier designs, Bloemsma chose a radical and unorthodox solution. FF Avance was given only asymetrical serifs. It was a way to avoid an all-too-obvious use of these elements and simultaneously emphasize the functional qualitities of the serif.

Bloemsma's initial source of inspiration for Avance was Adrian Frutiger's Icone, published by Linotype in 1980. Icone is a hybrid between a wedge serif or 'glyphic' and a half serif: the small, triangular serifs protrude on both sides of the stem, but are subtly asymmetric. Bloemsma's first sketches followed this model rather closely, and he even corresponded with Frutiger to ask his permission for incorporating the idea. Later, the triangular shape was abandoned for a horizontally stressed, curved form, which is more distinctly asymmetric.

Although for its designer it was a somewhat speculative experiment, Avance is quite a successful design – even more so, in fact, than its initial model. In small point sizes it is virtually indestructible – a kind of Century Schoolbook for the 21st century. When it is used in bigger sizes, interesting details become manifest. The typeface appears to possess a subtle 'swing' to the right; the undesirable effect of letters seeming to fall over to the left is thus avoided. Instead of making the verticals lean to the right, the designer constructed his characters almost completely with curved forms. Perhaps the latter is the main constant in Bloemsma's typefaces, so that all of his small but sophisticated body of work can be regarded as a tribute to his teacher Jan Vermeulen, whose dictum 'a straight line is a dead line,' has been a guiding light to Bloemsma throughout his career.

Legato: invisibly linked

In early 2004, FontShop published Bloemsma's fourth and final type family, FF Legato. For some time, Bloemsma had been toying with the idea of making a new sans-serif which was to be more agreeable to read that FF Balance, a typeface, which, with the passing of time, he had begun to dislike because of its conspicuousness. He had become convinced that FF Balance's horizontal stress had been somewhat of a self-conscious and mannered expedient. He had come to realize that the conventional diagonal stress still stands out as an indestructible means virtually to link single characters with ach other forming coherent words and lines. He had seen this confirmed in the Lexicon typeface – as a reader of the Dutch daily NRC Handelsblad, Bloemsma encountered Bram de Does's brilliant roman font on a daily basis. But while the traditional contrast between thick and thin strokes derives from writing with the broad-nibbed pen, Bloemsma wanted to avoid such a historical reference: there had to be a more original and more contemporary way to construct a sans-serif text face using diagonal contrast.

Evert Bloemsma liked to take inspiration from other design disciplines, such as architecture and car design. Shortly before he began working on Legato, he had enthusiastically pointed out to his friends the recent Renault automobiles: on the 1993 Laguna, the shape of the back doors did not run parellel to the back weel arch, but described its own path – an effect that has since been imitated by most car manufacturers (as Evert made a point of adding when reviewing this text). Brilliant! Wouldn't it be possible to use a similar idea in type design, by drawing counters that contradict the outer shapes? In mid-2002 Evert had sent me a sketch of a new alphabet in which this principle was tentatively worked out. The project did not yield any significant results until the hot summer of 2003 when, after a relaxing day with his young daughters on a lake near Arhnem, a more precise idea hit him. 'In the evening I started sketching in FontLab (directly on the computer) and suddenly, quite unexpectedly, a concept took shape that seemed to be very interesting. The next day, it still seemed to offer a lot of perspectives and I continued working on it, although designing type during the summer is not much fun. Work-

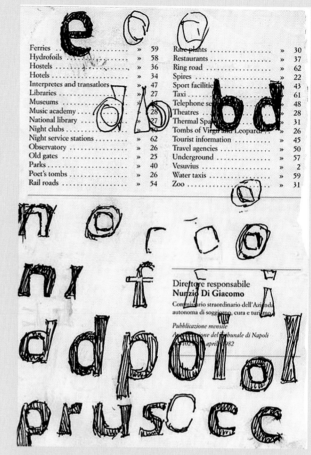

ing it out went very fast, because without fully realizing it, I had been preparing something for a really long time.'

One other factor that played a role was the fact that Bloemsma had intensively been teaching typography and type design at the Sint Joost Academy in Breda for a number of years. 'By working as an instructor I taught myself a lot, too. The classes I used to take at the Arnhem Art Academy were not really fundamental. Being a teacher forced me to do a lot of research, which helped me to get things straight for myself: one needs to formulate things clearly when talking to students.'

Special, yet normal

The Legato design started with a simple artifice: Bloemsma drew a circle and made it slant a few degrees to the right. A second, smaller circle was sloped to the left and put inside the first one. This led to an idiosyncratic basic shape from which an entire alphabet was quickly developed. It will not come as a surprise that the result was not exactly a beauty. Only five months and thousands of proofs later (but relatively quickly compared to Bloemsma's earlier typefaces) Legato had found its definitive form. While in earlier versions its peculiarities were extremely conspicuous, the typeface now looks quite unsensational in small sizes, and only when used at a fairly big size reveals its miraculous details. 'This was precisely my goal,' confirmed Bloemsma, 'to make an unsual, innovative, yet "normal" typeface. Contrary to previous designs, I wanted this time to avoid the situ-

---→
First sketches for the typeface that became FF Legato. Initally it was called Diagonal or Dia.

Het alfabet is het simpelste systeem van codering dat mogelijk is om klanken aan te duiden. Maar dat is ook de grote kracht van het alfabet. Omdat de componenten van het systeem geen bijbetekenissen of gevoelswaarden hebben kunnen ze gecombineerd worden in een eindeloze variëteit van teksttoepassingen. De duizenden Chinese karakters zijn echter stuk voor stuk boordevol culturele betekenis. Ze kunnen geassocieerd worden met klanken en concepten en het schrijven lezen van Chinese karakters schijnt voor sommigen een religieuze belevenis te zijn. De minder dan dertig letters van een alfabet vertegenwoordigen geen culturele gevoelswaarde (behalve misschien voor typografen), geen kleur en geen smaak. Juist daardoor is een voorwaarde geschapen voor een enorme 'operationele efficiency' (Bartlett, 1993) tengevolge v

light
generates a wide range of activities, from workshops **to specially des**
projects providing access to the company **for individuals and grou**
walks of life. The work is designed to **stimulate and develop under**

black
l'aérodynamique faire vive des progrès
coup publicitaire. C'est le genre de qu

light
nportante **encore, o**

FF Legato

Legato   oɟɐƃǝ˥

Legato   oɟɐƃǝ˥

Legato   oɟɐƃǝ˥

The quick lazy fox jumps
over the brown dog?

FF Legato

| *Counter of the 'o'* | *Outside shape of the 'o'* | *Counter of the 'o', enlarged* |

---

ation that the concept would hamper the self-evident functionality of the letterforms. I don't think that Legato is similar to any existing typeface, although there is an affinity with Hans Eduard Meier's Syntax. But Legato incorporates the contrast in a more radical way. That, I think, is its main innovation: the pronounced diagonal stress that had never been so determined in a sans-serif typeface. I have not adopted it in order to be true to the craft but to create an optical, slanting link between the letters, as with a braid.'

Thus, the typeface's name describes its aim: 'legato' (Italian for linked, or bound) is a musical term for playing a series of connected notes. Without literally hooking up the characters to each other, FF Legato connects the loose parts of a word to form a tight visual whole, thus enhancing legibility.

'What makes so many so-called "friendly" or "humanist" sans-serifs so uninteresting," wrote Bloemsma, 'is that they allude to calligraphy in a way that is hardly directed towards its ergonomic quality – to suggestively link physically unconnected unities – and only cite superficial details such as oblique stroke endings, an all-too-literal reference to the broad-nibbed pen. I have tried to avoid such decorative effects and only used the calligraphic perpective because of its ergonomic qualities. The crossed, braided visual connection makes for better word images.' ⊕

↑↑
Diagram by Bloemsma to show the diagonal stress or contrast in Times, the vertical stress in Helvetica and the diagonal stress in Legato. Readers are used to left-to-right diagonal contrast; this becomes all the more clear when the image is mirrored.

↑
Enlarging the counter of the 'o' to the same size as the outer shape brings out the differences.

↙
Fictive project designed (probably by Bloemsma) to show FF Legato's potential for identity design.

Filmstiftung **Schweiz**

deutsch

Schweizerische Stiftung für die Film
Fondation Suisse pour la Film
Fondazione Svizzera per la Pellicola
Swiss Foundation of Film

Filmstiftung Schweiz
Brendelstrasse 56
Zürich

Patrick Baglee
1999–2005

set in FF Meta Pro

FF Govan was originally designed for Glasgow 1999 UK City of Architecture and Design. At the time, MetaDesign had three studios – in Berlin, San Francisco and London. While Ole Schäfer and Erik Spiekermann worked on the typeface in Berlin, Patrick Baglee coordinated the project at the London office. Years later, Baglee wrote an article about the design process for Typographic, the periodical published by the International Society of Typographic Designers (ISTD); the piece was rewritten for this book.

FF GOVAN, THE TYPEFACE designed by MetaDesign for Glasgow 1999 UK City of Architecture and Design, was the result of a paid competitive pitch. The initial invitation to participate came via a one-page fax, late in 1996, initially requesting some evidence of MetaDesign's typographic credentials.

We knew straightaway that Glasgow's design community would be the first and main implementers of the chosen design. Putting ourselves in their place, we were certain that our typeface stood a better chance of winning through to the final stages if we could make it ever so slightly DIY: the ability to work the typeface into unique shapes and structures. If the type was worthy and trussed up, the creative community might reject it out of sheer boredom. More pressing though – it might not even have won through to the second stage of the competition.

There was another challenge. We wanted the panel of esteemed judges to understand that it would be unrealistic to suggest a typeface alone could give Glasgow 1999 and all the collateral involved a distinctive, differentiating look. We gave ourselves licence to extend our influence from designing FF Govan to offering ideas on how the whole family of communications might start to take shape.

Some weeks later, following the panel's scrutiny of our typographic CV, we received notice of selection to move into the second phase of the project where a handful of designers and type-design specialists would receive a modest development fee to produce an outline typographic treatment for the phrase 'Glasgow 1999 UK City of Architecture and Design'.

Time was at a premium, and all we could realistically produce for the initial submission was a broad concept. To help our case we showed rough workings 'in situ', illustrating how the typeface could grow in character and support the communication needs of the festival and the city. From the off, the project was a collaborative effort between MetaDesign's offices in London and Berlin, with London enjoying unfettered access to the knowledge and experience of Erik Spiekermann and the team of experts he had assembled.

Glasgow 1999

Edinburgh can not quite believe that Glasgow is capable of competing with it, Alan Taylor, deputy editor, The Scotsman

One quarter of all our conversations are made up from so words: the, and, to, a, in, that, of, it, I and you. The way we construct words gives language form. Glasgow 1999 offers numerous alternatives in the building of written language. The alternative characters designed within the face provide room to interpret the city of Glasgow in many ways; it provides variety without repetition.

Glasgow 1999 UK City of Architecture and Design

← Poster designed by Meta-Design as a demonstration of the playful possibilities of the Glasgow typefaces. (hi-res data not available)

↙ ↓ Stills from an on-screen presentation made by MetaDesign to convince the Glasgow 1999 judges of its grasp on the city's character.

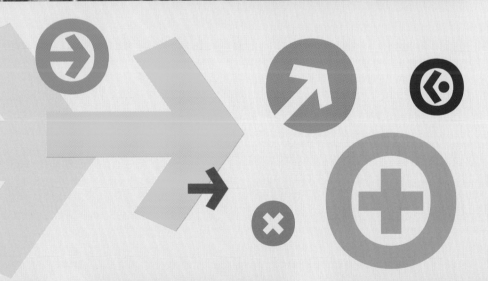

pedigree and American in its gridiro

nd American in its gridiron plan.

Scottish

The logo can be reproduced black on white, white out of black, reversed out of an image or in any colour from the colour palette (page 10).

The only rule is that when the logo is used in its basic form as illustrated here, parts 'a' and 'b' should be the same colour, and that the contrast with the background is strong enough to make it legible.

Parts 'a' and 'b' are available as key commands within the Glasgow 1999 Logo font. Instructions on how to create the ten versions are available in the Typeface User Manual. The Logo font is available on the Resource CD-ROM.

Glasgow 1999 Part 'a'
UK City of Architecture and Design Part 'b'

To create more dynamic and fluid layouts, the parts of the logo can be used expressively as abstracted elements.

The examples here have been scaled and overlayed, using the angles of 9.99 and -9.99. Keylines are also used (page 13).

The only rule is that part 'a' should be the more dominant.

To use the logo as an endorsement, place the logo square to the edge and maintain a reasonable distance between the edge of the layout and the logo.

The logo is the signature of the festival. It is based on the concepts of construction and flexibility – there are many versions of the same logo, using slightly different character combinations.

Each project where the signature is required could use a different logo. In fact, the more that are used, the better – they all represent the spirit of Glasgow 1999. You'll see that all the examples on these pages are different.

The logo is created by typing two characters within the Glasgow 1999 Logo font.

Within this font there are ten versions of each part of the logo, all available by simple key commands. So, inventive combinations can produce a variety of results.

Details of where to find these parts and character variations are given in the Typeface User Manual.

The abstracted logo can be used on different types of communication: posters, banners, publicity and signage. This adds another layer of flexibility to the identity.

The angle in which the two parts of the logo can appear is either 9.99°, -9.99°, or on the horizontal.

Within continuous text the name of the festival should appear as 'Glasgow 1999: UK City of Architecture and Design' using upper and lowercase, and spelling out 'and' in full.

Phonetic alphabet

The true possibilities of the design began to take shape early the following year when Spiekermann faxed over early outline concepts for a phonetic alphabet. He'd taken inspiration from a clipping he'd found in The Guardian that stated nearly a quarter of day to day conversation comprised just ten words (the, and, to, a, in, that, of, it, I and you). He'd started with these common phrases as the building blocks for FF Govan. With the addition of frequent letter combinations, dipthongs and character groups that could be turned into ligatures, we quickly realised that more written language than you would expect is fixed before you even set it down.

We set about designing an alphabet that echoed such idiosyncracies and oddities. The basic principle is not without precedent. Kurt Schwitters published his face 'Systemschrift' as far back as 1927 as an attempt to capture the sound of language. It ran counter to many principles of letterform structure and accepted typographic balance by representing vowels and other sounds in bolder type or by using adjoining characters. Each phrase became a piece of printed sculpture.

To build a typeface in such a way would be a remedy for the lack of diacritical marks in the majority of Roman alphabets that help distinguish between letter sounds and so form the phonetics and the clarity of spoken language. What we were designing was an alphabet that could automatically represent such patterns and quirks.

The spirit of the city

As the deadline approached, so the brief became clearer. We were being challenged to create a design that was distinctive and memorable, and that would reflect the spirit of a contemporary city. There was also the task to create from the alphabet a 'typemarque' to act as a logo for the festival. Easy enough to write on a brief, but not entirely straightforward when it comes down to execution. Creating a typeface that is memorable in isolation isn't too hard, but it's a challenge to create something to win through a competitive process with all the necessary impact that doesn't then become mannered and as a result quickly date. The typeface needed to be as much a supporting artist as it did a romantic lead depending on the situation.

In Berlin, Ole Schäfer, then director of Type Design at MetaDesign, started producing some outline ideas based on Spiekermann's original pencil sketches, who had chanced upon a note from Professor Andy MacMillan of the Mackintosh School of Architecture that described Glasgow as 'Scottish in its stone, European in its urban pedigree, American in its grid-iron plan'. Our idea, of a typeface that was 'built', was rooted in Glasgow's own physicality.

It remained important that an element of freedom was inherent in the design of FF Govan. So we included a higher than average number of variant sorts, ligatures and under-scores so letters could be bolted together by designers with simple keystrokes. We were keen to avoid rigid guidelines for use.

The Glasgow 1999 typeface and layouts are intended to be flexible to allow for a multitude of different designs to be constructed.

The combination of these elements and techniques is entirely the choice of the individual designer.

In order that the most delicate elements of the identity do not become lost, we recommend that illustrative/photographic images are simple and bold, especially where type or elements are overlayed.

The angles 9.99° and -9.99° are integral to the identity – they are one part of its overall personality. The headlines on this page are set to 9.99°.

The keylines used are 0.25pt, 0.5pt and 2pt. They are then overlayed on solid type with an image background. Information on specifying keylines can be found on page 13.

To the engineering of the alphabet, we also brought echoes of the work and hand-rendered type forms of Charles Rennie Mackintosh. FF Govan uses some of the essence of the underscores and other furniture that Mackintosh employed as well as taking its denser curves from the heavy, close-set photo-typefaces of the 1960s and 1970s. This was an alphabet that owed less to calligraphy and penmanship and more to the the quarry, the shipbuilder and the stonemason. It would suit being set tight but not touching. Used well, the additional sorts give FF Govan a peculiar and unexpected delicacy.

Common vocabulary

When Glasgow 1999 finally chose MetaDesign to proceed with the design and programming of the final typeface, we quickly set about supplementing our initial proposal (a very basic batch of letters and sorts) with a variety of weights and appropriate alternates. We also worked in partnership with the organisers to establish a common vocabulary where all parties had a clear understanding of the process of executing the complete alphabet and all its alternates.

It was our hope that once the typeface was in use, no two Glasgow 1999 typemarques would look the same. In its own way, FF Govan showed the important difference between a creative consistency (that offers nothing but slavish adherence to a corporate font swatch), and a creative harmony where all the elements we'd provided could be beautifully and enthusiastically orchestrated. ⊕

asatanaubebydsdedueien
esetfbfffhfififfifjfkflililm
nisitlalellnoofonstthto
ttquumyeyozu
yes do go in and the it of

Govan One Lined
Govan One Alt Lined
Govan Two Lined
Govan Two Alt Lined
Govan Three Lined
Govan Three Alt Lined

Double-page spreads from the Glasgow 1999 typography manual; the text typeface was Frutiger.

FF Govan comes in three versions with alternates, as well as extensive sets of ligatures and dingbats

91

Grandmother's bitmaps
FF Nelio

Jan Middendorp   set in FF Meta Pro
2004

FF Nelio is a reaction to the coldness of cell phone displays. As Sami Kortemäki from Finland - the land of Nokia - asks: 'Why should a technology that strives to make our lives more comfortable limit itself to the chilly hi-tech aesthetics of bare bones bitmaps?' FF Nelio suggests the possibility of investing pixel alphabets with a novel yet familiar human touch, building a bridge between grandma's embroidered towels and today's ubiquitous mobile telephones. FF Nelio is a family of bitmap-based scripts in which the different shapes of the pixels result in stylistic variations on the same construction.

BITMAP LETTERING EXISTED long before the advent of the personal computer. These square-grid-based embroidery letters were designed in a large variation of styles. As with FF Nelio, the biggest challenge was in attempting to make detailed and sophisticated, yet fluent, curves by placing crosses on a square grid. The lettering often imitated handwriting (particularly the curly cursive hand that results from writing with a pointed pen, which is also FF Nelio's calligraphic origin), but sometimes the design was directly sketched on the grid itself. When no paper sketches are used as a starting point or reference, it's easy to end up with dull, predictable results because the grid is so dominating.

Embroidered lettering is tailored; the manufacturer can immediately judge the final visual appearance of the lettering and adjust the forms to fit a specific purpose. In a digital typeface, every possible character combination should have an acceptable visual appearance without the need for manual adjustments. FF Nelio has a set of ligatures to correct, and give extra richness to, certain character combinations.

Commodore pixels

FF Nelio's designer, Sami Kortemäki, is part of the Commodore 64 generation. He was one of those boys who spent half of their waking hours playing games and designing their own. Those boys remember a software package called 'Shoot 'Em Up Construction Kit' a tool for creating one's own shooting games. It came with a fancy character editor for making new bitmap fonts for startup screens. Those fonts all had the same limitation: they were monospaced and based on an 8 x 8 pixel square – a standard on the C64.

This was the environment in which Kortemäki started FF Nelio's design process. Just for fun, he grabbed his old C64 from the basement, and, using that obsolete machine, began drawing a monospaced bitmap script font. Working within an 8 x 8 square proved to be quite a challenge – he had to cheat a bit.

Examples of embroidered script type.

The 'Alphabet de la brodeuse' is a sample book published by Editions Th. de Dillmont in Mulhouse, France, in 1900. The book sold around a million copies.

Courtesy of the St. Bride Printing Library, London.

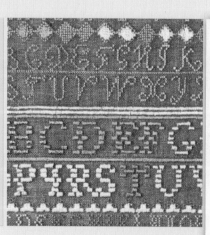

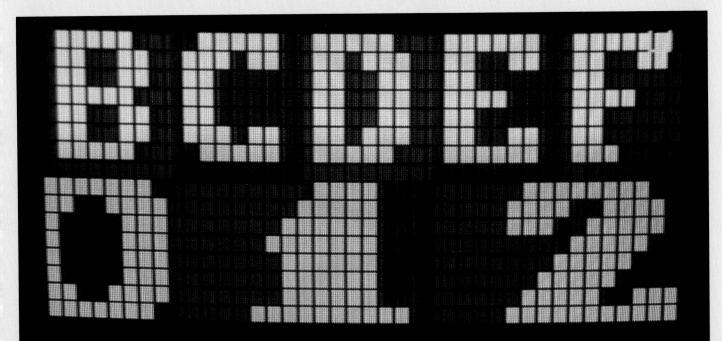

↑
Bitmap letters designed
by Sami Kortemäki on the
Commodore 64 computer,
and photographed from
the screen

⟵ ⟵
Set up in the studio –
the "tools"

⟵
Early versions

↙
The FF Nelio family.

FF Nelio Round & Light
FF Nelio Round Link
FF Nelio Round Bar
FF Nelio Square & Light
FF Nelio Square Bar

Ascenders and descenders were taken to separate character slots, leaving seven pixels for the x-height. Of course, a font is not really a font if one has to hit two or three keys to make a single character. So the design was soon brought into Fontographer on a Mac. The final typeface is no longer monospaced, but retains the same pixel proportions for x-height, ascenders, descenders, and capitals.

FF Nelio has seven styles of pixels – round or square, separated or connected – which have all been projected on the same bitmap construction. ⊛

Nelio in action: very very bad news

In 2001, FF Nelio became part of the FontFont library. Since then, it has been used for various purposes.
In one of the best examples, FF Nelio Round Regular Script is used extensively in Jordi Bernadó's photography book *Very Very Bad News*, published by Actar, Spain. FF Nelio makes a contextual twist for the title and adds humor to photos taken in the shantytowns of Brazil, the Peep Shows of Barcelona, on the beaches of Cape Town, and in many other far-flung locales.

Warm-hearted modernism
FF Profile

John D. Berry
2001

set in FF Profile

Typographer John D. Berry, former editor of ITC's typographic magazine U&lc, originally wrote this article for his column dot-font on the creativepro website. According to Berry, 'Martin Wenzel's typeface FF Profile shakes up our assumptions about sans serif fonts.'

Profile used for a banner on Potsdamer Platz, Berlin, publicizing the new Canadian embassy.

ONE OF THOSE rules of thumb we love to repeat to ourselves, especially in the United States, is that sans serif typefaces are inherently less readable in extended text than typefaces that have serifs. Sans serifs, the logic goes, are mechanical and lifeless; they've sacrificed the subtle warmth of an old-style serif typeface to the cold, cruel logic of the machine age. Yet this assumption has been challenged over recent decades by a significant number of type designers, most of them in Europe, who seem intent on creating a sort of warm modernism.

The humanist tradition

FF Profile is one of a growing number of typefaces that are sans serif, monoline (or almost so), and characteristically clean and spare in appearance, but that have very little to do with either the clunky 19th-century tradition of serifless grotesques or the rational, modernist 20th-century tradition of geometrical sans serifs. This newly expanding category is the humanist sans serifs – typefaces whose letterforms are based on the humanist handwriting of the 15th century, or on the old-style typefaces that followed them (and that dominated printing until nearly the time of the French Revolution). Today's humanist sans serifs follow those Renaissance forms – but stripped of their ornamentation and most of their contrast, reduced to their essential forms and then reconstituted in a variety of weights. One characteristic of almost all humanist sans serifs is that they have true italics, not just slanted romans as so many other sans serifs do.

Martin Wenzel, the designer of FF Profile, is a 32-year-old German designer from Berlin who studied in the Netherlands and now works in Delft with Buro Petr van Blokland + Claudia Mens. Even if you didn't know that he'd been a student at the Royal Academy for Fine and Applied Arts, in the Hague, it would be obvious to anyone with an eye for the fine points of type that he'd been influenced by the humanist Dutch typographic tradition. Profile clearly grows out of some of the same ideas and concerns that gave us Petr van Blokland's Proforma and Luc(as) de Groot's Thesis. (It also has some details in common with Erik Spiekermann's Meta, which approaches the same problems from a somewhat different direction.)

The trick that a sans serif typeface like this has to perform is to be varied enough for comfortable reading in long blocks of text, yet simple and unornamented enough to define its space on the page and suggest an uncluttered, modern, clearly delineated world.

I'm judging Profile entirely from printed samples; I've never put the fonts to use. And of

Lucifer: люцифер
256+Onethousand
Paddestoel: под стуломс, Pompoen: иум-иум
GoOn4Ever
Marten and MartenCyrillic
Goededag: хуй-дах

Two box fighters hunt Eva by Sylt.
Le rapide renard brun
saute par-dessus le chien paresseux.
edged Surface
Bringen sie diesen alten hellen Whiskey der eine
Pfeife raucht.
2,457,890 $€¥£€ et!?@

FOX IN BOX

Produzent von Flops ⊛ I hope it rocks
Bear on socks
🐍🐸🐝 Whiskey ⊛🐛🐵 on the rocks
So many knots
❶❾❾❹✦▶◀❙❙▶
DID YOU CHANGE THE LOCKS?

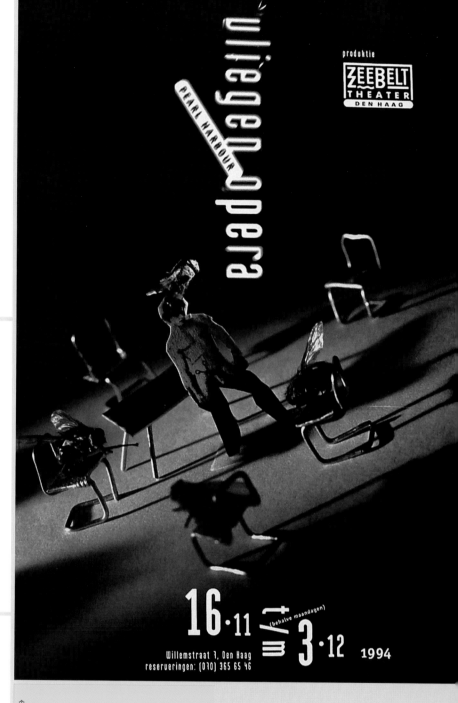

↑
FF Marten in use in a poster for the Vliegenopera
(Fly Opera); both the performance and the poster were
created by Studio Dumbar (designer: Bob van Dijk).

Before designing FF Profile, Martin Wenzel released
several other font families with FontShop.

↖ ↖
FF Marten was his first typeface, a compressed display
face built on geometric principles. It was one of the very
first FontFonts of which a Cyrillic version was released.
FF Primary (centre) is based on forms carved in stone;
it has a special version which allows the user to build
characters using different hues for top, bottom, left and
right to create a three-dimensional effect.
FF Rekord (bottom) is a surprisingly legible sans-serif
roman made with straight lines only. It comes with a set
of pictograms specially made with the music industry
in mind.

‑× **!"#$%&'()*+,‑./01;**
456789:;<=>?@ABCDE
GHIJKLMNOPQRSTUV
XYZ[\]^_`abcdefghijkl
nopqrstuvwxyz{|}~ÄÅ
ÑÖÜáàâäãåçéèêëíìïïñ

course the new type-specimen booklet from FontShop (the fifth in their FontFont Focus series) is handsomely designed, in a way that would show any typeface off to its best advantage. The samples make me want to try out the face in various designs and layouts, much the way Thesis appealed to me the very first time I saw it. Profile has the same clarity and slim elegance that Thesis has, and a similarly open, spacious appearance. But Profile has a slightly warmer, less stark look, because of detailing the small, skewed swellings at the ends of some strokes. Without jumping around or being too lively, Profile possesses a slight informality that makes it feel friendly.

Fine details

Wenzel has given Profile humanist characteristics in the roman, such as the open aperture and small eye on the lowercase 'a' and 'e', as well as a traditional two-story 'g'. The italic, he points out, 'is gently oblique and runs a little narrower and lighter than the respective roman.' Both roman and italic are spaced generously, not crowded together like an advertising headline face. The ends of some of the strokes are asymmetrical; in the 'v', for instance, the angles of the ends of the two arms are different.

Profile comes in five weights, each of which includes roman, italic, small caps, and no fewer than five different sets of numerals: old-style (the standard), lining, monospaced old-style (for tables and columns of figures, as in an annual report), and small lining figures in both the superscript and baseline positions (for making fractions,

among other things). Wenzel has provided a number of simple but useful ornaments, such as arrows in various directions and dotted lines and boxes, as well as such unusual characters such as a euro symbol with only one crossbar (in addition to the standard one with two crossbars) and an alternate "at" sign that, as Wenzel puts it, 'takes the "a" literally, as a ligature of a and t.' He even created appropriate versions of the various mathematical symbols that are part of every standard digital font, but that many type designers just let default to Symbol.

The recipe

After describing some of the influences on the design of Profile (and making the usual disclaimer that it wasn't based directly on any particular face), Wenzel whimsically describes what he calls 'the recipe':

'Take the forms of classical typefaces based on writing with a broad-nibbed pen (for example, a Garamond). Then, carefully reduce the contrast within the character shapes (the thicks and the thins) to a minimum. To finish, reduce the serifs so that only a little detail will remind us that they were once there. Serve unscaled and with enough leading.'

Not a bad recipe for the typographic cuisine of the 21st century. We have a lot of fine reading ahead of us. ⊕

↑
Proofs of
FF Profile Black,
with annotations
and corrections
by Martin Wenzel.

⟶ ⟶
Following pages:
Specimen of
FF Profile,
designed by
Martin Wenzel.

Although *thy hand* and faith By CHILDREN'S BIRTHS, and DEATH, Could make me any summer's story tell. Death is like the insect, Exhuberant, restless, Flesh of his excavated flesh. *Glory* is that bright tragic thing, I have nourish'd the wounded Journeyers with their own sublime KNOWING? No coward soul is mine. OH, LET ME OUT! Prison and palace and reverberation, **Quoth the Raven, nevermore. Some say GOODNIGHT at night, The riddle we can guess, Unto me?** *Violence leaped* **and appeared in the room. The 38 Women – or where there even more? – come and go talking of X-mas. Yearning** *toward* **Zero. Although THY HAND and faith By children's** *births*, **and** *death*, **Could make me any summer's STORY TELL.**

Li
Re
M
Bo
Bl

0	1	2	3	4	5	6	7	8	9	a	b	c	d	e	f	g
h	i	j	k	l	m	n	o	p	q	r	s	t	u	v	w	x	y
z	A	B	C	D	E	F	G	H	IJ	K	L	M	N	O	P	Q
R	S	T	U	V	W	X	Y	Z	0	1	2	3	4	5	6	7
8	9	A	B	C	D	E	F	G	H	IJ	K	L	M	N	O	P
Q	R	S	T	U	V	W	X	Y	Z	@	ą	á	à	â	ä	ã
å	æ	ª	ª	ð	œ	ø	º	º	þ	ß	Á	À	Â	Ä	Ã	Å
Æ	Ð	Œ	Ø	Þ	\	0	1	2	3	4	5	6	7	8	9	|
0⁰	1¹	1¹	2²	3³	4⁴	5⁵	6⁶	7⁷	8⁸	9⁹	[	¢	€	£	£	$
$	¥	¥	¼	½	¾	‰	%	]	&	&	#	¶	†	‡	*	§
•	Δ	µ	Ω	∏	π	◊	∞	∂	∑	∫	√	¦	(	®	©	℗
™	)	!	¡	?	¿	·	¿	¿	¡	¡	□	⫶	←	↑	→	↓
⋮	↙	↘	↖	↗	.	,	:	;	‹ ›	« »	, „	' "	' "	{	/	+
–	=	≈	≠	×	±	¬	÷	>	≥	<	≤	-	}	…	'	"

a *b* *c* *d* *e* *f* *g* *h* *i j* *k* *l* *m* *n* *o* *p* *q* *r* *s*

ß *t* *u* *v* *w* *x* *y* *z* *&* *0* *1* *2* *3* *4* *5* *6* *7* *8*

9 *A* *B* *C* *D* *E* *F* *G* *H* *I J* *K* *L* *M* *N* *O* *P* *Q* *R*

S *T* *U* *V* *W* *X* *Y* *Z* *&* *0* *1* *2* *3* *4* *5* *6* *7* *8*

9 *A* *B* *C* *D* *E* *F* *G* *H* *I J* *K* *L* *M* *N* *O* *P* *Q* *R*

S *T* *U* *V* *W* *X* *Y* *Z* *0* *1* *2* *3* *4* *5* *6* *7* *8* *9*

0 ^{0} 1 ^{1} 1 ^{1} 2 ^{2} 3 ^{3} 4 ^{4} 5 ^{5} 6 ^{6} 7 ^{7} 8 ^{8} 9 ^{9} *!?* *!?* @ ¶ ... * €

MONTAG NACHT: 2.36 Uhr. Typografen schlafen nicht? (Nicht bei £140,–/h) Doch, aber nur selten wenn es dunkel ist ("Schazile, es is schoh gans negadiv drœse."). Der Enthusiasmus hält sie wach und aufmerksam. Der Inhalt von Geschriebenem verschwindet hinter der Form, dem Bild einzelner Buchstaben oder dem ganzer typografischer Landschaften.

Die Euphorie, sich stundenlang in Welten von allerkleinsten Einheiten zu bewegen, ist für andere meist nicht nachvollziehbar. Selbst bei "Disseinern" – Kollegen? – ist diese Lust am Wortbild leider nicht so weit verbreitet. Es gibt ihnen ein unsicheres Gefühl, dass die Auswahl an Schriften nicht nur auf vier Familien beschränkt ist ("Also: Futura, Times, Industria, Garamond, (Hobo)? Äh … mehr fällt mir gerade nicht ein.") Niemand verlangt von jenen selber Schriften zu entwerfen – Gott bewahre? X-fach versuchten berühmteste Gestalter Werber davon zu überzeugen, dass die Schriftwahl den selben Stellenwert verdient, wie die Auswahl eines Fotos. Gelder fließen

– das Meiste bekommen die Werber – und der reichlich überlegte Gestalter geht leer aus.

Das ist aber eigentlich nicht das Schlimmste: Keiner scheint ihn zu verstehen. Seine Erwartungen werden nicht erfüllt, sondern übergangen. Der Gestaltungsauftrag mutiert zum Bürgerkrieg und Politik wird der *Gestaltungsfaktor.* Qualen quälen – der Spaß ist vorbei, CHANCE gehabt!

Man vertraut *DER BANK?* und seiner Zahnärztin, dem Taxichauffeur und dem Drucker. Dem *Typografen* aber **traut man nicht über den Weg („Was macht der DA FÜR NUR € 20.156,–** *eigentlich* **so lange rum?")**

Wer die Nuancen – quatsch: die weltweiten Unterschiede – verschiedenster Romane kennt, die nur das THEMA LIEBE behandeln, kann sich ein Bild machen vom *himmelweiten* **Unterschied zwischen Joanna und** *Trump Mediæval.* **Oder etwa immer noch nicht? Und: Wollen wir nicht IMMER NOCH EINEN nächsten Liebes-Roman? Verrückte Welt [Ypsilon**

Montag Nacht: 2.36 Uhr. *Typografen* schlafen nicht? (Nicht bei £140,– pro Stunde) Doch, aber nur selten wenn es dunkel ist («Schazile, es is schoh gans negadiv drœse.»). Der Enthusiasmus hält sie wach und aufmerksam. Der Inhalt von Geschriebenem verschwindet hinter der Form, dem Bild einzelner Buchstaben oder dem ganzer *typografischer* Landschaften. ¶ Die Euphorie, sich stundenlang in Welten von allerkleinsten Einheiten zu bewegen, ist für andere meist nicht nachvollziehbar. Selbst bei "Disseinern" – Kollegen? – ist diese Lust am Wortbild leider nicht so weit verbreitet. **Es gibt ihnen ein unsicheres Gefühl, dass die Auswahl an** *Schriften* **nicht nur auf vier Familien beschränkt ist ("Also: Futura, Times, Industria, Garamond, {Hobo}? Äh … mehr fällt mir gerade nicht ein."). Niemand verlangt von jenen selber** *Schriften* **zu entwerfen – Gott bewahre! ¶ X-fach versuchten berühmteste Gestalter Werber davon zu ÜBERZEUGEN, dass die** *Schriftwahl* **den selben Stellenwert verdient wie die Auswahl eines Fotos. Gelder fließen – das meiste bekommen die Werber. Der gut überlegte Gestalter**

Seitenverh. A4-Format: $1 : \sqrt{2}$. $\pi \approx 3{,}1415926535$ [Kugelumfang: $U \approx 4\,\pi\,r^2$, Kugelabschn.: $A \approx \pi \div 3 \cdot h^2 \cdot (3r - h)$]. *Löslichkeitsprod., AgCl:* 10^{-10}, $Ca(OH)_2$: $5{,}5 \cdot 10^{-6}$, $PbSO_4$: 10^{-8}. Magnetische Feldkonstante: $\mu_0 = 12{,}5664 \cdot 10^{-7}$ H m^{-1}.

Seemeile (1sm=1°:60)	1,852	km	**Gallone**	4,546	l
Engl. Meile	1,524	km	**Engl. Pfund**	0,4563	kg
Engl. Yard = 3 Fuß	0,9144	m	Engl. Unze	28,35	g
Engl. Fuß = 12 Zoll	0,3048	m	Registertonne	2,832	m³
Engl. Zoll (inch)	2,540	cm	Knoten = 1sm/h	0,5144	m/s

Looking into the old, learning something new: Designing FF Clifford

Akira Kobayashi
2003

set in FF Clifford Nine Roman

Having been born and raised in Japan, designing a latin text typeface was quite a task for Akira Kobayashi. Although he had designed more than a dozen latin alphabets for two Japanese type foundries between 1990 and 1994, these were limited character sets made to match Japanese text typefaces. His first full-fledged roman text type designed for use in Western countries was FF Clifford, the typeface you are now reading. The Clifford family has 25 fonts and took four years to complete. There is an old Chinese saying, 'Look into the old, learn something new.'

That, writes Kobayashi, was how he designed the type.

MY FIRST IMPRESSION of digital type was not good. I remember very clearly when I first used a digital version of the Bembo typeface. I had never touched a computer until 1999 when I began working for a type design studio in Tokyo. I had just come back from London where I learned calligraphy, studied English and read books on typography. The studio bought type design software from a European company that offered ten digital fonts from their library, and I was responsible for choosing the fonts. The fonts I chose included Bembo, Bembo Italic and Bembo Bold. The fonts arrived and I immediately installed them in the computer. Bembo Roman was the first font I opened with the type design software. The font layout appeared, and I double-clicked the lowercase 'g' just to check if the software worked all right. What I saw was a letter 'g' about ten-inches high, and I thought, 'Oh, I opened the wrong font, silly me!' because it did not look like a Bembo 'g'. Then I re-selected Bembo from the pull-down menu and opened the 'g' but the result was the same. After seeing the 'a' and another letter, I got into a slight panic. None of the letters looked like Bembo! For a moment I froze in front of the computer, thinking about writing a letter of complaint to the company for sending us the wrong font.

After a while I checked the Bembo Italic, and I slowly began to realise that the fonts were indeed a version of Bembo. I calmed down enough to recall that the typeface was originally designed for metal type, and most of the specimens and texts I was familiar with were set in metal type in text size. That was why the images of the characters did not correspond. I knew that a metal typeface was cut or designed separately for each size, but a film composition or digital face is a kind of compromise with proportions designed for reduction and enlargement. But I was overwhelmed to see such a huge gap. I looked into the types used in western offset-litho prints to see the digital Bembo types in use (this typeface was and still is unpopular in Japan). The typefaces originally designed for hot-metal often looked too light and feeble. I even purchased a digital rendering of a famous foundry type that cost 30,000 yen, but I still wasn't satisfied.

Monotype Bembo for hot metal typesetting, ca. 9pt, enlarged (top) compared to Adobe's PostScript Type 1 version.

abcdefghijklmn
opqrstuvwxyz ij
abcdefghijklmn
opqrstuvwxyz ij

·····➔
The model for FF Clifford:
Wilson's Long Primer
as used in a book printed
by the Foulis Brothers,
Glasgow, in 1751.

➘ ➘
drawings by
Akira Kobayashi
for FF Clifford and
FF Clifford Italic.

454 PLINII EPIST.
PLINIUS TRAJANO.
Ob diem imperii.

Diem, domine, quo fervafti imperi- 60 um dum fufcipis, quanta mereris laetitia celebravimus, precati deos, ut te generi humano (cujus tutela et fecuritas faluti tuae innifa eft) incolumem florentemque praeftarent. praeivimus et commilitoni- bus jusjurandum more folenni praeftanti- bus, et provincialibus, qui eadem certa- runt pietate, jurantibus.

TRAJANUS PLINIO.
Quanta religione ac laetitia commili- 61 tones cum provincialibus, te praeeun- te, diem imperii mei celebraverint, li- benter, mi Secunde cariffime, cognovi literis tuis.

C. PLINIUS TRAJANO.
De pecunia foenebri.

Pecuniae publicae, domine, providen- 62 tia tua, et minifterio noftro etiam exactae funt, et exiguntur, quae vereor, ne otio- fae jaceant. nam et praediorum compa-

Wilson's long primer

I began thinking about the need for a new digital text typeface suitable for offset-litho printing. The idea was still vague but the typeface had to be conventional or classical in design and robust, such as Monotype Plantin. My idea was further developed when Barry McKay, a friend of mine who I first met at the ATypI conference in 1990, gave me a book. It was a 16mo book printed by the Foulis brothers of Glasgow in 1751. The type used was Wilson's Long Primer roman type. The book was in Latin, which I could not read, but at first sight I could tell it was extremely legible. I liked the type immediately – it was so beautiful. The colour of the text was even and the letterspaces were consistent.

Inspired by the Wilson type, I started a few drawings of my new typeface. I had basic ideas to start with. The type was to be an oldstyle face with some robustness. The words set in the type were to be comfortable to read, each of the characters should be beautiful. The subtle curves and nuances would not be ironed out. However, I was not interested in rendering a faithful image of the printed letters with all the bumps and warts. No photographic enlargement was made. What I wanted to do was to distil the letterform from the prints by hand. My goal was to design a new text type of even letterspace and colour, not an imitation or a reproduction of the metal type.

I carefully drew several lowercase half-inch-high characters while thinking of a way in which they might be used. The drawings were scanned and traced by hand. The rest of the characters were drawn directly on-screen. Adjustments to the width and letterspacing followed. It was a long and slow process; I assume I spent more time working on letterfitting and kerning than drawing the characters. When the design process of the roman type on the Mac was nearly finished, I began drawing the italic type. As no italic type was shown in the Foulis book, I chose Joseph Fry & Sons' Pica Italic No.3 from their 1785 specimen as the model for the italic. Although the typeface was not made by the same hand nor in exactly the same period of time, I believed it would match the roman. Again there was no photographic enlargement. I retained all the vigorous swashes on the letter 'Q', 'T' and 'Y' that were typical of the Anglo-Dutch oldstyle typefaces.

page 103
Camille Silvy (1834–1910)
Hunting Still Life, 1858
9.19 x 6.38 in. (23.343 x 16.205 cm)
albumen print
1984.012.055

Silvy had already studied law and been a French diplomat before he began experimenting with photography. He had only been photographing a year when he produced this still life, which he dated and initialed in the image by writing on the wood with crayon or chalk. In 1859 he decided to move to London, where he became one of the most popular society portraitists. The only other known print that is similar to this, in the Victoria and Albert Museum, does not show the little projection of the gun barrel above the edge of the image.

page 104
Charles Marville (1816–79)
Marble Bas-Reliefs by Luca Della Robbia, 1853–54
5.5 x 14.0 in. (13.97 x 35.56 cm)
salt print
1994.030.151

Photographs of famous works of art were very popular in the early days of the medium. The sale of such prints was often a major source of income for the first commercial studios, especially in France.

See discussion on pages 21 and 56.

page 105
Louis-Rémy Robert (1811–82)
Porcelain from the Factory at Sèvres, 1855
10.13 x 12.63 in. (25.73 x 32.08 cm)
salt print
1984.012.053

page 106
Jean Nicolas Truchelut (active 1850s–1870s)
Two Models in a Studio, c. 1856–60
7.44 x 5.38 in. (18.898 x 13.665 cm)
albumen print
1985.010.018

The name of the painter who commissioned the four Truchelut figure studies—François-Victor Jeannenet—comes down to us from a signature on the photographs. So far, no painting has been found that includes the subjects of the Truchelut photographs, and little is known about Jeannenet.

See discussion on page 30.

FF Clifford in use.

↑
Detail of a page from *A Gift of Light: Photographs in the Janos Scholz Collection* by Stephen Moriarty, University of Notre Dame Press, 2002.

→
Erik Spiekermann and Susanna Dulkinys' design of the American magazine *Reason* uses FF Clifford alongside FF Meta

Optical weights

When the roman and italic faces were complete, I set various texts in different sizes. The type was not bad, but it obviously had limitations. When set larger than 18 point, it already started to look too bold and clumsy, and when used in 6 or 7 point, it looked too dark and compressed. I thought back on my disappointment when buying a digital typeface for the very first time. As long as the type has one master design, the limitation is inevitable. Usually a serifed typeface that looks all right in 10 point cannot look refined in 72 point.

The ultimate solution was 'optical scaling', i.e. designing different masters for different ranges of size. The idea was not innovative at all. In fact it had been the ordinary method of making a series of typefaces for five hundred years, as the punches – the original letters prepared for mass-production – had to be cut one by one and size by size. Most filmsetting and digital types currently available have only one letterform and the types are enlarged or reduced mechanically. The modern method was efficient from an economical point of view but rather disadvantageous for the reader, as many type critics have pointed out. Also, there was an excellent example of the use of 'optical scaling' in the digital type industry. ITC Bodoni was designed in three variations: Seventy-two, Twelve, and Six – a very appropriate decision for a 'modern face'. Otherwise the delicate hairline serifs would fade away in small sizes and look blunt in displays and headlines.

The greatest disadvantage of 'optical scaling' is that the type designer has to spend more time completing the family. But I had been designing the type for fun so I did not have to rush. The next drawback is the number of font families. The more variation the type has, the more computer memory it takes up. But in today's environment of type and graphic design, the amount of memory that a font family requires is very small when compared to, say, a CMYK image. So I decided to make the Clifford type a size-sensitive text type family.

First I had to develop a letterform appropriate to the function and the size of footnotes. There were no written criteria for designing variations for smaller sizes, so I studied specimens of metal type to see how the designers of this era overcame this task. In particular, I referred to the Caslon Old Style, which exhibits certain irregularities depending on its size as a part of its distinctive character, and the 6-point type of the Monotype Bembo series is extremely well designed. What I found in the specimens during the research excited me. In smaller sizes, the contrast of thick to thin was reduced, x-height was set a little higher, the extenders were designed shorter, and the fit of the letters was looser. The overall shapes of individual characters were sometimes altered as well. This is most discernible in the Caslon Old Style type. The curlicues in some swash characters, which often appear too complicated, were simplified in the small size, and gorgeously flourished in larger sizes. The modifications were so clever that I could not take my eyes off the old type specimens! All the modifications were made for the small size variation, and the result was fascinating.

However, one question remained. Should I add a bolder version to the already dark text type? I tried to design a bold variation but it looked awkward, so it was abandoned. Instead, I started designing the larger size meant for chapter headings, small headlines or large texts. At this point, the type had three optical size variations: for text, for footnotes and for headings.

The right time

In 1995, I had a chance to write the renowned calligrapher and type designer Hermann Zapf about the Clifford typeface in progress. He wrote back to me, giving a favourable comment on the design of the type, but he also warned me that it was not the right time period to submit a traditional text face to font companies. I also showed specimens of the type to Juzo Takaoka, who was running a letterpress workshop in central Tokyo. He also liked my typeface but said that I should choose my timing carefully, and in the meantime try to design something different. So I decided to temporarily freeze the Clifford project and wait for an appropriate time. In 1996 I began designing a sans-serif typeface family based on my handwriting, which I submitted to the International Typeface Corporation (ITC) in New York. It was named Woodland after my family name Kobayashi (which means small woods) and published by ITC.

In the autumn of 1997, I saw an advertisement for a typeface competition organised by U&lc, the graphic magazine published by the ITC. The competition had three categories: display, text, and picture fonts. It was a good opportunity for me to have my text type design assessed. I reviewed and revised almost every letter of the six variations before submitting them to the competition: it took longer than I had imagined. Eventually the Clifford type received both the 'Best of Category' (text) and the 'Best of Show' awards. Finally in the summer of 1999, FontShop International published the typeface under the name of FF Clifford. The FF Clifford family includes 25 typefaces, including lined figures, expert sets and borders. FF Clifford received the 'Certificate of Excellence in Type Design' in TDC 2000 from the Type Directors Club in New York.

The Clifford family is a bridge between the past and the present. I learned from 'the old fellows' through the fonts they produced and printed, implementing their ideas to my digital type when necessary. Electronic enlargement and reduction of single letterforms seems to be the prevailing practice, but it often looks monotone. A printed page set in variations of slightly irregular quality will be lively and more pleasant to read. A size-sensitive family of 25 fonts may sound like too many, but thanks to today's technology, it is certainly easier to handle than storing cases of metal type.

FF Acanthus and Henri Didot

Another typeface inspired by the past is FF Acanthus, published in 1998. It started when Clifford was almost finished. FF Acanthus is more faithful to its source of inspiration: the typeface used in De Imitatione Christi (Paris 1788) printed by Henri Didot (1765-1852). It may be classified in the 'modern face' category but it has few straight lines and razor-sharp corners. Again, I did not intend to imitate the original printed surface, but I thought the 'moderns' should look that way. The serifs of Acanthus are extremely thin, but they are very carefully emphasized at the extremes. Acanthus was designed for display work or large text.

As for the italic, it seemed to me that Henri Didot's solution did not match Acanthus roman: it was somewhat stiff and mechanical. Therefore, I decided to draw a new italic in the spirit of the period. I later added the 'text' variations for use at ca. 10 point.

In 1999, I designed another typeface, Conrad, this time based on the fifteenth-century type by Sweynheym and Pannartz: the two German printers active in Rome at that time. They produced a unique, slightly-out-of-balance-but-attractive type. The original print example acted merely as a reference. The distinctive lowercase 'a' and some of the other letters were inspired by Sweynheym and Pannartz's second roman type, but I revived the type in a more informal way. In this case, I used the historical type as a springboard. The resulting type looks different, taking on a rather contemporary and lively look. It received a prize in the text type category in the third Linotype International Type Design Contest in 1999 and has been released through the Linotype Library. I assume that the Linotype Conrad is the first revival of the Sweynheym and Pannartz type, though it does not closely resemble the original.

Designing new typefaces is fun. It is stimulating to look into the old type specimens and rediscover how clever the designs of the 'old fellows' were. Reviving old types in the digital era does not necessarily mean designing cheap imitations. The historical typefaces sometimes help me to create traditional-looking fonts and sometimes fonts that are fresh and lively. I am continuously looking for good typefaces from the past just waiting to be rediscovered. ❖

Akira Kobayashi's Clifford FFamily

Clifford Roman
Clifford Roman Expert
Clifford Italic
Clifford Italic Expert
CLIFFORD CAPS
CLIFFORD CAPS EXPERT
Clifford ✳ Borders

36 pt. ## It was only a vague idea
24 pt. inspired by a book printed in 1751 by
18 pt. the Foulis Bros., Glasgow, in sedicesimo format.

36 pt. *As an example for the italic*
24 pt. *he chose Pica Italic No. 3, as reproduced in*
18 pt. *Joseph Fry & Sons' excellent Type Specimen book, 1785.*

DE
AAR-
DIG-
STE
MAN
TER
WE-
RELD

De Vree

Freddy
De Vree DE
AARDIGSTE
MAN TER
WERELD

Book cover typography by Piet Schreuders (2002)

Size	Clifford Six Roman	Clifford Nine Roman	Clifford Eighteen Roman	Clifford Six Italic	Clifford Nine Italic	Clifford Eighteen Italic
6 pt.	Dependable, enduring	Dependable, enduring	Dependable, enduring	Dependable, enduring	Dependable, enduring	Dependable, enduring
7 pt.	Reliable, sturdy	Reliable, sturdy	Reliable, sturdy	Reliable, sturdy	Reliable, sturdy	Reliable, sturdy
9 pt.	No optical scaling	No optical scaling	No optical scaling	No optical scaling	No optical scaling	No optical scaling
12 pt.	Dependable	Dependable	Dependable	Dependable	Dependable	Dependable
14 pt.	Digital font	Digital font	Digital font	Digital font	Digital font	Digital font
18 pt.	Original	Original	Original	Original	Original	Original
24 pt.	Oldstyle	Oldstyle	Oldstyle	Oldstyle	Oldstyle	Oldstyle

Abcdefghijklmnopqrstuvwxyz1234

Clifford Eighteen Roman 36 pt.

Abcdefghijklmnopqrstuvwxyz1234

Clifford Eighteen Italic 36 pt.

ABCDEFGHIJKLMNOPQRSTUVWXYZ

Clifford Eighteen Caps 36 pt.

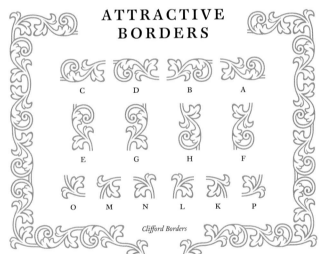

ATTRACTIVE BORDERS

Clifford Borders

Characters in Complete Font

ABCDEFGHIJ
KLMNOPQRS
TUVWXYZ & $
@ 1 2 3 4 5 6 7 8 9 0 %
a b c d e f g h i j k l m
n o p q r s t u v w x y z
. : , ; - ' ' ! ? – ( )
ff fi ffi fj fl ffl ft st

Clifford Nine Roman & Expert

FRACTIONS

¾ ¾ ¾ ¾ ¾
60 pt. 48 pt. 36 pt. 24 pt. 18 pt.

½ ½ ½ ½ ½
60 pt. 48 pt. 36 pt. 24 pt. 18 pt.

Characters in Complete Font

ABCDEFGHIJ
KLMNOPQRS
TUVWXYZ & $
@ 1 2 3 4 5 6 7 8 9 0 %
a b c d e f g h i j k l m
n o p q r s t u v w x y z
. : , ; - ' ' ! ? – ( )
ff fi ffi fj fl ffl ft st

Clifford Nine Italic & Expert

✎ Brigitte Willinger
2000

set in FF Danubia

FF Danubia is a typeface in the 'modern face' tradition – but it's not another Bodoni. Based on the first German classicist typeface, it has unusual forms and highly original details. And the newly designed script is gorgeous.

A GRADUATE OF the Höhere Bundeslehr- und Versuchs-anstalt in Vienna, Viktor Solt-Bittner (1970) has been working as an independent typographer and graphic designer since 1995. Since his college days, he has been designing typefaces as well as studying typographic history. He has also taught handwriting and typography at the Department of Information Design of the Fachhochschule Joanneum in Graz. During the past few years, besides working as a type designer, he has concentrated more and more on animation. His Vienna studio, Bonsai Cuts, conceives and produces 2D-and 3D-animated movies. According to Solt-Bittner, type design and animation have a lot in common: a higher degree of creativity compared to designing for print – where administrative and technical factors are often dominant – but also the need to work with great precision and to concentrate on details. As a connection between his two main lines of work, the designer made a short promotional trailer for his first FontFont, FF Danubia.

Although today's computer technology allows virtually everyone to 'make' a font, Solt-Bittner finds that the really extraordinary typefaces are precious few: 'Around 90 percent of the new fonts are copies and variations on ever the same examples'. He tends to buy the fonts that he likes, even if he does not need them for any particular project. He collects typefaces the way an art lover collects paintings.

Danubia's self-willed classicism

The majority of the text typefaces that have been released the past ten years are either sans-serifs, or fonts based on Renaissance romans and therefore modeled on typefaces whose historical origins lie in the 15th and 16th centuries. Their dynamics is based on the ductus, the path of the strokes. Solt-Bittner's FF Danubia, on the other hand, is modeled on an 18th-century classicist typeface, which draws its dynamics from the different thicknesses of the strokes – the contrast between the stronger and weaker elements of each character.

The starting point of the FF Danubia design was the Prillwitz-Antiqua, the first German classicist typeface, newly interpreted by Alfred Kapr more recently. The most conspicuous feature of Kapr's interpretation is that it has vertical triangular serifs (in letters such as 'E', 'F' and 'z/Z') instead of the usual cupped ones. Solt-Bittner has further developed this typeface in a new direction, taking it to the extreme. Besides the triangular serifs, it is characterized by abrupt changes in stroke width, which result in strikingly angular forms.

FF Danubia is a versatile family which can be used both as text and display face, thanks to its range of six weights: Regular, Italic, Bold, Bold Italic and Extra Bold.

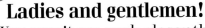

Viktor Solt-Bittner, www.bonsai-cuts.at

As an alternative to the italic weight, Solt-Bittner has developed a newly drawn script font, which is especially suited whenever the occasion calls for a typeface that is decorative, yet original. Many of FF Danubia's features are not very conspicuous and in fact are hardly visible when the typeface is used in normal text sizes. Only when adopted at display sizes do the unusual details stand out: the idiosyncratic descenders; the above-mentioned triangular serifs; the unorthodox stroke terminals that ensure that upper and lowercase letterforms – which are usually very similar to each other (such as 'S' and 's', or 'V' and 'v',) – are more clearly varied than in other typefaces.

Foreign elements

Although FF Danubia was based on an 18th-century classicist typeface, the designer has consciously avoided following his historical model too faithfully. He allowed 'foreign' elements to seep in wherever it seemed suitable to him – not unlike the way in which unusual elements were introduced in the original classicist types. This has leant a certain liveliness and versatility to his typeface; Solt-Bittner judged this to be of greater importance than achieving total perfection, with the risk of causing an effect of sterility. For instance, the Italic version refers to a Renaissance model that allowed for counters with triangular proportions, whereas the counters of the romans describe rectangular forms that are balanced by oval outside shapes. The connecting element between all the variants are formal principles such as proportions, extender lengths and contrasting stroke thicknesses.

Ski resort

The first sketches of FF Danubia were made in 1999 while traveling by train between Graz and Vienna. Its working title, 'Semmering', borrows from these trips, appropriately named after the famous Austrian ski area. When FontShop decided to release the type family as part of the FontFont library, Erik Spiekermann said he would prefer a name with more international appeal. In order to retain the association with Austria, Solt-Bittner decided in favour of FF Danubia – the Latin name for the river Danube.

Contrary to other alphabets designed by Solt-Bittner, based on hand-written letters, FF Danubia was drawn entirely on the computer – apart from a few initial doodles on paper. Even the first sketches were executed with the help of graphic software. Although FF Danubia is obviously a printing type that does not have the spontaneity and cheekiness of handwriting, its designer imagines the font to be used in ways that are charming and exciting, and somehow contradict the formal character of the font itself. Solt-Bittner, who judges himself to be more talented as a type designer than as a graphic designer, prefers to leave it to others to decide how far to go with FF Danubia. He cherishes the element of surprise that this process entails. ⊕

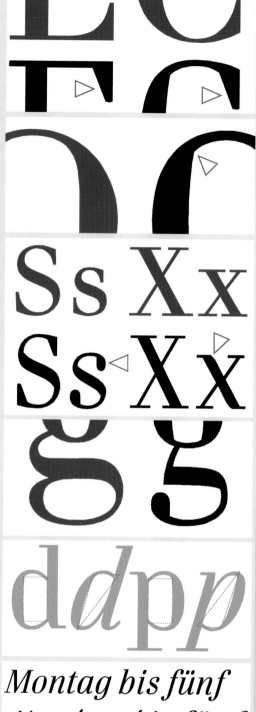

FF Danubia compared to Bodoni: the proportions and stress are similar, but the details are very different.

The counters of the roman are based on a rectangle, while the counters of the italic are triangular.

FF Danubia Italic follows the original classicist model; the playful script version was newly drawn.

While FontFont families such as FF Meta, FF Celeste and FF Quadraat have grown steadily over the years, Ole Schäfer's FF Fago was conceived as a mega-family right from the start. When it came out in early 2000, it had three widths, five stroke weights and three different types of numerals – almost 250 fonts in all. The designer had very precise intentions about what all these variations could be used for. The following article by Antje Dohmann, type reporter for Germany's PAGE magazine, was published on the occasion of FF Fago's release.

OLE SCHÄFER DOESN'T like a job half done – when he designs a typeface, he does it right. Meaning he wants his design to be equipped for all possible uses and prepared for any eventualities. For this reason, his FF Fago consists of 247 fonts – and this was not because he wanted to get into the *Guinness Book of Records* or to raise the bar for other designers. 'In every corporate design program that I supervised,' says Schäfer, 'certain things were missing from the typeface that was chosen. It either did not have small caps at all, or no italic small caps. Quite often table figures were the only kind available.'

The pharmaceutical sector is one area where Fago's versatility might be of use. Such firms need a corporate typeface that is both easy to read at very small sizes – for example on instruction leaflets, and in complicated words such as Hydroxypropyl. The same typeface, however, should also work well when used for the company's stationery, newsletter and, depending on the firm's size, advertising and internal signage system. Out of necessity, many companies opt for using a collection of similar-looking typefaces. 'At the moment, there are very few well-developed sans serif families with two or three widths,' says Ole Schäfer. 'Basically, the only families that qualify are Helvetica and Univers, plus a number of multiple masters fonts that nobody knows how to use. I found that we simply needed some kind of alternative – we couldn't just begin the new millennium with 1970s typefaces, could we?'

xHnƒg78

The five stroke widths of FF Fago Extended superimposed. Contrary to conventional praxis, heavier weights do not 'grow' vertically: even with the rounded shapes, baseline and height remain strictly the same.

!"#$%&'()*+,-./0123456789:;<=>?[\]^_`{|}~

†°¢£§•¶ß®©™´¨≠ÆØ∞±≤≥¥µ∂ΣΠπ∫ªºΩæø¿¡¬√ƒ

≈Δ«›»…Œœ——""''÷◊/€‹›fifl‡·,,,‰¹

ABCDEFGHIJKLMNOPQRSTUVWXYZ

abcdefghijklmnopqrstuvwxyz

ABCDEFGHIJKLMNOPQRSTUVWXYZ

Testansicht Normal, Caps, LF, Tab, Alternate (unvollständig), Expert (unvollständig), ohne Kerning, 20.02.99, © Ole Schäfer, Gp Projekt, Vorbereitung für TypeboardMeeting 14. Feb. 1999 für Release FF 25, Oktober 99, Text 9 pt, Ansicht 36 pt, Testsatz 18 pt

Ðð Ł ł Þ þ ¦ − × ¡ ∧ _ ⓘ ¶ ‹› ⟨⟩

' . ‚ 1 1 √ ®® ‖ ¿ Ⓟ G J M Q

Ŋ ʜ Ŧ ª º € a a ff g g j l t t ß ŋ ħ t đ ð ɑ u fb fh ffffifjfkffflft

stat$()0123456789[]{}¢£¥€()0123456789[]{}ÐŁÆ

ØŒÞSSFIFL

The Quick brown fox jumps over lazy đogman and Handgloves, Handgloves, Schrift, Groß Millionen, Jahrhundert, ʙʀᴏᴡɴ Testdokument – ʜᴀɴᴅɢʟᴏᴠᴇꜱ

Planning

An extensive project like ꜰꜰ Fago calls for thorough planning. Before drawing a single stroke, Schäfer already had very precise ideas about how many and what kind of weights he wanted to produce. It was also an advantage that Schäfer had acquired many of the necessary skills in earlier projects; the complex kerning values were based on experience rather than trial-and-error. Had this not been the case, this part of the process alone would have required months. It was time consuming enough as it was – the type designer sat in front of his computer for about nine months before he was satisfied with the result.

Schäfer made the first sketches by hand. These initial sketches were useful in trying out basic forms, but have little or nothing in common with the final result. Apart from these early trials, the complete design was done in Fontographer. When designing a typeface, the designer usually starts with the normal or regular weight and from the result, derives the bolder weights. Schäfer approached ꜰꜰ Fago from the other end. 'First, I drew the Black Condensed weight,' he explains. 'It is the darkest weight of the family, and I wanted to keep it as narrow as possible to make it suitable for headlines.' From there, Schäfer developed ꜰꜰ Fago Condensed Bold, which in turn became the starting point for the Condensed Regular. Subsequently he developed those same weights for the Normal and Extended versions.

Numeral systems

One distinct feature of ꜰꜰ Fago is the addition of three different systems of numerals. The Oldstyle Figures, or hanging figures, are mainly intended for use in body text. The Lining Figures are proportionally spaced, and because their height is slightly inferior to that of the capitals, they are not too conspicuous when used in running texts. Finally, the monospaced Tabular Figures stand out in that they take up the same width in each of the stroke weights of one sub-family. The monetary symbols that come with these Tabular versions have also been adapted to this standard width. It is particularly convenient that each of the three numeral systems is available for all the weights in the Fago family. As a result, there is no need to switch between different fonts when combining text – be it roman, italic or small caps – with a specific kind of numerals. ꜰꜰ Fago has three variants: Fago Normal, Fago Condensed and Fago Extended, each consisting of five stroke weights (Roman, Medium, Bold, Extrabold and Black). Due to the triple numerals, each of the stroke weights consists of: three upright, three italic, three caps, and three italic caps fonts, plus an Expert Set for each weight. Which results, summa summarum, in four times three fonts plus four expert sets equaling sixteen fonts for each stroke weight. Which ultimately brings the total to 240. The remaining seven fonts include a monospaced version (Roman, Medium and Bold plus the Expert Sets) and a variant called Extra Bold Condensed Rounded, made available as a bonus font on the FontFont Library CD.

No big capitals

The Expert Sets consists of characters not available in the standard character set; in the case of FF Fago these sets contain certain diacritical signs and arrows in widths matching the fonts and real fraction numerals, as well a large number of special ligatures: fi, fl, ff, fb, ft, ffi, ffl, fj and fk. Within one stroke weight, all characters have the same stroke thickness. 'Of course I know this is kind of unusual,' Schäfer states frankly, 'but I simply don't like big capitals that stand out.' Besides, the comparatively narrow capital letters help create a homogeneous overall image. The italics are more subtly sloped than many other typefaces and are therefore easier to identify. All of the FF Fago family, for that matter, stands out for its excellent legibility even in small point sizes. This is due to the sturdy construction of the letterforms and to the relatively large x-height. Another feature distinguishing FF Fago from most other type families is the weight difference of the letter 'n' between roman to bold. Usually when changing the weight of the letter 'n' from roman to bold, most typefaces show a slight heightening of the curve above the x-height in the bolder version. Conversely, this vertical value remains unchanged in FF Fago, because the weight increases towards the inside. This principle works well, provided the characters have an ample x-height to begin with. It makes for a more harmonious overall text image, says Schäfer, while the details become more lively: the bolder the type, the more outspoken the contrast within each character. Wouldn't it have made sense, considering the multitude of stroke widths, to produce FF Fago as a Multiple Master font? 'Technically speaking that may be the case,' says Ole Schäfer, 'but the problem with Multiple Master technology is that hardly anybody knows how to handle it. I have had meetings with art directors who have not even heard of ATM – let alone a clue as to what Multiple Masters are. Those who do know don't necessarily know how to work with them. I think that Multiple Master fonts will gradually die out. Most people prefer the stroke width to be established for them instead of choosing it themselves.' [Ole was right: Adobe discontinued the Multiple Master system a few years later. – JM 2006]

Ole Schäfer does not remember exactly how he thought of the name Fago. The important thing, he says, is that the name is short and easy. As far as he has been able to check, the word has no meaning. He only hopes that 'fago' does not mean dog turd or something similar in Surinam.

Making a living

Last year Ole Schäfer left MetaDesign to become an independent type designer. 'At the moment it is still a dream to be able to make a living exclusively by designing type. But if things go well, it may happen within the next two years or so.' The designer occasionally works for FontShop: apart from designing new fonts, Schäfer has also made updates and extensions for existing FontFont families such as FF Info.

Ole Schäfer is optimistic about FF Fago's future. 'I always try to develop typefaces for which there is a good reason. One should at least give the user an idea of what to do with the typeface, then there's a chance he will actually use it.' One example is the economic magazine Econy. For the re-launch of the magazine, designed by MetaDesign, both the publisher and the editors decided on Fago as the headline face. For a number of months, Econy will have exclusive use of FF Fago, with the typeface becoming available at FontShop after April.

Meanwhile, Ole Schäfer is already thinking about his next typeface, as well as a series of extensions to the Fago family. 'In any case, besides the monospaced version, we will produce Fago Office for correspondence with a set of serif fonts to be used where needed.' Schäfer is also working on Eastern European and Turkish character sets in order to prepare FF Fago for the international market. Naturally, these versions, too, will contain all widths and stroke weights – so maybe FF Fago really is a serious candidate for the *Guinness Book of Records* after all. ⊕

'The new advertising typeface' — with this slogan the Bauersche Gießerei (Bauer Typefoundry) in Frankfurt am Main released ❧ Bernhard Negro ❧, a display typeface designed by Lucian Bernhard, in 1930. Sixty years later the typeface was rediscovered and expanded by American designer David Berlow. The result was called FF Berlinsans — one of the few FontFonts that could, to some extent, be called a 'revival'.

AABBCCDDEEFFGG
HHIIJJKKLLMMNNOO
PPQQRRSSTTUUVV
WWXXYYZZ ·⚮·⊕·𝄢
ffi rf rt ftst ꜩ ck ch ff ffl
≫ 1234567890 ≪
❧ 1234567890 ❧ @€$
🐟 abcdefghijklmno
prstuvwxyzß 🐟

↑
Berlinsans character set.

⇢
Original specimen,

LUCIAN BERNHARD, who worked in the USA for a considerable time, enjoyed international prestige as a poster designer. Among his best known typefaces are Bernhard Gothic, Bernhard Roman, Bernhard Tango and Bernhard Imago. Sixty years after the publication of Negro, Font Bureau founder David Berlow chanced upon an original Bauersche Gießerei promotional brochure of the typeface. Being an admirer of Bernhard's work, he loved the Bernhard Negro concept. He decided to digitize the typeface and expand it into a family.

The original Negro, published as foundry type for hand-setting, came in one bold weight only — hence the name, simply the Spanish word for 'black'. Being a jobbing face, it was available in a wide range of display sizes: 12, 14, 16, 20, 24, 28, 36, 48, 60 and 72 points. At the time it was customary to specify the weight of a complete fount in the catalogue — for Negro it ranged from 6.5 kg at the smallest point size to 42 kg at the largest size. The character set was relatively modest. It consisted of an uppercase alphabet with a number of alternate, slightly narrower characters, a lowercase alphabet, numerals and the most common punctuation marks.

Today, a PostScript font needs to have many more characters in order to be distributed in the international market. Besides all the standard European diacritics and special signs (such as &, % and §), a basic character set must contain all possible punctuation marks, currency symbols, other special characters and a number of ligatures that are standard on the Mac and/or the PC. This amounts to more than 200 glyphs for a contemporary PostScript character set. Berlow, who worked on Berlinsans for over a year, expanded the original bold alphabet into a four-weight family: Light, Roman, Semibold and Bold, each including an Expert Set. [The narrower uppercase characters which formed the Expert Sets were later accomodated in a special series of Alternates.]

As a result, FF Berlinsans is a versatile family that can be used for purposes other than merely as a headline and poster font. It works well in larger text blocks and even as a medium-sized body face. When setting headlines, playing around with the alternate capitals to obtain a livelier text is an exciting game. ⊕

BERN HARD

NEGRO

DIE NEUE WERBE- SCHRIFT

BAUERSCHE GIESSEREI
FRANKFURT A · M · NEW YORK

✎ Antje Dohmann
2001

set in FF Zine Serif

The name of this typeface by Ole Schäfer refers to its intended medium: the FF Zine family is designed for magazine headlines and subheads - although it is also suitable for medium-size body texts. This article was published in May 2001 in Page, the German graphic design magazine, when FF Zine had just been released.

THERE IS HARDLY any editorial design today that can make do with only one typeface. Magazine designers therefore spend a lot of time trying to find compatible serif and sans serif fonts, painstakingly fine-tuning the various combinations.

Known for his thoroughness, Berlin type designer Ole Schäfer tackled this issue by drawing his FF Zine in three versions right away: Sans, Serif, and Slab Serif. Schäfer explains: 'In many cases, typefaces are created in two styles. However, I wanted to cover the whole spectrum by designing three compatible variants, providing the user with a typographic palette that is suited for both classical and modern editorial design.'

Remarkable details

The serifed roman came first. Schäfer started out with the Regular and then moved on to the bolder weights. As FF Zine is relatively narrow, the Regular is very close to a condensed font. As the weight increases, the characters not only get wider but also rounder.

Having completed the Serif, Schäfer then developed the Sans and finally the Slab Serif. The latter has remarkable details in the form of bent terminals at the bottom right of characters such as 'm', 'n' and 'u', which help to loosen up the overall image and distinguishes FF Zine Slab Serif from a classic Egyptian. All three variants are characterised by their clarity and sturdiness, producing acceptable results even when under bad printing conditions; even printed on poor-quality newspaper stock, the characters remain intact.

FF Zine consists of six packages: Serif, Sans and Slab, each in Roman as well as Italic. Each version comes in Regular, Medium, Bold, Extra Bold and Black, and all five weights are available with lining figures as well as table figures (TF). Furthermore, Schäfer developed Expert sets with extra glyphs such as arrows, which have been specially drawn for each weight. When considering this amazing quantity of variants, one should realise that the new type family is meant as a display typeface with a broad range of

FF Zine's prototype was Schäfer's 1996 redesign of the Sächsische Zeitung masthead.

applications, from headlines to subheads and streamers to short introductory texts. FF Zine can also be used in body texts, but in this case the designer should open up the letterspacing according to the context.

Sächsische Zeitung

Ole Schäfer created the basic forms of FF Zine as early as 1996, when designing a serifed headline alphabet in two weights for the Dresden-based daily, *Sächsische Zeitung*. The design was in limbo until 2000, when Schäfer completely redrew the forms and developed them into the present family.

'Typefaces work considerably better when one has been able to test what works and what doesn't,' says Schäfer, 'and therefore having the *Sächsische Zeitung* typeface as a forerunner made a lot of sense. To develop fonts not just according to one's whim but for a well-defined field of application - this means a lot to the type designer. When all goes well, experiences from daily practice are incorporated into the design. Details of a type design can only be optimally integrated into the whole family once the fundamental requirements of daily use have been recognised and analysed. A simple example being the fact that a newspaper headline face should be narrow in order to accommodate as many words as possible into a headline. Or the fact that a large number of kerning pairs is needed in order to create orderly lines. FF Zine, for instance, has more than 2000 hand-edited kerning pairs.'

As with his earlier type family, FF Fago, Schäfer symbolically assigned a specific colour to his new typeface: in this case, a dark hue of green. He finds it difficult to explain why a decision like that is a question of gut feeling rather than rational considerations. It certainly does not mean that Schäfer envisions a frequent use of the typeface in hunting and forestry magazines.

Fear and innovation

Schäfer can see the font family being used in a wide range of newspapers and magazines - from dapper dailies to glamorous glossies. The designer is convinced that many other publications would also profit from a somewhat more innovative and contemporary approach, reagarding both overall design and the choice of type. The use of ever-similar fonts, says Schäfer, is a sign of fear of innovation on the part of magazine designers, and especially, publishers. As type and design are always supposed to be a unity, it is easier work with what has been used before - when in doubt, use what the competition uses. North-American designers are inclined to attribute more importance to creating a stark contrast to the other participants. There is a stronger tendency to propose radical re-designs than in other parts of the world.

'It could be a refreshing exercise,' says Schäfer, 'to adapt the giant format of newspapers to more reader-friendly dimensions. Then a re-design would be called for in any case.' Whatever direction is taken: a greater degree of diversification certainly would not harm the world of European periodicals. ⊖

0123456789:;?!,-./
ABCDEFGHIJKLMN
OPQRSTUVWXYZ
abcdefghijklmnop
qrstuvwxyzß

FF Zine 1999/2000
Copyright by
Ole Schäfer, 100 pt
19.10.99

abcdefghijklmn
opqrstuvwxyz
ABCDEFGHIJKLMN
OPQRSTUVWXYZ
<0123456789> *
(@&§¶!)[$€£%+;?]

FF Zine
Sans
Display

FF Zine
Serif
Display

FF Zine
Slab
Display

roman *italic* medium *medium italic* **bold** ***bold italic***
+ tabular figs 1234567890 + experts ⊕ž☼↙🖴⊠
roman *italic* medium *italic* **bold** ***italic*** **extra bold**
italic **black** ***italic*** • roman *italic* medium *italic*
bold ***italic*** **extra bold** ***italic*** **black** ***italic***

FF Zine by Ole Schäfer ✎ SignBox

334

3312345

TEE-JAY {*type-jockey

NOW PLAYING

crystal clear

TUNES

n!e

extra bold *extra bold italic* black *black italic*

a fingerlickin' **57 910**

thousand km trip :

planet M E R C U R Y *par*

route touristique D52

aire de repos *und* BEVERAGES

Slangfont

Slangfont

Slangfont

Slangfont

Slangfont

Slangfont

Slangfont

Slangfont

ABCDEFGHIJ
KLMNOPQRS
TUVWXYZ

ABCDEFGHIJ
KLMNOPQRS
TUVWXYZ

IN 1999, FRESH out of college, I arrived in Berlin to work for the summer as MetaDesign's in-house type designer. I spent most of that summer working on a light version of Futura for one of their big corporate clients, and during one of our meetings about the typeface, Erik mentioned that although Futura is often associated with the Bauhaus, the designers and printers there actually used Schelter & Giesecke's Grotesk, which had slipped into obscurity. He also mentioned that he had always wanted someone to draw a proper revival of Schelter Grotesk, which would set itself apart from other grotesks through a combination of warmth, personality, guts and grime.

About a year later, back in the US, I came across a Schelter & Giesecke specimen from 1912 in a Dutch bookseller's catalog. The bookseller assured me that there was at least a page or two of Grotesk, and when it arrived I was delighted to discover all three of the original weights, in sizes ranging from 6 point to about 72 point (300 point for the Bold). It was fascinating to see how much the forms changed from one size to another without losing the basic essence of the typeface. The family had clearly been cut by quite a few punchcutters, with a range of skill levels.

At first, this project seemed like a fairly straightforward revival, but it turned out to be very tricky to find the right balance between creating a usable typeface for contemporary designers and a historically accurate replica of Scheltersche Grotesk. It was very tempting to change as little as possible, and justify that choice as historial accurary, but that would have resulted in an interesting but not very useful museum piece.

My first version of FF Bau was as faithful to the source material as I could make it, but this was just a starting point. We found that the caps needed to get narrower and lighter, because they were distracting in mixed settings. (Perhaps this is why the Bauhaus was so opposed to using capitals?) We wanted to let the family keep many of its inconsistencies between weights, but some forms in the Regular looked too mannered, and really stuck out when the weights were used together, so I toned them down. Enough of the recognizable forms remained – for example, the distinctive two-story 'g', the exaggerated tail on the 'a', and the twisting 'S' – that it didn't seem to lose any of its character. Finally, Erik urged me to create a Super weight for the family, which never would have existed in handset metal type in Germany at the turn of the 20th century, but I think it manages to look convincing. The italics, too, are nowhere to be found in the original material, but their slight awkwardness seems to match well with the romans. ☻

ARCHITEKTUR
LICHTBILDER

VORTRAG

FREITAG

26.

FEBRUAR

ABDS. **8H** IN DER AULA DES

FRIEDRICH - GYMNASIUM

KERTEN VOR VERKAUF BEI:
ALLNER ● OLBERG ● RAUCH

DER KREIS
DER FREUNDE
DES BAUHAUSES

PROFESSOR HANS

POELZIG BERLIN

bauhausdruck bayer

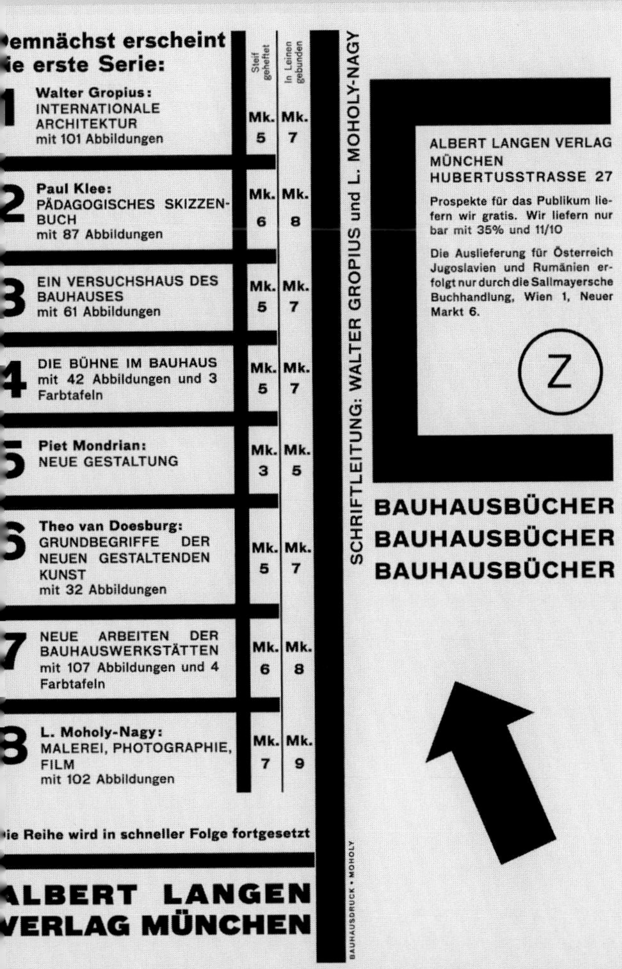

---

emnächst erscheint
ie erste Serie:

		Steif geheftet	In Leinen gebunden
1	Walter Gropius: INTERNATIONALE ARCHITEKTUR mit 101 Abbildungen	Mk. 5	Mk. 7
2	Paul Klee: PÄDAGOGISCHES SKIZZEN-BUCH mit 87 Abbildungen	Mk. 6	Mk. 8
3	EIN VERSUCHSHAUS DES BAUHAUSES mit 61 Abbildungen	Mk. 5	Mk. 7
4	DIE BÜHNE IM BAUHAUS mit 42 Abbildungen und 3 Farbtafeln	Mk. 5	Mk. 7
5	Piet Mondrian: NEUE GESTALTUNG	Mk. 3	Mk. 5
6	Theo van Doesburg: GRUNDBEGRIFFE DER NEUEN GESTALTENDEN KUNST mit 32 Abbildungen	Mk. 5	Mk. 7
7	NEUE ARBEITEN DER BAUHAUSWERKSTÄTTEN mit 107 Abbildungen und 4 Farbtafeln	Mk. 6	Mk. 8
8	L. Moholy-Nagy: MALEREI, PHOTOGRAPHIE, FILM mit 102 Abbildungen	Mk. 7	Mk. 9

ie Reihe wird in schneller Folge fortgesetzt

ALBERT LANGEN VERLAG MÜNCHEN

SCHRIFTLEITUNG: WALTER GROPIUS und L. MOHOLY-NAGY

ALBERT LANGEN VERLAG MÜNCHEN HUBERTUSSTRASSE 27

Prospekte für das Publikum lie-fern wir gratis. Wir liefern nur bar mit 35% und 11/10

Die Auslieferung für Österreich Jugoslavien und Rumänien er-folgt nur durch die Sallmayersche Buchhandlung, Wien 1, Neuer Markt 6.

Ⓩ

BAUHAUSBÜCHER
BAUHAUSBÜCHER
BAUHAUSBÜCHER

BAUHAUSDRUCK • MOHOLY

BREITE FETTE GROTESK

Nr. 6748. Nonpareille (6 P.)* 120 a 48 A = ¼ Satz ca. 3 kg	Nr. 6750. Korpus (10 Punkt)* 76 a 30 A = ¼ Satz ca. 4,8 kg	Nr. 6748. Petit (8 Punkt)* 90 a 36 A = ¼ Satz ca. 4 kg
Bei den raschen für den einzelnen kaum übersehbaren Fortschritten die unser modernes Kulturleben **KULTURLEBEN DER ARABER**	Corrispondenza privata **SI CALCOLA MINIMO**	Un vral classique, comme j'aimerais à l'entendre dé- **CODES DES LIBRAIRES**

Nr. 6751. Cicero (12 Punkte)* 60 a 24 A = ¼ Satz ca. 5,7 kg	Nr. 17778. Mittel (14 Punkte) 52 a 22 A = ¼ Satz ca. 5,7 kg
Lehrbücher für Photographie Kärnten UNGARN Salzburg	Ostdeutsche Eisenwerke Saison MEMEL Bauamt

Nr. 6752. Tertia (16 Punkte) 40 a 16 A = ¼ Satz ca. 6,9 kg	Nr. 6753. Text (20 Punkte) 30 a 12 A = ¼ Satz ca. 7,6 kg
Neue englische Mode	Höhenmessungen

No. 17779.* 2 Cicero (24 Punkte) 24 a 10 A = ¼ Satz ca. 7,3 kg	
Steinbaukasten	Hotel del Norte

Nr. 6754. Doppelmittel (28 Punkte)   20 a 8 A = ¼ Satz ca. 9,3 kg

Bilder amerikanischer Maler

Nr. 6755. 3 Cicero (36 Punkte)   14 a 6 A = ¼ Satz ca. 10,5 kg

Malerschule Dresden

Nr. 6756. 4 Cicero (48 Punkte)   8 a 4 A = ¼ Satz ca. 13 kg

Handelsberichte

J·G·SCHELTER & GIESECKE ☐D 72☐ SCHRIFTGIESSEREI·LEIPZIG

↑
Poster (after Herbert Bayer) set by Christian Schwartz in FF Bau

←--- ←---
original ad (by Moholy) from the Bauhaus print shop; set in Scheltersche Grotesk

←---
Specimen page from the Schelter & Giesecke 1912 catalogue

←--- ←--- ←---
Original caps (bottom); redesigned, lighter caps

Talking FontFont

Five interviews with FontFont designers

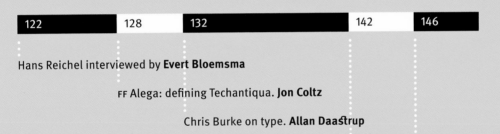

FontFont designer Evert Bloemsma admired the letterforms of his colleague Hans Reichel for their audacity and originality. In 2000 he travelled to Wuppertal to interview Reichel for the Dutch magazine PrePress.

A

WAITING
THE DAWN OF DACHSMAN
PLAYING THE TABLE MUSIC
AN OLD FRIEND PASSES BY
THINKING
DACHSMAN IN BERLIN

B

DACHSMAN MEETS THE BLUES
WATCHING THE SHADES
YMIR SHOWS UP
RETURN OF THE KNÖDLER SHOW
FORGOTTEN
AN OLD FRIEND PASSES BY AGAIN

SINCE DIGITAL MEANS began being deployed for the production, distribution and use of typefaces (or fonts), the market for new typefaces has rapidly evolved. Companies such as FontShop International, Émigré and the Font Bureau make a living by regularly publishing new series. Not all of the type that is newly produced is equally useable. The whole affair is somewhat like the release of collections by fashion designers or the motions of pop hits on a chart list. Some of the typefaces will find their way to the world of advertising and magazines to be used typically, in short-lived designs that depend on a striking, trendy appearance. Yet this does not imply that the quality is necessarily inferior. Some recent extraordinary designs show that it is still possible to create new means of typographical expression without getting lost in all too fashionable experiments.

Two interesting font families in this category are FF Sari and FF Dax, which have both been published as part of FontShop International's FontFont library. FF Dax has quickly become one of the series' bestsellers and has been put to a wide range of uses. FF Sari is also used more and more: from Perla coffee packaging at Albert Heijn, Holland's largest supermarket chain, to long copy in banking ads.

Just where do they come from, these typefaces that become ubiquitous in such a short time span? When we trace back FF Dax and FF Sari to their origin, we arrive at Hans Reichel (1949). Reichel is a German artist living and working in Wuppertal, a medium-sized city famous for its futuristic cableway ('Schwebebahn'), situated south of the industrial Ruhr region. Reichel is first and foremost a musician and composer, working occasionally as a graphic designer at several studios. When desiging or producing typefaces, he works from home.

Lost sheep
'I'm a kind of a lost sheep in the type world,' Reichel characterizes himself. 'I am not part of the scene the way that most type designers are. Not because I am not interested, but because I have other things to do. I am completely self-taught. I studied graphic design for only half a semester thirty years ago, and I was a typesetter for a few years, setting metal foundry type by hand. You could say that that was my first contact with the type designing craft. Furthermore, I have always been a musician.'

As a composer and musician, Hans Reichel is often invited to give concerts, touring regularly to perform around the whole world. His music is hard to characterize, but 'free jazz' and 'avant-garde' are notions that may describe it remotely. In any case, his music is always improvised. Says Reichel: 'I play the Daxophone, an instrument which I invented and built myself. Therefore the music sounds essentially like me. The Daxophone is an exceptional instrument. It allows

ABCDEFGHIJKLMNOPQRSTUVWXYZ
abcdefghijklmnopqrstuvwxyz123456
FF Sari

ABCDEFGHIJKLMNOPQRSTUVWXYZ
abcdefghijklmnopqrstuvwxyz123456
FF Schmalhans

Wirt SCHAFTS WunDer

ABCDEFGHIJKLMNOPQRSTUVWXYZ
abcdefghijklmnopqrstuvwxyz123456
FF Daxline

ABCDEFGHIJKLMNOPQRSTUVWXYZ
abcdefghijklmnopqrstuvwxyz123456
FF Dax

8, 9 en 10 OKTOBER 1998 ROTTERDAM CRUISE TERMINAL

SYMPOSIUM OVER GRAFISCHE COMMUNICATIE

georganiseerd door FontShop Benelux *en* de Academie van Beeldende Kunsten Rotterdam *with* Jonathan Barnbrook *en* W.&L.T. *en* Peter Bil'ak *en* Erik van Blokland *and* Neville Brody *en* 75B *en* DEPT. *and* Ed Fella *en* Luc(as) de Groot *en* Gerard Hadders *and* Rian Hughes *en* Max Kisman *en* Martin Majoor *en* Roelof Mulder *en* Robert Nakata *and* Reverb *en* Just van Rossum *en* Fred Smeijers *und* Erik Spiekermann *and* Tomato *en* V2_Organisatie

Prijs tot 15 augustus 1998 : studenten ƒ 245,- *en* professionals ƒ 495,-. Daarna : studenten ƒ 295,- *en* professionals ƒ 595,-.
Voor meer inlichtingen FontShop : Nederland tel. 0114 - 315 880 fax 0114 - 320 088. België tel. 09 - 220 26 20 fax 09 - 220 34 45*end*

www.thype98.com

Hans Reichel's FontFont families.

FF Dax Italic in use, in combination with FF Moderne Gothics. Designed by students of the Willem de Kooning Academy, Rotterdam (Hans Foks, Martijn Rietveld, Joey Vermijs) under the guidance of Rick Vermeulen and Jan Willem Stas. Photo Maarten Laupman

Hans Reichel, hand-lettering on a record sleeve; this alphabet later became FF Schmalhans.

light **FF Dax Condensed** mager
abcdefghijklmnopqrstuvwxyzäåæööœßü
ABCDEFGHIJKLMNOPQRSTUVWXYZÆÄÖÜÅØŒ
1234567890%(.,-:;!¡?¿–)·["„""»«]+-=/$£†*&§

regular **FF Dax Condensed** normal
abcdefghijklmnopqrstuvwxyzäåæööœßü
ABCDEFGHIJKLMNOPQRSTUVWXYZÆÄÖÜÅØŒ
1234567890%(.,-:;!¡?¿–)·["„""»«]+-=/$£†*&§

medium **FF Dax Condensed** halbfett
abcdefghijklmnopqrstuvwxyzäåæööœßü
ABCDEFGHIJKLMNOPQRSTUVWXYZÆÄÖÜÅØŒ
1234567890%(.,-:;!¡?¿–)·["„""»«]+-=/$£†*&§

bold **FF Dax Condensed** fett
abcdefghijklmnopqrstuvwxyzäåæööœßü
ABCDEFGHIJKLMNOPQRSTUVWXYZÆÄÖÜÅØŒ
1234567890%(.,-:;!¡?¿–)·["„""»«]+-=/$£†*&§

extrabold **FF Dax Condensed** extrafett
abcdefghijklmnopqrstuvwxyzäåæööœßü
ABCDEFGHIJKLMNOPQRSTUVWXYZÆÄÖÜÅØŒ
1234567890%(.,-:;!¡?¿–)·["„""»«]+-=/$£†*&§

black **FF Dax Condensed** black
abcdefghijklmnopqrstuvwxyzäåæööœßü
ABCDEFGHIJKLMNOPQRSTUVWXYZÆÄÖÜÅØŒ
1234567890%(.,-:;!¡?¿–)·["„""»«]+-=/$£†*&§

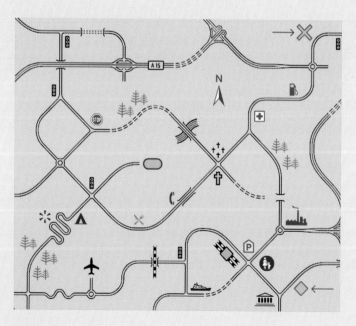

you to make all sorts of sounds; you can produce animal and human voices, sing, whistle – amazing. The sound is made by brushing a bow across wooden planks that are fixed to the Daxophone's resonanating box; the pitch is modulated by means of a rocking, oval-shaped block of wood. The Daxophone is a small, inconspicuous intrument which has no strings; its sound is amplified electronically.' Reichel sees no connection between his music and his typographic work. 'Music happens during a limited timespan – then it's gone. Type is not ephemeral in that way. I try to do both as well as I can. Perhaps I have a switch in my head.'

Hand-drawn
'I drew my first letterforms just for fun, for the lettering of a poster or one of my own record sleeves, and I liked the result a lot. Then I went on to draw an entire alphabet – by hand, of course. This was the early eighties. I then reduced and multiplied the drawings with a photocopier, cut them up, pasted up words by hand, photographed them and then printed the result in the dark room. You couldn't do it otherwise back then. The outcome was, of course, heavily influenced by the copier technology: the results varied according to the condition and the presets of the photocopy machine.'

'In 1981 I made a sample text and sent it to three type foundries: Berthold, ITC and Stempel (Linotype). Initially they all showed interest, but then I did not hear from ITC and Stempel and I ended up at Berthold AG. During forty years, the head of Berthold's typographic studio, located in Munich, was Günther Gerhard Lange. Although I never met him personally, I exchanged many phone calls and numerous letters with him. He said: "That alphabet has a character all of its own, we definitely want to publish it." Yet he also realized immediately that I was not an experienced craftsman. During more than a year the drawings of the typeface went back and forth by mail. His directions were always given in an amicable tone, never patronizing.'

'All this time, we were talking about one weight only. Then at a certain point he said: "Now you must also make the bold version." I had no idea how you were supposed to do that; I was only a beginner, really. So I made a lot of mistakes, but Lange kept diligently sending me lots of corrections. Well, and then one fine day it was finished and I had to think of a name for it. I lived in a neighbourhood of Wuppertal called Barmen, and thought: why don't we simply call the typeface Barmen. After a few years it became clear that this name could not be patented and so we changed the name into Barmeno. Berthold made a nice-looking full-colour catalogue. I got paid royalties: a share in the retail price. I did not get the impression that the typeface was particularly successful.'

'The Berthold brand stood for quality. But they realized too late that a digital revolution was about to

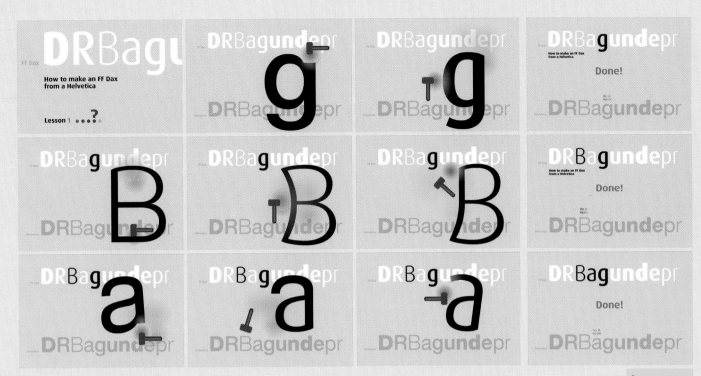

happen and went broke in the early 1990s. There were a couple of firms which tried to continue the exploitation of the renowned Berthold type collection. The juridical side of this is complicated. I have not heard or received anything from any of these people for years.'

'Barmeno was made in a period when there were no computers to draw a typeface with. When the nineties arrived, a friend of mine came to me saying: "I've got your typeface on my Macintosh". What's a Macintosh?" I asked. "A computer," he replied. I had no idea of what you could do with such a machine as a designer. Then, at some point, I started working on type again and my friend offered to "digitize" my skethes. That's how I discovered the possibilities of the computer and saw how you can make your own alphabet into a font and use it to type or typeset with. The first version of Dax Condensed was made on the computer after I had travelled to Düsseldorf by S-Bahn, bought a Macintosh and dragged the big boxes back up here. That friend of mine had one free day, he gave me a couple of programs and explained how they worked. We scanned all the Dax drawings and converted them into vector paths in Freehand. It was quite tiresome work. After having imported the paths into Fontographer as EPSs, everything had to be re-processed again.'

In 1994 Hans Reichel sent the result to Günter Gerhard Lange, whom he had not been in touch with for years. 'Lange was enthusiastic right away. He called me and said: "Erik Spiekermann happens to be visiting and has had a look at the typeface. He wants to publish the typeface!" So I sent the design to FontShop and made the other weights using interpolation. It was a narrow version and so we called it FF Dax Condensed. I had no idea of what an extended family it would become. FontShop entirely leaves the execution and production of the typefaces to the designer. Fortunately, I had learned a lot from working on Barmeno and had taught myself, among other things, to measure everything accurately. The first edition of FF Dax Condensed consisted of six weights, from light to extra bold.' After the 1995 condensed version, Reichel subsequently designed normal, wide and compact variations.

His next typeface for FontShop was FF Schmalhans, based on his lettering on early music posters and packaging. In 1997 Reichel drew FF Sari for FontShop, based on the work he had done for his very first typeface. Like Barmeno, Sari makes for an idiosyncratic text image that is hard to classify. The typeface lends itself for use in both headlines and text sizes.

One feature that FF Dax, FF Schmalhans and FF Sari have in common is the lack of spurs at the verticals of characters like 'a', 'b', 'd', 'm' and 'n'. This makes some of the letters look slightly unusual, such as the lowercase 'r'. Hans Reichel adds: 'Its reductive forms make FF Dax very clear. At the moment I am working on the Dax small caps and italic small caps. That's quite a lot of work! I hate doing italics. It's a tough job. When you work on them for a long time, it makes your whole brain go oblique. Then when you look at a normal straight roman, it seems to fall over to the left. It takes a week before you can look at things normally again.'

'When I work on something like that, I don't think of anything else. I forget about the family or the clock and just keep working until it's done.' ⊕

↑
Stills from an animation by Hans Reichel, showing how to quickly transform Helvetica into FF Dax.

←--- ←---
Reichel's FF Routes, a font families of elements for road maps.

FF Sari Light+Expert
FF SARI LIGHT CAPITALS+EXPERT
FF Sari Light Italic+Expert
FF Sari Regular+Expert
FF SARI REGULAR CAPITALS+EXPERT
FF Sari Regular Italic+Expert
FF Sari Medium+Expert
FF SARI MEDIUM CAPITALS+EXPERT
FF Sari Medium Italic+Expert
FF Sari Bold+Expert
FF SARI BOLD CAPITALS+EXPERT
FF Sari Bold Italic+Expert
FF Sari ExtraBold+Expert
FF Sari ExtraBold Italic+Expert
FF Sari Black+Expert
FF Sari Black Italic+Expert

1 PETTICOAT (WAIST TO ANKLES) AND A BLOUSE are the essential under-garments for the sari. Unfold your sari. Adjust the length up to your navel and tuck *the extra flat inside the petticoat.* FF SARI LIGHT

2 TAKE THE TOP END OF THE SARI in your right hand and circle it round your waist till you come to the front. *Now tuck the sari flatly inside your petticoat.* FF SARI REGULAR

5 YOUR MIDDLE FINGER AND INDEX FINGER will be slipping to and fro while your little finger and ring finger *will steady your right thumb.* FF SARI MEDIUM

6 WHEN YOU HAVE PLEATED UNIFORMLY, tuck the pleats neatly inside your petticoat and *smoothen the pleats to your choice.* FF SARI BOLD

3 YOU ARE NOW READY FOR PLEATING IN THE FRONT. Pleating is done with your right hand *while your left hand holds tight the remaining length of the sari.* FF SARI MEDIUM

4 ACTUAL PLEATING is done with your *middle* finger and *index* finger. FF SARI BOLD

7 Take the remaing length and pass it gently round the waistline and *bring it under your right arm.* FF Sari Extra Bold

8 Take the sari over your left arm covering roughly the position between your bustline and knees. *Such is the beauty of the sari.* FF Sari Black

Sari: the traditional dress of a Hindu woman. Actually, the sari is not a Hindu garment at all, but is a convenient way to wear thin layers of cloth that allow enough air circulation around the female form to keep cool, but still cover enough of the body to appear modest. A sari is most usually a very long piece of cotton cloth that is either dyed or embroidered with patterns. It is worn over a short, tight top with short arms and a thin underskirt of plain cotton. The sari is wound and pleated around the waist; as the layers are put on, they are tucked into each other. The end of the cloth is draped over the shoulder of the woman from front to back and can be used to cover the face and head when modesty is required.

Its technicality belies its unadorned beauty; its modernity conceals its classical roots; and its simplicity disguises it as a mere skeletal substructure. But this is no bag of bones; with Alega, Siegfried Rückel turns Gill's form-norm on its side, and the result is a unique hybrid of a face whose characteristics blur genre boundaries and whose eminent readability, notwithstanding its novelty, may just force us to reconsider our criteria for a good book face.

Here, Siegfried discusses the sans-serif branch of Alega.

JOHN COLTZ: Alega is a non-traditional text face: It possesses a unique, technical character, to the extent that some of the glyphs (e.g., the uppercase 'Q' and 'X') stray far from the archetypal forms; yet I perceive it as having a palpable warmth and familiarity. How do you feel these qualities are conveyed?

SIEGFRIED RÜCKEL: Alega is a technically constructed type. Most technical types leave a cold impression owing to their clear and austere forms. In contrast, Alega has letterforms that, apart from some exceptions, tend to the forms of an antiqua. This means that there doesn't exist a quadratic or rectangular 'a' or 'u' that fits into a prefabricated framework, but rather that the individual characters are well-balanced and proportioned, and create more or less the impression of antiqua signs from a distance. The italics in particular have the characteristics of a handwritten typeface.

Nonetheless, there are some characters that have nothing at all to do with antiqua forms. These work to the effect that the typeface differs from traditional types. Above all, there are glyphs such as the uppercase 'X' that are reminiscent of cave drawings or of primitive African art. In their creation, the normal strictness of a traditional type is livened up. The most important aspect, however, is the soft, curved form that dominates all letters. All letter endings are softened, and most interior shapes consist of curves. All of this, combined with the well-balanced letter proportions and different line thicknesses, lends Alega this warm impression.

In your notes on the FontFont site, you mention the motif that is present in the lowercase — particularly in the 'b', 'd', 'p', and 'q' — taking the form of a 90-90-115-65° polygon. How did you conceive of this form and its implementation?

I discovered this shape by experimenting with some fun faces in connection with a totally different type. I was of the opinion that it would be possible to create a totally new typeface. After some experimentation, I defined the forms for 'b', 'd', 'p' and 'q'. On basis of these forms I adapted all other letters. I did so because this 90-90-115-65° polygon affected me so much. I had the impression of the ultimate, technical form for the aforementioned glyphs.

Your letterforms are non-traditional, yet you've issued all of the complements — text figures, small caps, a wealth of ligatures — that are needed for traditional, careful book work. Was it your intention to create a new book face?

Yes — I intended right from the beginning that Alega shouldn't be just a new typeface but a very useful font for demanding typography.

You've noted also that Alega could be used for anthroposophic typography. Are you a devotee of Steiner, or were you schooled in the Waldorf pedagogy?

My only point of contact with the doctrine of Steiner is the fact that Joseph Beuys — a well-admired artist — has incorporated anthroposophic thoughts into his works and texts. Nevertheless, I am of the opinion that Alega is very suitable as a new interpretation of anthroposophic typography.

The Greek fonts were released very shortly after the Romans. Why did you choose to draw a Greek face, and did you encounter any problems — or uncover any new insights — in doing so?

The Greek version was planned right from the beginning. I'm always disappointed when a good design concept is undermined by the substitution of an unsuitable face for text in another language — for example, when

Alega

available at fontshop

Light	Light
Light Expert	Light Expert
Light Small Caps	Light Small Caps
light Small Caps Expert	Light Small Caps Expert
Light Italic	*Light Italic*
Light Italic Expert	*Light Italic Expert*
Light Small Caps Italic	*Light Small Caps Italic*
Light Small Caps Ita Exp	*Light Small Caps Ita Exp*
Normal	Normal
Normal Expert	Normal Expert
Normal Small Caps	Normal Small Caps
Normal Small Caps Expert	Normal Small Caps Expert
Normal Italic	*Normal Italic*
Normal Italic Expert	*Normal Italic Expert*
Normal Small Caps Italic	*Normal Small Caps Italic*
Normal Small Caps Ita Exp	*Normal Small Caps Ita Exp*
Bold	**Bold**
Bold Expert	**Bold Expert**
Bold Small Caps	**Bold Small Caps**
Bold Small Caps Expert	**Bold Small Caps Expert**
Bold Italic	***Bold Italic***
Bold Italic Expert	***Bold Italic Expert***
Bold Small Caps Italic	***Bold Small Caps Italic***
Bold Small Caps Ita Exp	***Bold Small Caps Ita Exp***

there is no Greek version of the selected type for the Greek text on packages or in instructions. Besides, I am simply fascinated by Greek letters. When I am in Greece I have fun deciphering Greek words even though I don't read the language. And there you notice that there are only fewmodern Greek types.

Lack of fluency is certainly a handicap when you want to design a face in another language or type system. When you cannot read or write the language you are inevitably dependent on having the type tested for its legibility by a native speaker. Even so, I've noticed that although you have to consider some important aspects of the other written language you can go much further than is done usually (i.e. you can depart from the traditional forms).

But my interest in foreign types in general is reason enough for me to create a Greek version. In the same vein, I began to design single signs of the Chinese type system in the manner of Alega and with the help of a Chinese calligrapher. But this was a just-for-fun project and won't be worked out in the end.

Alega is your first commercially available typeface. In what ways have you seen it used so far? Do you plan to expand the face further, or have you moved onto new forms?

At present, Alega has mostly sold in the USA, and so I haven't seen many examples of it in use. As mentioned above, I am occupied from time to time with the further development of Alega; a Turkish version is planned. And at the moment, I am still working on the revision of the serifed version that will come out soon as part of release 33 of the FontFont library.

Originally, I didn't plan to develop a serifed version, but then I began to try a few possible transformations of the basic idea. The result convinced me to the extent that I showed it to the FontFont type board, whose members were also enthusiastic about the idea. So a totally independent type was created — one that can be combined easily with the sans-serif, but that also offers new possibilities for use. Of course I have other type projects in mind, but at the moment it is not clear which one I'll begin with. ✪

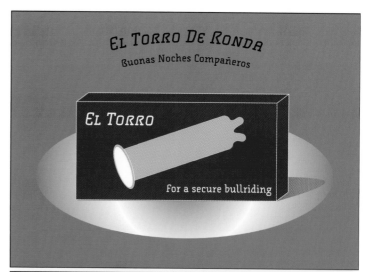

ffAlega Serif™ • light • normal • **bold** • *italic* • smallcaps

alega

designed by Siegfried Rückel • published by FSI • ©2003

FF Alega and Alega Serif in use: samples designed by Siegfried Rückel.

www.fontcredit.de

2004

ffAlega™

	W	T	F	S	S	M	T	W	T	F	S	S	M	T	W	T	F	S	S	M	T	W	T	F	S	S	M	T	W	T	F	S	S	M	T	W
April		1	2	3	4	5	6	7	8	9	10	11	12	13	14	15	16	17	18	19	20	21	22	23	24	25	26	27	28	29	30					
May			1	2	3	4	5	6	7	8	9	10	11	12	13	14	15	16	17	18	19	20	21	22	23	24	25	26	27	28	29	30	31			

Christopher Burke on type
FF Celeste, FF Parable

Allan Daastrup   set in FF Celeste Sans
2002

This is an edited version of the original English text of an interview conducted in 2002 by the Danish calligrapher and type designer Allan Daastrup with Christopher Burke, the designer of FF Celeste, FF Celeste Sans and FF Parable. The article was published in the Spanish-language, digital-format journal Typo-Red, which was conceived and edited by a group of designers residing in Barcelona.

Where do you think your interest in type primarily comes from?

I've always been interested in drawing, and perhaps more in what you might call technical drawing than artistic drawing. I am not very good at figurative art, but I always used to draw things with straight lines, which naturally led me on to letters. So before I had any training as a typographer, I had drawn quite a few letters without really knowing what I was doing. Parallel to that I have always had an interest in making language itself, in writing. I suppose that is kind of an ideal combination for becoming a type designer: you're interested in the form of the letters and also how they compose to form words. So my main interest as a type designer is in making type that is very legible for text, because I like printed language.

When did you realize that you were to become professionally engaged with typography, and what contributed to this realization?

I did a BA degree in Typography and Graphic Communication at Reading University; that's where the basis of my professional capabilities lies, I guess. I have practised as a typographer, but in my professional career I have always mixed the three - - writing about design and typography, practising typography and designing type; they are in reality difficult to separate for me. Becoming a type designer was something that I developed on my own initiative alongside being trained as a typographer. I think an education in typography is a very good basis for being a type designer, because apart from the basics that you learn about type – how it has worked historically and should work – you develop a visual awareness of typefaces. When you look very hard and in detail at what is available to you, not only does it make you a good typographer, but it can make you a type designer as well because you know what is there and where you can contribute something different.

Which was your first attempt to design letters for typographic use, and what made you start designing type?

I think it was in my third year of this four-year course in typography when I had a large, self-directed project to define and achieve for the final assessment, and I chose to do a typeface design, which was not a very common thing to do. I was the only one doing it at the time. It was in 1990 or 1991; that project eventually became Celeste. It was in fact my first serious attempt at designing a typeface. I was really starting from zero because I had no formal tutelage in how to do it. I just started drawing and my first attempts were not very good – trying to invent some completely new form of letter that had never been dreamed of before, which I think is almost impossible now. Obviously it did not work.

 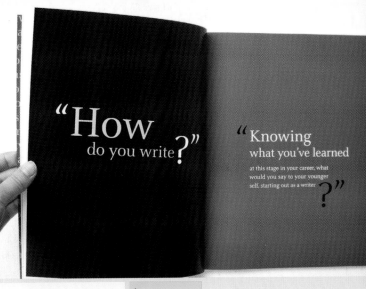

↑
Spreads from
Don Denton,
*First Chapter.
The Canadian
Writers.*
The Banff Center
Press, Alberta
2001.
Design by Janine
Vangool, Calgary,
Canada.

←···
Page from
Christopher
Burke's book
*Paul Renner.
The Art of
Typography*,
Hyphen Press
1999.
Burke's considera-
tions about small
text in footnotes
led to the design
of FF Celeste
Small Text.

↓
FF Celeste and
FF Celeste Sans in
four weights each.

Futura, Magere — Paul Renner 1927	Hamburgers
Bauersche Gießerei, Frankfurt a. M. 6, 8, 10, 12, 14, 16, 20, 24, 28, 36, 48, 60, 72	
Kabel, Leichte — Rudolf Koch	Hamburgers
Gebr. Klingspor, Offenbach a. M. 6, 8, 9, 10, 12, 14, 16, 20, 24, 28, 36, 48, 60, 72, 84	
Futura, Halbfette — Paul Renner 1927	Hamburgers
Bauersche Gießerei, Frankfurt a. M. 6, 8, 10, 12, 14, 16, 20, 24, 28, 36, 48, 60, 72, 84	

state.[76] In the first type specimen marking Futura's release in late 1927, entitled 'Futura: die Schrift unserer Zeit', some of the text employs these characters, but they were not present in a second edition of the Futura specimen (c.1928; see figures 65–6).[77] In this second type specimen non-ranging figures were still offered, but they too soon disappeared from use. Sanserif typefaces had never included non-ranging figures before Futura, and it is another signal of Renner's fresh approach to this style of type that he designed a set.

Renner remarked later that, when Futura was originally released, it did not exclusively contain the unconventional small letterforms. He implied that two versions of each were consciously developed:

> It is not so that Futura was initially released with the Constructivist (to use this horrid word) small letters, rather it was in two forms from the outset: you will see yourself from the files, which unfortunately I no longer have, that the a and g forms were cut at the latest in early 1926, if not earlier.[78]

It seems, then, that the typefoundry decided to finally opt for the more conventionally designed characters, perhaps fearing that any quirks might affect the sales of the typeface. Some early press comments contained doubts about the unconventional small letterforms.[79] In publicity material, it was soon stated that a second form of r had been produced in addition

67 Showing of Futura Light and Regular (with Kabel in-between) in the first supplement (1927) to Wetzig (ed.), *Handbuch der Schriftarten*. Light shows a, m, g; Regular shows a, m, g.

a g m n ä &
1 2 3 4 5 6 7 8 9 0
a g m n ä &
1 2 3 4 5 6 7 8 9 0

68 Alternative small letters and non-ranging figures initially provided for Light and Bold weights of Futura.

76 'Die alte und neue Buchkunst' (1927a) p.3. The first trade advertisement for Futura was in *Archiv für Buchgewerbe und Gebrauchsgraphik* (Band 64, Heft 5/6, 1927). Press advertisements in 1927 did not feature the bold weight of Futura extensively, neither did the first edition of the type specimen. Only in a further advertisement in *Klimschs Druckerei-Anzeiger* of February 1928 were all three weights shown in detail (Light, Regular and Bold), as in the second edition of the type specimen.

This implies that the first issue of Futura was only fully completed in February 1928. (See also Lane, 'Futura.') These dates are also discussed in a document about a copyright dispute concerning Futura & Elegant Grotesk (Stempel). See Burke, 'The authorship of Futura', p.37.
77 This specimen formed part of a folder called *Futura – die sich die Welt eroberte*, which also included loose examples of Futura in use. The large amount of material in the folder implies that it may well have appeared one or

two years after the initial release. Unfortunately the type specimens are undated. Further evidence of initial confusion about which letterforms to use in the typeface is provided by showings in the first supplement (1927) to Wetzig (ed.), *Handbuch der Schriftarten* (figure 67).
78 Letter to the Bauer Typefoundry, 5 April 1940.
79 For example, see Julius Rodenberg, 'Neues aus den Werkstätten der Schriftgießereien' in *Gutenberg Jahrbuch* (1927) p.230.

Snabg
Snabg

anorgicést
fjküvwxy;
z 256 ABC

That was the attitude with which you started – some sort of desire to invent?

Yes, I guess that is the idea that a lot of people have when they come to type design in the first place – perhaps not you, coming from a calligraphy background where you know an awful lot about the history of letters. But let's say graphic designers in general, who have some drawings for a new typeface: it is often a really strange and wacky thing, based on their own handwriting perhaps. They know normal typefaces, they've used them and see nothing special about them, so they think that the idea of type design is to do something really different. I was trying to work within variations of the tradition in letterform style, so mine was always a legible letterform from the beginning. However, I had some strange ideas, and so it didn't work. At that time we had an old Ikarus system with a digitizing tablet. I made some first proofs of a few letters, then made some text proofs, and it was immediately apparent that I wasn't doing the right kind of thing. So then I carried on and just started to relax a bit, drawing letters without any big plans of inventing the ultimate typeface, but instead just something that was a bit different. And that eventually turned into what is Celeste, which has some subtle differences and originalities within the tradition of text types – elements and combinations that had never been done in that particular way before. The idea behind Celeste is that it is refers to the tradition of the 'modern face' – in the sense of traditional type classification; meaning that it has vertical stress. Yet it has the hint of a calligraphic element: to use the terms of Swiss type theorists, it has a combination of the static and dynamic principles. It also has an uncommon form of serif which I've never seen used on that particular category of type.

Which features in particular do you think are calligraphic in Celeste?

There are certain terminals which are kind of reminiscent of a broad-edged pen, calligraphic terminations – let's say on the top curve of the lowercase 'a', and also in letters like the lowercase 'e' where the termination at the bottom doesn't curl right around and close in a circle like it does in a Bodoni type, for instance, but shoots out a bit towards the right. It creates a left-to-right direction – that was the idea. I was, and still am, quite an admirer of Baskerville types. They are a good historical example of a visually solid British type, and I suppose I was trying to make a solid new British type, although not consciously, simply because I happen to be British. Consequently I have recently described Celeste as being on the way back to where Baskerville is: a retrospective transitional type, if that is possible.

I always tend to think of calligraphic principle as more related to the modulation of stroke rather than actual terminals of letters...

Yes, that's because you're a proper calligrapher and I am not. When I say calligraphy, I am talking from a very inexpert

DERJKM
NOPSTU
VXYZ 7?

RRR angu an IR 3 3 796

Drawings for
FF Celeste

point of view, because I have never been a calligrapher – I don't really know how to do it. Well, I know how one should probably do it, but I can't do it, because I'm lazy and don't have the skill. So perhaps when I sometimes say calligraphy, I simply mean hand-written movement, and I am talking about a dynamic in the letters. In the same way one might say that there's a certain calligraphic dynamic in a typeface like Syntax because of the structure. In terms of stroke contrast, I wanted Celeste to have a noticeable difference between thick and thin parts, but I also wanted the thin parts not to be too thin. That is an issue with Baskerville. There is no really good digital version of it, and that was part of my intention: to make a type in that category of, let's say, transitional/modern, which was entirely suited to current technologies, and which did not have parts that were too thin that dazzle the eye.

Speaking of contemporary text type and technology, there are a great variety of books in my house of which a large part is set in lead type and then another part with type from the digital era – and my point is that with the supposed improvements in printing technology, I don't really see any significant improvement in the quality of typesetting. Do you think that we have gotten our priorities a bit mixed up in these first years of digital type?
In the first years of the digital (type) revolution, the priority of the type manufacturers – the big type manufacturers like Monotype and Linotype who were still powerful then – was

to make available in digital form the classical lead typefaces. This was not always done very intelligently. Some of those classical faces, such as Garamond or Bembo, got ruined. They have become too thin because there wasn't a proper process of adaptation. I find them unusable in digital form. With lead type – though I don't know whether it was entirely intentional – there is this thickening up of the type image that makes it kind of sturdy, and I'm sure it adds to legibility in certain cases. That was missed out in a lot of the early adaptations to digital technology. But there have been some intelligent adaptations since.

This makes me think of the fact that you first designed Celeste and then Celeste Small Text. Was it the experience of having used your own type that contributed to the necessity for developing another, sturdier version of Celeste?
Yes. When I was designing Celeste, as I said, I was kind of making it up as I went along and, because I was learning in the process, I made many mistakes, and it took me quite a number of years to complete it, but I think it came out okay in the end. I think I was always intending it for ordinary, normal text sizes in books, like 10-11 point, and it is really optimized for that kind of size. It is a relatively light and open text face and when I came to design the book that I wrote about Paul Renner,

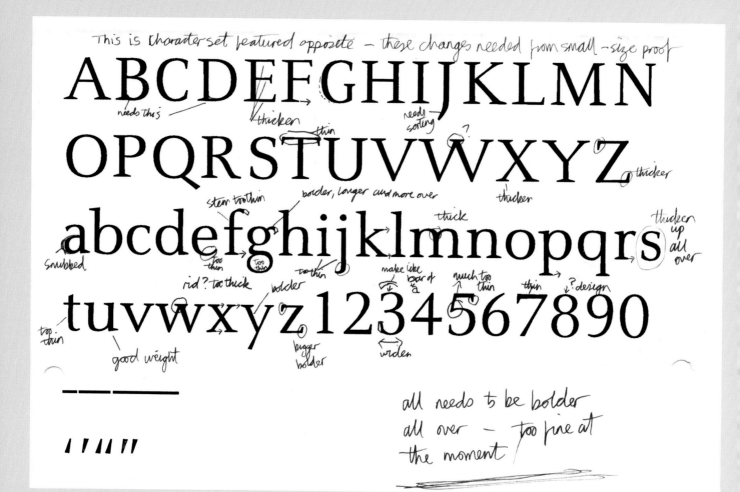

This is character set featured opposite – these changes needed from small-size proof

I was obviously wanting to use my typeface, and as someone who has always been sensitive to optical scale in typefaces, I instinctively knew that Celeste, if I scaled it down to 6 or 7 point for footnotes, wouldn't work too well – that it wouldn't be too legible. So I immediately started to make an optically compensated version of the typeface for the footnotes in that book. There's a very good article about optical scale in type design by the great scholar Harry Carter, with some useful illustrations, where he sets out the principles of how it used to be done during five hundred years of typefounding. Type designers would make things a bit bolder for smaller sizes and perhaps the proportions of the letters a bit wider, and the x-height would proportionally be bigger. It is something that they probably would not even articulate; it is just that working at true size, carving physically on small pieces of metal and having to proof them to be functional in those sizes, that is the way they resulted, and it seemed to work. I think observation shows that this is the way it should be done, so I followed those principles. I adapted Celeste for footnotes and it eventually became known as Celeste Small Text. So, it is a version of the same typeface, only compensated in various ways.

In the process of designing Celeste, how did you make proofs to evaluate the type?

As it was intended as a text type, I printed A4 sheets with two columns of some 10 point text as soon as I could. For me that's the most exciting part of type design, when you get almost a whole lowercase digitized and basically spaced so that you can make text. From then onwards it's downhill – it can be very mechanistic and a bit boring. Obviously I made proofs of letters at larger sizes as well, to see the forms, and what was going on in the outlines.

On a laser printer?

Yes – a 300dpi machine initially, which isn't much use when you intend your typeface to work with professional high-resolution imagesetters. So I had some high-resolution output done as early as I could. From that I saw that the stroke weight was generally too thin, so I had to go over everything in Fontographer and beef up the strokes, which was a very laborious thing to do at the time. Now I know more or less how bold one needs to draw letters to work at a small size a lot bolder than one would expect. You can easily test this by printing a certain type, the weight of which you like in text, at a very large size and then look at the weights of strokes and things like that. During my education as a typographer I had become acquainted with studies about legibility: the basic knowledge that dates from the late nineteenth century about what endangers the legibility of a lettershape, the fact that we basically recognize the top half of letters, and so on. But in terms of designing a letter for optimum legibility I didn't go about it in any scientific way. It was all intuition. I like to think that when I look at proofs of my own typefaces, I am able to look with eyes that are not just my own; that I am able to imagine someone else looking at this thing, and notice possible dangers of a lettershape not surviving very well under certain printing or reading conditions, or that it doesn't seem to be itself because of a certain stroke or feature. All this is really intuitive to someone who is attached to the idea of legibility. When I read a lengthy text I don't like my reading to be molested or interfered with by the letters being in some way strange or peculiar.

Were there any particular shapes in Celeste that at a very late stage you realized had to change?

The state that the typeface was in when I presented it at my Bachelor's degree was not exactly what it was by the time it was released as FF Celeste in 1994. Originally there were practically no straight lines in it – not even the bottoms of the serifs were flat. I had this idea, perhaps as a twist on the modern-face tradition, that all the stems would be waisted, or with a certain kind of inverted entasis. When proofing the type at small sizes on 600 dpi printers and certainly on 300 dpi printers, this makes for jagged edges and just ruins your typeface. So I thought: there will be designers who will be proofing this typeface on these kind of low-resolution printers until it gets printed; do I really want it to look like this to them? I asked myself whether the subtle curves were really doing anything for a digital typeface that was made to be used at about 10 points. And finally I got rid of all those subtle curves and I didn't think that it lost anything – in fact I preferred it like that.

What references would you give as a guideline for someone wanting to design type?

Well, close observation and measuring of existing types, and then read what has been written about the process of type design, which isn't an enormous amount, but there are some things written by Jan Van Krimpen, William Dwiggins or Walter Tracy in particular that have been good sources for me.

You spoke at one point about the relationship between curves in Celeste: would you say that the actual curves in a typeface, say, for instance, the bowl of the 'a', indicates or outlines a path that adds fluency to the way the letters relate to each other? For example, the upper joint in the bowl of the 'a' may lead the eye in a diagonal direction as opposed to horizontal, and in that way relate to, say, the top serif of an 'n' or 't'...

Yes, I am talking about how it works in combination with all the other letters, because type design is to some extent about designing the letters as isolated entities, but then, if it is to work in text, you have to look at them all in combination, and obviously the rhythmic or directional flow of a typeface is created by certain directional strokes or by the way the stroke of the 'a' has to agree with – or at least contribute to – a rhythm. If you are talking about a text type and you don't want the 'a' to stand out, then it has to harmonize with the rhythm created by the curves in the rest of the characters.

Looking at Celeste I found that so me characters, which are kind of key characters like b, p, q and d, compared to other curves with perhaps less tension, have

Hamburgefonstiv

Humanist: Garamond

Hamburgefonstiv

Transitional: Baskerville

Hamburgefonstiv

'modern face' or Didone: FF Acanthus

Hamburgefonstiv

FF Celeste

frage

urgefons

I instinctively knew that Celeste, if I scaled it down to 6 or 7 point for footnotes, wouldn't work too well – that it wouldn't be too legible. So I immediately started to make an optically compensated version.

FF Celeste Regular
24 and 6,8 pt

urgefons

I instinctively knew that Celeste, if I scaled it down to 6 or 7 point for footnotes, wouldn't work too well – that it wouldn't be too legible. So I immediately started to make an optically compensated version

FF Celeste Small Text
22 and 6 pt

←···· ←····
Corrected proofs of FF Celeste.

←····
Outline of FF Celeste superimposed on a digital version of Baskerville. Note the difference in thickness in the thin stroke parts.

←····
FF Celeste Small Text was specially designed for use in small sizes, such as footnotes and captions.

⬆
Drawings of the typeface that followed FF Celeste: FF Parable, a typeface designed for small point sizes.

⋯➔
Page from the Oxford Companion to English Literature, set in FF Celeste.

earth's history, maintaining deistic views and the unity of all creation with man as its centre and crown. Buffon was a notable stylist. His ideals of order, harmony, and decorum are set out in his *Discours sur le style* (1753), originally his address on being received into the *Académie française, later published as a supplement to the *Natural History*; it contains the celebrated dictum: *'Le style, c'est l'homme même.'*

Buffone, Carlo, in Jonson's **Every Man out of his Humour*, 'a public scurrilous profane jester', from the Italian *buffone*, 'jester', the origin of the English 'buffoon'.

Bufo, a character in *Pope's *Epistle to Dr Arbuthnot* (ll. 230–48), a patron of the arts 'fed with soft Dedication all day long' who may represent some of the traits of the earl of Halifax and of *Dodington.

Bug Bible, a name given to versions of the English Bible (Coverdale's and Matthew's) in which the words in Psalm 91: 5 are translated,

sacred vocal compositions and virginals, however, important of their day. Th included a modest *Ayre manuscript being lost, nov cent. copy; it bears an inte the tune of *'God Save th been claimed as the origin anthem. Any connection w nationalism stops with his left England in 1613, in offi returned.

Bull, John, see JOHN BULL.

Bull-dog Drummond, se

BULLOUGH, Geoffrey (1 head of the department College, London (1946–68 were an edition of *Grevi (1939) and his definitive ac *and Dramatic Sources of 1957–75).

got a particular pull which actually adds a nice kind of dynamic and flow to Celeste, creating a balance between more static elements of the type. Did you work on the letters on a very individual basis?

I did, partly through intention and partly through ignorance, not knowing how to make the process faster and make it easier for myself – but in the end that probably added something positive to the typeface. There is a temptation and a possibility in digital type design, because of the cut-and-paste way of working, to make type quite modular and to repeat shapes, which can potentially add to a certain lifelessness. This is a contentious view and I know that there are good and respected type designers who would disagree with me, who think that type design, for text at least, is about a comfortable repetition of shapes and that the exactness of digital technology can add to that and accentuate it as a positive thing; but I think that a certain kind of humane, non-repeated element can sometimes be advantageous. Given that Celeste is, to a certain extent, a type in the modern-face tradition, with a very modular and regular appearance in terms of the vertical strokes and how they work in a line, I thought that some kind of asymmetric structure was going to provide a difference, a certain unpredictability – if that's the right word – in the rhythm and make it more interesting than simply a very strict modern-face type.

Does this relate to what could be perceived as a sometimes too precise reproduction of letters in high resolution output for modern offset printing?

It does. In the typeface I have recently been designing, FF Parable, I tried to make softer shapes, which somehow resemble the slightly more blurred and fuzzier outlines that you get with lead type. I do think it's great that we have a really precise technology that can reproduce the shapes that type designers make. It is probably the most favourable time to be working for a type designer, because it is such precise technology, but sometimes I get a little bored with the extreme cleanness and crispness of the forms you get in digital and offset-lithography techniques. I did take advantage of the possibility of this sharpness with the serifs in Celeste, for example, which are purely rectilinear and orthogonal: they don't have any bracketing. It's a form of serif that is not very old – the earliest typeface I can think of was Trump Mediaeval, and it was also used in Gerard Unger's typeface Swift. It struck me as a kind of serif which was still ripe for picking and could be used in new ways.

Could you briefly describe the design process of Celeste: did you sketch or make drawings? What sort of proofs did you need in evaluating the type…?

I started by just drawing letters in pencil, with a capital height of about 5 centimetres. I drew the lowercase first, because I probably still do find the lowercase letters more interesting. I remember at the time feeling that once I had done the lowercase I would have to do the capitals, which was a bit boring (laughs). Then, actually I did not use Ikarus for doing Celeste – I scanned my drawings, then imported them as bitmaps into Fontographer and traced

them manually. So a lot of the work in refining and redesigning the outlines was done on the screen of the computer.

I think I only went back to drawing on paper when I came to do the italic. Being naturally lazy, I took the easy option and started it by sloping the roman: but I knew that I wanted it to be a proper italic with forms that were different from the regular. There were certain letters that at that time I couldn't originate on screen: I wasn't able to make the shapes that I wanted by drawing with a mouse, so I had to go back and draw a few letters on paper. But mostly it was done on the computer. Obviously I output proofs on a laser printer at large sizes – letters of an x-height of about 4 or 5 centimetres – of entire character sets and of certain letters which were proving problematic. Then as soon as I could I made text proofs at about 10 point size, evaluating how the type performed that way. And that's really the principal way in which I evaluated the type, making slight adjustments to the form, weight and shape from looking at text proofs – ideally high-resolution text proofs. It's all a process of trial and error. I remember it took me quite a while to work out the length, angle and form of the termination of downstrokes in the italic, like on the right hand side of the 'n'. It is a very basic thing for an italic type, because it gets repeated many times. And that angle of course has to tie in with the angle of the upstroke – the stroke that begins the curves of letters like 'n, m, h and r' – and those two things have to tie up and create either a regular, or perhaps irregular, rhythm. That's something that took me quite a long time to work out, by trying things on screen and proofing. That's another good thing about working with digital media – you can quite easily and quickly make variations.

Did you take a peek at any other italics or designs to try and figure out how it works?

Sure. You're always influenced by many things as you're working; I can't consciously remember anything in particular. But I remember having my own specific idea of how I wanted Celeste Italic to work: it was not to be too cursive, and not too condensed; it should provide quite a strong angled differentiation from the regular, but not be a very scripty italic like both the conventional modern-face italics and the old-face italics, which can be very cursive. It was to be a proper italic in structure but mainly differentiate itself by angle, so that it provided a relatively calm interruption to the rhythm of the regular version – a differentiation that wasn't too strident. I had very calming ideas about the structure – I wanted Celeste to work well in long texts and all the parts of it to harmonize well. You could say that having an italic that differentiates itself very strongly could be useful in certain situations, and I would agree with you, but I thought that in other situations it might be good to have an italic which didn't interrupt the rhythm too much. If there was to be a text with an enormous amount of italic – certain kinds of dictionaries, or listings, for example – then I thought it might be useful. There is an edition of the Oxford Companion to English Literature that uses Celeste and it works quite well in this sense, because there's a lot of book titles in every paragraph, in every entry.

It is actually a specific quality particular to Celeste.

Yes. There is also the intention I had about the capital letters in Celeste, which are following conventional wisdom to a certain extent in being not as tall as the ascenders of the lowercase, but also they are hardly any bolder in stroke weight than the lowercase. In older classical types the capitals are often quite a lot heavier. But I didn't want to emphasize the capitals too much – I think the spirit of a text typeface is basically in the lowercase letters.

A final question. I have had the fortune to get a rudimentary introduction to composition in lead type in the Graphic Museum of Denmark, where I studied for six months. In an average printing workshop, there used to be a stock of maybe six or perhaps ten complete founts of type in various sizes – they wouldn't have that large a collection. My question is: how do you see the role and function of the type designer with so many types already in existence?

It is easy to be pessimistic – you could say that we have all the typefaces we could possibly need for print. Honestly, I don't think that what I do is very important, but designing type is something that I like doing, and I like to try to give a new typeface a kind of functional intention.

That is that case with my new typeface, Parable. It was a kind of general text type, and I got bored with it at one point and I left it for about two years without touching it. And when I took it out of the drawer again and looked at the proofs I thought: 'What would be the justification for me finishing this type; it is going to be a lot of work – do I really believe in it, and what would make it relevant?' It has a few original stylistic ideas, which is perhaps enough – I think one good or original or slightly different idea, just one, and it may be a small idea, is enough to justify a typeface – but I decided to make it into a typeface that is optically compensated for really small sizes, which gave me a theme with which to work, a vehicle with which to carry the type along and to give it an identity. It is an interest I have developed from making FF Celeste Small Text. It seemed to me that instead of just making another general text type that had a certain stylistic quality, why not give this one a very strong functional identity. So I have tried to make it very robust and legible for those small sizes and consequently it is quite bold in its regular version; it doesn't have an awful lot of stroke contrast and has relatively short ascenders and descenders. People could use it for whatever they want, but I also wanted it to work very well for a specific purpose. And given that I am interested in complex typography myself, I guess that my typeface designs are partly driven by my own interests as a typographer. I can see myself using my FF Parable in designing books with a lot of complicated text – dictionaries, listings, bibles; it would also work well in newspapers.

The question strikes me as being interesting because I have followed for instance the releases of FontFont and other digital type distributors. A recent release, FF Atma, has about 56 variants in 4 weights! Do the demands of visual communication today really require such an extensive typographic palette – or is more of an excuse to create a kind of typographic playground for people who enjoy that sort of activity?

I think that people who master the digital techniques of type design can do that kind of thing quite easily – make tens or even hundreds of variations of a typeface. It can be confusing to the user, and I am not sure that the reader will be able to assimilate that many distinctions in terms of typographic differentiation. There is a kind of reaction against that kind of thing. I have had conversations with type designers and students who say: 'What I want to do is to make basically useful and small families of typefaces. I don't see any reason for this massive proliferation of weights'. I wouldn't want to stop anybody doing it – it's fine with me, but I've never seen a great use for it myself. I don't have any strong ideological point to make about that – it's just something I wouldn't do myself, because it would take up too much of my time (laughs). Are we done? ⊕

FF *Parable*

CHRIS BURKE 2002

Ein Sommernachtstraum in Deinem Garten. Ja, das war ein Glücklicher Gedanke! Ein kleines Fest im Kreise lieber Freunde und Bekannten. Der milde Abend regt zu besinnlichen Gesprächen an. In bunter Folge ertönt nette Musik, denn das Radiogerät bringt jeden Sender. Ein Tanz krönt den Höhepunkt der frohen Stimmung. WIR TANZTEN IM DREIVIERTELTAKTE

ITALIC, REGULAR, BOLD, SMALL CAPS 6/9 PT

L'omaggio è alla donna bionda o a quella bruna? L'omaggio è alla bella donna italiana, alle anti-Hollywood, al tipo che rinnega nella sua grazia, nella sua figura, nei lineamenti del viso e del-lo spirito il modello internazionale che deve la sua standardizzazione e la sua diffusione alla COSTUME DI SANTA CHRISTINA

ITALIC, REGULAR, SMALL CAPS 7/10.5 PT

Und während Du auf Deinem Balkon gelöst und leicht bekleidet Ruhe hälst, die kühle Erfrischung auf dem Tisch, da jagen Funk-Reporter hin und her, um Berichte zu geben von wichtigem Geschehen. Hier wird ein Autorennen SCHÖNE STUNDEN IM HEIM

ITALIC, REGULAR, SMALL CAPS 8,5/12 PT

Onze collectie Zoomerkleeding voor Heeren is thans gereed. Wij bieden U hier een klein overzicht uit onze sorteering om U te overtuigen dat wij, zoowel wat smaak en moderne stijl betreft, als ook wat kwaliteit in HEEREN-ZOMERKLEEDING

ITALIC, REGULAR, SMALL CAPS 9,5/13 PT

A man who will know exactly what his automobile is doing, who has an accurate, constant and precise indication of all its consumption and who has any TRAVEL PROFESSIONALLY

ITALIC, REGULAR, SMALL CAPS 11/15 PT

12345
67890
12345
67890

12345
67890
12345
67890

12345
67890
12345
67890

FF PARABLE AND
FF PARABLE LF
(LINING FIGURES)

In den Moment, da wir in den Qualitätsbegriff die Gestaltung der Form einbeziehen, kommen wir aus dem wirtschaftlichen in das kulturelle Gebiet hinein. In rein technischer Beziehung, GESTALTUNG ALS QUALITÄT

BOLD ITALIC, BOLD, BOLD SMALL CAPS 7/11 PT

Let us explain our dilemma to you. It is distinctly understood that the lessees will not sublet any part of their space or allow third parties to RULES AND REGULATIONS

BOLD ITALIC, BOLD, BOLD SMALL CAPS 9/13 PT

Offsetdruck, das geeignete Verfahren zur Herstellung von Bild-Plakaten aller Art STEINDRUCK ERFUNDEN

BOLD ITALIC, BOLD, BOLD SMALL CAPS 12/16 PT

The success of the tours depends not alone on the beautiful ships, spotlessly clean and faultlessly

EXTRA BOLD ITALIC, EXTRA BOLD 10/15 PT

Royal Mail Line
REGULAR 32 PT

West Indies
EXTRA BOLD 40 PT

Casino El Dorado
GRAND HOTEL ARLEQUIN
BOLD ITALIC 29 PT AND BOLD SMALL CAPS 19 PT

*Handels*bank
ITALIC AND EXTRA BOLD 68 PT

SMALL CAPS HAVE BEEN GIVEN EXTRA LETTERSPACING. TEXTS ADAPTED FROM VEB TYPOART DRESDEN TYPE SPECIMEN, 1953

Ian Lynam   set in FF Atma
2004

FF Atma gives users a bag of tricks: small caps in three sizes with corresponding figures and punctuation. Ian Lynam interviewed the designer, Alan Greene.

| Jj | Ee | Gg | Kk |
| Nn | Pp | Qq | Yy |

What led you to the realization that you wanted to create a typeface? And what ultimate goal did you have in mind when starting on this path/conceptually, what were you looking to create?

When I saw that type design software was available, I knew wanted to try it out. It was a great feeling to see letters that I had drawn (albeit as unimaginably hideous as they were) being used as abstract components of an image, or as text on a page. I wanted to have created every element of my school projects, starting with the type. It was an ego thing.

For FF Atma, my goal was simply to create a distinctive, polished, useful text face. I wanted something that I could really take seriously, something that would allow me to explore my take on letter forms in a focused setting. Of course, things didn't quite work out right away. There were many points along the way where I experienced the conceptual equivalent of starting from scratch. Although I was rethinking my intentions for an existing structure, the kinds of changes being made may have been best carried out by drawing the forms over. But I'm just guessing. Naturally, these major overhauls became less frequent later in the development process. (By 'major', I mean huge changes in the overall look and feel of the typeface that are immediately apparent from reading distance.)

	1	1	1
1	2	2	2
2	3	3	3
3	4	4	4
4	5	5	5
5	6	6	6
6	7	7	7
7	8	8	8
8	9	9	9
9	0	0	0
0

1 Atma Serif Expert Figures
2 Atma Serif Regular Figures
3 Atma Serif Proportional Lining Figures
4 Atma Serif Tabular Lining Figures

Atma Serif Book Roman

Atma Serif Medium Roman

Atma Serif Bold Roman

Atma Serif Black Roman

Atma Serif Book Italic

Atma Serif Medium Italic

Atma Serif Bold Italic

Atma Serif Black Italic

CAPITALS

What are the historical/theoretical jumping–off points for the face? What informs the formal qualities of the face? How did you determine the geometry and lines of the face?

I started by looking at typefaces that seemed to be very ubiquitous, but which I had never considered using. These would be mainstays like Times, Helvetica, and Trajan. I also looked to Democratica for philosophical guidance, as I was initially determined to create a typeface whose characters had all been drawn individually, without copying and pasting. FF Atma would eventually reveal only nominal evidence of such an approach, whereas Democratica embraces this concept at a structural level.

Through this casual research, I saw that the Baskerville types and their revivals (in particular, Mrs Eaves) were most pleasing to me. That FF Atma seems to take cues from other transitional typefaces is probably not accidental; I love the Baskervilles and it's only natural that their aesthetic seep into mine.

What determines readability/legibility in your eyes?

Not as any disrespect to you or your question, but I really don't think my opinions count when it comes to the issue of legibility. I have much more to learn

about this subject before I go touting my own theories and pretending to know something that someone else doesn't.

What I have learned from others (and have subsequently noticed for myself and incorporated into FF Atma) is that text typefaces rely fairly heavily on optical trickery to be serviceable at reading sizes. There are too many little tricks to mention at once, but they all share one thing in common: they all look wrong at first!

How does the face stack up against what you had envisioned as the end result?

Since it took so long to complete, my vision of the end result inevitably changed quite drastically over the course of the development period. I would say that FF Atma satisfies what I was aiming for, though a bit more involved than what I had initially planned.

How long did it take you to create the face?

From the first drawings to the final family, four years. However, it has not been without hiatus. The first couple of years were off and on, thinking it was done and working on other fonts. The past two years or so have been the much more intense development time. Most of that time was spent on just the most basic font

What sizes will it be released in? What variety of weights? What informed these decisions on your part and what is different about the varying weights of the family?

The first release is a collection of serif types for use at normal reading sizes: about 10pt to 12pt, but they also work at larger sizes. The weights are Book, Medium, Bold, and Black. From there, all of the weights have eight styles: regular lowercase and three sizes of small caps, in both roman and italic. Each of these styles in turn has three sets of figures: proportional old-style, cap-height or small cap-height proportional lining figures, and cap-height or small cap-height tabular lining figures.

The decision to make various sizes of small caps just came from personal experience. There have been countless times when I wished for small caps that were between x-height and cap-height, or that were slightly smaller than cap-height, in addition to the more traditional small caps closer to x-height. By making all three sizes, I hope to have provided enough possibilities to be serviceable in many situations. I would certainly not recommend that a user employ all three small cap sizes in a single setting, instead choosing one or two and sticking to them. As for also providing them in italic and each with its own numbers, I wanted to make sure that nothing was left out. I also would certainly not recommend that anyone set

a document in FF Atma Serif Black Italic Mid Caps with tabular figures. The idea of multiple small cap sizes is not my idea, by the way. It was done this way with Mrs Eaves, and perhaps others. I just extended it a little bit to include three small cap sizes in roman and italic, and in all weights.

How do you envision the face being used in a utopian situation (i.e.: ultimate project that you'd love to see it used in)?

If it were used for the liner notes of a gigantic Philip Glass box set, I would die of glee instantly. ☉

THIS LONG PLAYING RECORDING *was made possible through the use of the* FINE & INGENIOUS MARGIN CONTROL *process — a technique whereby it has become possible for us to produce for the record buying public a disc of truly superior quality, especially with respects to brilliance, clarity, dynamic range and reliable stylus tracking. This record can be played on any 33 ⅓ R.P.M. turntable equipped with microgroove pick-up, as long as pick-up playing stylus is not* WORN *or* DAMAGED.*

* Text adapted from the 1997 POLYGRAM RECORDS Reissue CD of Clark Terry's 1955 LP »Clark Terry«

Gordon Protz designed the FF Atma specimens and illustrations

45pt Text typefaces *rely* FAIRLY HE

32pt Text typefaces *rely* FAIRLY HEAVILY on Op

24pt Text typefaces *rely* FAIRLY HEAVILY on OPTICAL TRICK

18pt Text typefaces *rely* FAIRLY HEAVILY on OPTICAL TRICKERY to be *serviceabl*

15pt Text typefaces *rely* FAIRLY HEAVILY on OPTICAL TRICKERY to be *serviceable* at **reading** si

12pt Text typefaces *rely* FAIRLY HEAVILY on OPTICAL TRICKERY to be *serviceable* at **reading** sizes. Text typefaces *rely*

9pt Text typefaces *rely* FAIRLY HEAVILY on OPTICAL TRICKERY to be *serviceable* at **reading** sizes. Text typefaces *rely* FAIRLY HEAVILY on OPTICAL TRICK

7pt Text typefaces *rely* FAIRLY HEAVILY on OPTICAL TRICKERY to be *serviceable* at **reading** sizes. *Text inspired by a POLYGRAM RECORDS Reissue CD of **Clark Terry** ´s 1955 LP »Clark Terry«*

5pt Text typefaces *rely* FAIRLY HEAVILY on OPTICAL TRICKERY to be *serviceable* at **reading** sizes. Text typefaces *rely* FAIRLY HEAVILY on OPTICAL TRICKERY to be *serviceable* at **reading** sizes. Text typefaces *rely* FAIRLY HEAVILY on OPTICAL TRICKERY to be *serviceable* at rea

3pt Text typefaces *rely* FAIRLY HEAVILY on OPTICAL TRICKERY to be *serviceable* at reading sizes. Text typefaces *rely* FAIRLY HEAVILY on OPTICAL TRICKERY to be *serviceable* at reading sizes. Text typefaces *rely* FAIRLY HEAVILY on OPTICAL TRICKERY to be *serviceable* at reading sizes. Text typefaces *rely* FAIRLY HEAVILY on OPTICAL TRICKERY to be *serviceable* at re

Book /italic/CAPS/ITALIC	Atma SPHERE	Atma SPHERE	Atma SPHERE	Atma SPHERE
Medium/italic/CAPS/ITALIC	Atma SPHERE	Atma SPHERE	Atma SPHERE	Atma SPHERE
Bold/italic/CAPS/ITALIC	Atma SPHERE	Atma SPHERE	Atma SPHERE	Atma SPHERE
Black/italic/CAPS/ITALIC	Atma SPHERE	Atma SPHERE	Atma SPHERE	Atma SPHERE
	Regular+SMALL CAPS	Regular+MEDIUM CAPS	Regular+QUARTER CAPS	Regular+REGULAR

Medium Roman
abcdefghijklmnopqrstuvwxyz1234567890
ABCDEFGHIJKLMNOPQRSTUVWXYZ

MEDIUM ROMAN QC
ABCDEFGHIJKLMNOPQRSTUVWXYZ

MEDIUM ROMAN MC
ABCDEFGHIJKLMNOPQRSTUVWXYZ

MEDIUM ROMAN SC
ABCDEFGHIJKLMNOPQRSTUVWXYZ

Medium Roman/ Medium Roman Expert
æ á à â ä ã å ç ð é è ê ë í ì î ï ł ñ œ ø ó ò ô ö õ š ú ù û ü ý ÿ ž ß þ ð Þ ff fi fl
Æ Á À Â Ä Ã Å Ç Ð É È Ê Ë Í Ì Î Ï Ł Ñ Œ Ø Ó Ò Ô Ö Õ Š Ú Ù Û Ü Ý Ÿ Ž
" ‹ « ([{ , ; : . · • ˇ ^ ´ ¯ ≤ ≠ × ± ≥ \ | / % # § & ~ - ¬ = _ ½ ³⁄₄ ¼ ² }]) » › "
$ ¢ £ € ¥ ∏ π ∂ ∫ ◊ √ ∑ ∆ ∞ Ω ¤ Ⓟ © ™ ®

Roman/MC/SC

SC TABULAR FIGURES

SC PROPORTIONAL FIGURES

Talking about FF Kievit
An interview with Mike Abbink

Jon Coltz
2003

set in FF Kievit

Jon Coltz – type enthusiast and co-organiser of the annual TypeCon event – has interviewed a number of type designers for his weblog *daidala.com*. This e-mail conversation with FF Kievit designer Mike Abbink was first published there; this is the first time it's seen in print.

Utility = *Identifiability + Interoperability + Inclusiveness*

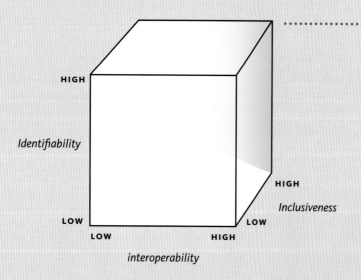

I HAVE MY pet theories about type, as you undoubtedly do too. Mine warp and mutate more-or-less continually, and at present, I regard myself a utility-based gestaltist. Fancy that! So what do I mean?

Well, I happen to view typefaces not in terms of a few, select characters, but as whole blocks spanning 0 to 255 (and beyond), the virgule as important as the ampersand as important as the Z. Designers who produce book faces perhaps share this perspective. If a face is thoughtfully and carefully designed, the whole is indeed much more than the sum of its parts; but if reduced effort is applied, the net result may be much less. That's the gestalt part; it forms the metaphorical trunk of the tree. Utility, then, comprises all of the branches and leaves.

Sincere efforts at crafting book faces may assume a gestaltist perspective and do well to have utility as a central aim. I'll define utility as the sum of three factors:

1. **identifiability**, or unambiguity – that is, the ease of identification of each of the letters, numbers, and other glyphs in the face; also, the canonical or archetypal nature of their forms

2. **interoperability**, or cohesiveness – the manner with which the different glyphs work together on the page and truly constitute a single typeface with one, unified voice

3. the **inclusiveness** or completeness of the face – the extent to which it has all of the necessary components for setting text well: small caps, text figures, and ligatures among them; through all of Bringhurst's secondary level and at least part of his tertiary (v. 2.5, p 54)

Only the third component of utility is somewhat quantifiable, yet certainly open to debate; the first and second are more qualitative and subjective. It's no trivial matter to take qualitative sums, but again, for schematic purposes, utility = identifiability + interoperability + inclusiveness. For me, then, a truly good book face is one that possesses maximal utility; it must score highly on all three factors, and therefore, it occupies the upper right, rear space in *this* figure.

But how many typefaces actually do maximize utility? Clearly several serifed faces, but markedly fewer sansserifs. Of the latter, however, one that springs first and foremost to mind is Mike Abbink's FF Kievit. Admittedly, I thought it rather plain when it was first introduced two years ago. That only shows the extent to which I missed the point! Kievit is a strong and unpretentious, yet ultimately versatile sans-serif face, and that is precisely what Abbink intended to produce.

As modest and unassuming as Kievit is, its story nonetheless deserves to be told.

INTERN. PONY | PAUL BRTSCHITSCH | L'USINE | QUAKE-FILME | CLAUS LEGGEWIE | POLITIK-DIGITAL | 236 REVIEWS

MONATSZEITUNG

DE:BUG 62

ELEKTRONISCHE LEBENSASPEKTE

August 2002. EUR 2.80
Schweiz: SFR 5,50

MUSIK MEDIEN KULTUR SELBSTBEHERRSCHUNG

DE:BUG

AUDIOGALAXY
Die Filesharing Homestory.

Kennon Ballou, ehemaliger Programmierer bei der Tausch-Community Audiogalaxy, blickt wehmütig auf die Geschichte der Filesharing-Börse zurück und erklärt, warum man gegen die RIAA nicht gewinnen kann. Von juristischen Muskelspielen, außergerichtlichen Einigungen und einem wilden Trip.

SCION
Basic Channel neu erfunden.

Scion zerlegen auf ihrer neuen CD Basic Channel-Tracks und reichen damit die längst überfällige und von allen sehnsüchtig erwartete Compilation der alten Klassiker nach. Geholfen hat ihnen dabei die Software "Live". Tradition, Respekt und lebendiges Fortschreiben in Perfektion.

SODAPOP
Kuschelzoo auf dem Rechner.

Es ist die Konsenswebsite der letzten Jahre. Mit dem "Sodaconstructor" kann man lauter lustige Kreaturen bauen und die dann hüpfen, tanzen, manche sogar fliegen lassen. Ed Burton hat sich das ausgedacht. Ein Hoch auf die Künstliche Intelligenz und Java sowieso.

 Q As someone who cares a great deal about the environment, I would like to invest in **environmentally responsible mutual funds.** Where can I find out about them? —Charles Fischer, Philadelphia

Answer You've got plenty of company. Buoyed by the interest of do-good investors, so-called socially responsible funds now hold $32 billion, up more than 150% from five years ago. Morningstar tracks more than 80 such funds. Most **screen out weapons makers, environmental polluters and alcoholic-beverage makers** from their portfolios. (There are also a few conservative funds, which buy defense stocks, and religious offerings,

which ban companies involved in birth control.) Beyond that, each fund has its own definition of "socially responsible," which may not match yours. For example, **Pax World Balanced** (PAXWX) favors companies that demonstrate "environmental responsibility," but it owns oil and gas stocks, while **Sierra Club Stock** (SCFSX) excludes fossil-fuel companies.

To find a fund that fits your convictions, first go to socialfunds.com or to social invest.org, where you can

find lists and brief descriptions. Then visit fund websites to get more details about how stocks are chosen, and go over a recent annual report to see what stocks the fund holds. Finally, take a close look at expense ratios, since many of these funds are costly. Two less expensive options: **Ariel** (ARGFX), a small growth fund in the MONEY 50 with a reasonable 1.07% expense ratio, and **Vanguard Calvert Social Index** (VCSIX), with a miserly 0.25% expense ratio.

Q Is it correct that the **federal government protects investors in some retirement plans,** such as 401(k)s and 403(b)s, from creditors in the event of bankruptcy, but not IRAs? —Barbara Segal, New York City

YALE
ALUMNI MAGAZINE

14.91 | JAN/FEB 2003

35 years after Black Power
Doonesbury's antebellum ancestor
How to decode food labels

One walks,

the other doesn't

Bioengineer Erin Lavik invented a device that healed a rat's spinal cord. Could it ever help humans?

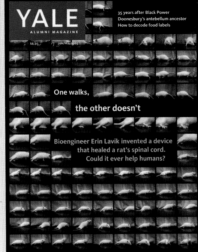

WELCOME | WILLKOMMEN | BIENVENUE

< = >

Less is more.
The thickness and weight of the FontFont Catalogue has increased steadily since FSI FontShop International launched the FontFont library in 1990.

When the editors began work on this edition, it became clear that a new, condensed layout would be necessary if the catalogue was to include the many new FontFonts and continue reaching thousands upon thousands of designers worldwide. So the catalogue has been re-designed: more fonts, less paper.

This new design provides just what is needed. Characteristics of each typeface or family are visible at-a-glance. Emphasis is placed on those families in the "Typographic" category where seeing character sets and text specimens is important. Those categories containing display faces are now handled with simplified showings adequate to convey the nature of each face and show available weights/styles (character set showings of these faces are readily available online or from your FontFont distributor).

This catalogue shows the entire FontFont Library sorted using FSI's unique classification system (see page 29). If you know the name of the font you seek, refer to the Package Index (pp. 2–28) for the page number.

The goal of the FontFont Library has always been to showcase contemporary type design. The members of the FSI Type Board who have actively assembled the collection over the years (Erik Spiekermann, Neville Brody, Erik van Blokland and David Crow, amongst others) have ensured that only novel and distinctive designs enter the Library.

The FontFont Library now contains over 3000 fonts and continues to grow with regular releases. FontFonts are available worldwide through a selected network of resellers. Contact your local FontFont distributor for details.

Weniger ist mehr.
Der Umfang des FontFont-Katalogs ist kräftig gewachsen, seit FSI FontShop International 1990 die ersten FontFont-Schriften veröffentlichte.

Als das Redaktionsteam die aktuelle Ausgabe in Angriff nahm, war schnell klar, dass eine neue, kompaktere Form gefunden werden musste, damit der Katalog nicht nur die neuen FontFonts aufnehmen kann, sondern den Tausenden Designern weltweit einen besseren Überblick verschafft.

Der neue Aufbau liefert genau das, was wichtig ist. Die Eigenschaften jeder Schrift oder Schriftfamilie werden auf einen Blick deutlich. Den Schwerpunkt bilden jetzt die Familien der Kategorie "Typografisch", wo es wichtig ist, komplette Zeichensätze und Textschriftmuster zu sehen. In den Kapiteln mit Display-Schriften gibt es vereinfachte Darstellungen, die sowohl den Charakter der Schriften verdeutlichen als auch die lieferbaren Strichstärken und Stile (die kompletten Zeichenvorräte dieser Schriften finden Sie online oder bei Ihrem FontFont-Distributor).

Dieser Katalog enthält die komplette FontFont-Bibliothek, sortiert nach FSIs einzigartiger Klassifizierung (mehr dazu auf Seite 29). Wenn Sie den Namen der Schrift wissen, finden Sie im Paketindex (S. 2–28) rasch die Seitenzahl.

Das Ziel der FontFont-Bibliothek war immer, zeitgemäße Schriftentwürfe zu veröffentlichen. Die Mitglieder des FSI TypeBoards, die die Kollektion seit ihrem Start betreut haben (Erik Spiekermann, Neville Brody, Erik van Blokland, David Crow u.a.) garantieren dafür, dass nur neuartige und außergewöhnliche Entwürfe in die Bibliothek aufgenommen werden.

Die FontFont-Bibliothek umfasst über 3000 Schriften und wächst mit ständig neuen Veröffentlichungen. FontFonts sind weltweit über ein Netzwerk von ausgewählten Händlern erhältlich. Bitte wenden Sie sich an Ihren FontFont-Händler vor Ort für weitere Informationen.

Moins, c'est plus.
Le catalogue FontFont s'est très largement étoffé depuis 1990, date de la publication des premières polices de caractères FontFont par FSI FontShop International.

Au moment d'entamer la rédaction du présent catalogue, l'équipe responsable a rapidement constaté qu'il fallait opter pour une nouvelle formule plus compacte. Cette nouvelle forme devait permettre au catalogue d'accueillir les nouvelles FontFont nées depuis la dernière édition et faciliter la consultation aux milliers de designers qui, dans le monde entier, utilisent cet ouvrage de référence.

Le catalogue nouvelle formule va droit à l'essentiel, en présentant très clairement les propriétés de chaque police ou de chaque famille de polices. Priorité est accordée cette fois-ci aux polices de la catégorie «Typographiques», qu'il est important de présenter avec des jeux de caractères complets et des exemples de textes composés. Les chapitres contenant des polices «Display» fournissent des présentations simplifiées, qui font ressortir le caractère des polices ainsi que les épaisseurs de traits et styles disponibles (l'intégralité de ces polices est disponible en ligne ou chez votre distributeur FontFont).

Ce catalogue contient l'ensemble de la typothèque FontFont, classée selon le système propre à FSI (cf. page 29). Si vous connaissez le nom de la police de caractères que vous recherchez, vous trouverez rapidement la page correspondante dans l'index des paquets (p. 2–28).

La typothèque FontFont a toujours eu vocation à publier des polices de caractères contemporaines. Les membres du FSI TypeBoard, qui accompagnent la collection depuis sa naissance (Erik Spiekermann, Neville Brody, Erik van Blokland, David Crow, etc.), veillent à ce que seules des créations de conception nouvelle et très originales viennent enrichir la typothèque.

La typothèque FontFont comprend plus de 3000 fontes et elle ne cesse de s'agrandir au fil des publications. Les polices FontFont sont disponibles dans le monde entier grâce à un réseau de revendeurs soigneusement sélectionnés. Si vous souhaitez un complément d'information, veillez vous adresser à votre revendeur FontFont.

F

Easy. Sophisticated. It's about to become your favorite camera.

Ergonomically Designed The grip fits comfortably in your hand. The entire camera is perfectly balanced. The most common controls are within easy reach. It's like your favorite pair of sneakers, in camera form.

Auto or Manual LCD Brightness The automatic setting will always display the brightest image. The manual setting will display the image to match the camera exposure.

Articulated Color LCD Monitor You can shoot through the monitor in normal position. Or you can flip it down 20° for accurately framed overhead shots. Or flip it up 90° for extremely low angle shots without having to lie on the ground.

 Auto-Connect USB The E-20N is designed to be quick and convenient. Plug it into nearly any USB computer (including those with Windows XP and Mac OS X), and it connects automatically. No software. No conflicts. No setup. No hassle.

 Dual Media Slots Which media type do you prefer? You can use SmartMedia™ in one slot, CompactFlash™ (Types I and II) or IBM Microdrive™ in the other. Even transfer information from the card in one slot to the card in the other.

 95% Accurate SLR Viewfinder and LCD To a serious photographer, accuracy is critical. The E-20N SLR viewfinder and LCD monitor are centered horizontally and vertically, and give an accurate 95% viewing of the image area.

 Video Out Want to review the day's images on a large screen? Even in your hotel room? You can connect the E-20N directly to any NTSC TV or monitor.

 Lens Hood More control over light means better photographs. The E-20N lens hood is designed specifically to match the requirements of its 4x zoom lens.

 RM-1 Wireless Remote A self-portrait. A long exposure. With the RM-1, you can both release the shutter from a distance and minimize camera shake.

best + restaurants

moveable feast

What restaurants can't use, they donate. What's donated trains hopeful chefs. What the chefs cook feeds the hungry. And that's how Second Helpings changes lives.

BY MIKE KNIGHT
ILLUSTRATION BY JON KRAUSE

173

The Berlin monthly newspaper de:bug, devoted to 'aspects of electronic life', used FF Kievit for all its typography during the first years of its existence (2001–2002).

Money magazine uses FF Kievit as a secondary typeface for headlines, subheads and boxed text. Format design by J.Abbott Miller.

When re-designing Yale Alumni Magazine as Consulting Art Director, J. Abbott Miller chose FF Kievit as headline

The 2004–2005 FontFont Catalogue was designed by Mark van Bronkhorst (MVB Design) using FF Kievit for the main text and captions

Catalogue for Olympus cameras

In the Indianapolis Monthly, FF Kievit is used as headline typeface and secondary text face.

FF Kievit

◆◆◆◆◆◆◆◆◆◆◆◆◆◆◆◆◆◆◆◆◆◆◆◆◆◆◆◆◆◆◆◆◆◆◆◆◆

Mr Bennet, how can you abuse your children in such a way?

YOU TAKE DELIGHT IN VEXING ME.

You have no compassion on my poor nerves.

You mistake me, my dear.

I HAVE A HIGH RESPECT FOR YOUR NERVES.

They are my old friends.

I HAVE HEARD YOU MENTION THEM WITH

consideration these twenty years at least.

fi fl ff ffi ffl *fi fl ff ffi ffl*

0123456789 *0123456789*

◆◆◆◆◆◆◆◆◆◆◆◆◆◆◆◆◆◆◆◆◆◆◆◆◆◆◆◆◆◆◆◆◆◆◆◆◆

A typeface by Mike Abbink

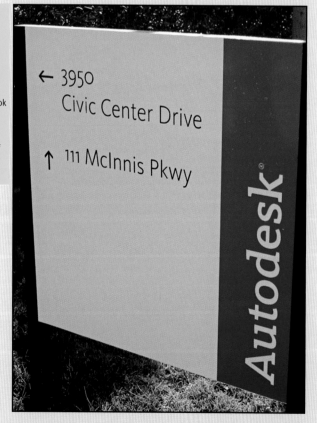

↑ and ⋯→ ⋯→
FF Kievit
specimens by
Jon Coltz.

⋯→
For a signage
project that took
FF Kievit as a
basis, Abbink
drew a custom
serif version of
the typeface.

Jon Coltz: A couple of years have passed since Kievit was released. Has the way you feel about the face changed at all?

Mike Abbink: Sort of; I guess it depends on how it's used. There are times when I feel Kievit really works well and other times when I think it needs a bit more character or something more unique; but after all, it was the intent to create a very neutral typeface with no real character other than its lack of character (if that makes any sense). Kievit is meant to take on some characteristic or personality from the environment it's used in, kind of like the Woody Allen film, Zelig. If it's in a formal environment, then it feels somewhat bland; if it's in a more exciting environment, then it has more life. Overall I'm pleased with Kievit and just want to focus on some other fonts I'm working on.

What was your reaction upon seeing Kievit used as the main text face in the 2002 FontFont catalogue?

I had no idea that it was going to be used until Erik Spiekermann told me the new catalogue was at the printer. I was very pleased of course, and I hope people respond to it well. Hopefully it will last as long as Meta and Info did. I think it's a good place to use a typeface like Kievit. It really shows how neutral it can be, but it also shows that in the right environment it can take on a bit of personality.

On the Method site, you mentioned some of your goals with Kievit: to produce a face without character…to achieve extreme legibility. I imagine that this would require a great deal of discipline and restraint. How did you manage to keep focused on the canonical forms, and were any letters/styles especially difficult?

The typeface Frutiger was an inspiration for Kievit. It has the same kind of restraint that I wanted to achieve. I just wanted to add the humanist (oldstyle) characteristics and proportions to improve legibility.

A digital lifestyle magazine/newspaper called DE:BUG in Germany used Kievit for all the text, and when I saw they used 6pt text it was still very legible. It was nice to see it in the context of something real. It was the first time I saw Kievit used in such a text heavy format. Christian Schwartz recently told me that he and Roger Black used it for headlines and text in the redesign of ADWEEK as well, so I'm looking forward to seeing how it looks/works in that setting. I think DE:BUG and ADWEEK were good case studies for Kievit. It really shows the legible nature of the face.

While designing Kievit the focus was on the stroke of the letterforms; I just tried to keep each letter free of elements other than a somewhat even, simple stroke. I always like to think of it as having the skeleton of an old style, but the flesh of a modernist typeface (like Frutiger). I really learned a lot about drawing letters digitally because Kievit needed to be refined to achieve the goals for its modern side. The humanist side was less challenging since it was more about the basic shape and structure.

The path to Kievit's release was perhaps somewhat sinuous. Could you describe: (a) the decision to hire Font Bureau (FB) to assist in completing the face, (b) your interaction with Christian Schwartz, and (c) your eventual decision to release the face through Font Shop International (FSI)?
I don't think of it as sinuous; it was just a matter of finding help to complete the font for a client that was interested in using it as their corporate typeface. Kievit was complete in the regular weight (roman, italic, small caps, and italic small caps) and needed a black version to interpolate some other weights. The only way to get the font done for the client was to get help and FB was recommended to me by Tobias Frere-Jones. I chose FB over FSI because they were more cost effective at the time. Christian was a major help of course, and my interaction with Christian was good; I only got a little frustrated early on in the process. As you can imagine, it's not easy to talk about the details of a letterform over the phone. Overall, it was a good experience and one I would like to continue with other fonts, but it's probably not the kind of work Christian wants to do.

My final decision for FSI came in the end; I had worked at MetaDesign for three years and Erik Spiekermann had encouraged me to get the font finished for FSI. He had seen the progress on Kievit for years and was hoping to have it in the FSI collection. There was also a time when I thought I would release it myself and start a foundry with another friend of mine (Josh Distler), but in the end I went with FSI. I still struggle over this idea with Josh; part of me wants to have a foundry, but going with someone like FSI makes it a bit easier on the workload. I never really discussed releasing Kievit with FB although they asked what my intentions were when Kievit was done. At the time I was not sure and that's what I told them.

The shiftype site currently shows an interesting sample of some of your recent work. Could you tell us more about it?
I have a font in progress that I'm calling Router. It has a long way to go, but I'm hoping I can get something out to the public next year. I'm excited about this one and I hope it turns out well. It's based on some routed letters I've seen on address and name plates in the Netherlands. There will be a sans and serif version if I can ever get the time to finish it. I'm further along with a font called Milo, which should be finished in the next 6–8 months. It's quite a utilitarian letter with short ascenders and descenders. The forms are a bit more mechanical and stiff, but with a hint of character this time.

How has the nature of your work changed since you moved to Apple, and in what ways do you interact with type there?
Primarily I've been working on packaging for hardware and software, but have done some other typographic related things since I've been here; unfortunately it's not something I can talk about in detail right now. The packaging is starting to get out there (like the new black Powerbook boxes). There is a great team here now and we're trying to do our best to improve

graphic design. You may have noticed the recent change to Myriad as the corporate font, instead of Garamond. This has led to a specific design challenge within the company as you can imagine. A sans serif is a big step for Apple!

Overall, however, I don't think the nature of my work has changed. I just wish I had more time to focus on letterform design. I'm very anxious to finish Router and Milo and move on to an oldstyle Kievit. Which reminds me, there is also a slab Kievit in the works and that may be out within the next year (if I'm lucky). ⊕

3

Making FontFont

FontFont designers visualize their motives, methods and sources

Berlin type designers Ole Schäfer and Verena Gerlach took a close look at the typefaces used on the street signs in both halves of their city – and did so before it was too late. They digitized the two distinctly different alphabets and went on to make a small family of text fonts based on these letterforms that are so familiar to Berliners.

FF City Street Type (2000)

Since the Iron Curtain crumbled in 1989–1990, the huge visual differences between the two halves of Europe have rapidly been evened out – and nowhere as rapidly as in Berlin. Many typophiles find that this is a shame. In the Eastern part of Berlin, light boxes in corporate colours have replaced most of the time-worn commercial lettering that had so long been left intact (under communist reign, there was no urge to update it, as competition did not exist). The street names, too, got levelled down. Formerly, the East and the West each had their own alphabets. Since the early 1990s, new street signs are invariably set in the western alphabet – as if it were naturally superior.

Shortly after the 'Wende' (the big change the reunited Germany) Ole Schäfer and Verena Gerlach, two type-loving city strollers, began documenting the street signs on both sides of the former Wall. Instead of researching the technical drawings that might be hidden in some city archive, they preferred to refer to the signs themselves – to use the actual lettering rather than some engineer's ideal vision of it.

While the newest street signs are more or less standardized, the original signs showed an almost infinite number of variants of both alphabets – marked differences in both letterspacing and character width. The Western typeface is related to Erbar by Joseph Erbar, a pre-WWII precursor of popular sans-serifs such as Helvetica. Its most characteristic and charming variant could be found on old enamel signs which Gerlach and Schäfer tenaciously localized and inventoried. The typeface used in East-Berlin was drawn more recently, possibly around 1950, and has a more industrial look: a typical engineer's constructed alphabet along the lines of DIN Engschrift. The fact that it is so much narrower that the Western face may have to do with the street names proposed by the GDR government, often celebrating Communist heroes, first names and all.

West

ÅBCDEFGHIJKLMÑÓ PQRSTÛVWXŸZÆŒØ

Original   Original Round

abcdêfghijk lmñopqrstuvw xyzßæœøfifl

Regular   Medium   Bold

{[[0123456 789€¢£$¥?!;*&%@©®

Regular   Original Round

Ost

West

ÅBCDEFGHIJKLMÑÓ

Original

PQRSTÛVWXŸZÆŒØ

Original Round

abcdêfghijk lmñopqrstuvw

Regular   Medium

xyzßæœøſtʒ

Bold

{[[0123456 789€¢£$¥?!;*&%@©®

Regular   Original Round

From many variants, the two designers distilled three typefaces which they labelled as 'original': Berlin East Original and Rounded, and Berlin West Original. Many Glyphs were newly designed by the two. In order to make City Street Type (CST) into more than a novelty font, they designed a series of smoother, reader-friendly variants of both alphabets, creating two balanced sub-families of three weights – Regular, Medium and Bold.

These fonts are considerably less eccentric than the original ones but still have enough character to lend a characteristic touch to a headline or a shop sign – or even to text in a smaller point size, as the current example shows.

A brief history of Fontesque

By **Nick Shinn**

EMBLEMA XLII. *De secretis Naturæ.*   177

In Chymicis verſanti Natura, Ratio, Experientia & lectio,
ſint Dux, ſcipio, perſpicilia & lampas.

1618 This wobbly type, which wasn't locked up firmly enough, is an extreme display of the haphazard quality present to some extent in all letterpress printing. Now we're surrounded by precise, mass-produced articles, and this faulty old type becomes a thing to cherish, an icon of what it means to be human, to be imperfect. It's a feeling I set out to express in Fontesque. *Atalanta Fugiens.*

earlier types,

1921 **Frederic Goudy** drew his imperfections impeccably: "I made no attempt to eliminate the mannerisms or deficiencies of his [Garamond's] famous type, realizing that they came not by intention, but rather through the punch-cutter's handling, to his lack of tools of precision and his crude materials; for he worked "by eye" and not by rule … Drawings like mine which were made free-hand, were not the sort usually worked from at the Monotype Company, so there was a constant fight to see that the workmen did not "correct" what seemed to them to be bad drawing on my part. If I intentionally gave a letter an inclination of one degree, they straightened it up. My serifs, which had a definite shape, were changed to meet their own ideas, since they "had always made them that way."
—F. W. Goudy, *Goudy's Type Designs*, 1946

Columbia

1947 Precursor: mid-century, there was a lovely, loopy style of lettering practised by artists like **Alex Steinweiss.**

1999 In Canada, Fontesque has become very popular for restaurants and food packaging. Now, about that ff ligature…

La rosa no buscaba la rosa inmóvil por el cielo buscaba otra cosa

1991 In this piece of calligraphy I had begun to experiment with controlled irregularity.

Deconstruction
Grunge Irony

1994 The New Typography of the Heroic Desktop Era had many factions, mostly anarchic.

1995 The FontFont corporate yellow is a strong branding but lacked the techno glamour of flyers from Quark and Adobe, so the Fontesque specimen booklet was filled with ritzy, colorful eye-candy, and the cover rendered in Pixar Typestry.

FF Fontesque by Nick Shinn   Nick Shinn

abcdefghikz
lmnprrrs
tuvwxyz
np
ʌ ʌ ʌ ʌ ʌ
ABCDEFG
HIJKLMN
OP2QR
RSTUVV

1993 I worked on a Mac for several years before taking the plunge into Fontographer—I was busy enough wrestling with the everchanging Quark, Illustrator and Photoshop.

What got me going was an event organized by David Michaelides of FontShop Toronto in the Fall of 1993, with Neville Brody and Matthew Carter showing their stuff. It was great to see two people with such differing visions of type design doing their own thing: so why not me?

The initial sketches were drawn quickly in one take, to try and capture an intuitive sense of letter-form.

Your Good Looks

Look perfect even on rainy days!

It's easier than you think to weather-proof your hair and makeup!

Weather-proof your makeup

▼ PROBLEM Shiny skin

▼ PROBLEM Lipstick that won't stay put

1996 North American typography is fast and carefree. The designer here uses a dropshadow and some serious horizontal scaling to get the type to stand out and fit. **Woman's World.**

1994 The first settings (right, top) were made from unaltered scans of letters traced, with a Fineliner felt-tipped pen, over the original sketch (above).

The letterforms of the final font (right, bottom) are close to the original drawing, but done with a stronger, more deliberately typographic color, in particular by enlarging the very small counters.

BUSLINGTHORPE

She scratches a letter into a wall that's made of stone.
Matelot, matelot, where you go my heart goes too.

BUSLINGTHORPE

She scratches a letter into a wall that's made of stone.
Matelot, matelot, where you go my heart goes too.

FF Fontesque

Regular
Italic
Bold
Bold Italic
Extra Bold
☆☼⚘♡❀
☆☼⚘♡❀
★☀✿♥♣
☆☼⚘♡❀

FF Fontesque Sans

Ultra Light
Light
Light Italic
Regular
Italic
Bold
Bold Italic
Extra Bold

FF Fontesque Text

Regular
Italic
Bold
Bold Italic

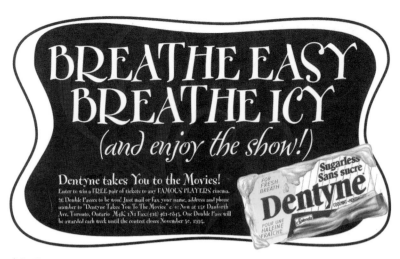

1995 The art director has fun with several styles of Fontesque, and the Ornaments!

1997 (Right)
An art director conjures
a watery metaphor from
the wavy wordforms
of Fontesque Bold.

1999 (Below)
Fontesque's irregularity
allows designers to change
letter proportions (C),
or even invert them (s).

Ever wonder why oceans are so big?

The average Humpback whale weighs more than four times a Tyrannosaurus rex!

When you're between 12 and 15 metres long like the Humpback whale, and you tip the scales at around 30,000 kilograms, you need a habitat that offers a little room to move. To learn more about these legendary sea creatures, visit the **Whales** exhibit at the Royal Ontario Museum and experience the Ontario Place where IMAX® Theatre film presentation of **Whales**. While at the ROM, participate in special programs, browse for educational _____ satisfy your appetite in our deli or dining-room. For more information call the ROM today at (416) 586-8000 or _____ 00. Discounted ROM/Cinesphere packages available.

_____ Government of Ontario. *Masters of the Ocean Realm: Whales, Dolphins and Porpoises at the ROM was organized and is circulated by the Natural History Museum _____ ction of National Wildlife Federation, Destination Cinema and Zephyr Productions Limited.*

TORONTO STAR   pizza pizza   CHFI FM98

Whales
Royal Ontario Museum
& Ontario Place

1998 Fontesque Text characters (right) have thicker hairlines, larger counters.

2001 Why didn't I do this before? It finally dawned on me that a number of serifed FontFonts, such as Scala, Quadraat and Eureka, had spawned sans versions, and so I thought it was about time that Fontesque joined in.

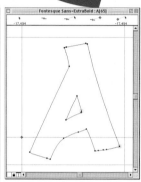

1. Fontesque Extra Bold is used as reference.

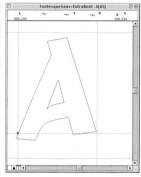

2. The Sans letter is pencil-traced over the serif.

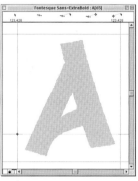

3. Tracing is scanned, filled, cleaned up in Photoshop.

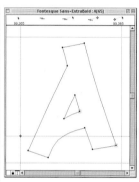

4. Scan imported into Fontographer template.

5. "Autotrace" creates rough outline path.

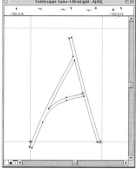

6. Outline path cleaned up point-by-point.

7. Adjustments made in relation to other letters.

8. Serifed character outline is pasted into the template layer of the Ultra Light Fontographer file.

9–10. Skeletal paths drawn by eye, using the pen tools in Fontographer.

11. "Expand stroke" creates a perfectly even weight.

12. Extra Bold and Ultra Light are "merged", in varying proportions, to create the intermediate weights.

2000 Fontesque encourages designers to play with words.

Nick Shinn (www.shinntype.com) has collected these samples of Fontesque in use in Canada. He apologizes for not knowing the names of the art directors and graphic designers who created the packages and ads.

Roman

Strada

BLACK

BOLD

SEMI BOLD

Condensed

Tabular Figures

Italic

Modulo

Ligatu

Roman

x-height-TF

Modulo

Form

FF

Tabular Figures

857

04

18

FF Strada by Albert Pinggera   Albert Pinggera

80

Mono

FF Strada™
was originally created in 1997 as a graduation project at the Royal Academy of Fine Arts (KABK) in The Hague, the Netherlands. The designer's home is in Südtirol/Alto Adige, a part of northern Italy where German is spoken alongside Italian; this is a reason why he was interested in creating a typeface that would be particularly suited for bilingual administrative forms. The family of fonts was further developed and diversified for corporate design projects as well as complex book typography.

FF Strada has a very economically condensed version. It is not too narrow and can therefore be read with ease; this also leaves room for a future compressed version.

Strada Cond

FF Strada

▲ Kerning
2.781 p

OSF

FF Strada is a low-contrast sans-serif with an agreeable and harmonious word image. As the development of the family started with the italic, it was not treated as a secondary face and therefore has a strength of character and originality often found lacking in contemporary sans-serif italics.

FF Strada was designed by Albert Pinggera

Small Cap

Text	Text Italic	Condensed	Condensed Italic	Text Small Caps	Text Small Caps Italic
Light	*Light Italic*	Cond Light	*Cond Light Italic*	SC LIGHT	*SC LIGHT ITALIC*
Regular	*Regular Italic*	Cond Regular	*Cond Regular Italic*	SC REGULAR	*SC REGULAR ITALIC*
Semi Bold	***Semi Bold Italic***	**Cond Semi Bold**	***Cond Semi Bold Italic***	**SC SEMI BOLD**	***SC SEMI BOLD ITALIC***
Bold	***Bold Italic***	**Cond Bold**	***Cond Bold Italic***	**SC BOLD**	***SC BOLD ITALIC***
Black	***Black Italic***	**Cond Black**	***Cond Black Italic***	**SC BLACK**	***SC BLACK ITALIC***
OSF 0123456789	*0123456789*	0123456789	*0123456789*		
TF 0123456789	*0123456789*	0123456789	*0123456789*	0123456789	*0123456789*
EXP 0123©®℗↑↗→	*0123©®℗↑↗→*	0123©®℗↑↗→	*0123©®℗↑↗→*	0123©®℗↑↗→	*0123©®℗↑↗→*

Condensed

FF Strada

The initial characters of what later became FF Strada Italic were created during stone-carving classes at the Royal Academy in The Hague.

0123456789 0123456789 0123456789
abcdefghijklmnopqrstuvwxyz
abcdefghijklmnopqrstuvwxyz
ABCDEFGHIJKLMNOPQRSTUVWXYZ
ABCDEFGHIJKLMNOPQRSTUVWXYZ
&#%!?@[ø]®©™/æœéèêëß
←↖↑↗→ 0123456789 ⁘⁖⁙… ®©℗

Italic eyyYYE

Roman – Italic – Small Caps

A typeface that is being used in complex projects – be it corporate identities, book typography or signage – has to provide the user with a sufficient range of styles. It needs to come with an italic that it clearly distinguished from the roman. In the tradition of The Hague Academy, FF Strada's italics are, of course, 'real' italics (as opposed to oblique romans). The x-height of its small caps is slightly higher than that of the romans in order to give them the same optical size.

weights – interpolation

FF Strada's weights have not been derived from each other in a mechanic, linear way. For each weight separate drawings were made afresh, resulting in an optically harmonious sequence. Strada's weight range allows for careful balancing of positive and negative text – for instance, a negative text printed in semi-bold combines well with a positive text set in regular. For normal use, it is best to skip one grade in order to obtain an ideal bold companion:
Regular > **Bold**, Semi Bold > **Black**

afe *afe* AFE 25 25 25 *bbbbb*

roman · italic · small caps · osf · tf · x-height-tf

numerals

Strada has three complete sets of figures: oldstyle (or hanging) figures; tabular figures and x-height or small-caps figures. Each set contains currency and mathematical symbols whose form, height and width match those of the numbers.

Karbid

Karbid Display

Verena Gerlach 1998

 FF Karbid by Verena Gerlach / Verena Gerlach

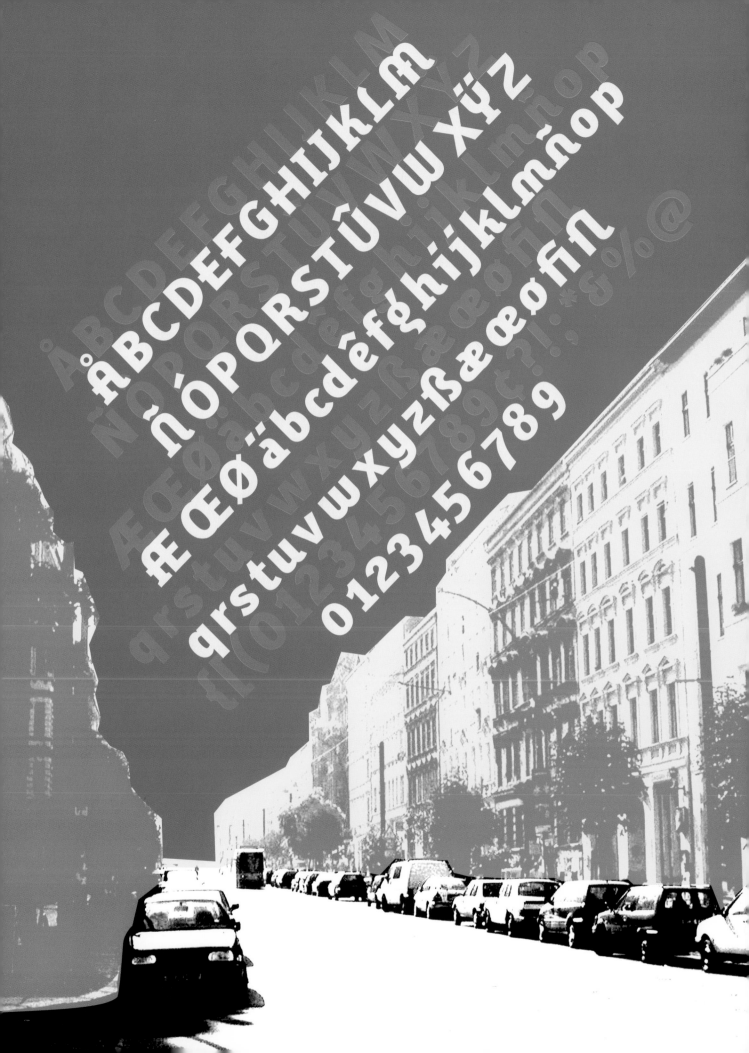

Karbid Regular

KARBID REGULAR CAPS

Karbid Bold

KARBID BOLD CAPS

Karbid Extra-Bold

KARBID EXTRA-BOLD CAPS

Karbid Display Bold

Karbid Display Extra- Bold

+ Experts

+ Lining Figures

When setting a wide variety of texts, a display type to complement the text face will often be needed. Around the turn of the last century typesetting and founding machines were commonly used in book and news printing. The process involved typing the letters on the machine to create the matrices which would then be assembled into lines of text. However, in order to be able to use text and display faces toge-ther, two sets of matrices were necessary. As there was plenty of room on the long matrix segment a second typeface could be set at the same time. This type of matrix was called **'double-type matrix'**. Nonetheless, it was difficult to mix different types of fonts, simply because the different proportions of the various typefaces made proper baseline alignment difficult. The introduction of the **German stan-dard baseline** specification in 1905 aimed to rectify this problem by defining a standard for the descender lengths at each size of a font. Due to the fact that at the time typesetting in Germany still most-ly used **GOTHIC FACES**, words of non-German origin were set using roman display faces. **Because using these two kinds of typeface next to each other required a common baseline and roman faces were less widely used than gothic ones with their shorter descenders, foundries started to truncate the descenders of roman faces. Thus the 'natural' baseline of roman faces was eventually raised.**

The resulting unique look was perceived to signal modernity and applied to façade lettering as well, although there was technically no need for this.

THE ELEMENTS THAT MAKE UP KARBID HARK BACK TO ORIGINAL SIGNAGE AND FAÇADE LETTERING AT THE TURN OF THE LAST CENTURY, MOST OF WHICH HAVE BEEN LOST IN THE COURSE OF THE ONGOING REDEVELOPMENT OF THE BERLIN CITYSCAPE AFTER THE FALL OF THE WALL. RESISTING A SENSE OF MERE REVIVAL, THE FONT ESCHEWS NOSTALGIC GLOSS BUT ATTEMPTS A FRESH INTERPRETATION OF THE ORIGINALS IN THE LIGHT OF MODERN DESIGN PRINCIPLES.

Karbid-Text has been trimmed down to the bare essentials of a text face which makes it eminently readable, especially at small point sizes. Despite this back-to-basics reduction, **Karbid-Text** is a font that captivates through its sheer liveliness. The sweeps that replace the serifs and link the characters create a flowing movement. The font is quite wide and should be set with a generous amount of leading.

How to get from a to a

by Martin Wenzel

For me, successful type design has been a process of internalizing the principles of character drawing with a broad- and pointed-nibbed pen. It's an intuitive response to the basic understanding of how type is built and how its elements work together. Creating type has been a journey of insight and experiment for me and has taken years to achieve the kind of results I'm really pleased with.

I got into type design because it attracted me. I had a knack for recognizing the forms and remembering the names of fonts and played "guess the typeface" on CD covers with friend and colleague Just van Rossum. It was early on that I remember looking closely at the capital T of a *Garamond* and noticed that the serif on the left-side of the horizontal bar differed from the right side. How could this be? I wondered how asymmetry could contribute to the gracefulness of the effect.

My approach in the beginning was to see type design as a kind of geometry exercise.

I was a typesetter in Berlin in 1990, working on Mac and greatly inspired by my Dutch friends in the field. I wanted to design a typeface but had no training so I began spontaneously, drawing geometric shapes and angles and experimented how far I could get with vertical and horizontal forms. I produced simple shapes with a minimum of elements and an overall modular style. The result was my first published font, *FF Marten*, a narrow-running headline typeface used for art and music posters and sports product adverts.

This first success sparked my interest in making a real text typeface. However without the proper training I soon realized that I couldn't produce the results I imagined. I applied to the Royal Academy of Fine and Applied Arts in The Hague, The Netherlands, where I started studying in 1993.

FF Marten. A simple principle produces simple shapes. A headliner. Later added, a cyrillic version.

A FUSE font – *F InTegel* – that demands a lot of work from the user: he has a range of basic shapes (different types of 'pixels') to choose from – typing them line for line – will supply him with a complete character.

NoTitle. This "a" belongs to a typeface which I somehow mislaid. I had to redraw it at this point. Didn't take long.

Daela – the name of this font – is actually a further development of the font NoTitle. I added some contrast and ended up with something quite calligraphic.

Daela was the basis for this FUSE font: *F Schirft*. I rearranged the elements of each character so that every word becomes a secret. The theme of this FUSE issue was code.

The philosophy behind the program in Typography at the Academy is to introduce the principles of calligraphic writing as a background for the development of type design and it was here that I was introduced to writing with a broad-nibbed and pointed-nibbed pen.

Except for adhering to certain rules of proportion such as the width of pen and height of characters, no grid is used and the characters are freely drawn. Whereas before I had used (and reused) geometric lines in each character I produced, now I was free to develop shapes at will, a sense of harmony developing with more and more practice. I learned, through my own exercises, that the pen explains how and why text typefaces look the way they do today. The "asymmetry" which I first found confusing in Garamond now made sense.

This knowledge enabled me to develop my own new characters and I was anxious to put it into practice and create a full text font. After the first lessons, I made my first serif, sans serif and italic alphabets which were based on the writing model.

No matter what sort of typeface one wants to create, it's possible to use the pen as a base and then remove oneself from it. I felt I had to learn the rules and then let go of them – like the need to know the spelling of a word to be able to pronounce it correctly. From there the skill becomes subconscious.

I spent a good deal of time practicing and carefully looking at what others have done and how they did it. Through that I grew to have a more definite idea of what my text face, my ideal one, would look like and my ability to reach that goal was becoming internalized.

→

FF Rekord. After being so extremely strict while designing *FF Marten* it was time for change. This one is just made up of sraight lines only. Rough shapes that remind one – in smaller sizes – of book printing.

This is one of my first "a"s that directly derives from drawing with a broad-nibbed pen.

After following a few lessons of type design I impatiently drew all the lowercase characters for two roman and one italic font.

NoTitle becomes *Daela* which becomes *FF Primary.* In this font I moved further away from a modular system to create my outlines.

One of my first pointed-nibbed pen drawings.

The groundwork for my first textfont begun at the Academy, although the first drawings (1995) were awkward and indefinite. By 2000 when the font was published, I felt I had achieved the fluidity and definition I was looking for: *FF Profile*.

FF Profile. A modern classic typeface

Many contemporary font designers became bored by the closed, oversimplified, almost "heartless" shapes of all sorts of Helveticas. The idea that the lowercase ascenders should align perfectly with the uppercase, and that everything should fit either ninety or zero degrees was a thing of the past. Those were the rigorous statements of the 20th century. Modern font designers were energized by the rediscovery of the principles on which type designers based their work before. This inspiration led to designs that have become more vivid and legible. We end up with text typefaces that have two things in common: new shapes with classic proportions. And *FF Profile* is one of them.

It took five long years to complete *FF Profile*. In between the waves of intensive work were the long breaks which I felt were necessary to gain distance, allowing me to judge my work more objectively.

Big and fat. The other characters are just as pretty.

High and low: These two derive from the same basis except that one has high and the other low contrast.

A futher development of the headliner, *FF Primary*. This typeface, which is for more than just headlines, is called Prima. The design is more traditional and more removed from a modular system.

Another digital sketch for a text font.

Let's try a pointed-nibbed pen design.

This was my first serious approach towards a text typeface, called *Book*.

What is it used for

FF Profile is flexible in its possible field of use, since it consists of a wide range of weights and styles. It has 5 sets of figures: hanging figures, mono spaced hanging, mono spaced lining as well as lining figures superscript and on the baseline. I have seen it being used for corporate designs, displays, book typography, signage systems, poster campaigns and magazines.

The recipe

Take – metaphorically speaking! – the forms of classical typefaces that are based on writing with a broad-nibbed pen (for example a *Garamond*). Then, carefully reduce the contrast within the character shapes – the difference between the thick and the thin – to a minimum. Simultaneously the serifs are reduced so far that only a little detail will remind us that they were once here.

The result

A typeface with friendly, balanced shapes. The relation of x-height, capital height and the length of the ascender, the openly drawn shapes and the subtly exceeding angled ends prove to be very legible in small sizes. In bigger sizes *FF Profile* is immediately recognizable because of the just mentioned 'serifs' and certain asymmetric endings. Serve un-scaled, with generous leading!

In between designing what is now known as *FF Profile* I amused myself by drawing this swash version of it.

I was never asked to think about what a *TrinitéSans* could look like, but I just couldn't resist. Take a look at Bram de Does' beautiful *Trinité* at www.teff.nl (The Enschedé Font Foundry)

FF Profile. Five weights, many styles.

BEEKMAN'S ALPHABETS

Based in Amsterdam, Donald Beekman works as a musician, producer and graphic designer. Most of his FontFonts are based on the alphabets he drew for his designs of 12' record covers, CD packaging, posters and packaging of legal 'smart drugs.

ABCDEFGHI
JKLMNOPQ
RSTUVWXYZ
1234567890

FF Overdose

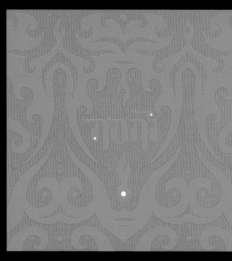

ABCDEFGH
IJKLMNOPQ
RSTUVWXYZ
1234567890

FF Noni Wan Regular

ITALIC
ALTERNATE REGULAR
ALTERNATE ITALIC
NONI TOO REGULAR
ITALIC
ALTERNATE REGULAR
ALTERNATE ITALIC

FF Flava Regular

FLAVA LO
FLAVA HI
FLAVA ROUND

ABCDEFGHIJKLM
NOPQRSTUVWXYZ
abcdefghijklm
nopqrstuvwxyz
1234567890

ABCDEFGHIJKLM
NOPQRSTUVWXYZ
abcdefghijklm
nopqrstuvwxyz
1234567890

FF Stargate

ITALIC

FF Manga Stone

ITALIC
OUTLINE
OUTLINE ITALIC

ABCDEFGHI
JKLMNOPQ
RSTUVWXYZ
1234567890

FF Imperial Bone

LONG BONE
SPIKE
LONG SPIKE

ABCDEFGHIJKLM
NOPQRSTUVWXYZ
1234567890

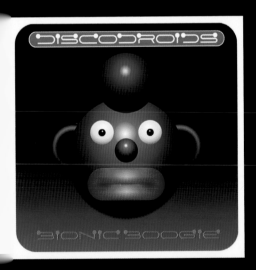

FF Droids Regular

ITALIC
LIGHT
LIGHT ITALIC
BOLD
BOLD ITALIC
SANS LIGHT
SANS LIGHT ITALIC
SANS REGULAR
SANS ITALIC
SANS BOLD
SANS BOLD ITALIC

ABCDEFGHIJ
KLMNOPQRS
TUVWXYZ$?
abcdefghij
klmnopqrs
tuvwxyz&%
1234567890

ABCDEFGH
IJKLMNOP
QRSTVXYZ
1234567

FF Tsunami Extended

ITALIC
BOLD
BOLD ITALIC

Mr. Alessio
presents:

Handwriter & a lot of other beau tiful type faces.

Q. Why use the computer if you could use your brain?!

this is FF Handwriter Regular

A. Because the brain does not support OpenType.

this is FF Handwriter Bold Regular

Q. Is there anything that a typedesigner could do beside drawing typefaces?

A. I will ask my psychologist.

this is FF Baukasten Four

Q. Now seriously: Do you hate pets?

this is FF Baukasten One

A. No, it's just that I can't install TrueType Cats & Dogs in my house.

this is FF Baukasten Six

Q. Look at the catalogues: there are already thousands of fonts. Do you think people REALLY need new typefaces?

this is FF Baukasten Three

A. Yes, the next one that I will design.

this is FF Baukasten Two

Q. Your favourite typeface?

this is FF Baukasten Five

A. The next one that I will design.

this is FF Priska Serif Regular

Q. What do you think about Emigrè?

this is FF Priska Serif Little Creatures

A. Well, damm question! Next, please.

this is FF Priska Serif Not That Fat

Q. Do you believe in a God?

this seems to be FF Priska Serif Little Creatures again!

A. Guess who the Hell is changing the fonts here?!

Everything is under control, no reason for PANIC!

FFGraffio

this is a very nervous typefaces family by the normally quiet Alessio Leonardi.

THIS SIDE UP

OUR MOTTO: we take cares you FUCK!

The story of Letterine is made out of many, weird and somehow unbelievable strange stories of tiny people named Archetippetti.

These people created Letterine in order to express themselves in a colourful way. We have stolen the letters and captured some of these little sweet drawings and we now force them to work for us and make Alessio a very RICH & respec-ted member of our community. We are so bad! Aren't we? Oh, YES!

FFAlessio

THE KITCHEN=AID SET FOR DESIGNERS

PRESENTS:

Nobody

is perfect!

FF COLTELLO A FILM ABOUT CUT LETTERS, FF FORCHETTA

FF Mulinex Twirled Characters,

Legible Vegetables FF Cavolfiore

AND PERFECT SIGNS & Pi

FF COLTELLO FIGURE

SOME BASIC

Stephan Müller, FF Container (FF Backstage Pack)

INGREDIENTS

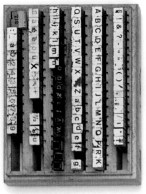

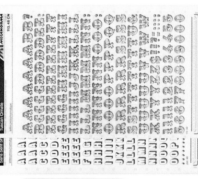

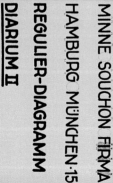

FF Super Grotesk, Typestar, Screenstar, Xcreen ✎ Eboy

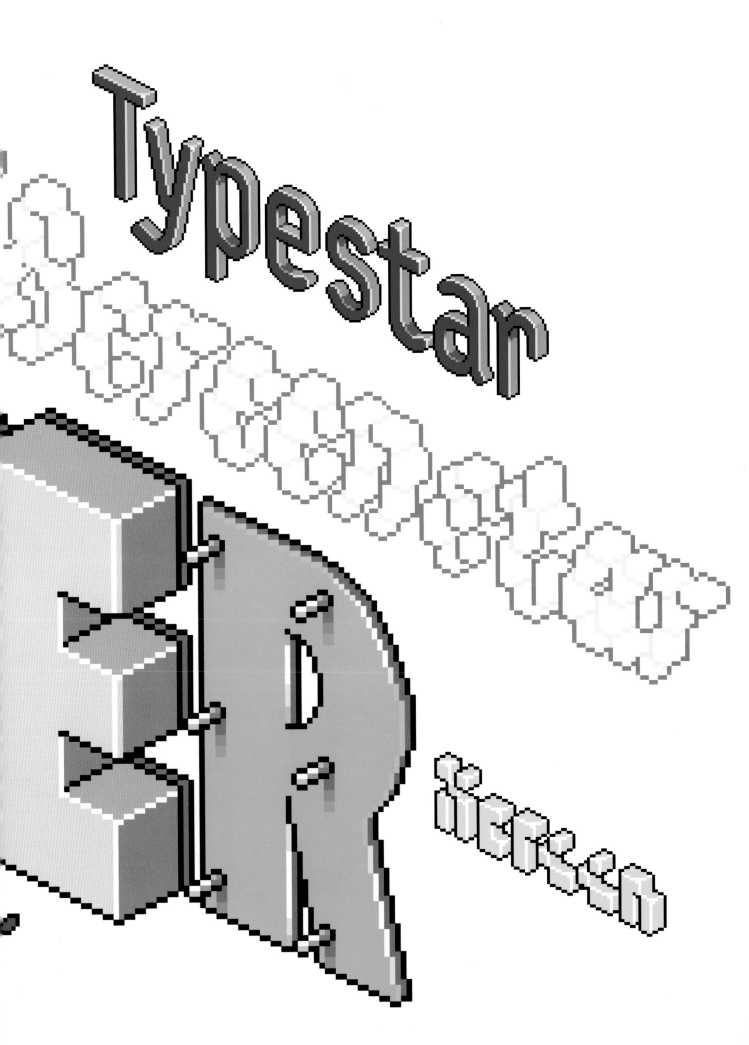

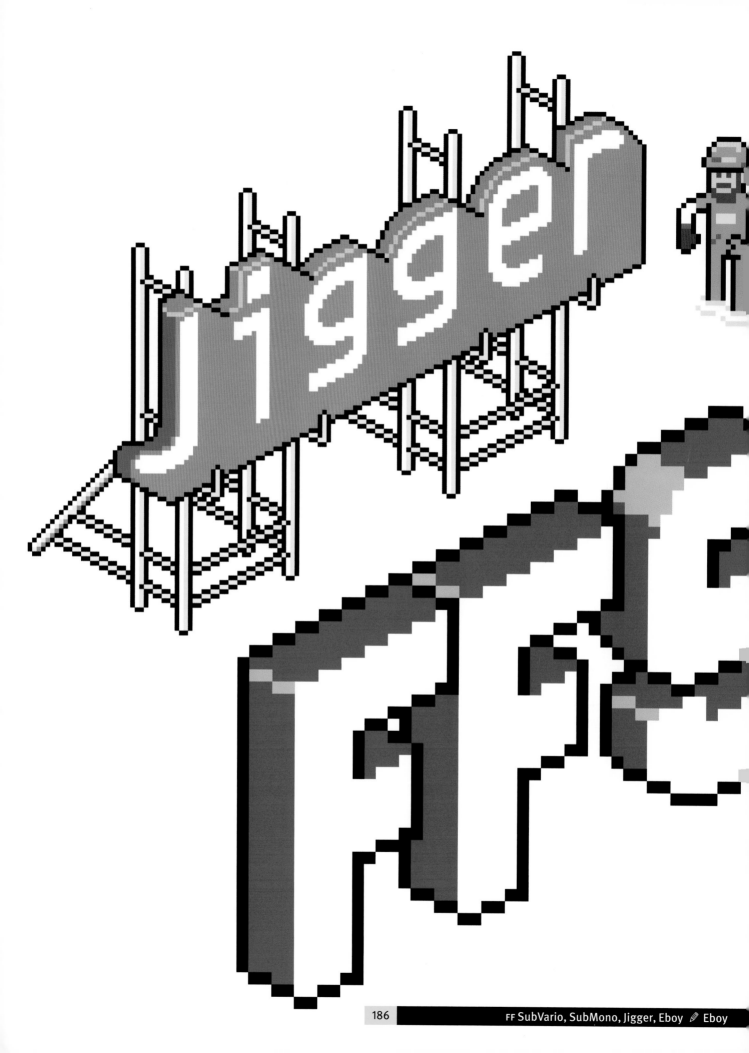

FF SubVario, SubMono, Jigger, Eboy ✎ Eboy

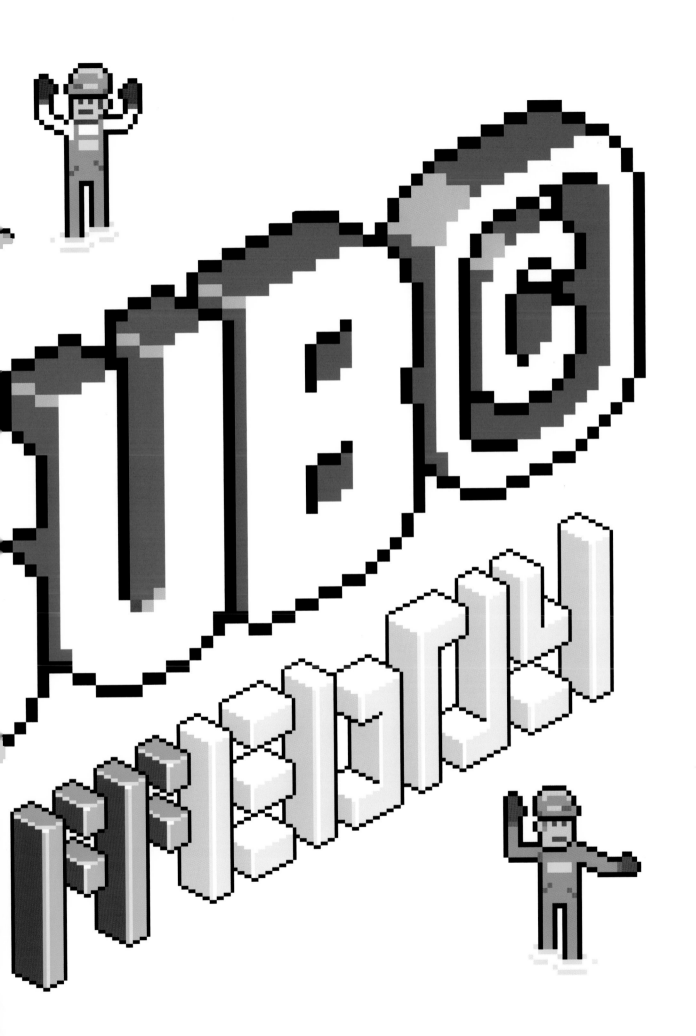

FF Beadmap by Ian Wright & David Crow ✏ Ian Wright

BOX No. 1

PAIR OF HANDS

3
WEIGHTS
Sistema → FF CARTONNAGE
☑ ALTERNATE ☑ Roman ☑ Pict

KNIFE

FF CARTONNAGE

PRIMERA CLASE

AUTOTRANSPORTERS / PASAJEROS

MERIDA - PROGRESO

Este boleto es bueno únicamente por un viagje en la fecha y para la hora que se expide al Seguro del Viajero y hasta 25 Kgs de equipeje y deberá mostrarlo a los inspectores siempre que le soliciten.

abcdefghijklmnopqrstuvwxyzAB
CDEFGJKLMNOPQRSTUVWXYZ
#1234567890©®@™$€£¢¥
ffi&%¶*+†‡.,.:;...!i?¿„""''‚'»«•
–_=<> ()[]{}|/ ˛ˆ˚<> fiflß§ªº
áàâäãåæçéèêëíìîïñóòôõöœøúùûüÿ
ÀÁÂÃÅÄÆÇÉÈÊËÍÌÎÏÑÓÒÔÕÖŒØ
ÚÙÛÜŸ

5 CONTAINERS

| 5 |
| 4 |
| 3 |
| 2 |
| 1 |

300905 42UMB

GLOBAL

7 GLASES

Co 300963

THIS SIDE UP

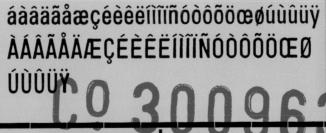

A TRUCK

1 1
— —
2 8

SIZES AVAILABLE

START HERE

FF CARTONNAGE | presented by Yanek Iontef

Dingbats from both
Ottofont and
Klunder Script
text set in Ottofont

"Get up offa that thing"
James Brown

"Will you, won't you,

ill you, won't you, will you join the dance?"
Lewis Carroll 1832-1898

El tipo Pepe
es una tipografía caligráfica
que recoge en su estructura formas naturales y aleatorias,
formas libres que dotan a la caja de texto de un aspecto fresco,
delicado, desinhibido y ecléctico.
Se pueden obtener excelentes resultados
aplicando diferentes cuerpos
de letra dentro de la misma palabra.
También resulta interesante el aspecto que ofrece
al aplicarla sobre líneas suavemente onduladas
y un tanto caprichosas.

FF Pepe by Pepe Gimeno   ✎ Pepe Gimeno

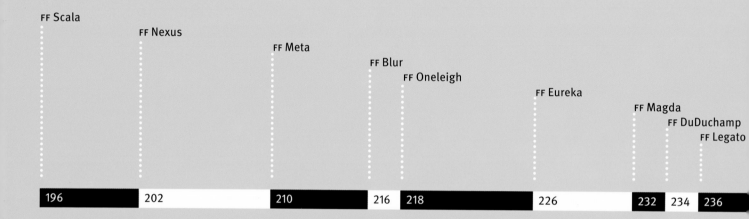

FF Scala

FF Nexus

FF Meta

FF Blur
FF Oneleigh

FF Eureka

FF Magda
FF DuDuchamp
FF Legato

| 196 | 202 | 210 | 216 | 218 | 226 | 232 | 234 | 236 |

Showing FontFont

A collection of contemporary type specimens

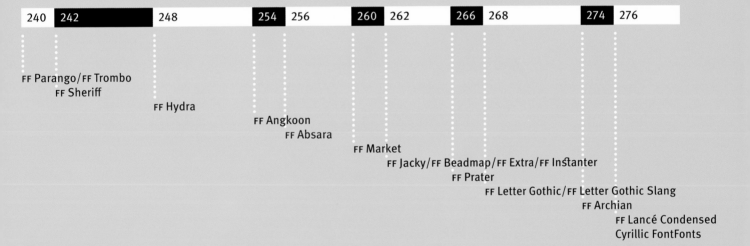
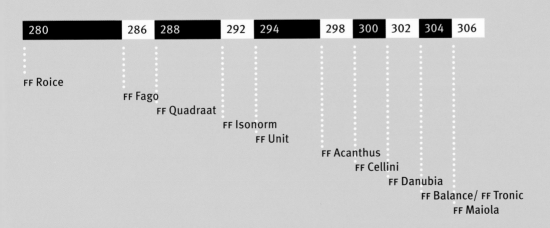

WRITING WITH

Scala

TYPE SPECIMEN | WRITING SAMPLE

writing by Ellen Lupton

WRITING WITH
SCALA *Scala by Martin Majoor*

I FIRST USED SCALA IN 1991, when Robin Kinross mailed it to me in New York City on a floppy disk. Robin was writing an essay for an exhibition catalogue I was editing, *Graphic Design in the Netherlands: A View of Recent Work*. His essay was about typeface design, and this is what he had to say about Scala, designed by the brilliant young typographer Martin Majoor:

> Scala sums up many characteristics of recent Dutch type design.
> It is an "old style" face, perhaps, but it follows no established model—
> it invokes memories of W. A. Dwiggins and Eric Gill. Scala has a
> definite, sharp character of its own, which escapes the Van Krimpen
> mold. As usual with the Dutch, *the italic has a strong, insistent rhythm,*
> *perhaps to an extreme.* Much love and attention has gone into the
> "special sorts,"—there is even an x-height ampersand (&)—and the
> figures are, of course, non-lining.[1]

Presented on the following pages are specimens of texts that I have written over the years, sampled and reconfigured to provide a showing of this amazing typeface. All of these texts were originally written in Scala. As a writer who is also a designer, I often compose my words directly on the page, and I am happiest when writing in Scala. Its crisp geometry and humanist references make Scala at home with both the visual and literary qualities of the written word. Scala's x-height, which may be unfashionably large by today's standards, has always sat well with me, reminding me of my own bottom-heavy figure. Scala's distinctively shaped characters call attention to the physical presence of typography; at the same time, their design allows the letters to recede into the texture of words, enabling the process of reading to move forward with comfort and ease.

FF Scala family, designed by Martin Majoor, beginning in 1991.

1. Robin Kinross, "Non-Lining Figures: On Recent Dutch Type Design," in Ellen Lupton, editor, *Graphic Design in the Netherlands: A View of Recent Work* (The Cooper Union and Princeton Architectural Press,). Published in Scala, 1992.

22/28 pt

Advertising and design serve to amplify *Bold*
the value of useful things, *transforming* *Italic*
functional tools into alluring FETISHES *Jewel (Pearl)*
that promise to satisfy emotional as well as
material needs. A Eureka vacuum cleaner *Regular*
claims not only to sweep clean the rug,
but to give its user all her heart desires.

14/18 pt

Scholars of religion use the word FETISH to describe objects *Jewel (Diamond)*
that societies invest with the magical ability to control the forces of nature. *The witch's broom, a* FETISH *appearing in Euro-* *Jewel (Crystal)*
pean folklore, is a cleaning tool employed for magical purposes;
the witch is a dangerously bad housekeeper, a single woman with
cobwebs in every corner. KARL MARX *borrowed the word* FETISH *Caps*
to characterize the cult object of capitalism: THE COMMODITY, a
product manufactured primarily to be sold, and only second-
arily to satisfy a human need. The object becomes a FETISH
as its functional role gives way to psychological incentives.

12/17 pt

The commodity FETISH speaks through advertising, packaging, styl- *Jewel (Sapphire)*
ing, and brand name recognition. *The corporate personality invoked by a*
familiar brand image such as logos for Hoover or Maytag can raise the value
of an appliance, regardless of its functional difference from other brands. Marx
assigned a feminine personality to the commodity FETISH *by describing*
the alluring, extra-functional features of the consumer product as "amorous
glances" that solicit the inner hopes and passions of the buyer. Freud used the
word FETISH to name an object or body part that stands in place of a
forbidden sex object. A foot or a shoe, a hand or a handbag—each can
become the target of desire, invested with emotional significance.

Text from Ellen Lupton, *Mechanical Brides: Women and*
Machines from Home to Office (New York: Princeton
Architectural Press and Cooper-Hewitt, National Design
Museum.) Written in Scala, 1993.

justified

JACQUES DERRIDA's theory of *deconstruction* asks how representation inhabits reality. How does the external image of things get inside their internal essence? How does the surface get under the skin? Western culture since Plato has been governed by such oppositions as *inside/outside* and *mind/body.*

flush left

The intellectual achievements of the West— its science, art, philosophy, literature—have valued one side of these pairs over the other, allying one with truth and one with falsehood. Deconstruction attacks such oppositions by showing how the devalued, negative concept inhabits the valued, positive one.

flush right

Consider, for example, the Judeo-Christian concept of the body as an external shell for the inner soul, a construction that elevates the mind as the sacred source of thought and spirit, while denigrating the body as mere mechanics. The original work of art carries an authenticity that its copy lacks—the original is endowed with the spirit of its maker, while the copy is mere empty matter.

centered

If *writing* is but a copy of spoken language,
typography
is even further removed from
the primal source of meaning
in the mind of the author.
The alphabet aims to represent
the sounds of speech with a finite set of marks.
Derrida used the term
GRAMMATOLOGY
to name the study of writing as a
distinctive form of representation.

mixed

A study of *typography* informed by
DECONSTRUCTION
would reveal a range of structures
that dramatize the intrusion of visual form
into verbal content, the invasion of ideas
by graphic marks,

gaps,

and differences.

Derrida proposed *grammatology* as a field of inquiry for which deconstruction is a crucial mode of research, a manner of questioning that frames the nature of its object. Falling within the domain of grammatology are the material forms and processes of typography. Robin Kinross's *Modern Typography* (1992) charts the progressive rationalization of the forms and uses of letters across several centuries of European history. As Kinross argues, printing was a prototypically *modern* process that engaged techniques of mass production.

The seeds of modernization were present in Gutenberg's first proofs; their fruits are born in the self-conscious methodologies and standardized visual forms of printers and typographers, which, beginning in the late seventeenth century, replaced an older notion of printing as a hermetic art of BLACK MAGIC, its methods guarded by a caste of craftsmen.

If Kinross's history of modern typography spans five centuries,
so too might a history of deconstruction,
running alongside and beneath
the evolution of transparent
formal structures.
Derrida's own writing draws on experimental
forms of page layout,
and countless forms of irrational order
appear across the discourses of
THE PRINTED LETTER.

FF Scala
8/12 pt
Regular, Italic, and Caps

FF Scala
9/12 pt
Regular, Italic, and Caps

External/internal, image/reality, representation/ presence, such is the old grid to which is given the task of outlining the domain of a science. And of what science? Of a science that

Text adapted from Ellen Lupton and J. Abobtt Miller, "Deconstruction and Graphic Design," *Design Writing Research: Writing on Graphic Design* (London: Phaidon Boooks). Written in Scala, 1996.

can no longer answer to the classical concept of the episteme because the originality of its field— an originality that it inaugurates—is that the opening of the 'image' within it appears as the condition of 'reality,' a relationship that can no longer be thought within the simple difference and the uncompromising exteriority of 'image' and 'reality,' of 'outside' and 'inside,' of 'appearance' and 'essence.' JACQUES DERRIDA

FF Scala Sans

Bold

MODERN DESIGNERS, WORKING IN 22 pt

THE AMBITIOUS DECADES BETWEEN THE LAST 18 pt

CENTURY'S TWO WORLD WARS, EMPHASIZED 16 pt

AND TRANSFORMED THE TECHNOLOGIES OF MECHANICAL REPRODUCTION. 10 pt

Regular

THEY SOMETIMES BURIED EVIDENCE 20 pt

OF THE HAND IN ORDER TO OBJECTIFY THE MACHINE. 14 pt

Caps

THE MASS MANUFACTURERS 30 pt

OF THE NINETEENTH CENTURY HAD PROVEN THAT INDUSTRIAL 14 pt

PRODUCTION COULD REPLICATE THE WORK OF TRADITIONAL ARTISANS. 11 pt

Regular

Avant-garde designers aimed, instead, 24 pt

to express the techniques of production in the form and appearance of the object. 11 pt

Italic

They sought to expose technology and loosen 22 pt

its constraints, viewing the processes of manufacture as devices equipped with 12 pt

Caps

CULTURAL AND AESTHETIC CHARACTER. 22 pt

Bold, Regular, Caps, Italic

Modernism fetishized the very means of manufacture, using the systems of MECHANICAL REPRODUCTION to build a mode of design that openly endorses its technical origins. The *ruler* and *compass*, the *camera* and *halftone block*, the *letterpress shop* and the *offset press*: these were technologies charged with meaning, their presence heroically narrated in the visual forms they served to produce. 12/15 pt

Bold, Regular, Caps, Italic

Artists and designers tapped the CULTURAL ENERGY OF THE MACHINE, viewing industrial production as a vehicle for utopian social change. Although the visual languages of the avant-garde were suppressed in the Soviet Union, they continued to grow in the West, where *graphic design* emerged as a practice that translates the technologies of communication into compellling visual forms.

Text adapted from Ellen Lupton, "Design and Production in the Mechanical Age," Graphic Design in the Age of Mechanical Reproduction: Selections from the Merrill C. Berman Collection, Maud Lavin, ed. (New Haven: Yale University Press.) Written in Scala, 1998.

In the 1980s and early 1990s, many experimental graphic designers embraced the idea of the readerly text. Inspired by theoretical ideas such as Roland Barthes's "death of the author," they used layers of text and interlocking grids to create works of design that engaged the reader in the making of meaning. In place of the classical model of typography as a crystal goblet for content, this alternative view assumes that content itself changes with each act of representation. Typography becomes a mode of interpretation, and the designer and reader compete with the author for control of the text.

Bold

Another model surfaced at the end of the 1990s, borrowed not from literary criticism but from human-computer interaction (HCI) studies and the fields of interface and usability design. The dominant subject of our age has become neither reader nor writer but user, a figure conceived as a bundle of needs and impairments—cognitive, physical, emotional. Like a patient or child, the user is a figure to be protected and cared for but also scrutinized, tested, and controlled.

Regular

How texts are used becomes more important than what they mean. Someone clicked here to get there. Someone who bought this also bought that. The interactive environment not only provides users with a degree of control and self-direction but also, more quietly and insidiously, it gathers data about its audiences. Text is a game to be played, as the user responds to signals from the system. We may play the text, but it is also playing us.

Italic

FF Scala Sans

9/11 pt

Graphic designers can use theories of user interaction to revisit some of our basic assumptions about visual communication. Why, for example, are readers on the Web less patient than readers of print? It is a common assumption that digital displays are inherently more difficult to read than ink on paper. Yet HCI studies conducted in the late 1980s proved that crisp black text on a white background can be read just as efficiently from a screen as from a printed page.

The impatience of the digital reader arises from culture, not from the essential character of display technologies. Users of Web sites have different expectations than users of print. They expect to feel "productive," not contemplative. They expect to be in search mode, not processing mode. Users also expect to be disappointed, distracted, and delayed by false leads. The habits of the screen are driving changes in design for print, while also affirming print's role as a place where extended reading still occurs.

Another common assumption is that icons are a more universal mode of communication than text. Icons are central to the GUIs (graphical user interfaces) that routinely connect users with computers. Yet text can often provide a more specific and understandable cue than a picture. Icons don't actually simplify the translation of content into multiple languages, because they require explanation in multiple languages. The endless icons of the digital desktop function more to enforce brand identity than to support usability. In the twentieth century, modern designers hailed pictures as a "universal" language, yet in the age of code, text has become a more common denominator than images.

FF Scala Sans

8.5/11 pt

Perhaps the most persistent impulse of twentieth-century art and design was to physically integrate form and content. The Dada and Futurist poets, for example, used typography to create texts whose content was inextricable from the concrete layout of specific letterforms on a page. In the twenty-first century, form and content are being pulled back apart. Style sheets, for example, compel designers to think globally and systematically instead of focusing on the fixed construction of a particular surface. This way of thinking allows content to be reformatted for different devices or users, and it also prepares for the afterlife of data as electronic storage media begin their own cycles of decay and obsolescence.

In the twentieth century, modern artists and critics asserted that each medium is specific. They defined film, for instance, as a constructive language distinct from theater, and they described painting as a physical medium that refers to its own processes. Today, however, the medium is not always the message. Design has become a "transmedia" enterprise, as authors and producers create worlds of characters, places, situations, and interactions that can appear across a variety of products. A game might live in different versions on a video screen, a desktop computer, and a cell phone.

The beauty and wonder of "white space" is another modernist myth that is under revision in the age of the user. Modern designers discovered that open space on a page can have as much physical presence as printed areas. White space is not always a mental kindness, however. Edward Tufte, a fierce advocate of visual density, argues for maximizing the amount of data conveyed on a single page or screen. In order to help readers make connections and comparisons as well as to find information quickly, a single surface packed with well-organized information is sometimes better than multiple pages with a lot of blank space. In typography as in urban life, density invites intimate exchange among people and ideas.

FF Scala Sans

7.5/11 pt

Text adapted from Ellen Lupton, *Thinking with Type: A Critical Guide for Designers, Writers, Editors, and Students* (New York: Princeton Architectural Press). Written in Scala, 2004.

FF Nexus

CONNECTIONS IN TYPE

DESIGNED BY MARTIN MAJOOR, 2002—04

FF Nexus Serif · Aa Bb Cc Dd Ee Ff Gg Hh Ii Jj Kk Ll Mm Nn Oo Pp Qq Rr Ss Tt Uu Vv Ww Xx Yy Zz · ABCDEFGHIJKLMNOPQRSTUVWXYZ · (1234567890)0987654321 · [£+@<!>$%–*&~?] · {fiflfffjftffifflctst}

THIS SPECIMEN DESIGNED BY MARK THOMSON

FF Nexus Serif Italic · Aa Bb Cc Dd Ee Ff Gg Hh Ii Jj Kk Ll Mm Nn Oo Pp Qq Rr Ss Tt Uu Vv Ww Xx Yy Zz · ABCDEFGHIJKLMNOPQRSTUVWXYZ · (1234567890)0987654321 · [£+@<!>$%–*&~?] · {fiflffffjftffiflctst}

Martin Majoor's FF Nexus is a three-way

FF Nexus Serif Bold · Aa Bb Cc Dd Ee Ff Gg Hh Ii Jj Kk Ll Mm Nn Oo Pp Qq Rr Ss Tt Uu Vv Ww Xx Yy Zz · ABCDEFGHIJKLMNOPQRSTUVWXYZ · (1234567890)0987654321 · [£+@<!>$%–*&~?] · {fiflfffjftffifflctst}

conversation in type: one language, three voices;

FF Nexus Serif Bold Italic · Aa Bb Cc Dd Ee Ff Gg Hh Ii Jj Kk Ll Mm Nn Oo Pp Qq Rr Ss Tt Uu Vv Ww Xx Yy Zz · ABCDEFGHIJKLMNOPQRSTUVWXYZ · (1234567890)0987654321 · [£+@<!>$%–*&~?] · {fiflfffjftffiflctst}

one form, three expressions; one structure, three

FF Nexus Sans · Aa Bb Cc Dd Ee Ff Gg Hh Ii Jj Kk Ll Mm Nn Oo Pp Qq Rr Ss Tt Uu Vv Ww Xx Yy Zz · ABCDEFGHIJKLMNOPQRSTUVWXYZ · (1234567890)0987654321 · [£+@<!>$%–*&~?] · {fiflfffjftffifflctst}

constructions. Variations in serif treatment and

FF Nexus Sans Italic · Aa Bb Cc Dd Ee Ff Gg Hh Ii Jj Kk Ll Mm Nn Oo Pp Qq Rr Ss Tt Uu Vv Ww Xx Yy Zz · ABCDEFGHIJKLMNOPQRSTUVWXYZ · (1234567890)0987654321 · [£+@<!>$%–*&~?] · {fiflfffjftffiflctst}

stroke contrast create different 'voicings', unified

FF Nexus Sans Bold · Aa Bb Cc Dd Ee Ff Gg Hh Ii Jj Kk Ll Mm Nn Oo Pp Qq Rr Ss Tt Uu Vv Ww Xx Yy Zz · ABCDEFGHIJKLMNOPQRSTUVWXYZ · (1234567890)0987654321 · [£+@<!>$%–*&~?] · {fiflfffjftffifflctst}

by an exceptionally lucid letterform structure.

FF Nexus Sans Bold Italic · Aa Bb Cc Dd Ee Ff Gg Hh Ii Jj Kk Ll Mm Nn Oo Pp Qq Rr Ss Tt Uu Vv Ww Xx Yy Zz · ABCDEFGHIJKLMNOPQRSTUVWXYZ · (1234567890)0987654321 · [£+@<!>$%–*&~?] · {fiflfffjftffiflctst}

¶ The family grew organically in the same way

FF Nexus Mix · Aa Bb Cc Dd Ee Ff Gg Hh Ii Jj Kk Ll Mm Nn Oo Pp Qq Rr Ss Tt Uu Vv Ww Xx Yy Zz · ABCDEFGHIJKLMNOPQRSTUVWXYZ · (1234567890)0987654321 · [£+@<!>$%–*&~?] · {fiflfffjftffifflctst}

as FF Scala before it, but this time with another

FF Nexus Mix Italic · Aa Bb Cc Dd Ee Ff Gg Hh Ii Jj Kk Ll Mm Nn Oo Pp Qq Rr Ss Tt Uu Vv Ww Xx Yy Zz · ABCDEFGHIJKLMNOPQRSTUVWXYZ · (1234567890)0987654321 · [£+@<!>$%–*&~?] · {fiflfffjftffiflctst}

dimension: Nexus serif *begat* Nexus sans *begat*

FF Nexus Mix Bold · Aa Bb Cc Dd Ee Ff Gg Hh Ii Jj Kk Ll Mm Nn Oo Pp Qq Rr Ss Tt Uu Vv Ww Xx Yy Zz · ABCDEFGHIJKLMNOPQRSTUVWXYZ · (1234567890)0987654321 · [£+@<!>$%–*&~?] · {fiflfffjftffifflctst}

Nexus mix. A monospaced sans serif and a range

FF Nexus Mix Bold Italic · Aa Bb Cc Dd Ee Ff Gg Hh Ii Jj Kk Ll Mm Nn Oo Pp Qq Rr Ss Tt Uu Vv Ww Xx Yy Zz · ABCDEFGHIJKLMNOPQRSTUVWXYZ · (1234567890)0987654321 · [£+@<!>$%–*&~?] · {fiflfffjftffiflctst}

of swash characters extend the family's reach

FF Nexus Typewriter · Aa Bb Cc Dd Ee Ff Gg Hh Ii Jj Kk Ll Mm Nn Oo Pp Qq Rr Ss Tt Uu Vv Ww Xx Yy Zz · (1234567890) 0987654321 · [£+@<!>$%-*&~?]

back and forward in time.

a b c d e f

g h i j k l

m n o p q r

s t u v w x

y z

TEXT FROM SIMON PATTERSON AND MARK THOMSON: A–Z, 2005

FF Nexus · MARTIN MAJOOR, 2002–04

A

André-Marie Ampère
(1775–1836)

Å

Anders Jonas Ångström
(1814–74)

Bq

Antoine Henri Becquerel
(1852–1908)

C

Charles Coulomb
(1736–1806)

Ci

Marie Curie
(1867–1934)

D

DIOPTRE

dB

Alexander Bell
(1847–1922)

°F

Daniel Gabriel Fahrenheit
(1686–1736)

gr

GRAIN

H

Joseph Henry
(1797–1878)

Hz

Heinrich Rudolf Hertz
(1857–94)

in

INCH

J

James Prescott Joule
(1818–89)

K

William Thomson,
Lord Kelvin
(1824–1907)

kn

KNOT

lx

LUX

µm

MICRON

N

Isaac Newton
(1642–1727)

Ω

Georg Simon Ohm
(1789–1854)

oz

OUNCE

Pa

Blaise Pascal
(1623–62)

pk

PECK

q

QUINTAL

°R

William John
MacQuorn Rankine
(1820–72)

°r

René Antoine
Ferchault
de Réaumur

S

Karl Wilhelm
(William) Siemens
(1822–83)

T

Nikola Tesla
(1856–1943)

Alessandro Volta
(1745–1827)

James Watt
(1736–1819)

x

Wilhelm Conrad
Röntgen
(1854–1923)

All life on earth can be classified into a number of separate, major units (or 'taxa') known as *kingdoms*, each representing an ancient lineage that has evolved into a multiplicity of modern species. (14/20 pt)

Just how many kingdoms might appropriately be recognised to encompass this multiplicity of species is, however, still uncertain. The simplistic view recognised just two kingdoms, 'plants' and 'animals', and followed classical beliefs established

long before the foundation of modern systematics by Linnaeus in the mid-eighteenth century. This comfortable tradition continued almost unchallenged for close on three centuries, and only quite recently, in the latter part of the twentieth century, has it been radically reviewed and replaced. This change has largely reflected progress in the study of micro-organisms, involving ultrastructural and biochemical characters and especially the application of molecular systematics, advances which have finally shown (12/18 pt)

that a two-kingdom system is hopelessly inadequate to encompass the huge diversity and complexity of life on Earth. A multi-kingdom classification is clearly needed, at least for scientists and researchers, even though the public at large has generally been happy to retain just two kingdoms. Although fungi, as well as protozoa and bacteria, had occasionally been considered separate kingdoms at various times since the seventeenth century, no consensus on this view was held until comparatively recently. Margulis and Schwartz (1988) were the first to propose (11/16 pt)

the classification of living organisms into five kingdoms, following earlier suggestions by Whittaker (1969). No-one now disputes the several-kingdom structure of life, but the number of kingdoms and their delimitation remain unsettled. In one of the more recent classifications (Cavalier-Smith, 1998), a six kingdom system has been suggested, although it now seems that Woese et al. (1990) were correct in splitting one of these kingdoms (the *Prokaryota*) into two. These prokaryotic organisms, the *Archaea* and the *Bacteria*, are single-celled structures, the most ancient of all organisms, with which life on Earth (10/15 pt)

9/13 pt began. Their cells completely lack any membrane-bound organelles; they have no nuclei or mito-chondria, and their DNA is dispersed. Prokaryotes probably evolved at least 4,000,000,000 years ago and were, for an immense period of time, the only life forms on Earth. Eventually, after at least two billion years of slow evolution, they gave rise to the more complex 'eukaryotes', organisms with sophisticated cells containing separate membrane-bound

8/12 pt organelles. The most important of these eukaryotic organelles are the 'nucleus', which governs the cell and in which the DNA is packaged, and the 'mitochondria', which provide energy. All life on Earth other than bacteria is eukaryotic, highly evolved and diversified over the last 2,000,000,000 years into five separate kingdoms. These are the plants (kingdom *Plantae*), the animals (kingdom *Animalia*), the true fungi (kingdom *Fungi*), and the less well-known kingdoms of the *Chromista* and the *Protozoa*

7/11 pt (Cavalier-Smith, 1998), both of which contain some fungus-like organisms. In Cavalier-Smith's system, the Protozoa is the most ancient of the eukaryotic kingdoms and includes a total of thirteen 'phyla'. These are the next main taxa below kingdoms, at a level which distinguishes human beings (phylum *Chordata*) from jellyfish (phylum *Cnidaria*). Animalia comprises 23 such phyla, Plantae and Chromista have five each, and four phyla make up the Fungi. Most of the organisms traditionally called 'fungi' belong within the kingdom Fungi according to this system, but some are

6.5/10 pt placed within the Protozoa and Chromista. Although this seven-kingdom system is not yet fully accepted, it does seem to be gaining favour as the current standard model. Nonetheless, significant changes are still being proposed and it seems likely, therefore, that even the highest levels in the classification of life will remain in a state of flux for a long time to come. Each of the seven kingdoms, as with all taxa, has its own unique features. In the old two-kingdom view of life, fungi were placed with plants mainly because, unlike animals, they do not move around. This is undeniably true, but is hardly a good scientific definition.

6/9 pt The fungal mode of nutrition, for example, is quite different from that of plants. Like animals, they are 'heterotrophs', unable to make their own food and requiring organic carbon derived from plants or other organisms. Unlike animals, however, which ingest their food, fungi digest and absorb nutrients externally. Plants, in contrast, are 'autotrophs', making their food by photosynthesis, their cells containing chlorophyll and able to use sunlight to convert carbon dioxide into sugars through the carbon reduction cycle. Fungi also differ structurally from plants, in particular lacking cellulose which is characteristic of plant cell walls. Instead, fungi are mainly composed of

5.5/8.5 pt chitin, the same basic material that makes up insect exoskeletons. Recognition of a separate kingdom for fungi was a major advance, although it was soon evident that the kingdom was not yet homogeneous but included organisms placed there because of similarities in their mode of nutrition, now known to have arisen independently from a different ancestor. As long ago as 1864, de Bary had proposed that slime moulds were not fungi but actually protozoa, a conclusion which received no acceptance until comparatively recently because of the fungus-like nature of their fruitbodies. Slime moulds (*Myxomycota*) are actually 'phagotrophs', ingesting bacteria and fungi by means of amoeboid stages, typical of protozoa. Again, the

TEXT FROM BRIAN SPOONER & PETER ROBERTS: FUNGI, NEW NATURALIST SERIES, COLLINS, 2005

AIX		
BECK'S		
SEX		
DECKS		
FECKS		
CZECHS		
HEX		
AJAX		
JACKS (NZ)	JACKS (US)	
KEKS	CACK	
LEX	LACKS	
MEX	MACS	MIX
NEXUS	**KNACKS**	**KNICKS**
OX	WHACKS	WICKS
PECS	PAX	PIX
QX	QUACKS	QUICK
REX	RACKS	RICK
SEXUS	SAX	SIX
TEX	TAX	TICKS
BIVOUACS	BIVOUACS	UNIX
VEX	VACC.	VICK'S
WEXFORD	WAX	WICKES
EX	YAKS	YORICKS
ZEX (D)	ZAKS	ZOOLOGICS
FF Nexus Serif SC	FF Nexus Sans SC	FF Nexus Mix SC

*Purg*ation *Priv*ation *Starv*ation *Vex*ation *Tax*ation

FF Nexus Serif Italic Swash One & Two

§1234567890-=
QWERTYUIOP[]
ASDFGHJKL;'\
`ZXCVBNM,./
qwertyuiop[]
asdfghjkl;'\
`zxcvbnm,./
FF Nexus Typewriter

§1234567890-=
QWERTYUIOP[]
ASDFGHJKL;'\
`ZXCVBNM,./
qwertyuiop[]
asdfghjkl;'\
`zxcvbnm,./
FF Nexus Typewriter Bold

FF Nexus Serif   Januart

FF Nexus Sans   Februarian

FF Nexus Mix   Marchile

FF Nexus Serif Bold   **Aprilious**

FF Nexus Sans Bold   **Mayal**

FF Nexus Mix Bold   **Junite**

FF Nexus Serif Italic   *Julienne*

FF Nexus Sans Italic   *Augustate*

FF Nexus Mix Italic   *Septembrent*

FF Nexus Serif   Octoberine

FF Nexus Italic Swash   *Novemberesque*

FF Nexus Typewriter   Decembric

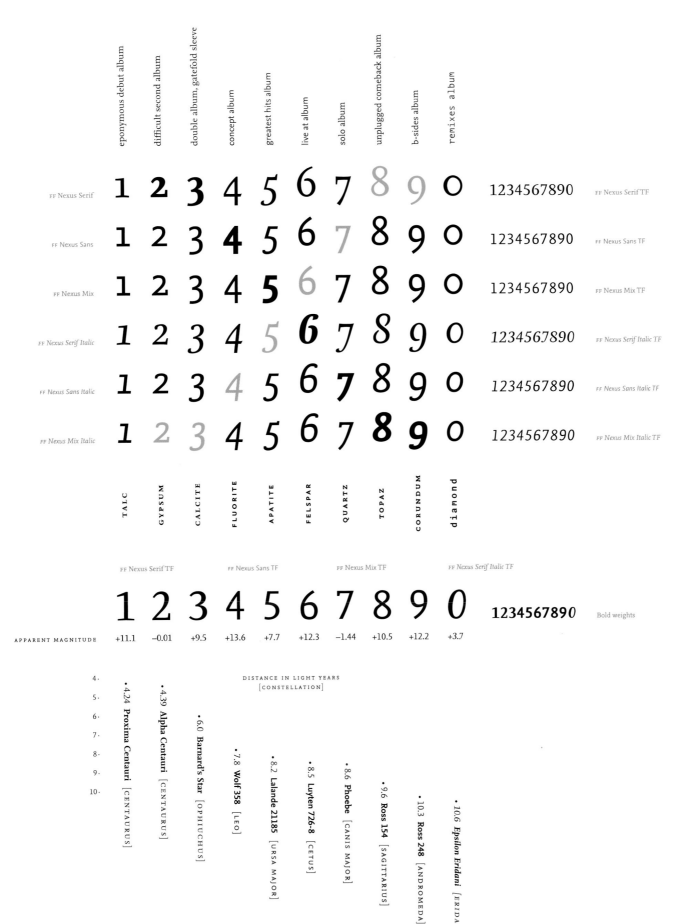

FF Nexus · MARTIN MAJOOR, 2002–04

CAREER PROGRESSION

Column headers: eponymous debut album · difficult second album · double album, gatefold sleeve · concept album · greatest hits album · live at album · solo album · unplugged comeback album · b-sides album · remixes album

	1	2	3	4	5	6	7	8	9	0		
FF Nexus Serif	1	2	3	4	5	6	7	8	9	0	1234567890	FF Nexus Serif TF
FF Nexus Sans	1	2	3	4	5	6	7	8	9	0	1234567890	FF Nexus Sans TF
FF Nexus Mix	1	2	3	4	5	6	7	8	9	0	1234567890	FF Nexus Mix TF
FF Nexus Serif Italic	1	2	3	4	5	6	7	8	9	0	1234567890	FF Nexus Serif Italic TF
FF Nexus Sans Italic	1	2	3	4	5	6	7	8	9	0	1234567890	FF Nexus Sans Italic TF
FF Nexus Mix Italic	1	2	3	4	5	6	7	8	9	0	1234567890	FF Nexus Mix Italic TF

MOHS' SCALE OF HARDNESS

TALC · GYPSUM · CALCITE · FLUORITE · APATITE · FELSPAR · QUARTZ · TOPAZ · CORUNDUM · diamond

FF Nexus Serif TF   FF Nexus Sans TF   FF Nexus Mix TF   FF Nexus Serif Italic TF

1 2 3 4 5 6 7 8 9 0   1234567890   Bold weights

THE TEN NEAREST STARS

APPARENT MAGNITUDE	+11.1	−0.01	+9.5	+13.6	+7.7	+12.3	−1.44	+10.5	+12.2	+3.7

DISTANCE IN LIGHT YEARS [CONSTELLATION]

4·
5·
6·
7·
8·
9·
10·

•4.24 Proxima Centauri [CENTAURUS]
•4.39 Alpha Centauri [CENTAURUS]
•6.0 Barnard's Star [OPHIUCHUS]
•7.8 Wolf 358 [LEO]
•8.2 Lalande 21185 [URSA MAJOR]
•8.5 Luyten 726-8 [CETUS]
•8.6 Phoebe [CANIS MAJOR]
•9.6 Ross 154 [SAGITTARIUS]
•10.3 Ross 248 [ANDROMEDA]
•10.6 Epsilon Eridani [ERIDANUS]

ALPHABETS	CRIMINALS	BRA SIZES	DISASTERS	ERICS	FAKERS	GEOMETRICAL FIGURES	HAIRCUTS	INDICES	JINXES	KLINGON	LINES	MESSAGES

Aquiline
Backline
Baseline
Bassline
Bikini line
Circle Line
Cunard Line
Dotted line
Equator
Feline
Forgotten lines
Greenwich Meridian
Halfway line
Hot line
International Date Line (IDL)
Jubilee Line
Laughter line

Binding Spells
Breakup Spells
Cassandra's Curse
Custom Spells
Divorce Spells
Fertility Spells
Fidelity Spells
Hex Removal Spells

Ley line
Line Dance
Linea Alba
Linea Negra
Maginot Line
Oder-Neisse Line
Offline

Airplane Accidents
Avalanches
Blizzards

28 A–G Droughts
30 A–JJ Earthquakes
32 A–JJ Floods
34 A–JJ Hurricanes
36 A–JJ Ice Jams
38 A–JJ Landslides
40 A–J Mudslides
42 B–J Nuclear Disasters
44 B–H Oil Spills
46 B–H Power Outage
48 B–H Rockslides
50 B–FF Structural Failures
52 B–FF Tsunamis
54 B–FF Volcanoes
56 B–FF Wrecks

Major George Byron
Thomas Chatterton
Charles Dawson
Elmyr de Hory
William Henry Ireland
Geert Jan Jansen
Konrad Kujau
Ferdinand Legros
Han van Meegeren
George Psalmanasar
Claude Emile Schuffenecker
Ignatius Timothy
　Trebitsch Lincoln
Milli Vanilli
Otto Wacker

Back, Sack and Crack
Bob
Brazilian
Craig David
Crew
Hoxton Fin
Kojak
Landing Strip
Mohican
Mullet
Number One
Pudding Bowl
Short Back and Sides
Yul Brynner

Jinxes for the Jinxed
Job Spells
Love Spells
Love Return Spells
Luck Spells
Marriage Spells
Misspells
Money Spells
Protection Spells
Revenge Spells
Sailor's Curse
Success Spells
The Curse
The Curse of Tutankhamen
The Travellling Curse

Party line
Plimsoll Line
Plumb line
Queue
Red line
Saline
Sex line
Shoreline
Tropic of Capricorn
Tropic of Cancer
Unsteady line
Visible Panty Line (VPL)
White line (double)
Cross line
Yellow line
Zenithal line

A B C D E F G H I J K L M

Arabic
Burmese
Cherokee
Devanagari
Etruscan
Fraser
Glagolitic
Hebrew
International Phonetic
　Alphabet (IPA)
Japanese
Korean
Latin
Mongolian
N'Ko
Ogham
Pollard Miao
Runic
Sutton SignWriting
Tai Lue

David Berkowitz
　(Son of Sam)
Kenneth Bianchi
Ian Brady
Ted Bundy
William Burke &
　William Hare
Alphonse Capone
Andre Chikatilo
Jeffrey Dahmer
Albert DeSalvo
John Wayne Gacy
Ed Gein
Myra Hindley
Ronnie & Reggie Kray
Peter Kurten
Donald Neilson
Pietro Pacciani (Il Mostro)
Robert Leroy Parker
　(Butch Cassidy)
Richard Ramirez
Harold Shipman
Benjamin 'Bugsy' Siegel
Peter Sutcliffe
Fred West

Eric **Blair**
Eric **Cantona**
Eric **Gill**
Eric **Hebborn**
Eric **Idle**
Eric **Morecambe**
Erik **Satie**
Erik **Spiekermann**
Eric **Sykes**
Eric **the Red**
Eric **Troncy**
Wreckless Eric

Acute angle Triangle
Circle
Decagon
Dodecagon
Ellipse
Equilateral Triangle
Heptagon
Hexagon
Isosceles Triangle
Kite
Nonagon (Enneagon)
Obtuse angle Triangle
Octagon
Parallelogram
Pentagon
Rectangle
Right angle Triangle
Rhombus
Scalene Triangle
Spiral
Square
Trapezium
Undecagon (Hendecagon)

'a Chinese encyclopaedia'
Byzantine Manuscript
　Indices
Climate Indices
Dow Jones Sustainability
　Indexes
Egypt Hermes Index
FTSE 100
FTSE Smallcap Index
Fractional Indices
Geomagnetic Indices
Gene Indices
Google
Hang Seng
Index finger
Index of Indices
Indices of deprivation
Jasdaq
Kosdaq
Laws of Indices
Magnetic activity indices
Nasdaq
Negative indices
Other indices
Pollen Index
Refraction Index
Retail Price Index
Routing Indices
Stability Indices
Superscript indices
Subscript indices
This index
Urinary Indices
Virtual index
Weather Indices

be'Hom *n.* girl
cha *n, pl.* torpedoes
cha'pujqut *n.* dilithium crystal
DuS *n.* torpedo tube
ghup *vb.* swallow
Hugh *n.* throat
Hurgh *n.* pickle (cucumber)
jach *vb.* scream, cry out,
　shout, yell
je' *vb.* feed (someone else)
laQ *vb.* fire, energize (e.g.
　thrusters)
lutlh *vb.* be primitive
mIv *n.* helmet
nuH *n.* weapon
plqaD *n.* Klingon writing
　system
qab *vb.* be bad
qa'vam *n.* Genesis
SIS *n.* rain
SoD *n.* flood
tut *n.* column
vergh *n.* dock
vergh *vb.* dock
wuQ *vb.* have a headache
wuS *vb.* lip
yach *vb.* pet, stroke
yIQ *vb.* be wet
yonmoH *vb.* satisfy
yopwaH *n.* pants
yuQjIjQa' *n.* United
　Federation of Planets

Bin Laden message
Cryptic message
Error message
Hidden message
Love message
Message Access Protocol
Message board
Message clock
Message-digest algorithm
Message stick
Message threading
Mixed message
On-message
Off-message
President's message
Spam message
The Queen's Christmas
　message
Test message
txt msg
Underlying message

ORGANS QUEUES STUNT PLAYERS UNDERWEAR WINDS YELLOWS

NARCOLEPTICS PHOBIAS REMAKES THEOREMS VANGUARDS KISSES AND CROSSES ZENITHS

ORGANS

The Austin Organ, Forbidden City Concert Hall, Beijing
Brentwood Cathedral's organ
The Cavaillé-Coll Organ of Saint-Antoine des Quinze-Vingts, Paris
The Cavaillé-Coll Organ of Saint-Sulpice, Paris
The dual-temperament organ for Saint Cecilia Cathedral
The Grace Cathedral Organ, Topeka, Kansas, Ohio
The Grand Organ of Liverpool Cathedral
The Great Silbermann Organ of Freiburg Cathedral
The Harrison & Harrison Organ of Westminster Abbey
The Mander Organ of Chichester Cathedral
The Mexico City Cathedral Organ
'Old Jupiter', the 9,999-pipe Willis Organ of the Royal Albert Hall
The Organ of Riga Dom Cathedral
The Organ of St Paul's Cathedral
The Passau Cathedral Organ
The Stumm Brothers Organ of St. Ulrich Church, Neckargemünd
The Visser-Rowland Tracker Pipe Organ at St. Mary's Cathedral
The Willis Organ of Winchester Cathedral

QUEUES

Activation queues
Asynchronous queues
Bank queues
Batch queues
Bus queues
Double ended queues
Episodic queues
First Class queues
Generic RTP input
Heaps and priority queues
Hurricane Katrina soup kitchen queues
Interest queues
Message queues
NHS queues
Phone queues
Polling Station queues
Post Office queues
Printer queues
Restoration queues
Rock cluster queues
Stacks and queues
Theatre queues
Theory of queues

STUNT PLAYERS

Roy Arbogast
Bill (Billy) Burton
James Day Camomile
Eddie Donno
Jeannie Epper
Logan and Terry Frazee
Sandra Gimpel
Buddy Joe Hooker
Garth Inns
A. J. (Alf) Joint
Phillip Knowles
Joseph J. (Joe) Lombardi
Dwayne McLean
Teruyoshi Nakano
Bill Orr
Pat Patterson
John Quinlivan
Giannetto (Bomberdoni) de Rossi
Eoin C. Sprott
John Thomas
Joseph A. Unsinn
Val van de Veer
Kit West
X
Bob Yerkes
Gary Zeller

UNDERWEAR

Balconette bra
Bandeau
Basque
Boxer shorts
Bustier
Cami-knickers
Camisole
Corset
Crotchless knickers (Ouvert knickers)
Demi-cup bra
Disposable knickers
Full briefs
Full-cup bra
French knickers
G-string
Gel-filled bra
Quarter-cup bra
Ouvert knickers (Crotchless knickers)
Maternity bra
Open string
Peephole bra
Plunge bra
Push-up bra
Slip
Strapless bra
Suspender belt
Suspender briefs
T-shirt bra
Thong
Y-fronts

WINDS

Hurricane **Arlene**
Hurricane **Bret**
Hurricane **Cindy**
Hurricane **Dennis**
Hurricane **Emily**
Hurricane **Franklin**
Hurricane **Gert**
Hurricane **Harvey**
Hurricane **Irene**
Hurricane **Jose**
Hurricane **Katrina**
Hurricane **Lee**
Hurricane **Maria**
Hurricane **Nate**
Hurricane **Ophelia**
Hurricane **Philippe**
Hurricane **Rita**
Hurricane **Stan**
Hurricane **Tammy**
Hurricane **Vince**
Hurricane **Wilma**

YELLOWS

Cadmium Yellow
Chrome Yellow
Cobalt Yellow
Indian Yellow
Lead Tin Yellow
Lemon Yellow
Naples Yellow
Orpiment (King's Yellow)
Yellow Ochre

N O P Q R S T U V W X Y Z

NARCOLEPTICS

Arthur Lowe
Mike Waters
Rip van Winkle

PHOBIAS

Ablutophobia
Bacillophobia
Cacophobia
Decidophobia
Ecclesiophobia
Febriphobia
Galeophobia
Hadephobia
Iatrophobia
Japanophobia
Kainolophobia
Lachanophobia
Macrophobia
Nebulaphobia (Homichlophobia)
Obesophobia
Pagophobia
Radiophobia
Samhainophobia
Tachophobia
Uranophobia
Vaccinophobia
Walloonphobia
Xanthophobia
Zelophobia

REMAKES

Breathless
The Bride Stripped Bare by her Bachelors, even (The Large Glass)
California Calls You
Cape Fear
El Mariachi
The Fly
Get Carter
The Italian Job
The Ladykillers
Ocean's Eleven
Planet of the Apes
The Postman Always Rings Twice
Psycho
Scarface
Shaft
Solaris
The Texas Chainsaw Massacre

THEOREMS

Archimedes' Principle
Brouwer's Fixed Point Theorem
Cantor's Theorem of the Denumerability of the Rational Numbers
Desargues's Theorem
Euler's Generalization of Fermat's Little Theorem
Fermat's Last Theorem
Gödel's Incompleteness Theorem
Hexagon Theorem (Pascal)
Infinitude of Primes (Euclid)
Königsberg Bridges Problem (Euler)
Laws of Large Numbers
Mean Value Theorem (Cauchy)
Newton's Binomial Theorem
Pi is Transcendental (Lindemann)
Quadratic Reciprocity, Gauss's Law of
Sum of an Arithmetic Series (Babylonians)
Sum of a Geometric Series (Archimedes)
The Birthday Problem
Undecidability of the Continuum Hypothesis (Cohen)
Wilson's Theorem

VANGUARDS

Constructionism
Constructivism
Cubism
Expressionism
Fauvism
Futurism
Hyperrealism
Impressionism
Neo-Expressionism
Neoplasticism/De Stijl
Orphism
Post-Impressionism
Postmodernism
Surrealism
Symbolism
Vorticism

KISSES AND CROSSES

Butterfly kiss
Eskimo kiss
French kiss
Glaswegian kiss
Charing Cross
Maltese Cross
Inverted cross
Stolen kiss

ZENITHS

Acme
Apex
Apogee
Climax
Cloud Nine
High Noon
Peak
Petit mort
Pinnacle
Summit
Vertex

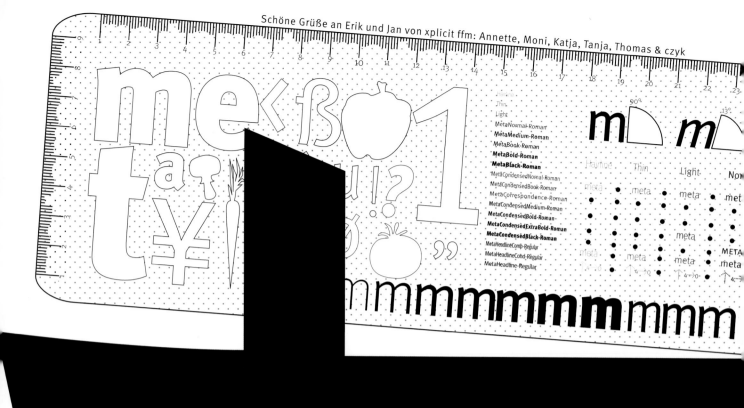

YPOMETA

Medium | Book | Bold | Black

meta *meta* meta *meta* **meta** *meta* **meta** *meta*
meta meta meta meta meta meta
meta meta meta meta meta meta
META *META* META *META* **META** *META* **META** *META*
meta meta meta meta **meta** *meta* **meta** *meta*

mmmmmm

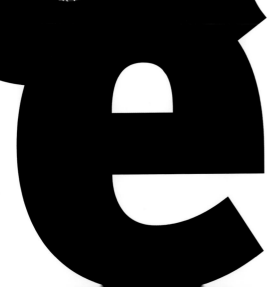

Meta Black LF
MetaBold LF
Meta Book LF
Meta Condesed Black
Meta Condensed Black LF
Meta Condensed Black Roman
Meta Condensed Black LF Italic
Meta Condensed Bold LF-Roman
Meta Condensed Bold LF-Roman
Meta Condensed-Book
Meta Condensed-Book LF-Italic
Meta Condensed Extra Bold
Meta Condensed Extra Bold LF-Roman
Meta Condensed Medium
Meta Condensed Medium LF-Italic
Meta Condensed Normal
Meta Condensed Normal LF-Roman
Meta Condensed Normal LF-Italic
Meta Headline
Meta Headline Comp
Meta Headline Condensed
Meta Medium LF
Meta Medium LF
Meta Normal
Meta Normal LF

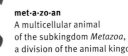

met·a·zo·an
A multicellular animal
of the subkingdom *Metazoa*,
a division of the animal kingdom
in traditional two-kingdom
classification systems

MetamorphosiS

metamorphose

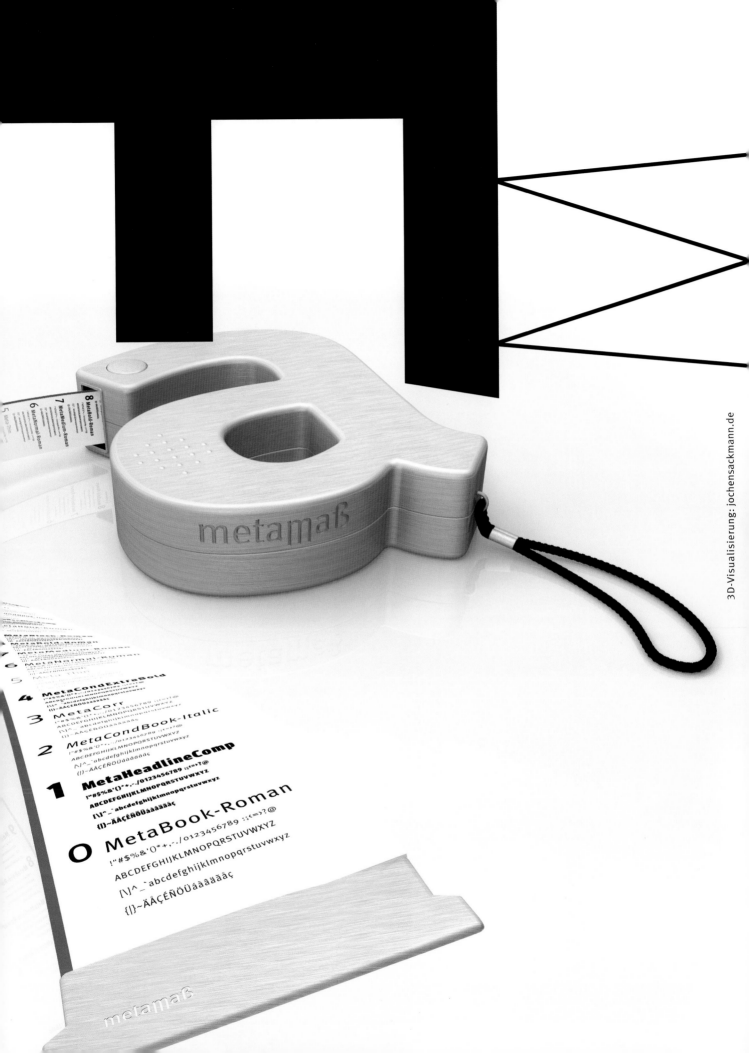

metamaß

3D-Visualisierung: jochensackmann.de

8 MetaBold-Roman
7 MetaNormal-Roman
6 MetaNormal-Roman
5 Meta-Thin

4 MetaCondExtraBold
!"#$%&'()*+,-./0123456789 :;<=>?@
ABCDEFGHIJKLMNOPQRSTUVWXYZ
[\]^_`abcdefghijklmnopqrstuvwxyz
{|}~–ÄÅÇÉÑÖÜáàâäãåç

3 MetaCorr
!"#$%&'()*+,-./0123456789 :;<=>?@
ABCDEFGHIJKLMNOPQRSTUVWXYZ
[\]^_`abcdefghijklmnopqrstuvwxyz
{|}~–ÄÅÇÉÑÖÜáàâäãåç

2 *MetaCondBook-Italic*
!"#$%&'()+,-./0123456789 :;<=>?@*
ABCDEFGHIJKLMNOPQRSTUVWXYZ
[\]^_`abcdefghijklmnopqrstuvwxyz
{|}~–ÄÅÇÉÑÖÜáàâäãåç

1 MetaHeadlineComp
!"#$%&'()*+,-./0123456789 :;<=>?@
ABCDEFGHIJKLMNOPQRSTUVWXYZ
[\]^_`abcdefghijklmnopqrstuvwxyz
{|}~–ÄÅÇÉÑÖÜáàâäãåç

O MetaBook-Roman
!"#$%&'()*+,-./0123456789 :;<=>?@
ABCDEFGHIJKLMNOPQRSTUVWXYZ
[\]^_`abcdefghijklmnopqrstuvwxyz
{|}~–ÄÅÇÉÑÖÜáàâäãåç

metamaß

BLUR

FontFont digital typefaces convince the reader through their clarity and sharpness. The quality of type is a question of know-how and expertise. What was true for metal type and, during a tense era of transition, for photo-typesetting, is still true for digital type: only through craftsmanship and

FF Blur Light 9/10,5

FontFont digital typefaces convince the reader through their clarity and sharpness. The quality of type is a question of know-how and expertise. What was true for metal type and, during a tense era of transition, for photo-typesetting, is still a

FF Blur Light 11/13

FontFont digital typefaces convince the reader through their clarity and sharpness. The quality of type is a qu estion of know-how and expertise. What was true for metal type and, d

FF Blur Light 12/14,5

N. Brody
1991
An Original FontFont

ABCDEFGHIJKLMN
OPQRSTUVWXYZ
abcdefghijklmnopqrstuvwxyzß
1/123456789
(¡!'"§$%&,:;'"''"„"""¿?£$€¥@)
[†‡•''' #°+÷=™]
YÄÁÂÀÃÅÆÇÍÎÏÍÑÖÓÔÒÕØO
EÉÊÈÙÚÛÙŸ äáâàãåæçëéêê
ïíîìñöóôòõøoeüúûùÿfifl

With negative letterspacing
With normal letterspacing
With extra letterspacing
With extreme letterspacing

In general, body types are measured in the typographi cal point size. However, be tween typefaces of the sam e point size, the optical size may vary considerably acco rding to the lenghts of ascen ders and descenders. This is also true for sizes of Font Font digital typefaces. For measuring point size, a tran sparent size gauge is recom mended. To determine the

FF Blur Light 16/19

Zweedse ex-vips geven behoorlijk quantumfysica. FontShop's quick brown fox

FF Blur Light 18pt

Zweedse ex-vips geven behoorlijk quantumfysica. FontShop's quick

FF Blur Light 20pt

Zweedse ex-vips geven behoorlijk quantumfysica. FontS

FF Blur Light 24pt

Zweedse ex-vips geven behoorlijk quantumfysica

FF Blur Light 28pt

Zweedse ex-vips behoorlijk quantumfy

FF Blur Light 36pt

Zweedse ex-vips behoorlijk quantu

FF Blur Light 40pt

Zweedse ex-vips behoorlijk q

FF Blur Light 48pt

Zweedse ex-vips behor

FF Blur Light 60pt

FontFont digital typefaces convince the reader through their clarity and sharp ness. The quality of type is a question of know-how and expertise. What was true for metal type and, during a tense era of

FF Blur Light 11/11

Size		Line spacing			100 char.	
mm	pt	kp	Ep	Ex	0	−1
1,33	5	1,75	2,06	2,00	90	87
1,60	6	2,06	2,50	2,50	106	98
1,86	7	2,38	2,88	3,00	122	115
2,15	8	2,75	3,31	3,50	139	129
2,40	9	3,06	3,75	3,75	155	144
2,65	10	3,38	4,13	4,25	172	158
2,92	11	3,75	4,50	4,75	188	174
3,20	12	4,13	4,94	5,25	204	188
3,45	13	4,44	5,38	5,75	220	204
3,72	14	4,75	5,75	—	236	218
3,98	15	5,06	6,19	—	252	234
4,25	16	5,44	6,56	—	268	248

FontFont digital typefaces con vince the reader through their clarity and sharpness. The qual ity of type is a question of know how and expertise. What was a

Blur Light 14/11

FF Blur by Neville Brody   Jan MIddendorp

BLUR

FontFont digital typefaces convince the re ader through their clarity and sharpness. The quality of type is a question of know-h ow and expertise. What was true for metal type and, during a tense era of transition, for photo-typesetting, is still true for digit

FF Blur Medium 9/10,5

FontFont digital typefaces convince the reader through their clarity and sharpness. The quality of type is a question of know-how and experti se. What was true for metal type and during a tense era of transition, for

FF Blur Medium 11/13

FontFont digital typefaces convi nce the reader through their clari ty and sharpness. The quality of type is a qu estion of know-how and expertise. What was true for

FF Blur Medium 12/14,5

N. Brody
1991
An Original FontFont

ABCDEFGHIJKLMN
OPQRSTUVWXYZ
abcdefghijklmnopqrstuvwxyzß
1/123456789
(i!"§$%&,.;'""„"«‹¿?£$€¥@)
[†‡*'''' #°+÷=™]
YÄÁÂÀÃÅÆÇÍÏÎÌÑÖÓÔÒÕØO
EËÉÊÈÜÚÛÙŸ äáâàãåæçëéêè
ïíîìñöóôòõøoeüúûùÿfifl

With negative letterspacing
With normal letterspacing
With extra letterspacing
With extreme letterspacing

In general, body types are measured in the typogra phical point size. Howev er, between typefaces of the same point size, the o ptical size may vary cons iderably according to the lenghts of ascenders and descenders. This is also t rue for sizes of FontFont digital typefaces. For me asuring point size, a tran sparent size gauge is rec

FF Blur Medium 16/19

Zweedse ex-vips geven behoorlijk quantumfysica. FontShop's quick b

FF Blur Medium 18pt

Zweedse ex-vips geven behoorlijk quantumfysica. FontShop's

FF Blur Medium 20pt

Zweedse ex-vips geven behoorlijk quantumfysica. F

FF Blur Medium 24pt

Zweedse ex-vips geven behoorlijk quantum

FF Blur Medium 28pt

Zweedse ex-vips behoorlijk quantu

FF Blur Medium 36pt

Zweedse ex-vips behoorlijk qua

FF Blur Medium 40pt

Zweedse ex-vips behoorlij

FF Blur Medium 48pt

Zweedse ex-vips beh

FF Blur Medium 60pt

FontFont digital typefaces convince the reader through their clarity and sharpness. The quality of type is a question of know-how and experti se. What was true for metal type and

FF Blur Medium 11/11

Size		Line spacing			100 char.	
mm	pt	kp	Ep	Ex	0	−1
1,33	5	1,75	2,06	2,00	90	87
1,60	6	2,06	2,50	2,50	106	98
1,86	7	2,38	2,88	3,00	122	115
2,15	8	2,75	3,31	3,50	139	129
2,40	9	3,06	3,75	3,75	155	144
2,65	10	3,38	4,13	4,25	172	158
2,92	11	3,75	4,50	4,75	188	174
3,20	12	4,13	4,94	5,25	204	188
3,45	13	4,44	5,38	5,75	220	204
3,72	14	4,75	5,75	—	236	218
3,98	15	5,06	6,19	—	252	234
4,25	16	5,44	6,56	—	268	248

FontFont digital typefaces convince the reader through their clarity and sharpness. The qual ity of type is a quest ion of know how and expert

Blur Medium 14/11

"That poster reminds me . . . a horseback scene like this would make
a good cigarette advertisement . . ."
"Sure, call it 'Thoroughbreds' and it would be perfect for Chesterfield!"

THEY'RE MILD
and yet THEY SATISFY

©1928, LIGGET & MYERS TOBACCO CO.

Shinn Design Inc., Toronto, May 1999.

That Which Speaks
of its Own Voice

FF ONELEIGH

This type

Self-reference is the theme of a specimen booklet for the typeface FF Oneleigh. What else is new?—type specimens have long played that game, says *Nick Shinn*

Learning to read, you become able to recognize certain images—first letters, then words, then phrases—as signs, and this process becomes a subconscious reflex. In fluent reading the medium (images) is engaged at a subconscious level, allowing consciousness to attend to the message (signs).

When conscious of a word as a sign, you are not conscious of it as an image. And vice versa. But it's hard to turn off a reflex, so you'll keep coming back to a message which signifies its own medium, such as the headline on this page, in a loop of feedback. Hence the fascination of self-reference.

Type specimens present words as images, showcasing the physical attributes of type, its size, detail, style, etc. But words are also signs, and whatever they may say, even if it's complete nonsense, they will be read as signs. So any text in a type specimen will be viewed as both image *and* sign.

It's a peculiar effect, akin to self reference.

Copy treatments such as alphabets, straight prose, and fake ads take no account of it. But the specimen's propensity for a kind of automatic concrete poetry has given rise to several unique genres, most evident in size declensions. "Look," they say, "these words don't mean a whole lot. They don't go anywhere. They're type-book words. Linger awhile, amused by the nonsense, and when that little bit of meaning wears off, you'll be left just looking at type."

Latin. *Quousque tandem…etc.* An unknown language to most these days, with connotations of typography's weighty history.

Pangrams. *The quick brown fox…etc.* These refer to their constituent letters as images, prompting a head count, with an inspection of distinguishing features.

Satire. Perfected by the Bard of specimen writers, Thomas MacKellar: *Driftsnow, Banker/Capital Invested in Ice Houses/Good for Sudden Runs* (MacKellar, Smiths and Jordan, 1868).

Magniloquence. Bombastic and exotic: *Incidental Notices of Manchooria & Kamschatka/Great Amoor River Country* (James Conner's Sons, 1873).

Lyricism. Verse, with a haiku-like quality: *Perfect specimen/simple design exhibited/considered very artistic/for modern typography* (American Type Founders, 1923).

Surrealism. Strange tales: *Reporting/aliens land in Boston/crashed/jumper cables/interstellar engine troubles/63.2 volts/they require a mechanic, pronto…*(Frere-Jones, Font Bureau, 1997).

Junk. Collage of random snippets from mass media and/or the printer's lexicon: *Sixteen Automobiles Wrecked/Perfect Register* (Bauer, 1936). Pure Dada, very *Naked Lunch.*

Self-reference has a key place in the history of art. Marcel Duchamp's ready-mades, such as *Fountain* of 1917 (a urinal), mark absolute zero, the culmination of centuries of progress towards pure art-about-art. Denied the validity of the art object (it's junk, signifying nothing), the viewer is referred to the meta-medium of art—the social setup of artist, critic, gallery,

❡"Of course, the bottle rack and the urinal are not art…Art has been thought through to a conclusion. Nothing, nihil, is all that is left."—Hans Richter, *Dada: art and anti-art*

❡"…The choice of these 'ready-mades' was never dictated by aesthetic consideration. The choice was based on a reaction of *visual indifference* with a total absence of good or bad taste…in fact a complete anaesthesia."—Marcel Duchamp, *From the Green Box*

Quousque tandem abutere, Catalina patientia nostra? quamdiu nos etiam furor iste tuus eludet? as Cicero said, and Caslon, and Bodoni, and Oswald Bruce Cooper, and Jonathan Hoefler.

Venerable phrases these, lending a flavor of erudition to generations of type specimens, and now finding themselves paraded in the vulgar panoply of an "advertising" type. Indignity! For this, Reader, is a kind of pre-view of a new face—FF Oneleigh. The designer is conscious of its crudity, and of its irreverence for the best traditions. But he believes that there are enough good types already—that the need is for poor types that can be used! And since he admits this to be a poor one, there now remains to be found out only whether it is usable or not. FontShop is publishing it in three weights, Roman and Italic, with Small Capitals for the Regular Roman, and the designer dares to hope they will sell enough to pay them for their trouble.

ABCDEFGHIJKLMNOPQR
STUVWXYZ&
abcdefghijklmnopqrstuvwxyz
$1234567890!?

Discover the comfort of historical precedent

IN 1911, Mitchell Kennerley, the New York publisher, asked N.W. Shinn if he would care to plan the arrangement, and make whatever decorative features he deemed necessary, to an American edition of *The Sword of Welleran,* by the Irish author Lord Dunsany. Shinn initially set trial pages in 12-point Caslon Old Face, but was disappointed with the orthodox appearance of the page proofs. While the type was of suitable vintage, he nonetheless felt that the effect of the Caslon was too firmly associated with the genuine events of history to do justice to such an elaborate fantasy. Consequently Shinn produced a new type, true to the Old Style genre, yet with considerable idiosyncrasy of both form and detail. This he named ONELEIGH.

Discover the comfort of historical precedent.

It's 1966. Drop out of the rat race. Go far away. Or long ago. Use a funky old face. Something weird and hand-made. Like Nicky Shinn's Oneleigh. But don't be shy about it. Make it bold.

And blow it up.

Discover The Comfort Of Historical Precedent.

It was more than sixty years ago that Oneleigh was first released, to wide acclaim.

Now it is reborn.

After exhaustive study and trial development, Nick Shinn has created a new version of the classic, eminently able to meet the needs of graphic usage in the 1980s.

New Oneleigh exhibits a subtlety of line and tight fit which make it inviting and easy to read.

The face was drawn free of ruling pen and straight edge; natural nuances are seen in each letter, slight differences in serifs and stroke weights which soften appearances when letters combine into words.

Each weight was drawn without computer software or re-proportioning camera shots.

Just good old style hand lettering.

Discover

the comfort of historical precedent

FF Oneleigh is a post-modern parody of old style typefaces. Designer Nicholas Shinn has plundered the past in cut-and-paste fashion, cannibalizing characters, serifs, and thematic effects from the heyday of the old style revival, the 1920s.

The lower case 'l', for instance, with its cap-like upper serif and cursive foot serif, is appropriated from Rudolf Koch's *Antiqua;* the capital 'W', with its condensed central space, is sampled from the *Initials* of Emil Weiss; the eccentric angle of the stress in the lower case italic—'bottom left to top right'—comes courtesy of Frederic Goudy's *Companion*...and so on.

In all events, Shinn has sought the most recherché material, and for good measure has complemented his larceny of history by liberally rewriting it.

Time stood the old house of Oneleigh.

I know not how many centuries had lashed against it their evanescent foam of years; but it was still unshattered, and all about it were the things of long ago, as cling strange growths to some sea-defying rock. Here, like the shells of long-dead limpets, were armour that men encased themselves in long ago; here, too, were tapestries of many colours, beautiful as seaweed; no modern flotsam ever drifted hither, no early Victorian furniture, no electric light.

Meanwhile, while it yet stood, I went on a visit there to my brother, and we argued about ghosts. My brother's intelligence on this subject seemed to me to be in need of correction. He mistook things imagined for things having an actual existence; he argued that second-hand evidence of persons having seen ghosts proved ghosts to exist. I said that even if they had seen ghosts, this was no proof at all. . . . Finally I said I would see ghosts myself, and continue to argue against their actual existence.

[2]

ABCDEFGHIJKLMNOP
QRSTUVWXYZ&ÆŒ
abcdefghijklmnopqrstuvwxyz
₵@fiflß™►æœctst*†‡§-[©®]
.,''";:!?(€$£¥¢)#1234567890%
Speaking of earlier types,
Shinn says: The old fellows
stole all of our best ideas.

CRITICAL COMMENT

THE size of 12 Point Oneleigh is small compared with other faces cast upon the same body, which makes it desirable for use on an open page. There is a *peculiar distinction* in a page with wide leading provided the balance is kept harmonious.
The small cap running head is from Aldus, who first felt the need of smaller characters which preserved the exact form of their larger prototypes.
The margins shown here are for 30½ × 36 paper (untrimmed).

THE SWORD
OF WELLERAN

I

THE GHOSTS

NOW Oneleigh stands in a wide isolation, in the midst of a dark gathering of old whispering cedars. They nod their heads together when the North Wind comes, and nod again and agree, and furtively grow still again, and say no more awhile.

The North Wind is to them like a nice problem among wise old men; they nod their heads over it, and mutter about it all together. They know much, those cedars, they have been there so long. Their grandsires knew Lebanon, and the grandsires of these were the servants of the King of Tyre and came to Solomon's court. And amidst these black-haired children of grey-headed

[1]

DESCRIPTION
Written Language
Means of Communication

A B C D E F G H I J K L M N
O P Q R S T U V W X Y Z a b c
d e f g h i j k l m n o p q r s t u v w x y z
& $. , - : ; ! ? ') " " 1 2 3 4 5 6 7 8 9 0

The fabulist's description portrays a traditional recital, a mythical narrative, history, memoir, memorial, specification, or saga. Delineation enters into particulars, describes the report. The exposé sets forth an epic scenario of life, AUTOBIOGRAPHICAL SUMMARY OF FACTS

A well-drawn brief pictures the work of fiction, a short story, or a novelette. The romance is an expository story, a eulogy that characterizes monographs, historiography, realistic fortunes PENNY DREADFUL NECROLOGIES

Chronography unfolds autobiographical allegory, giving an account of details, recapitulating the shilling shockers of a GRAPHIC SPINNER OF YARNS

Confessions of a raconteur sum up circumstantial journals of legend and render an account of memoirs BIOGRAPHICAL SKETCH

Rehearsed and recapitulated the adventures and anecdotes of the fairy-tale romancers in PLOT AND VIGNETTE

Narrate Graphic Catalogs
Descriptive Guide Books
FABULOUS ANNALS

A Factual Statement
Expository Parables
STORIED MYTH

Fictional Tale
Epic Novelette
SCENARIO

Particularized
OBITUARY
Suggestive
EXPOSÉ
Historic
FABLE
Relate
SAGA

Eureka

A TYPEFACE DESIGNED BY PETER BIĽAK, 1996–2001

sketches

fonts
in use

The first drawings for *Eureka* date back to 1995. The basic designs for Eureka Serif and Eureka Sans were completed in 1997 for the bilingual book *Transparency*, a study on graphic design and language. Western typefaces sometimes have x-heights that are too large to support languages with many accented characters. The *Transparency* project became a testing ground for Eureka's goal: the adaptation of a typeface's proportions to the diacritic-rich Slovak language.

Prvé škice písma *Eureka* sú z roku 1995. V roku 1997 boli dokončené digitálne verzie písiem Eureka a Eureka Sans pre dvojjazyčnú knihu *Transparentnosť*, diplomovú prácu na tému grafický design a jazyk. Písma, vznikajúce na západe majú často príliš vysoké minusky, a preto nie sú vhodné pre jazyky, ktoré používajú mnoho akcentov. Projekt *Transparentnosť* sa stal platformou na testovanie vytýčeného cieľa Eureky: *adaptáciu proporcií písma pre Slovenčinu.*

Roman	Roman Expert	CE Roman
Italic	*Italic Expert*	*CE Italic*
SMALL CAPS	SMALL CAPS EXPERT	CE SMALL CAPS
Medium	Medium Expert	CE Medium
Bold	**Bold Expert**	**CE Bold**

EUREKA ROMAN

abcdefghijklmnopqrstuvwxyz
ABCDEFGHIJKLMNOPQRSTUVWXZ
YÄÁÂÀÃÅÆÇÍÎÏÌÑÖÓÔÒÕØŒËÉÊÈÜÚÛÙŸ
äáâàãåæçëéêèïíîìñöóôòõøœüúûùÿfifl
[0123456789.,:;÷+-=<>µ€£$¥] (&@§¶ß©®™!?*)

EUREKA EXPERT

ꞇꞇꞇꞇ&Qfbffffkffhfflfjaznth
{≤≥≈×∞∂∑∏π∫Ω√Δ♈}

EUREKA CAPITALS

ABCDEFGHIJKLMNOPQRSTUVWXYZ
[0123456789] (⅍§¶ss©®™!?*)

EUREKA ITALIC

abcdefghijklmnopqrstuvwxyz
ABCDEFGHIJKLMNOPQRSTUVWXZ
YÄÁÂÀÃÅÆÇÍÎÏÌÑÖÓÔÒÕØŒËÉÊÈÜÚÛÙŸ
äáâàãåæçëéêèïíîìñöóôòõøœüúûùÿfifl
[0123456789.,:;÷+-=<>µ€£$¥] (&@§¶ß©®™!?*)

EUREKA CE

ąāáäčćďđěęéēėģįīíķľĺłļńňņőóôöōõŕřŗśśťůūűųüúýżźž
ĄĀÁÄČĆĎĐĚĘÉĒĖĢĮĪÍḰĽĹŁĻŃŇŅŐÓÔÖŌÕŔŘŖŠŚŤŮŪŰŲÜÚÝŻŹŽ

Eureka Sans Regular & Expert

abcdefghijklmnopqrstuvwxyz

ABCDEFGHIJKLMNOPQRSTUVWXZ

YÄÁÂÀÃÅÆÇÍÎÏÌÑÖÓÔÒÕØŒËÉÊÈÜÚÛÙŸ

äáâàãåæçëéêèïíîìñöóôòõøœüúûùÿfifl

[0123456789.,:;÷+-=<>µ€£$¥] (&@§¶ß©®™!?*)

{≤≥≈≠∞∂∑∏π∫Ω√∆◯}

Eureka Capitals

ABCDEFGHIJKLMNOPQRSTUVWXYZ

[0123456789] (⒜§¶ss©®™!?*)

Eureka Italic

abcdefghijklmnopqrstuvwxyz

ABCDEFGHIJKLMNOPQRSTUVWXZ

YÄÁÂÀÃÅÆÇÍÎÏÌÑÖÓÔÒÕØŒËÉÊÈÜÚÛÙŸ

äáâàãåæçëéêèïíîìñöóôòõøœüúûùÿfifl

[0123456789.,:;÷+-=<>µ€£$¥] (&@§¶ß©®™!?*)

Eureka CE

ąāáäčćďđěęéēėġjīíķĺľ łļńňņőóôöòōõŕřŗšśťůūűŭüúýžżž

ĄĀÁÄČĆĎĐĚĘÉĒĖĢJĪÍĶĽĹŁŁĻŃŇŅŐÓÔÖÒŌÕŔŘŖŠŚŤŮŪŰŬÜÚÝŽŻŽ

The height of the ascenders and descenders of *Eureka* is 1.7 times the x-height. This relatively small x-height leaves room for longer descenders and ascenders which in turn better accomodate accents and punctuation. Because of the small x-heights, Eureka can be perceived 1–2 points smaller than other text fonts.

Výška doťažníc *Eureky* je 70% výšky minusiek, čo sú proporcie klasických renesančných písem. Malá výška minusiek vzhľadom na doťažnice umožňuje väčší priestor pre akcenty a interpunkciu. Výsledkom je, že Eureka vyzerá 1–2 body menšia ako iné písma vysádzané v rovnakej bodovej veľkosti.

Light	Light Expert	Light Caps & Expert	CE Light	CE Light Caps
Light Italic	*Light Italic Expert*		*CE Light Italic*	
Regular	Regular Expert	Regular Caps & Expert	CE Regular	CE Regular Caps
Regular Italic	*Regular Italic Expert*		*CE Regular Italic*	
Medium	Medium Expert	Medium Caps & Expert	CE Medium	CE Medium Caps
Medium Italic	*Medium Italic Expert*		*CE Medium Italic*	
Bold	**Bold Expert**	**Bold Caps & Expert**	**CE Bold**	**CE Bold Caps**
Bold Italic	***Bold Italic Expert***		***CE Bold Italic***	
Black	**Black Expert**	**Black Caps & Expert**	**CE Black**	**CE Black Caps**
Black Italic	***Black Italic Expert***		***CE Black Italic***	

Eureka Sans Condensed & Expert

abcdefghijklmnopqrstuvwxyz
ABCDEFGHIJKLMNOPQRSTUVWXZ
YÄÁÂÀÃÅÆÇÍÏÎÌÑÖÓÔÒÕØŒËÉÊÈÜÚÛÙŸ
äáâàãåæçëéêèïíîìñöóôòõøœüúûùÿfifl
[0123456789.,:;÷+-=‹›µ€£$¥] (&@§¶ß©®™!?*)
{‹≥≈≠∞∂∑∏πΩ∫√∆◯}

Eureka Sans Condensed Capitals

ABCDEFGHIJKLMNOPQRSTUVWXYZ
[0123456789] (㏐§¶ss©®™!?*)

Eureka Italic

abcdefghijklmnopqrstuvwxyz
ABCDEFGHIJKLMNOPQRSTUVWXZ
YÄÁÂÀÃÅÆÇÍÏÎÌÑÖÓÔÒÕØŒËÉÊÈÜÚÛÙŸ
äáâàãåæçëéêèïíîìñöóôòõøœüúûùÿfifl
[0123456789.,:;÷+-=‹›µ€£$¥] (&@§¶ß©®™!?*)

Eureka Sans Condensed CE

ąâăäåçćčďđěęëëîíľĺńňóóôôŕŗşśšťţůúûüýźžž
ĄÂĂÄÅÇČĆĎĐĚĘ ÉËÎÍĽĹŃÑŐÓÔÖŔŖŞŠŚŤŢŮÚŰÜÝŹŽŽ

Eureka's proportions result in an space-saving typeface and allow the letters to be spaced more loosely, since it is the white space that we unconsciously read, not the actual letterforms. Looser spacing helps to avoid typographic noise inside a text, and retains the individuality of letters. Eureka comes with real Italics for all the weights in Sans and for the text weight of the Serif version. Italics are rather condensed and their angle is 5°.

Eureka je ekonomické písmo s charakteristickými širšími medzipísmenovými medzerami, kedže podvedome čítame biely priestor okolo písmen a nie ich samotné tvary. Toto presvetlenie pomáha zlepšiť čitateľnosť a celkový obraz písma. Všetky rezy Eureky Sans ako aj textová verzia Eureky Serif majú svoje vlastné kurzívy. Kôli odlíšeniu v texte boli kurzívy dosť zúžené. Ich uhol sklonu je však iba 5°.

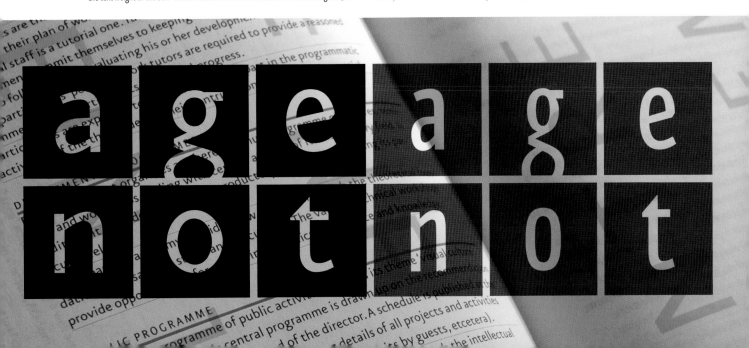

Part IV. **Eureka Mono**

abcdefghijklmnopqrstuvwxyz
ABCDEFGHIJKLMNOPQRSTUVWXZ
YÄÁÂÀÃÅÆÇÍÎÏÌÑÖÓÔÒÕØŒËÉÊÈÜÚÛÙŸ
äáâàãåæçëéêèïíîìñöóôòõøœüúûùÿfifl
[0123456789.,:;÷+-=<>µ€£$¥] (&@§¶ß©®™!?*)
{≤≥≈≠∞∂∑∏π∫ΩΔ♂}

abcdefghijklmnopqrstuvwxyz
ABCDEFGHIJKLMNOPQRSTUVWXZ
YÄÁÂÀÃÅÆÇÍÎÏÌÑÖÓÔÒÕØŒËÉÊÈÜÚÛÙŸ
äáâàãåæçëéêèïíîìñöóôòõøœüúûùÿfifl
[0123456789.,:;÷+-=<>µ€£$¥] (&@§¶ß©®™!?*)

ąāáäčćďđěęéēėġįīíḱľíłļ
ńňņőóôöōõŕřŗšśťůūűųüúýżźž
ĄĀÁÄČĆĎĐĚĘÉĒĖĢĮĪÍḰĽŁĻ
ŃŇŅŐÓÔÖŌÕŔŘŖŠŚŤŮŪŰŲÜÚÝŻŹŽ

Eureka takes into account the vast possibilities of type usage today, and has been designed accordingly. Eureka Mono was designed for screen rendering. All three typefaces, Sans, Serif and Mono, have the same skeleton and can easily be combined in text.

Eureka bola navrhnutá tak, aby spĺňala všetky požiadavky použitia písma v súčasnosti. Eureka Mono je určená predovsetkým pre obrazovku. Všetky tri rodiny písiem Eureky; Sans, Serif a Mono majú podobnú konštrukciu a dajú sa dobre kombinovať v texte.

Light	Light Expert	CE Light
Light Italic	*Light Italic Expert*	*CE Light Italic*
Regular	Regular Expert	CE Regular
Regular Italic	*Regular Italic Expert*	*CE Regular Italic*
Medium	Medium Expert	CE Medium
Medium Italic	*Medium Italic Expert*	*CE Medium Italic*
Bold	**Bold Expert**	**CE Bold**
Bold Italic	***Bold Italic Expert***	***CE Bold Italic***
Black	**Black Expert**	**CE Black**
Black Italic	***Black Italic Expert***	***CE Black Italic***

Eureka Mono Condensed & Expert

abcdefghijklmnopqrstuvwxyz
ABCDEFGHIJKLMNOPQRSTUVWXZ
YÄÁÂÀÃÅÆÇÍÎÏÌÑÖÓÔÒÕØŒËÉÊÈÜÚÛÙŸ
äáâàãåæçëéêèïíîìñöóôòõøœüúûùÿfifl
[0123456789.,:;÷+-=<>µ€£$¥] (&@§¶ß©®™!?*)
{ ≤ ≥ ≈ ≠ ∞ ∂ ∑ ∏ π ∫ ∩ ∆ ♂ }

Eureka Mono Condensed Italic

abcdefghijklmnopqrstuvwxyz
ABCDEFGHIJKLMNOPQRSTUVWXZ
YÄÁÂÀÃÅÆÇÍÎÏÌÑÖÓÔÒÕØŒËÉÊÈÜÚÛÙŸ
äáâàãåæçëéêèïíîìñöóôòõøœüúûùÿfifl
[0123456789.,:;÷+-=<>µ€£$¥]
(&@§¶ß©®™!?)*

eureka!

Eureka Mono Condensed CE

ąāáäčćďđěęéēèġįīíķľĺłļńňņőóôöòõŕřŗšśťůūűůÿüúýżźž
ĄĀÁÄČĆĎĐĚĘÉĒÈĢĮĪÍĶĽĹŁĻ́ŃŇŅŐÓÔÖÒÕŔŘŖŠŚŤŮŪŰŲÜÚÝŻŹŽ

mōñö ¡ môńõ

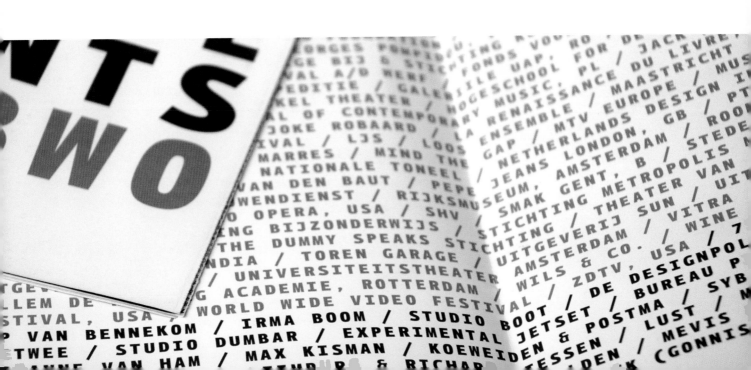

FF MAGDA MAGDA CLEAN

REZA ABEDINI

Bilak

FF Magda, FF Magda Clean ✏ Reza Abedini

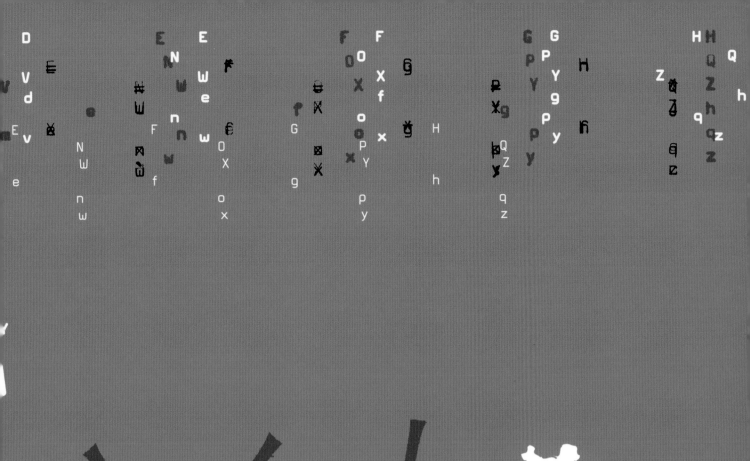

FF DuDuchamp by Dung van Meerbeeck ✎ Reza Abedini

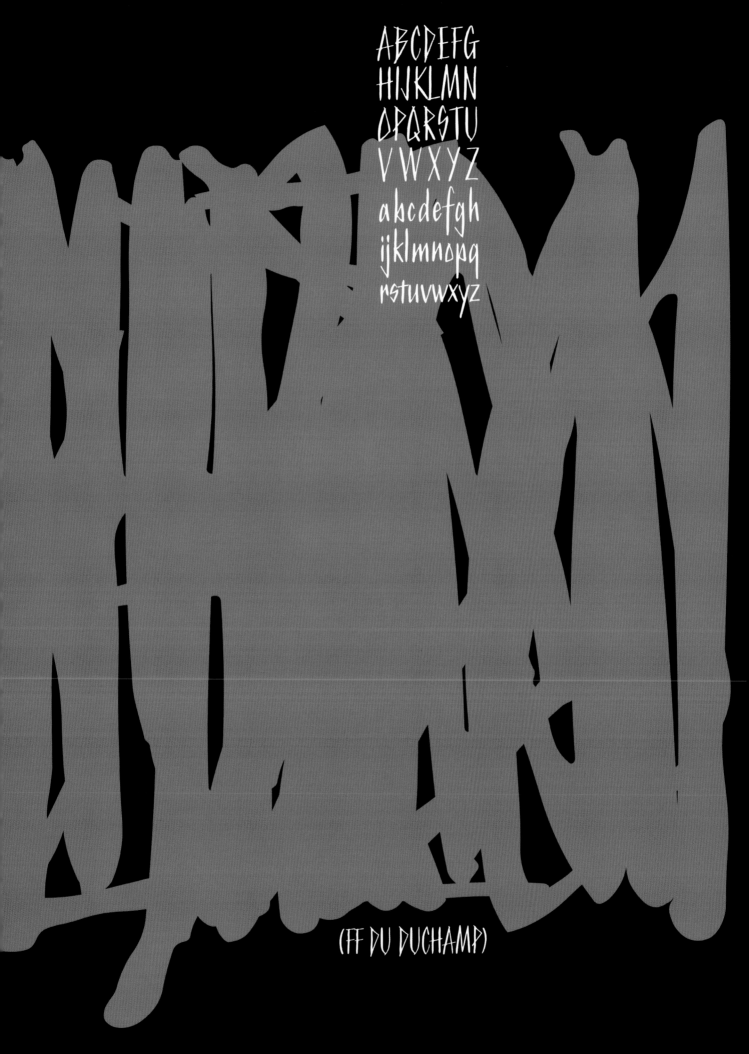

ABCDEFG
HIJKLMN
OPQRSTU
VWXYZ
abcdefgh
ijklmnopq
rstuvwxyz

(FF DU DUCHAMP)

FFLegato
FFLegato
FFLegato
FFLegato

typeface by evert bloemsma

((((The purpose of keyboards is to enable the 2 hands (e.g. on a pianoforte) or the 2 hands and 2 feet (organ) readily to control the sounds from a much larger number of strings, reeds, or pipes than could otherwise be controlled. Developed over a long period, it has come to be universally adopted: it is by no means the *most convenient method imaginable, but the conservatism of musicians will probably prevent its supersession unless some drastic change in the scales used in music makes such a change imperative.*

6/7½ **bold**, semi-bold, regular, light & *italics*

((((**There are records of the existence of crude instruments of the class of the organ long before the opening of the Christian era (cf. *Hydraulus*). By the 10th century development had got so far as (in very advanced specimens) 2 manuals each with a range of 20 notes and each note with as many as 10 different pipes, making 400 in all: the keyboard (if there was one) had broad notes requiring the blow of the whole fist, but it is possible that other means than a keyboard, such as sliders moving from front to back, were used (an ecclesiastical organ at the time served a purely melodic accompaniment of the plainsong). In the period which *followed there were 2 types of organ, a portative organ (cf. Regal) which could be carried in processions, and one fixed in its position, a positive organ.***

7/8½ **bold**, semi-bold, regular, light & *italics*

((((**In the beginning merely the melodic plainsong was played, at first thumped out on keys as broad as the fists that operated them. In those days, and for long after the keys had been adapted for pressure by the fingers, music was still modal (cf. Modes). Evolution of the modern organ from this simple infancy took place largely in northern Germany, and France at some periods. By the 17th century something like the present form of the instrument had come into being.** The pedal-board, of German introduction, dates from at least as early as the mid-15th century. In the Netherlands during the 16th and 17th centuries, competing cities built prestigious church organs, in answer to the *rising popularity of secular public concerts. The swell device from the early 18th century and pneumatic action (1832), are of English origin. The first American church organ was installed in Philadelphia, about 1694.*

8/9½ **bold**, semi-bold, regular, light & *italics*

((((**In recent times the American development of the organ has profited by the attention of many ingenious inventors. Ship organs used *steam* instead of compressed air. Churches and concert halls, dance and cinema theatres were fitted with organs (*cf. Radio City Music Hall* or *The Singing Detective*), and reproducing organs until they were made obsolete by recorded sound – the sound film and the deejay (disk jockey) – and the invention of** the DIGITAL SYNTHESIZER.

9/10½ **bold**, semi-bold, regular, light, *italics* and small caps

((((**Today's version of the organ is a LAPTOP computer operated on stage, performing** a digital musical score (*cf. Ballet Frankfurt* and pop music) from a manual reduced to *a simple* QWERTY-*keyboard*.

10/12 **bold**, semi-bold, regular, light, *italics* and *italic small caps*

((((¶ The **hurdy-gurdy** is a stringed instrument played by turning with the right hand a rosined wheel which serves as a bow, while the left operates a small keyboard with a few finger-keys like those of a piano. Two of the strings produce the low key-note, so resembling the drone of a bag-pipe (*cf.* Bourdon). Music has been provided for this instrument by serious composers (Haydn). It is still in some use.

¶ The **carillon** or **bell organ** is an ancient institution especially in Belgium and the Netherlands, consisting of anything up to 70 bells played by fists and feet on manual and pedal consoles like those of an organ but more cumbrous and mostly up a tower, near the bells. Tunes and accompanying harmonies can be performed. At the hours, halves and quarters the carillon is set in operation by a power driven clockwork.

¶ The **barrel organ** is a true organ of normal size, with instead of keyboards a barrel-and-peg mechanism operated by turning a handle. From the 1770's or earlier it was common, even in churches. A domestic size was also common and its repertory included dance music, etc. Cafés, dance and cinema halls especially in Flanders boasted elaborate built-in barrel organs until the ascent of the *juke box*. A street version survives by adapting up-to-date tunes.

¶ **Electrophonic organs** of various makes produce their tone not from pipes but, initially, by means of rotating disks with pick-ups working on the electro-magnetic or electrostatic principle. Its pioneers seem to have been Coupleux and Givelet. In 1931, Ranger exhibited a pipeless organ and in 1935 the HAMMOND CO. of Chicago put on the market their organ, which has been widely taken up. Out of such electro-mechanical devices various electronical instruments have evolved. In 1983, sales of **electronic keyboards** outnumbered acoustic keyboard instruments. Improved key-stroke sensitivity and digital sound lead to ever refined imitations of acoustic instruments. Not unlike the registers of an organ, piano, harpsichord, marimba, strings and percussion now are 'options', next to digital recording and reproducing facilities. Some high quality *acoustic* keyboard instruments can be switched to electronic operation and the use of *headphones*.

8/9½ **bold**, light, regular & *italic*

((((The purpose of keyboards is to enable the 2 hands (e.g. on a pianoforte) or the 2 hands and 2 feet (organ) readily to control the sounds from a much larger number of strings, reeds, or pipes than could otherwise be controlled. Developed over a long period, it is now universally adopted: *it is by no means the most convenient method imaginable, but*

the conservatism of musicians will probably prevent its supersession unless some drastic change in the scales used in music makes such a change imperative.

14/18 light, regular, semibold, **bold** and *italics*

portative organ
a fold out, bible-form *regal*
the composer César Franck at a *concert organ*
an elaborate *entertainment organ*
Hammond organ record sleeve
playing the *Hammond organ* manuals
early 1960's *synthesizer*
6½/10 light, *regular italic*

compiled by jaap van triest • dedicated to evert bloemsma
sources: p.a. sholes, *the concise oxford dictionary of music*, oxford university press 1975;
g. hindley (ed.), *larousse encyclopedia of music*, hamlyn publishing group 1971

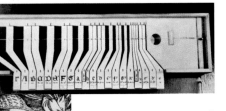

monochord
harpsichord
Hammerklavier
grand piano

20/20 light, regular, **semibold**, **bold**

((((

At first the longer fingerkeys, as we still have them, were all we needed. With the coming into use of the practice of *musica ficta* a B flat was found to be desirable and space for it was made by placing a short finger-key between the A and the B natural (a few keyboards like this still existed as late as the early 17th century). Other finger-keys were similarly added. Our present keyboard of 7 different long and broad keys and 5 short and narrow ones so came into existence.

This still leaves out many notes (e.g. *B sharp*, if required, has to be played as *C*, *F flat* as *E*, and so on). The restricted number of keys which the individual can manipulate, and the necessity of avoiding the high cost of providing a large number of extra organ pipes, strings, &c., precluded the provision of further finger-keys, and the difficulty was overcome by methods of tuning at first, partially, with MEANTONE tuning and then, fully, with EQUAL TEMPERAMENT tuning.

There have been many attempts at the invention of a keyboard which would be free (or largely free) from this principle of compromise, but none of them have proved of value practically in the making of music.

10/13 **bold**, semi-bold, regular, light, *italics* and CAPS

((((

Harpsichord. A stringed keyboard instrument of major importance from the 16th to the 18th centuries. Operation of the keys causes the strings to be plucked (rather than struck as in the modern piano) and it is virtually impossible to achieve gradations of volume by the degree of pressure on the key. When the key is released the jack falls back, a spring-operated escapement preventing the quill from plucking the string on its descent. A damper falls back on the string, stopping its vibrations. Until the 17th century most instruments had one keyboard, and each note had a single string or course of strings tuned to the unison. In later models duplicate sets of jacks and strings, to be selected by moving a hand stop, made it possible to vary the tone quality. In the 18th century, double-manual harpsichords were common, some with pedal boards. Revived in the 20th century, its limited volume, and *loss of the secret of making the sound board* in particular have led some makers to use electrical methods of sound amplification.

7/8½ regular, light, and *italic*

((((

Perforated roll instruments are operated pneumatically b paper rolls in which holes of varying lengths and in due po ition, represent the notes. They date from 1842 and range from small organs, with the roll or cardboard leporello op ted by a handle or by electric power, to the famous *Piano* (patented 1897) and similar instruments of which the mo power is supplied by means of pedals by the operator or l electricity. In one form a master roll is mechanically punc by the playing of some pianist of high repute, and the roll made from it reproduce very exactly his interpretation of music. This form is generally described as *reproducing pia* The same principle has been applied to organs of large si: A spectacular sight is a mechanical keyboard, moving 'all itself' in operation. Some require an operator to add swe pedal effects to the mechanical performance (*cf.* PLEYEL)

9/13 light, regular, semi-bold, **bold**, *italics*, CAPS +50

((((

By means of a special code on a punched tape, a reproducing grand piano exactly duplicates original music performances by Paderewski, Hoffman, Busoni, *and other pianists of world renown. Every nuance of style, touch of the pedal, or other distinctive artistic characteristic is retained, in a physical-acoustic experience. Much in demand between about 1905 and 1935, leading reproducing grand piano makes were* WELTE, AMPICO, DUO-ART, TRIOPHONOLA *and* AEOLIAN *(referring to its pneumatic mechanism). The reign of the reproducing piano was ended by broadcast radio and by competing forms of recorded sound: the gramophone record and the sound film. One of the finest reproducing grand pianos preserved is a* STEINWAY-WELTE *of 1905 in the* Mekanisk Musik Museum *of Copenhagen, Denmark.*

7/9 *regular italic*, *light italic* with ROMAN & *ITALIC* CAPS +50

((((

Piano, grand piano. A stringed instrument in which the strings are vibrated by felt-covered hammers operated from a keyboard. Essentially different from the harpsichord is its ability to produce varying gradations of volume according to the force with which the key is struck. Cristofori (1709) in his ›*gravicembalo col piano e forte*‹ used wooden hammers with leather covered heads, combining the clavichord *struck string* action with harpsichord jacks fitted to form cloth dampers. Attaining a compass of at least six octaves, the ›Hammerklavier‹ was perfected by Silbermann (1740s), Stein (1770) and Erard (1777, 1818). An escapement allows the hammer to fall back when the key is still held down – when it is released a damper falls back on to the string, unless a 'sustaining' pedal is used to hold the dampers off the strings. A 'soft' pedal reduces the travel of the hammers, or shifts them so that they strike fewer of the strings available. The piano has more than one string to each note, except on the very lowest notes. From the early 18th century, the pianoforte takes the position of the harpsichord. By the 1770s, C.P.E. Bach, Haydn and other major composers are writing for it. Nearly all of Mozart's keyboard music is written for the piano. Beethoven rapidly adopted it. Their first quiet pianofortes retain the harpsichord shape, or that of a ›square piano‹. The iron frame, invented in 1825, allows heavier stringing and by the 1840s the ›concert grand‹ has become a fully mature solo concert instrument, praised by Liszt. A much smaller ›upright‹ piano starts its conquest as a domestic intrument in 1811. During the 19th century it serves, to some extent, the function of the gramophone and radio.

7½/9 **semi-bold**, regular, and *italic*

the 22-key *monochord*
a *portable* keyboard instrument
First Musicke Printed for the Virginalls, 1611
harpsichord, 1571
spinet and *harpsichord* in one case
J.S. Bach's *Silbermann-klavier*: '*legato*-Spiel'
a modern *grand piano* (Robert Casadesus).

Legato, **legando**, *legabile* (It.), 'Bound', 'binding', 'in a binding fashion', i.e. performed with a smooth connexion between the notes (opposite of *Staccato*). *Legatissimo* is the superlative.

9/10 **bold**, semi-bold & *italic*

FFLegato
FFLegato
FFLegato
FFLegato

typeface by evert bloemsma

Rosenberg 'typographic keyboard', 1842.

Tschulik's 'Lettern Setzmaschine', 1846.

Sørensen's successful use of nicked type: 35 years ahead of Linotype's nicked matrice.

•• The Koenig cylinder press of 1811 and Hoe's rotary press, 1860, urge hand typesetting to mechanize. Some 200 inventors for a century work on this problem: could an *apparatus* replace the fingers of a skilled compositor in setting pieces of lead type in the order required?
The earliest idea is simply to place founder's type in channels and by the use of keys release them in the right order to reach a central point by gravity. This still involves distribution (the time-consuming sorting of type after use) and hand justification.

founder's type

•• In 1822, **Church** arranges type in inclined channels mounted in a wooden frame. By the operation of a keyboard the type is ejected onto a horizontal plate, where rocking arms sweep it to the centre to be devided up and line justified by hand. Type-setting takes place at such pace that the immediate recording of speech by a keyboard-operator is considered. It is Church who suggests to *cast type as required*, to eliminate the process of distributing type after printing. Sixty years later, this idea solves the problem – for the letterpress era.

In 1840, Young & Delcambre patent a first commercially adopted machine, the **Pianotyp**. Respective pieces of type are in long narrow boxes, and a touch of a key (like those of a piano-forte) detaches the type required on an inclined plane. A second mech-anism devides the letters into lines, building up a column of type matter. Seven operators are needed: one for typing, one for justification, two to fill the cases, two for the separate distribution of used type, and one for traction. A later version demands a crew of only three.

Sørensen before 1851 invents the **Tacheotyp**, a key-operated machine which composes and distributes simultaneously by two cylinders, one above the other. The upper rotates and carries used type: type *nicks* correspond with the channel entran-ces of the lower composing cylinder. Admired in Crystal Palace, 1851 and praised at the 1855 Paris world fair, it sets 50.000 characters per day, but every attempt at selling the machine to a conservative printing trade fails. Decades later, its qualities reappear in the **Thorne** typesetter of 1884.

Mergenthaler at the Linotype keyboard, 1886. Nicked matrices automatically return to their magazines. One linecaster replaces 5 hand compositors.

Monotype: the punched spool and the justification dial serve as a 'monitor' for the keyboard operator.

linotype

•• In search of a typesetting method for lithography, Mergenthaler is intro-duced to the problem of composing characters. Stereotyping inspires 'impression' trials: dies pressed into soft material. It leads to mechanized *setting with matrices instead of type*, the **Linotype** linecasting machine of 1885. Operated from a keyboard, selected type matrices and spaces form a mould for a *whole line* of letter-press type, to be cast within seconds. Justification is by wedge spaces. The nicked matrices automatically return to their 90 channels.

In 1886 a first 'line o'type' produces *New York Tribune* news columns — a year later they have 14 machines in operation. 'The slug as the unit of composition in stead of single types' simplifies handling & page make-up. No falling apart, no damaged type, and no time-consuming distribution: used slugs go into the melting-pot. Around 1900, a two-letter matrice, multiple magazine Linotype offers the equivalent of several type cases, and a *single operator* can compose complex advertisements and fine lay-outs with different sizes and

typefaces 'without getting up from the keyboard' Most economical, the machine will *compose, cast, justify,* and make distribution obsolete. One linecaster can do the work of *5 hand compositors*. The keyboard-operator is advised to 'think as little as possible' operating the machine: complex setting, questions of layout, corrections (retyping of entire lines) slow down production. This makes slug casting machines most suitable for the production of newspaper columns and other less demanding typesetting jobs.

monotype

•• The **Monotype** single-type setting and casting machine, patented by Lanston in 1887, is quite different. The keyboard, a paper ribbon perfo-rator operated by compressed air, is separate of the casting apparatus. Punched paper, collected from one or several keyboard operators, is fed into the caster, which composes individually cast single type mechan-ically placed in a galley, allowing for correction as in hand setting. It will also produce founts of type for the case, borders and spaces. In 1897, a first production model is on sale.

Phototype patent 1899: key-stroke moves trans-parent type-forms in front of a lense.

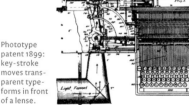

Control panels evolve into 'video screen' copy editing, photosetting and layout 'simulation' – fully digital page make-up, text and image integrated.

photo type

•• As early as 1867, Alisoff uses trans-parent sheets printed with musical symbols, cut and pasted in position for photograpic platemaking.
In 1896, Porzsolt patents a single alphabet machine utilising keybars bearing characters, to be illuminated and exposed on a sensitized plate. Friese-Greene, 1898, photographs an assembled line of type, and in 1925 Smothers places type negatives in the matrices of a slug caster. Following this principle, a *photo-typesetter* of 1936 has 114 keys, 4 magazines and 8 lenses, producing 32 type sizes.

In 1941, Zuse builds a fully *program-mable digital computer*. In 1944, Higonnet introduces *stroboscopic exposure* of a revolving type negative disc and provides some ›electronic memory‹ to set and correct prior to film exposure. His design leads to the **Photon-Lumitype** phototypesetter of the 1950s: punched tape instructs a spinning type disc for electronic flash tube *exposure on paper or film* in sizes of 5-72 points, using lenses. In 1946 the **Intertype Fotosetter**, an adapted slug casting machine, is the first reliable photosetting device.

The **Linofilm System** of 1954 works with a special 44-key electric type-writer, an electronic computer, a tape perforator, and control panels to select typeface, size, line measure and advance, justification and letter-spacing. The keyboard operator can directly set from 18 founts of 88 characters each in 6 sizes, punching 15-hole tape for the *Photographic Unit*. 'Working on artificial satellites, scientists were faced with an enor-mous quantity of essential data, spewing out of the teleprinters in such volume and quantity and so illegible and hard to handle that the Linotype Company came to the researchers' help by constructing the Linofilm machine to transcribe computer data into ordinary type.'

digital type

•• Mid 1960s computers will answer keyboard commands. The new *video terminals* display 128 characters and elementary graphics by electron rays. 1965 Hell **Digiset** crt typesetter. 1967 Berthold **Diatronic** keyboard-controlled phototypesetter. 1968 **Compugraphic** photosetter. 1968 'video display' *copy editing*. Photo type matter is cut and pasted in position for offset platemaking. 1970 Engelbart x-y indicator or *mouse* control. Xerox prototype **'personal' computer**, Alto. Display is by memory stored picture elements or 'pixels'.

'Cembalo scrivano' typewriter, 1858.

Fraser's machine of 1872 follows both Church and Hattersley.

Mackie's ideas, separation of keyboard and composition and the use of punched ribbon, will reappear in the Monotype.

The first practical typewriter, 1873, has only capitals. Shift-key and lower case follow in 1878: origin of a qwerty-keyboard of 40 keys representing 80 characters.

In 1857 Hattersley uses a compact 'type-writer' keyboard to compose type into a short line immediately accessible to the compositor who can readily space out the matter to the requisite length. Founder's type is held in tubes, refilled by means of a distribution mechanism. Hardly any

faster than hand setting, it leads to the pedal-driven **Kastenbein** of 1869, a relative success with a keyboard of 84 keys arranged in four rows. 'Sorting machines' of this kind are in use for over 30 years. A contemporary salesman admits that many of them are 'que des machines théoriques'.

coded copy::

In his **Steam Type Compositor**, 1867, Mackie applies the Jacquard system – a coded instruction, used in weaving. The separate *perforator* is like a small pianoforte (a telegraph) keyboard of 14 keys, most of them marked with 2 characters. Key-stroke perforates a paper ribbon on a drum which moves

after every perforation. Typists (often women and children) take a keyboard home to punch handwritten copy. In a steam-operated *type composing machine*, punched ribbon activates the mechanical selection of founder's type. Justification is by hand, refilling of the type boxes by use of the ribbon.

Kastenbein keyboard, 1869.

1885–2005 1885–2005 1885–2005

In 1899 the 225-character keyboard and corresponding casting mould are available. The vast keyboard has keys for up to *seven* alphabets (roman and small capitals, and lower case; italic capitals and lower case; bold capitals and lower case) plus a complete range of figures, ligatures, punctuation marks, space and justification keys. Its operator punches the copy, adding calculated justification commands using a type unit system. In the caster the paper ribbon is backwards so that each line is headed by its individual justification command.

A double-spool keyboard is used for parallel editions, tabular and complex book work (footnotes, different faces and sizes). In 1926 an observer notes: 'The monotypists, the girls operating the keyboard of the Monotype typesetting machine, are working in a separate department for an undisturbed performance of their duty, which demands great accuracy. It can easily be understood that these swift hands will have to deliver many perforated spools to keep the raging casting machines of the apparatus permanently occupied.'

In the 1970s, eighty years after its invention, the established Monotype machine offers 275-character sets of high quality type designs – and casts the finest letterpress type available. With a skilled keyboard-operator, the caster can produce almost *complete pages*, building up in the galley letter by letter, from the bottom line up. Mourned by book people, its reign as a *grand piano of fine typography* ends with the rise of photosetting and offset printing.

teletype::

After 1928, and more regularly from the 1950s, slug casting machines can also be operated by *perforated paper ribbon*, separating copy input from the actual casting (as Monotype had done from its start). **Teletypesetting** thus changes Linotype and Intertype machines into automated tape-driven slug casters, with *idle* keyboards. Coded copy is received by telegraph or from specialized punch typists, now responsible for copy entry and corrections.

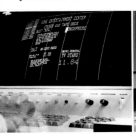

In 1971 **digital outline typesetting** systems appear. Vector outlines, computer calculated and completed, simplify storage, output and design. 1971 **Imlac c15** photosetter improves screen display, using vector outlines. 1974 Karow presents **Ikarus** vector outline type design software. Mid 1970's newspapers start using 'video display' for *page make-up*. 1981 Author Enzensberger criticizes **phototypesetting**. During exposure, development or re-reproduction for offset printing, type looses sharpness and corrections will show.

1981 Xerox's **Star computer work-station**, incorporating a *keyboard*, a graphical user interface of *icons*, *menus* and *mouse control*, vector out-line fonts and 'wysiwig' display screen launches desktop publishing (named after its user interface metaphor). Less advanced, IBM's 1981 **personal computer** will replace office type-writers and calculators world wide. In the **Aesthedes** graphics computer, 1982, all operating, colour and style menus and a flat qwerty-keyboard are touch-keys in a vast control desk; six monitors, but limited display.

Berthold's 1984 filmsetter combines on screen editing and layout with traditional fixed-negative exposure: a matrix of 128 produces an entire text layout on film at 27,7 characters per second, in sizes up to 60 points. The **Apple Macintosh** desktop com-puter, introduced in 1984, applies a graphic user interface, mouse and vector outline fonts, using *PostScript* graphic description language. Display equals output: new *laser prints* or high resolution **Linotron** laser filmsetting of text *as well as* raster image proces-sed halftone and line images.

Within a decade, desktop computers are in general use. Phototypesetter manufacturers and typesetting firms close down, and new names emerge.* *Digital font design*, *layout* and *imaging* software make the desktop revolution complete, just before the Internet. *Type design* regains freedom and gains exactitude. *Graphic design* flourishes, taking on the compositor's craft. **Typographer**, imagine a keyboard *as large as your character set*.

7,2/9 **bold**, regular, *italic* +4
* fontshop international digital fonts since 1990.
sources: j. moran, *the composition of reading matter*, 1965; l.w. wallis, *a concise chronology of typesetting developments 1886-1986*, 1988; jaap van triest, *regelzetters en monotypisten*, *loodvrij en digitaal*, 2001
compiled by jaap van triest • dedicated to evert bloemsma

Il Pleut (1918, Guillaume Apollinaire)

Il pleut des voix de femmes comme si elles étaient mortes même dans le souvenir

c'est vous aussi qu'il pleut merveilleuses rencontres de ma vie ô gouttelettes

et ces nuages cabrés se prennent à hennir tout un univers de villes auriculaires

écoute s'il pleut tandis que le regret et le dédain pleurent une ancienne musique

écoute tomber les liens qui te retiennent en haut et en bas

(Xavier Dupré)

FF Parango

ABCDEFGHIJKLMNOPQRSTUVWXYZÇÉÖ
abcdefghijklmnopqrstuvwxyzßfiflçéö
1234567890 ?.;,""'"$%‰&*#fj¿¤

ABCDEFGHIJKLMNOPQRSTUVWXYZÇÉÖ
abcdefghijklmnopqrstuvwxyzßfiflçéö
1234567890 ?.;,""'"$%‰&#fj¿¤*

ABCDEFGHIJKLMNOPQRSTUVWXYZÇÉÖ
ABCDEFGHIJKLMNOPQRSTUVWXYZSSFIFLÇÉÖ
1234567890 ?.;,""'"$%‰&*#fj¿¤

ABCDEFGHIJKLMNOPQRSTUVWXYZÇÉÖ
abcdefghijklmnopqrstuvwxyzßfiflçéö
1234567890 ?.;,""'"$%‰&*#fj¿¤

SMALL CAPS REGULAR, ITALIC, SMALL CAPS, BOLD + EXPERTS

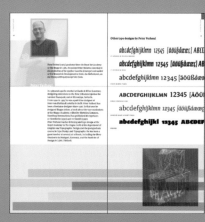

FF Sheriff in practice

het voltooien van zijr

ontwerpen. Aan de zu

lopende *Sheriff* begor

in 1989, maar pas in 1

kon deze egyptienne

FontShop uitgebrach

worden. Het meest op

lende vormkenmerk

dat de bogen recht

– zonder insnijding –

de stokken verbonder

Eerder verscheen bij

FontShop Verheuls ov

vallende script *Newbe*

pqrstuvwxyz
MNOPQRSTUVWXYZ
rstuvwxyz
MNOPQRSTUVWXYZ
pqrstuvwxyz
MNOPQRSTUVWXYZ
PQRSTUVWXYZ
67890

FF Sheriff

FF Sheriff is a sturdy, economical text typeface with crisp shapes. Its low contrast and relatively large x-height enable it to function excellently in small to very small type sizes. Its unusual details also make it suitable for use as a display type. The face was designed by Peter Verheul, a type designer and typographer in The Hague.

Sheriff characteristics

8 / 10,5 pt

FF SHERIFF is a sturdy, economical typeface with a clear form. Its low contrast and relatively large x-height enable it to function excellently in small to very small type sizes. Its unusual details also make it suitable for use as a **display type**. The face was designed by Peter Verheul, a type designer and typographer in The Hague. When designing printed and electronic publications, Verheul's aim from the very beginning was to use custom-designed typographic material – including typefaces. As a type designer of the *Hague School*, his basic principle is that printing is a form of writing. In the words of his tutor Gerrit Noordzij, 'typography is writing with prefabricated letters'. In other words, the printed letter was not born alongside, but out of, handwriting.

FF SHERIFF demonstrates that this view does not necessarily have to lead to classical characters with calligraphic undertones. Verheul's first published book face is an unprecedented design: one cannot point to a single existing face with the same characteristics. *Sheriff* is a somewhat stiff Egyptian or slab serif face, which means it has heavy, rectangular serifs. This also explains the name: *sheriff* is simply a personal corruption of *serif*. Starting from a single character – the lowercase 'n' – Verheul designed an alphabet with striking features derived from two basic shapes: the oval and the rectangle. This led to unusual details, such

9 / 11,5 pt

as the characteristic curve in the elongation of the top serif. In small type sizes the letter reads like a train – the unusual shapes are no distraction at all. But it does create a lively image that holds the attention.

In the eighties, when the first versions of Sheriff were designed, digital faces designed on and for the personal computer were a **novelty**. Young type designers had animated discussions on the demands the medium made on this sort of face. Many of the *revivals* by the major type foundries showed how not to do it. Digital versions of the great classics were too often a reproduction of existing large-format working drawings for photosetting – with the result that because the characters were so finely formed, they were not up to the job in an average size of 8 to 10 points. All that remained was a poor copy of the original letter which in some cases was barely legible. Like other examples such as Peter Matthias Noordzij's Caecilia, Gerard Unger's Oranda and Fred Smeijers' FF QUADRAAT, FF SHERIFF belongs to a new generation of type designs which take the

10 / 12,5 pt

qualities of digital design as their guiding principle. Printing techniques play a part too. The impact of metal letters on paper in letterpress printing produced a powerful **black impression**, whereas offset printing requires type which by nature already possesses this solidity and blackness. By keeping these demands in mind from the very beginning, Peter Verheul has created a typeface that, while unconventional, proves its practical utility under the most extreme conditions. It was a deliberate choice not to call the italicised version of FF SHERIFF *italic*, but *Italian*. The construction of a face actually determines whether it is a proper italic or not. This is the case when it is a continuous script with upstrokes. Oblique Roman types are often, but incorrectly, called italic. In the way the curve emerges from the serif, the Italian version of Sheriff has same characteristics as the Roman, which means it can never be a true italic. This increases the

11 / 13,5 pt

legibility of the *italic* in longer texts. At the same time, Sheriff Italian is relatively narrow and is therefore exceptionally economical. The proportions of capitals are so well attuned to each other that they give an optimal appearance to each word.

FF SHERIFF is a complete family suited to complex typographical jobs. SMALL CAPITALS are available in all weights: *roman, italian, bold, bold italian*. The figures in each weight are the same width. Figures for tables, the height of small capitals, can be found in the caps fonts.

Peter Verheul (1965) graduated from the Royal Art Academy in The Hague in 1989. He assisted Peter Matthias Noordzij in the production of the typeface Caecilia (Linotype) and worked at Océ Research & Development in Venlo, the Netherlands, on the

12 / 13,5 pt

bitmap editing of laserprinter fonts. In 1989 and 1990 he worked at Banks & Miles (London), designing extensions to the New Johnston typeface for London Transport, and at **Monotype**, Salfords. From 1991 to 1995 he was a part-time designer at Peter van Blokland's studio in Delft. Peter Verheul has been a freelance designer since 1996. In that year he designed Haagse letters, a book about the type curriculum at the Hague Academy, edited by Matthieu Lommen. FontShop International has published his typefaces FF NEWBERLIN (1991) and FF SHERIFF (1996). Peter Verheul teaches lettering and type design at the Royal Academy in The Hague, both at the department of Graphic and Typographic

13 / 14,5 pt

Design and the postgraduate course in Type Design and Typography. He has been a guest teacher at several art schools, including the Merz Akademie in Stuttgart, Germany, and the Institute of Design in Lahti, Finland.

FF SHERIFF is a sturdy, economical text typeface with a clear form. Its low contrast and relatively large x-height enable it to function excellently in small to very small type sizes. Its unusual details also make it suitable for use as a **display type**.

Quasi
210 pt

runner
172 pt

frequent
140 pt

florentine
120 pt

instrumentation
72 pt

scientific education
60 pt

mathematical icebreaker
48 pt

Sheriff, Type Specimen Roman, ROMAN CAPS, *Italian*,
ITALIAN CAPS, **Bold**, **BOLD CAPS**, *Italian bold AND BOLD CAPS*
24 pt
21 pt

FF Sheriff is a complete family suited to complex typographical jobs. small capitals are available in all weights: roman, italian, bold, bold italian. the figures in each weight are the same width. figures for tables, the height of small capitals, can be found in the caps fonts. Peter Verheul (1965) graduated from the Royal Art Academy in The Hague in 1989. He assisted Peter

Matthias Noordzij in the production of the typeface Caecilia (linotype) and worked at Océ Research & Development in venlo, the netherlands, on the bitmap editing of laserprinter fonts. in 1989 and 1990 he worked at Banks & Miles (london), designing extensions to the new Johnston typeface for London Transport, and at Monotype, Salfords. From 1991 to 1995 he was a part-time designer at Peter

van Blokland's studio in Delft. Peter Verheul has been a freelance designer since 1996. In that year he designed Haagse letters, a book about the type curriculum at the Hague Academy, edited by Matthieu Lommen. FontShop International has published his typefaces ff NewBerlin (1991) and ff Sheriff (1996). Peter Verheul teaches lettering and type design at the

Royal Academy in The Hague, both at the department of Graphic and Typographic design and the postgraduate course in Type Design and typography. he has been a guest teacher at several art schools, including the Merz Akademie in Stuttgart, Germany, and the institute of de

FF SHERIFF ROMAN ABCDEFGHIJKLMNOPQRSTUVWXYZ 1234567890abcdefghijklmnopqrstuvwxyz1234567890ÆŒ æœ&ßfifl~.,.:;?!¿¡...(/)[\]{|}""„"','‹›«»*†‡°'"'ªº§¶@®©™%‰$¢ £¥ƒ+#± <=>·÷/•ÅÇÉÑ ÒØÜáàäâãåçø¬

FF SHERIFF ITALIAN *ABCDEFGHIJKLMNOPQRSTUVWXYZ 1234567890abcdefghijklmnopqrstuvwxyz1234567890ÆŒæœ &ßfifl~.,.:;?!¿¡...(/)[\]{|}""„"','‹›«»*†‡°'"'ªº§¶@®©™%‰$¢£¥ƒ+#± <=>·÷/•ÅÇÉÑ ÒØÜáàäâãåçø¬*

FF SHERIFF BOLD **ABCDEFGHIJKLMNOPQRSTUVWXYZ 1234567890abcdefghijklmnopqrstuvwxyz1234567890Æ Œæœ&ßfifl~.,.:;?!¿¡...(/)[\]{|}""„"','‹›«»*†‡°'"'ªº§¶@®©™% ‰$¢£¥ƒ+#± <=>·÷/•ÅÇÉÑ ÒØÜáàäâãåçø¬**

FF SHERIFF BOLD ITALIAN ***ABCDEFGHIJKLMNOPQRSTUV WXYZ1234567890abcdefghijklmnopqrstuvwxyz123456789 0ÆŒæœ&ßfifl~.,.:;?!¿¡...(/)[\]{|}""„"','‹›«»*†‡°'"'ªº§¶@®©™% ‰$¢£¥ƒ+#± <=>·÷/•ÅÇÉÑ ÒØÜáàäâãåçø¬***

FF SHERIFF ROMAN CAPS ABCDEFGHIJKLMNOPQRSTUV WXYZ1234567890ABCDEFGHIJKLMNOPQRSTUVWXYZ123456 7890ÆŒÆŒ&SSFIFL~.,.:;?!¿¡...(/)[\]{|}""„"','‹›«»*†‡°'"'ªº§¶@® ©™%‰$¢£¥ƒ+#2 <=>·÷/•ÅÇÉÑ ÒØÜÁÀÄÂÃÅÇØ0

FF SHERIFF ITALIAN CAPS *ABCDEFGHIJKLMNOPQRSTUV WXYZ1234567890ABCDEFGHIJKLMNOPQRSTUVWXYZ12345678 90ÆŒÆŒ&SSFIFL~.,.:;?!¿¡...(/)[\]{|}""„"','‹›«»*†‡°'"'ªº§¶@®©™% ‰$¢£¥ƒ+#2 <=>·÷/•ÅÇÉÑ ÒØÜÁÀÄÂÃÅÇØ0*

FF SHERIFF BOLD CAPS **ABCDEFGHIJKLMNOPQRSTUV WXYZ1234567890ABCDEFGHIJKLMNOPQRSTUVWXYZ123 4567890ÆŒÆŒ&SSFIFL~.,.:;?!¿¡...(/)[\]{|}""„"','‹›«»*†‡°'"'ªº§ ¶@®©™%‰$¢£¥ƒ+#2 <=>·÷/•ÅÇÉÑ ÒØÜÁÀÄÂÃÅÇØ0**

FF SHERIFF BOLD ITALIAN CAPS ***ABCDEFGHIJKLMNOPQR-STUVWXYZ1234567890ABCDEFGHIJKLMNOPQRSTUVWXYZ1 234567890ÆŒÆŒ&SSFIFL~.,.:;?!¿¡...(/)[\]{|}""„"','‹›«»*†‡°'"'ªº§ ¶@®©™%‰$¢£¥ƒ+#2 <=>·÷/•ÅÇÉÑ ÒØÜÁÀÄÂÃÅÇØ0***

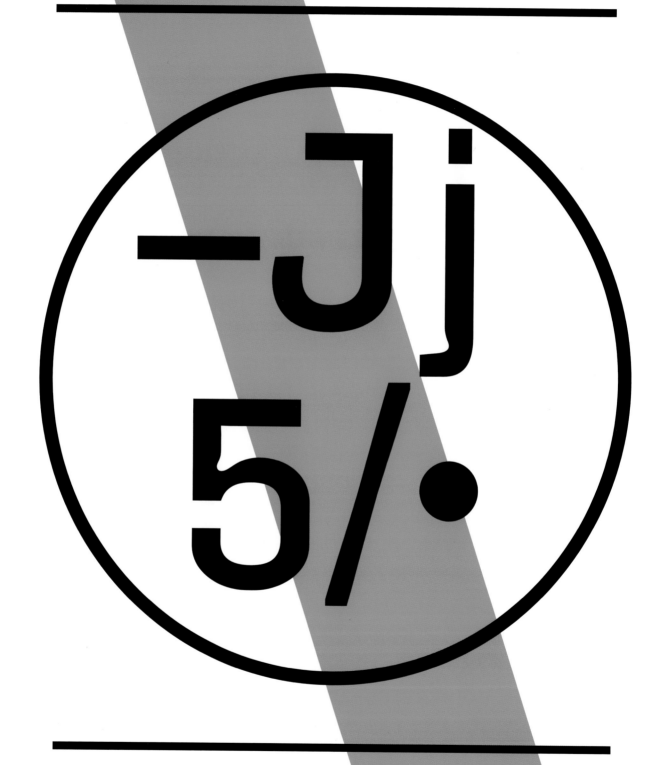

FF Hydra by Silvio Napoleone ✎Vincent van Baar, StudioDumbar

HYDRA TEXT-LIGHT	HYDRA TEXT-REGULAR	HYDRA TEXT-BOLD	HYDRA TEXT-BLACK	HYDRA EXT-BOOK	HYDRA EXT-MEDIUM	HYDRA EXT-BOLD	HYDRA-BOOK	HYDRA-MEDIUM	HYDRA-BOLD
Aa	Aa	Aa	Aa	Aa	Aa	Aa	Aa	Aa	Aa
Bb	Bb	Bb	Bb	Bb	Bb	Bb	Bb	Bb	Bb
Cc	Cc	Cc	Cc	Cc	Cc	Cc	Cc	Cc	Cc
Dd	Dd	Dd	Dd	Dd	Dd	Dd	Dd	Dd	Dd
Ee	Ee	Ee	Ee	Ee	Ee	Ee	Ee	Ee	Ee
Ff	Ff	Ff	Ff	Ff	Ff	Ff	Ff	Ff	Ff
Gg	Gg	Gg	Gg	Gg	Gg	Gg	Gg	Gg	Gg
Hh	Hh	Hh	Hh	Hh	Hh	Hh	Hh	Hh	Hh
Ii	Ii	Ii	Ii	Ii	Ii	Ii	Ii	Ii	Ii
Jj	Jj	Jj	Jj	Jj	Jj	Jj	Jj	Jj	Jj
Kk	Kk	Kk	Kk	Kk	Kk	Kk	Kk	Kk	Kk
Ll	Ll	Ll	Ll	Ll	Ll	Ll	Ll	Ll	Ll
Mm	Mm	Mm	Mm	Mm	Mm	Mm	Mm	Mm	Mm
Nn	Nn	Nn	Nn	Nn	Nn	Nn	Nn	Nn	Nn
Oo	Oo	Oo	Oo	Oo	Oo	Oo	Oo	Oo	Oo
Pp	Pp	Pp	Pp	Pp	Pp	Pp	Pp	Pp	Pp
Qq	Qq	Qq	Qq	Qq	Qq	Qq	Qq	Qq	Qq
Rr	Rr	Rr	Rr	Rr	Rr	Rr	Rr	Rr	Rr
Ss	Ss	Ss	Ss	Ss	Ss	Ss	Ss	Ss	Ss
Tt	Tt	Tt	Tt	Tt	Tt	Tt	Tt	Tt	Tt
Uu	Uu	Uu	Uu	Uu	Uu	Uu	Uu	Uu	Uu
Vv	Vv	Vv	Vv	Vv	Vv	Vv	Vv	Vv	Vv
Ww	Ww	Ww	Ww	Ww	Ww	Ww	Ww	Ww	Ww
Xx	Xx	Xx	Xx	Xx	Xx	Xx	Xx	Xx	Xx
Yy	Yy	Yy	Yy	Yy	Yy	Yy	Yy	Yy	Yy
Zz	Zz	Zz	Zz	Zz	Zz	Zz	Zz	Zz	Zz
123	123	123	123	123	123	123	123	123	123
456	456	456	456	456	456	456	456	456	456
789	789	789	789	789	789	789	789	789	789

[1] It is obvious that ultimate cutter life can only been achieved through proper usage and maintenance of the tool. These tools are manifactured with the faces of the teeth either in radial or undercut plane, spirally or straight gashed, and must be sharpened accordingly. Any deviation produces taper on the O.D. of cutter and inaccurate threads. It is also important to resharpen thread cutters at regular intervals to avoid excessive dulling which could result in cutter failure and damage to the work.

[2] Nos accessoires pour montage de tuyuateries ont été développés à l'aide des expériences faites dans la pratique et sont considérés partout comme un grand progrès dans l'outil-lage pour le montage de tuyauteries. Ils garantissent, en effet, l'exécution de filets impeccables, une éten-chéité parfaite et un meilleur rendement, tout en facilitant le travail du monteur.

Random text fragments from Catalogs of Industry & Trade from the collection Van Baar, The Hague. Titles & Companies: see page bottom.

Die Spannkloben können umgedreht werden.

[3] Unsere Planscheiben sind besonders kräftig, sie haben aus Stahl geschmiedete und gehärtete Spannkloben, die voneinander unabhängig durch Stahlbindeln bewegt werden und bei No. 1a–5a und 1n–4n sich gegen die Scheibe festklemmen lassen. Die Spannkloben können umgedreht werden. Wir halten Planscheiben mit glatter Bohrung auf Lager, so daß sie auf jeder beliebigen Drehbank oder anderen Werkzeugmaschine verwendet werden können. Es kann auch das Gewinde für die genormten Spindelköpfe eingeschnitten werden. Es empfiehlt sich, das in Frage kommende Spindelgewinde in den Planscheibenkörper selbst einzuschneiden, damit dieser möglichst nahe am Spindellager sitzt.

[4] Depuis 1918, le progrès technique en sidérurgie ne s'est manifesté par aucun procedé fondamental nouveau, mais bien par le perfectionnement des procédés et d'outillage existant et par le récupération toujours plus poussée des sous-produits. Ainsi, le nombre de hauts fourneaux en ordre de marche ou en activité a baissé, mais cette diminution fut compensée par une augmentation de la capacité de production des haut fourneaux.

[5] Wij hebben het genoegen U hierbij te overhandigen den eersten Nederlandschen catalogus der TERRY-producten, welke wij met stijgend succes sedert verscheidenen jaren importeren. De groote en steeds uitbreidende vraag naar onze artikelen heeft ons doen besluiten een catalogus in het Hollandsch te doen verschijnen, omdat het begrijpen van catalogi in een vreemde taal, hoe prachtig ook uitgevoerd, voor velen eigenaardige bezwaren oplevert.

Wij hopen, dat wij door aanbieding van deze catalogus wederom een stap nader mogen komen tot het doel, n.l.: het brengen van de uitgebreide series TERRY-artikelen in handen der Nederlandsche verbruikers.

Van deze gelegenheid maken wij gebruik Uw aandacht te vestigen op het feit, dat wij, naast de TERRY-producten, voor Nederland en Koloniën de alleenvertegenwoordiging voeren van

BENTON & STONE LTD., BIRMINGHAM

fabrikanten van ENOTS grease guns, verfspuiten, oliespuiten, hydraulische crics, parfum-spuiten, benzinekranen, oliekranen, luchtpompen, enz. enz.

ABINGDON WORKS LTD., BIRMINGHAM

fabrikanten der beroemde KING DICK schroefsleutels, dopsleutels, enz. enz.

POWEL & HANMER LTD., BIRMINGHAM

fabrikanten van rijwiel-, motor-, en automobiellampen, hoorns, spiegels, klaxons, ruitenwisschers, mistlampen, richtingwijzers, enz. enz. enz.

TAN SAD CHAIR Co. LTD., LONDON

fabrikanten van kantoor- en werkplaats-stoelen, zooals o.a. geleverd aan Postcheque- en Girodienst, Amsterdamsche Bank en vele andere groote instellingen.

Voor al deze artikelen houden wij ons beleefd aanbevolen tot het doen eener aanbieding onder toezending van prijslijsten en modellen.

[6] Zur gefl. Beachtung: Die Garnituren No. 140, 150, 160, 170, 180, 190 und 200 enthalten ausslißlich Werkzeuge von ausgesuchter, einwandfreier Bearbeitung und Qualität. Die Laubsägbogen, Drillbohrer, Hämmer usw. sind fein vernickelt, (bei Nos. 190 und 200 hochfein poliert), die Holzhefte hochfein poliert. Bei der Auswahl der Werkzeuge wurde besonder wert darauf gelegt, daß nur wirklich erstklassige, für den Laubsäger praktische Werkzeuge Verwendung fanden.

[7] Gearing Rack - A simple traversing motion which, by the use of standard chain, pinion, and end attachments eliminates costly gear and rack cutting. A wide variety of chain and wheel sizes is available, also end attachments for all methods of mounting. For example, using 0.75 in. pitch chain and a pinion of 19 teeth, one revolution of the pinion will produce a traverse of 14.25 inches.

[1]	[2]	[3]	[4]	[5]	[6]	[7]
GO & GO CO	+GF+	Loewe Werkzeuge	Talabot	Herbert Terry &	Blosta	Renold
Goddard & Goddard	Geoges Fischer	Ludw. Loewe & Co	S.A. des Hauts Fourneaux	Sons Ltd.	Carl Blombach	Renold Chains
Company Detroit	Société Anonyme	Actiengesellschaft	Forges et Aciéries	Redditch (U.K.)	Wuppertal (D)	Limited
(Mich. USA)	Schaffhouse (CH)	Berlin (D)	du Saut-du-Tarn	(Dutch catalog)	1932.	Manchester (U.K.)
1959	1952	1929	(F) 1935	1929		1955

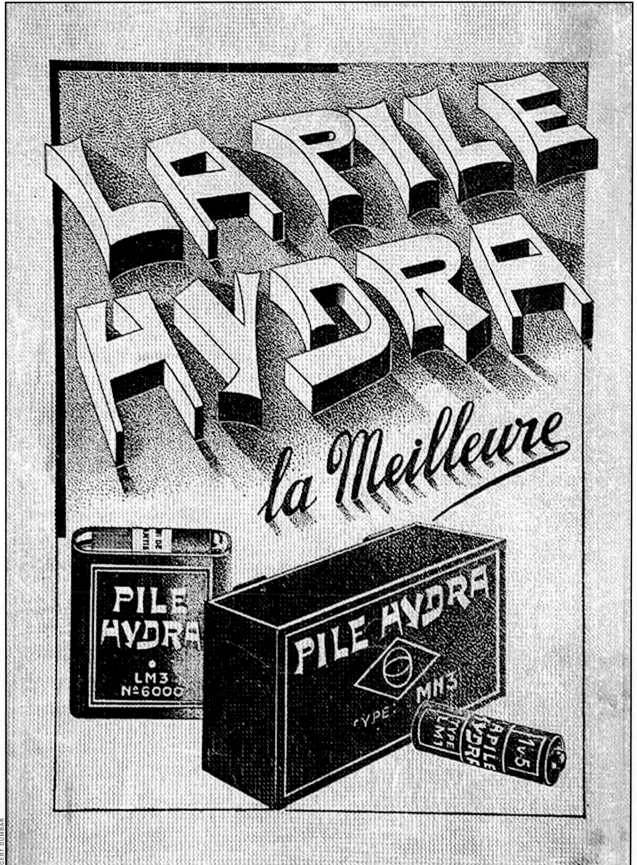

COLL. GERT DUMBAR

DECIMAL EQUIVALENTS

Fraction	Decimal
1/64	.015625
1/32	.03125
3/64	.046875
1/16	.0625
5/64	.078125
3/32	.09375
7/64	.109375
1/8	.125
9/64	.140625
5/32	.15625
11/64	.171875
3/16	.1875
13/64	.203125
7/32	.21875
15/64	.234375
1/4	.25
17/64	.265625
9/32	.28125
19/64	.296875
5/16	.3125
21/64	.328125
11/32	.34375
23/64	.359375
3/8	.375
25/64	.390625
13/32	.40625
27/64	.421875
7/16	.4375
29/64	.453125
15/32	.46875
31/64	.484375
1/2	.5
33/64	.515625
17/32	.53125
35/64	.546875
9/16	.5625
37/64	.578125
19/32	.59375
39/64	.609375
5/8	.625
41/64	.640625
21/32	.65625
43/64	.671875
11/16	.6875
45/64	.703125
23/32	.71875
47/64	.734375
3/4	.75
49/64	.765625
25/32	.78125
51/64	.796875
13/16	.8125
53/64	.828125
27/32	.84375
55/64	.859375
7/8	.875
57/64	.890625
29/32	.90625
59/64	.921875
15/16	.9375
61/64	.953125
31/32	.96875
63/64	.984375
1/1	1.

TO THE TRADE WE PRESENT THIS CATALOG WITH HOPE IT WILL BE OF REAL SERVICE TO YOU. ON ITS PAGES WE HAVE ENDEAVORED TO SET FORTH HELPFUL DATA ON A GREAT VARIETY OF TOOLS AND SUPPLIES USED GENERALLY BY ALL INDUSTRY. OUR WAREHOUSE, AS WELL AS OUR SOURCES OF SUPPLY ARE AMPLY STOCKED SO THAT WE ARE ABLE TO MAKE IMMEDIATE DELIVERY OF ALMOST ANYTHING YOU NEED. IT WOULD BE OUR PLEASURE TO SHOW YOU THROUGH OUR WAREHOUSE ANYTIME SO THAT YOU MAY SEE JUST WHAT FACILITIES WE HAVE FOR SERVING YOU. OCCASIONALLY YOU MAY HAVE NEED FOR AN ITEM NOT SHOWN IN THIS CATALOG. WHEN YOU DO, JUST LET US KNOW AND WE WILL GLADLY SEND SPECIAL CATALOGS. ALL INQUIRIES AND ORDERS FOR MATERIAL, WHETHER SHOWN IN THIS CATALOG OR NOT, WILL RECEIVE OUR BEST ATTENTION. **STERLING SUPPLY CO.** DETROIT 1948

Q

2g

Anc

abcdefghijklm
ABCDEFGHIJ
1234567890...12

{ Light | LIGHT SC | *Light italic* | *LIGHT ITALIC SC* } + Expert
{ Regular | REGULAR SC | *Regular italic* | *REGULAR ITALIC SC* } + Expert

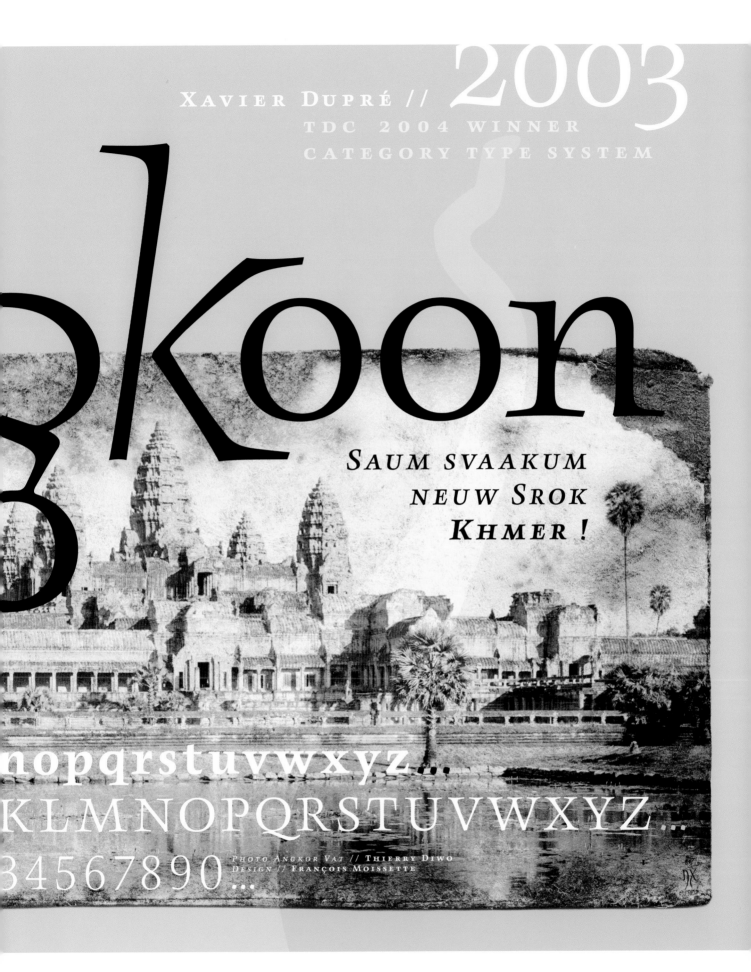

gkoon

SAUM SVAAKUM
NEUW SROK
KHMER !

nopqrstuvwxyz...

KLMNOPQRSTUVWXYZ...

34567890...

PHOTO ANGKOR VAT // THIERRY DIWO
DESIGN // FRANÇOIS MOISSETTE

Expert + { Medium | MEDIUM SC | *Medium italic* | MEDIUM ITALIC SC }

Expert + { **Bold** | **BOLD SC** | ***Bold italic*** | ***BOLD ITALIC SC*** }

FF Angkoon by Xavier Dupré ✎ François Moissette

XAVIER DUPRÉ — 2004

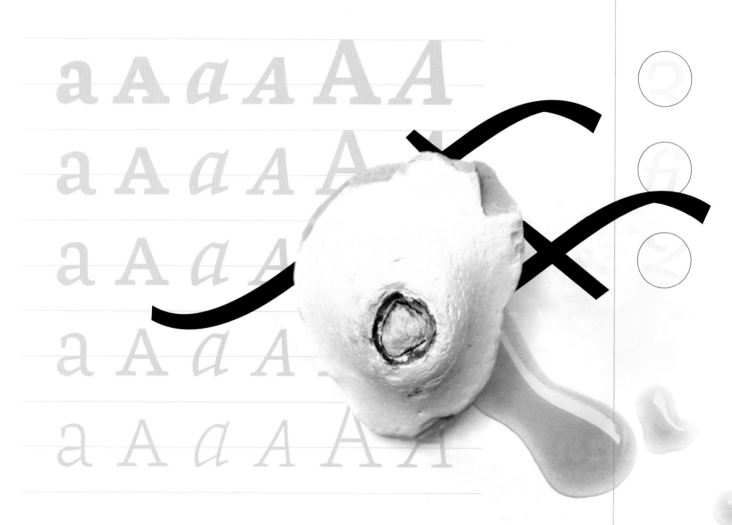

FF Absara by Xavier Dupré ✎ François Moissette

^{FF}Absara

ABCDEGHIJKLM
NOPQRSTVWXYZ
&abcdefghijklmn
nopqrstuvwxyz

Le terme **ABSARA**, désigne des divinités féminines, issues du *barattage de la mer de lait.* Danseuses et courtisanes célèbres pour leur beauté...

...essence gracieuse des eaux, de la légèreté de son écume. Évanescentes comme telles, CES NYMPHES CÉLESTES symbolisent *les possibilités informelles éternelles.*

Photos & design . FRANÇOIS MOISSETTE

Absara sans

a A A A A A A A A A

a A A A A A A A A

a A A A A A A A

a A A A A A A A

a A A A A A

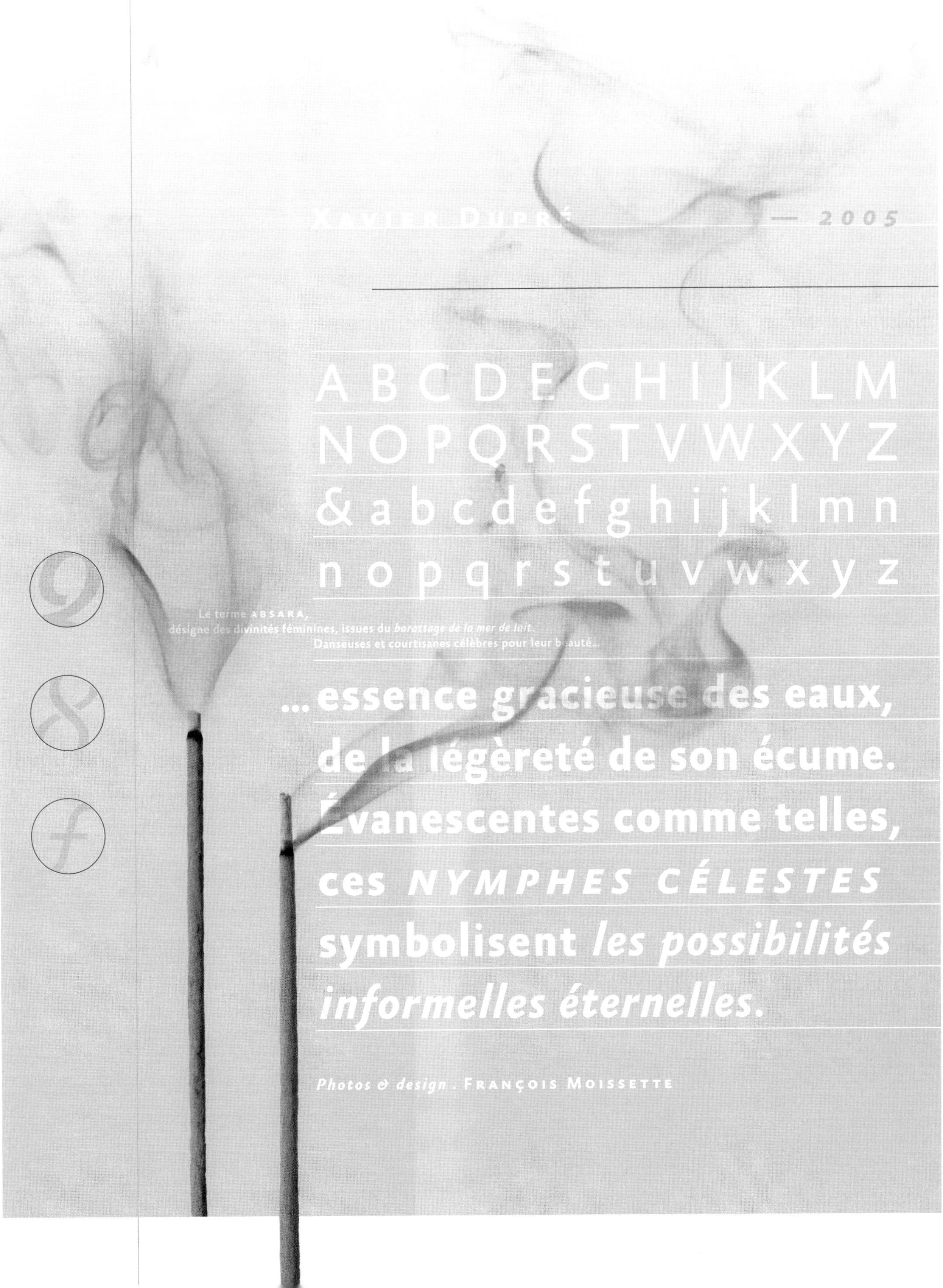

ABCDEFGHIJKLM
NOPQRSTVWXYZ
&abcdefghijklmn
nopqrstuvwxyz

Le terme **ABSARA**,
désigne des divinités féminines, issues du *barattage de la mer de lait*.
Danseuses et courtisanes célèbres pour leur beauté..

... essence gracieuse des eaux,
de la légèreté de son écume.
Évanescentes comme telles,
ces *NYMPHES CÉLESTES*
symbolisent *les possibilités*
informelles éternelles.

Photos & design . FRANÇOIS MOISSETTE

the Market
DISTRICT

ABCDEFGHIJKLMNOPQRSTUVWXZ abcdefghijklmnopqrstuvwxyz

YÄÁÂÀÃÅÆÇÍÎÏÌÑÖÓÔÒÕØOEËÉÊÈÜÚÛÙŸäáâàãåæçëéêèïíîìñöóôòõøoeüúûùÿfiflfrkrFrFF

[0123456789.,:;÷+-=<>µ$£$¥] (&@§¶ß©®TM!?*)

FF MARKET + MARKET EXPERT

ABCDEFGHIJKLMNOPQRSTUVWXZabcdefghijklmnopqrstuvwxyz

FF MARKET CONDENSED MEDIUM + EXPERT

ABCDEFGHIJKLMNOPQRSTUVWXZabcdefghijklmnopqrstuvwxyz

FF MARKET BOLD + EXPERT

H.A. SIMON, 1996

ABCDEFGHIJKLMNOPQRSTUVWXZabcdefghijklmnopqrstuvwxyz
ABCDEFGHIJKLMNOPQRSTUVWXZabcdefghijklmnopqrstuvwxyz

YÄÁÂÀÃÅÆÇÍÎÏÌÑÖÓÔÒÕØOEËÉÊÈÜÚÛÙŸäáâàãåæçëéêèïíîìñöóôòõøoeüúûùÿfifl

[0123456789 · 0123456789.,:;÷+-=<>µ$£$¥] (&@§¶ß©®TM!?*) [0123456789 · 0123456789]

FF DISTRICT LIGHT + ITALIC + TABLE FIGURES

ABCDEFGHIJKLMNOPQRSTUVWXZabcdefghijklmnopqrstuvwxyz
ABCDEFGHIJKLMNOPQRSTUVWXZabcdefghijklmnopqrstuvwxyz
1234567890 · 1234567890 · 1234567890 · 1234567890

FF DISTRICT REGULAR + ITALIC + TABLE FIGURES

ABCDEFGHIJKLMNOPQRSTUVWXZabcdefghijklmnopqrstuvwxyz
ABCDEFGHIJKLMNOPQRSTUVWXZabcdefghijklmnopqrstuvwxyz
1234567890 · 1234567890 · 1234567890 · 1234567890

FF DISTRICT MEDIUM + ITALIC + TABLE FIGURES

ABCDEFGHIJKLMNOPQRSTUVWXZabcdefghijklmnopqrstuvwxyz
ABCDEFGHIJKLMNOPQRSTUVWXZabcdefghijklmnopqrstuvwxyz
1234567890 · 1234567890 · 1234567890 · 1234567890

FF DISTRICT BOLD + ITALIC + TABLE FIGURES

ALBERT BOTON, 2002–2004

M E N Ú

ENTRANTES

Amanida Verda
Empedrat de bacallà
Ous al plat

2º PLATO

Bistec amb patates
Lluç a la planxa
Llom amb pebrots

Pan, Vino y Postre

9€ +7% IVA

Bed & Breakfast
KN
21,
Nice Street
·New York·

CHOCOLATES
"LA SABROSA"
BARCELONA

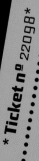

* Ticket nº 22098 *

TANDOORI
LENOIR
presents a show in 6 colours

SALA APOLO·Nou de la Rambla 113 · 08004 Barcelona

Rythm & Blues
Festival
Tuesday 13
September
Doors open at 9,00 p.m

The
LUX
Club

Jacky Regular
Jacky RegularExpert
Jacky RegularAlternate
Jacky RegularAlternateExp
Jacky RegularFull
Jacky RegularLigatures
JACKY REGULARSWASH

Jacky Bold
Jacky BoldExpert
Jacky BoldAlternate
Jacky BoldAlternateExp
Jacky BoldFull
Jacky BoldLigatures
JACKY BOLDSWASH

Jacky Block
Jacky BlockExpert

ALSJEBLIEFT
JACKY
DOE NIET ZO
HYSTERISCH*

Instanter-light
Instanter-bold

BEADMAP-INLINE
BEADMAP-OUTLINE

*Please Jacky, don't be so hysterical

EXTRA-BLACK
EXTRA-CONDENSED

A

FF Prater Serif One Bold

YES

FF Prater Sans One Bold

north

FF Prater Sans Two Bold

FF Prater Block One Regular/Block One Back

HOT

tomorrow

FF Prater Script One/FF Prater Script Tw

FF Prater Sans One Regular/Sans Two Regular

Sunshine

FF Prater Serif One Bold

FF Prater Serif One Bold

old

?

FF Prater Serif One Regular/Serif Two Regula

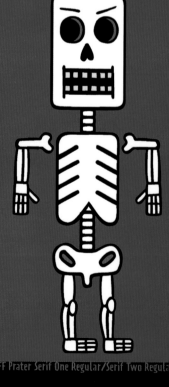

hell

heaven

FF Prater Serif One Regular/Serif Two Regular

Prater Block Two Regular/Block Two Back

!

FF Prater Sans One Bold

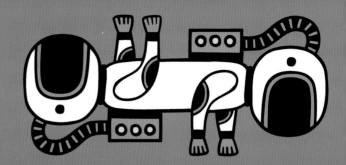

FF Prater Script One Regular/Script Two Regular

yesterday

COLD

Thunderstorm

FF Prater Sans One Regular

FF Prater Serif One Bold

New

FF Prater Sans Two Bold

south

FF Prater Sans One Bold

NO

FF Prater Serif One Bold

Z

all illustrations: tobot–automated illustration systems

font design: Steffen Sauerteig, Henning Wagenbreth

unta Finale 3.516m
tztaler Wildspitze 3.770m
an di Zucchero 3.505m
ima Fiammante 3.219m
ima Altissima 3.480m
ianca Alta 3.281m
ima Anima 3.470m
armolada 3.340m

jargʘn
watch

a pʘcket dictiʘnary
fʘr the jitterati*

as Øverheard by Gareth Branwyn

*1. What the digital generatiʘn
becʘmes after tanking up ʘn
and
nʘt
n,
ʘf

FF Letter Gothic

In the mid-1990s, FontShop
decided to adopt a number
of classic non-designed
typefaces and relaunch them
after thorough revision.

Jan Apma, specialist in een perifeer ziekenhuis:

« Meer dan ooit voel ik mij ondernemer »

Het Internationaal Bureau Fraudeinformatie
(IBF) helpt uitvoeringsinstellingen bij
de handhaving van de wetten en regels voor
de sociale verzekeringen. Tot over de hele
wereld voert het IBF verkennend onderzoek
uit naar mogelijke fraude met sociale
verzekeringen.

het voor de rechtshandhaving goed is om
in dit opzicht samen te werken. Een
gemeenschappelijke aanpak van internationale fraude met sociale verzekeringen
is volgens Haap ook bittere noodzaak.
Door mogelijke afspraken verwagen de
landsgrenzen, waardoor niet alleen het
economisch verkeer maar ook internatio-

rechtsaangelijkheid te ontstaan Sociale
verzekeringsfraude binnen Nederland
wordt binnen wel aangepakt. Bovendien
zou het ontbreken van internationale
fraudebestrijding voor kwaadwilligen een
uitnodiging zijn hun slag te slaan.
De omvang van de internationale fraude
met sociale verzekeringen is niet precies

FF Letter Gothic Slang by Susanna Dulkinys

FF Letter Gothic by Albert Pinggera   Wim Westerveld

Information Dominance
Military term for having superior intelligence and the ability to cripple an enemy's information infrastructure. "In the Gulf War, the coalition clearly had information dominance; in Somalia, it was Aideed." See also **Infowar**.

Information Gridlock
The traffic jams on the information superhighway that may eventually lead to full-blown Net collapse. See also **Web Brownouts**.

Infowar [or Cyberwar or Netwar]
Infowar is the use of information and information systems as weapons in a conflict in which information and information systems are the targets. Infowar is divided into three classes: Class I: personal privacy; Class II:

industrial and economic espionage; Class III: global (nation-state vs. nation-state) information warfare. Infowar has also been referred to as "Third Wave Warfare." See also **Information Dominance**.

Intel
[from the sci-fi novel Snow Crash]
Term used to describe any useful information found in cyberspace. "Just got some cool intel on UNIX shortcuts from FringeWare."

Intellectual Gillnetting
The process by which Hollywood studios scoop up all conceivable intellectual rights to a given property by burying perpetual, universal "multimedia" rights within the contractual boilerplate.

De **Feiten**

Benut nu uw allerlaatste kans De
uitvoeringsinstellingen beschikken niet altijd 5
meer rust dankzij kunst van PC over de kennis en de
met sociale verzekeringen aan te zitten 4
over de nieuwe ontwikkelingen.

Jan Aphia, specialist in

» **Meer dan o**
onder

De fraudeteams van de zoru
uitvoeringsinstellingen besch
altijd over de kennis in de me
om op internationaal niveau a
fraude met sociale verzekerin
zitten. Daarom gird vor
periode ain twe jaarp
bureau
vijf jaarp
pro het 1 niet
hel tebeli lle samer
anism oien goed

Beauty

belle, ô mortels ! comme un rêve de
sein, où chacun s'est meurtri tour à
pour inspirer au poète un amour
re ... que la matière.
erem Sektion St. Martin in Passeier
met ainsi

un sphinx incompre
l'azur comme la blancheur des
de neige à déplace les lignes,
vement qui jamais je ne ris
pleure et
mes grandes
mprunt

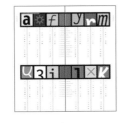

Like DIN and OCR, both of which were originally designed for industrial uses, Letter Gothic has gone through a veritable renaissance. In the course of the 1990s, graphic designers became saturated with the extensive choice of perfectly crafted typefaces, and as a result developed an interest in the archetypes of the computer age. DIN was appreciated for its bare systematic qualities, while OCR and Letter Gothic were liked because of

their tense, monospaced rhythm. Technical limitations gave these typefaces a straightforward, sincere character. Type designers responded to this new interest among type users by designing such artefacts as FF Blur, FF Confidential, FF Dynamoe, FF Magda and FF Trixie. These fonts imitated and exaggerated the deformation of letterforms caused by the use of primitive technologies. However, in the case of a revived classic like Letter Gothic, the original image of the type was left as intact as possible. Consequently, FF Gothic is more suitable for headlines and body text.

The Bitstream version of Letter Gothic was based on the typeface designed between 1956 and 1962 by Roger Robertson, a condensed, monospaced typewriter face for IBM electric typewriters. The renewed interest in the typeface in the 1990s brought to light a number of disadvantages. It lacked certain diacritics and other special signs, while its lack of bold weights was limiting. FontShop wanted to remove these drawbacks and commissioned type designer Albert Pinggera to adapt and complete Letter Gothic so as to better meet the needs of graphic designers. As the name Letter Gothic Text suggests, Albert Pinggera's first adaptation of the typeface was not monospaced. This decision had been prompted by the fact that many designers wanted to use Letter Gothic for longer body texts, making legibility an important issue. Varying letter widths and a proportional fit were obviously called for.

Albert added a large number of mathematical symbols, such as fractions and Greek characters usually found in symbol fonts, and designed mediaeval figures. In 1996 FF Letter Gothic Text was released in light, roman and bold versions. Early users of the font appreciated the thorough, sophisticated design and the extended character set, but some expressed disappointment at the loss of the monospaced character. Albert Pinggera appreciated the criticism and went to work again, taking FF Gothic back to its roots – the principle of monospacing. In 1998 the Monospaced version was released. FF Letter Gothic and FF Letter Gothic Text combine well. For instance, FF Gothic's tabular figures are a good alternative to the mediaeval figures found in the Text version. Albert Pinggera also drew 'real' italics for each of the four versions, and the family grew to twelve members. Meanwhile, American designer Susanna Dulkinys designed her own playful version of Letter Gothic by putting the characters to improper use – by swapping them with others, rotating and flipping them. She used her new typeface (called 'A day' at the time) for the Wired booklet Jargon Watch. In 2000, a definitive version based on FF Letter Gothic came out under the name FF Letter Gothic Slang.

Letter
 Łetter
BE
Tyļ
©Łøø
fixquark

er Gothic

Gothic $Lang

NCH

oisch

©KWØ®K

und boxkämpfer

FF Letter Gothic
Light
Light Expert
Light Italic
Light Italic Expert
Roman
Roman Expert
Roman Italic
Roman Expert Italic
Bold
Bold Expert
Bold Italic
Bold Italic Expert
Text Light
Text Light Expert
Text Light Italic
Text Light Italic Expert
Text Roman
Text Roman Expert
Text Roman Italic
Text Roman Expert Italic
Text Bold
Text Bold Expert
Text Bold Italic
Text Bold Italic Expert
$Lang Light
$Lang Light Σxþεrt
$Lang ®✳man
$Lang ®✳man Σxþεrt
$Lang ß✳ᄂd
$Lang ß✳ᄂd Σxþεrt
Tεkst $Lang Light
Tεkst $Lang Light Σxþεrt
Tεkst $Lang ®✳man
Tεkst $Lang ®✳man Σxþεrt
Tεkst $Lang ß✳ᄂd
Tεkst $Lang ß✳ᄂd Σxþεrt

Łεttεɾ G☀thic $Łαng Łight

Δß©ÐƩFGHIJKŁMNØÞQ®$TUVWXYZ12Ƹ
456789✱αþcdƐfghijkŁʍn✱þqrstuv
w×yz12Ƹ456789◊ÆŒæœ&ßfifl~·.,:;?!
¿¡…(/)[\]{|}""„"'ʻ,'‹›«»*†‡º'"ª
º§¶@®©™‰‰$¢£¥ƒ+#±<=>·÷/•Ḁ̊ƇƩÑÒ
ØÜáàäâãåƈø¬

Łεttεɾ G☀thic $Łαng ɾ☀man

Δß©ÐƩFGHIJKŁMNØÞQ®$TUVWXYZ12Ƹ
456789✱αþcdƐfghijkŁʍn✱þqrstuv
w×yz12Ƹ456789◊ÆŒæœ&ßfifl~·.,:;?!
¿¡…(/)[\]{|}""„"'ʻ,'‹›«»*†‡º'"ª
º§¶@®©™‰‰$¢£¥ƒ+#±<=>·÷/•Ḁ̊ƇƩÑÒ
ØÜáàäâãåƈø¬

Łεttεɾ G☀thic $Łαng þ☀Łd

Δß©ÐƩFGHIJKŁMNØÞQ®$TUVWXYZ12Ƹ
456789✱αþcdƐfghijkŁʍn✱þqrstuv
w×yz12Ƹ456789◊ÆŒæœ&ßfifl~·.,:;?!
¿¡…(/)[\]{|}""„"'ʻ,'‹›«»*†‡º'"ª
º§¶@®©™‰‰$¢£¥ƒ+#±<=>·÷/•Ḁ̊ƇƩÑÒ
ØÜáàäâãåƈø¬

Łεttεɾ G☀thic $Łαng þ☀Łd Ɛxþεɾt

∞≤≥∂Ʃ∏π∫Ω√≈Δ◊≠/fifl˥˘˙˚˝˜Łisɪff
ffiffllfj‹›■¼ÐðŁ7ƈ ŠšÝýÞþŽž½¼ ¾ ² ¦
–×Łisɪff ffiffllfj‹›◼©□®¤fu¶◄►┃•fu

Letter Gothic Light

ABCDEFGHIJKLMNOPQRSTUVWXYZ123
456789oabcdefghijklmnopqrstuv
wxyz1234567890ÆŒæœ&ßfifl~.,:;?!
¿¡…(/)[\]{|}""''‹›«»*†‡°'""ª
º§¶@®©™‰$¢£¥ƒ+#±<=>·÷/·ÅÇÉÑÒ
ØÜáàäâãåçø¬

Letter Gothic Text Light

ABCDEFGHIJKLMNOPQRSTUVWXYZ12
34567890abcdefghijklmnopqrstuvw
xyz1234567890ÆŒæœ&ßfifl~.,:;?!¿¡
…(/)[\]{|}""",'‹›«»*†‡°'""ªº§¶@®©
™%‰$¢£¥ƒ+#±<=>·÷/·ÅÇÉÑÒØ
Üáàäâãåçø¬

Letter Gothic Light Italic

*ABCDEFGHIJKLMNOPQRSTUVWXYZ123
456789oabcdefghijklmnopqrstuv
wxyz1234567890ÆŒæœ&ßfifl~.,:;?!
¿¡…(/)[\]{|}""''‹›«»*†‡°'""ª
º§¶@®©™‰$¢£¥ƒ+#±<=>·÷/·ÅÇÉÑÒ
ØÜáàäâãåçø¬*

Letter Gothic Text Light Italic

*ABCDEFGHIJKLMNOPQRSTUVWXYZ12
34567890abcdefghijklmnopqrstuvw
xyz1234567890ÆŒæœ&ßfifl~.,:;?!¿¡…
(/)[\]{|}""",'‹›«»*†‡°'""ªº§¶@®©™
%‰$¢£¥ƒ+#±<=>·÷/·ÅÇÉÑÒØÜáà
àäâãåçø¬*

Letter Gothic Roman

ABCDEFGHIJKLMNOPQRSTUVWXYZ123
456789oabcdefghijklmnopqrstuv
wxyz1234567890ÆŒæœ&ßfifl~.,:;?!
¿¡…(/)[\]{|}""''‹›«»*†‡°'""ª
º§¶@®©™‰$¢£¥ƒ+#±<=>·÷/·ÅÇÉÑÒ
ØÜáàäâãåçø¬

Letter Gothic Text Roman

ABCDEFGHIJKLMNOPQRSTUVWXY-
Z1234567890abcdefghijklmnopqr
stuvwxyz1234567890ÆŒæœ&ßfi
fl~.,:;?!¿¡…(/)[\]{|}""",'‹›«»*†‡°""
ªº§¶@®©™%‰$¢£¥ƒ+#±<
=>·÷/·ÅÇÉÑÒØÜáàäâãåçø

Letter Gothic Italic

*ABCDEFGHIJKLMNOPQRSTUVWXYZ123
456789oabcdefghijklmnopqrstuv
wxyz1234567890ÆŒæœ&ßfifl~.,:;?!
¿¡…(/)[\]{|}""''‹›«»*†‡°'""ª
º§¶@®©™‰$¢£¥ƒ+#±<=>·÷/·ÅÇÉÑÒ
ØÜáàäâãåçø¬*

Letter Gothic Text Italic

*ABCDEFGHIJKLMNOPQRSTUVWXYZ1
234567890abcdefghijklmnopqrstu
vwxyz1234567890ÆŒæœ&ßfifl~.,:;
?!¿¡…(/)[\]{|}""",'‹›«»*†‡°""
ªº§¶@®©™%‰$¢£¥ƒ+#±<
=>·÷/·ÅÇÉÑÒØÜáàäâãåçø*

Letter Gothic Bold

**ABCDEFGHIJKLMNOPQRSTUVWXYZ123
456789oabcdefghijklmnopqrstuv
wxyz1234567890ÆŒæœ&ßfifl~.,:;?!
¿¡…(/)[\]{|}""''‹›«»*†‡°'""ª
º§¶@®©™‰$¢£¥ƒ+#±<=>·÷/·ÅÇÉÑÒ
ØÜáàäâãåçø¬**

Letter Gothic Text Bold

**ABCDEFGHIJKLMNOPQRSTUVWXY
Z1234567890abcdefghijklmnopqr
stuvwxyz1234567890ÆŒæœ&ßfi
fl~.,:;?!¿¡…(/)[\]{|}""",'‹›«»*†‡°""
ªº§¶@®©™%‰$¢£¥ƒ+#±<
=>·÷/·ÅÇÉÑÒØÜáàäâãåçø¬**

Letter Gothic Bold Italic

***ABCDEFGHIJKLMNOPQRSTUVWXYZ123
456789oabcdefghijklmnopqrstuv
wxyz1234567890ÆŒæœ&ßfifl~.,:;?!
¿¡…(/)[\]{|}""''‹›«»*†‡°'""ª
º§¶@®©™‰$¢£¥ƒ+#±<=>·÷/·ÅÇÉÑÒ
ØÜáàäâãåçø¬***

Letter Gothic Text Bold Italic

***ABCDEFGHIJKLMNOPQRSTUVWXYZ
1234567890abcdefghijklmnopqrst
uvwxyz1234567890ÆŒæœ&ßfifl~
.,:;?!¿¡…(/)[\]{|}""",'‹›«»*†‡°'""ªº§
¶@®©™%‰$¢£¥ƒ+#±<=>·÷/·
ÅÇÉÑÒØÜáàäâãåçø¬***

Normal

abcdefghijklmnopqrstuvwxyz 1234567890
ABCDEFGHIJKLMNOPQRSTUVWXYZ
[.,;:?!$&-] {ÄÖÜÅÆŒÇ} [äöüßåæœç]

Night

abcdefghijklmnopqrstuvwxyz 1234567890
ABCDEFGHIJKLMNOPQRSTUVWXYZ
[.,;:?!$&-] {ÄÖÜÅÆŒÇ} [äöüßåæœç]

Initial

abcdefghijklmnopqrstuvwxyz 1234567890
ABCDEFGHIJKLMNOPQRSTUVWXYZ
[.,;:?!$&-] {ÄÖÜÅÆŒÇ} [äöüßåæœç]

Plastic

abcdefghijklmnopqrstuvwxyz 1234567890
ABCDEFGHIJKLMNOPQRSTUVWXYZ
[.,;:?!$&-] {ÄÖÜÅÆŒÇ} [äöüßåæœç]

Wilmos

abcdefghijklmnopqrstuvwxyz 1234567890
ABCDEFGHIJKLMNOPQRSTUVWXYZ
[.,;:?!$&-] {ÄÖÜÅÆŒÇ} [äöüßåæœç]

Boogie- Woogie

abcdefghijklmnopqrstuvwxyz 1234567890
ABCDEFGHIJKLMNOPQRSTUVWXYZ
[.,;:?!$&-] {ÄÖÜÅÆŒÇ} [äöüßåæœç]

FF Archian by György Szönyei ✎ György Szönyei

ARCHIAN Normal

abcdefghijklmnopqrstuvwxyz 1234567890

ARCHIAN NIGHT

abcdefghijklmnopqrstuvwxyz 1234567890

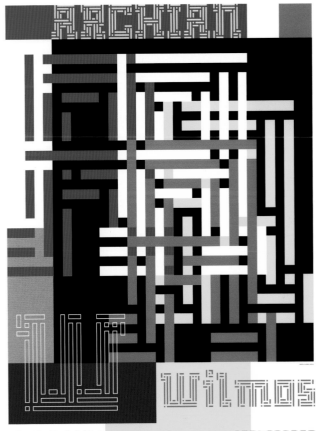

ARCHIAN Plastic

abcdefghijklmnopqrstuvwxyz 1234567890

ARCHIAN Wilmos

abcdefghijklmnopqrstuvwxyz 1234567890

Système Typographique Simplifié

Using the Space-saving Alphabet Devised by Dr. LANCÉ, San Francisco (USA)

Aa	Bb	Cc	Dd	Ee	Ff	Gg	Hh	Ii	Jj
01	02	03	04	05	06	07	08	09	10
Kk	Ll	Mm	Nn	Oo	Pp	Qq	Rr	Ss	Tt
11	12	13	14	15	16	17	18	19	20
Uu	Vv	Ww	Xx	Yy	Zz				
21	22	23	24	25	26				

FF Lancé Condensed
by JOACHIM MÜLLER-LANCÉ

Aa	Bb	Cc	Dd	Ee	Ff	Gg	Hh	Ii	Jj
01	02	03	04	05	06	07	08	09	10
Kk	Ll	Mm	Nn	Oo	Pp	Qq	Rr	Ss	Tt
11	12	13	14	15	16	17	18	19	20
Uu	Vv	Ww	Xx	Yy	Zz				
21	22	23	24	25	26				

LightMediumBold
No Italics! No SmallCaps! No Oldstyle Figures!

Aa	Bb	Cc	Dd	Ee	Ff	Gg	Hh	Ii	Jj
01	02	03	04	05	06	07	08	09	10
Kk	Ll	Mm	Nn	Oo	Pp	Qq	Rr	Ss	Tt
11	12	13	14	15	16	17	18	19	20
Uu	Vv	Ww	Xx	Yy	Zz				
21	22	23	24	25	26				

$£€%&!?§±/@*

Award-Winning Economy Since 1997

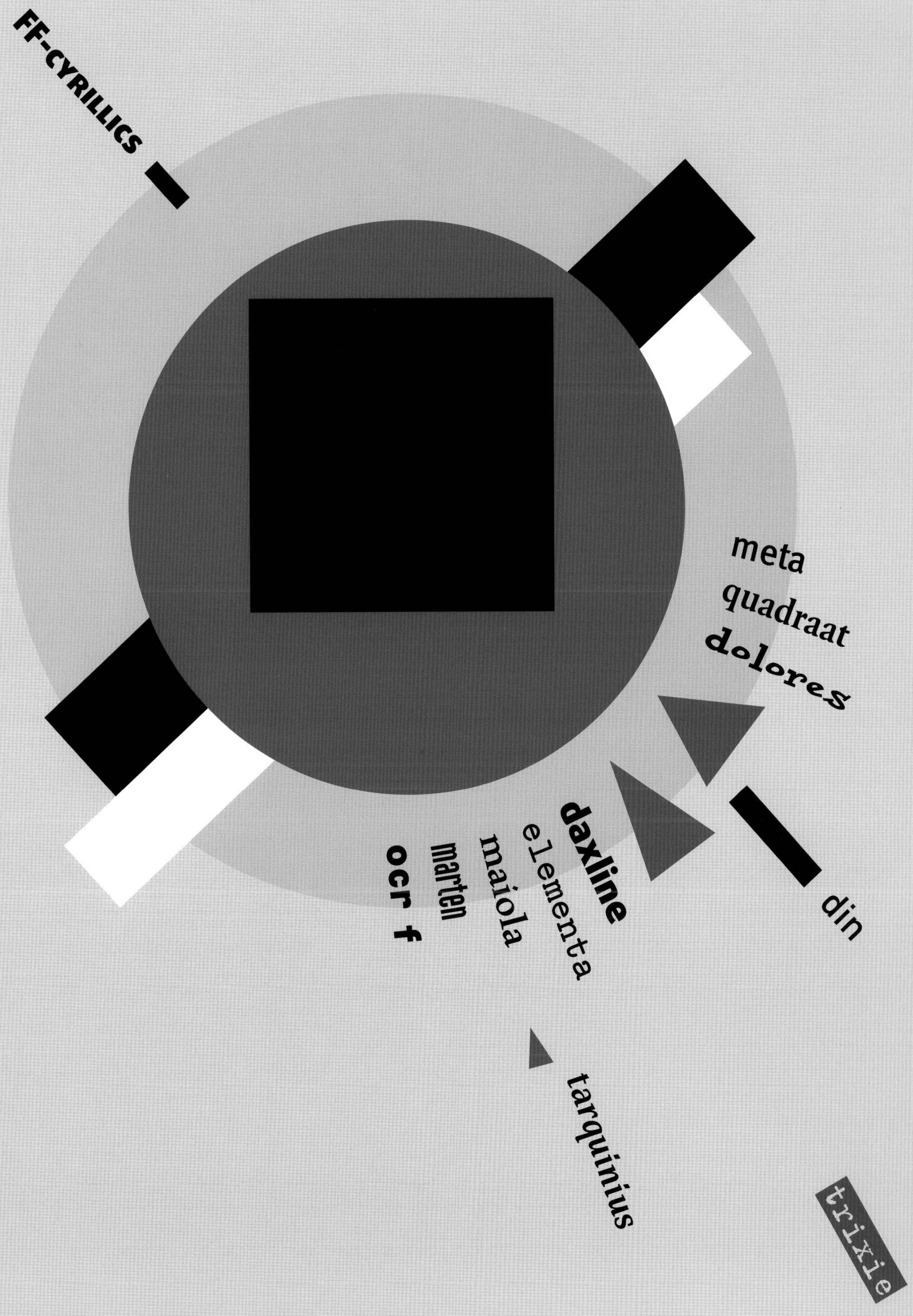

FF-CYRILLICS

meta

quadraat

dolores

daxline

elementa

maiola

marten

ocr f

din

tarquinius

trixie

АБВГДЕЁЖЗИЙКЛМНОПРСТУФХЦЧШЩЪЫЬЭЮ
абвгдеёжзийклмнопрстуфхцчшщъыьэ•
АБВГДЕЁЖЗИЙКЛМНОПРСТУФХЦЧШЩЪЫ ЭЮ
абвгдеёжзийклмнопрстуфхцчшщъыьэю
АБВГДЕЁЖЗИЙКЛМНОПРСТУФХЦЧШЩЪЫЬЭЮ
абвгдеёжзийклмнопрстуфхцчшщъыьэю

Trixie Cyrillic: Cameo/Light/Plain

АБВГДЕЁЖЗИЙКЛМНОПРСТУФХЦЧШЩЪЫЬЭЮ
абвгдеёжзийклмнопрстуфхцчшщъыьэю
АБВГДЕЁЖЗИЙКЛМНОПРСТУФХЦЧШЩЪЫЬЭЮ
абвгдеёжзсийклмнопрстуфхцчшщъыьэю
АБВГДЕЁЖЗИЙКЛМНОПРСТУФХЦЧШЩЪЫЬЭЮ
абвгдеёжзийклмнопрстуфхцчшщъыьэю
АБВГДЕЁЖЗИЙКЛМНОПРСТУФХЦЧШЩЪЫЬЭЮ
абвгдеёжзийклмнопрстуфхцчшщъыьэю

Quadraat Cyrillic: Bold/Bold Italic/Regular/Italic

АБВГДЕЁЖЗИЙКЛМНОПРСТУФХЦЧШЩЪЫЬЭЮ
аб'вгдеёжзийклмн◦прстуф×цчшщъыьэю
АБВГДЕЁЖЗИЙКЛМНОПРСТУФХЦЧШЩЪЫЬЭЮ
аб'вгдеёжзийклмн◦прстуф×цчшщъыьэю
АБВГДЕЁЖЗИЙКЛМНОПРСТУФХЦЧШЩЪЫЬЭЮ
аб'вгдеёжзийклмн◦прстуф×цчшщъыьэю
АБВГДЕЁЖЗИЙКЛМНОПРСТУФХЦЧШЩЪЫЬЭЮ
аб'вгдеёжзийклмн◦прстуф×цчшщъыьэю
АБВГДЕЁЖЗИЙКЛМНОПРСТУФХЦЧШЩЪЫЬЭЮ
аб'вгдеёжзийклмн◦прстуф×цчшщъыьэю

Dolores Cyrillic: Black/Extra Bold/Bold/Regular/Light

АБВГДЕЁЖЗИЙКЛМНОПРСТУФХЦЧШЩЪЫЬЭЮ
абвгдеёжзийклмнопрстуфхцчшщъыьэю
АБВГДЕЁЖЗИЙКЛМНОПРСТУФХЦЧШЩЪЫЬЭЮ
абвгдеёжзийклмнопрстуфхцчшщъыьэю
АБВГДЕЁЖЗИЙКЛМНОПРСТУФХЦЧШЩЪЫЬЭЮ
абвгдеёжзийклмнопрстуфхцчшщъыьэю
АБВГДЕЁЖЗИЙКЛМНОПРСТУФХЦЧШЩЪЫЬЭЮ
абвгдеёжзийклмнопрстуфхцчшщъыьэю

Marten Cyrillic: Grotesque/Grotesque Rough/Regular/Rough

АБВГДЕЁЖЗИЙКЛМНОПРСТУФХЦЧШЩЪЫЬЭЮ
абвгдеёжзийклмнопрстуфхцчшщъыьэю
АБВГДЕЁЖЗИЙКЛМНОПРСТУФХЦЧШЩЪЫЬЭЮ
абвгдеёжзийклмнопрстуфхцчшщъыьэю

OCRF Cyrillic: Bold/Regular/Light//OSF

АБВГДЕЁЖЗИЙКЛМНОПРСТУФХЦЧШЩЪЫЬЭЮ
абвгдеёжзийклмнопрстуфхцчшщъыьэю
АБВГДЕЁЖЗИЙКЛМНОПРСТУФХЦЧШЩЪЫЬЭЮ
абвгдеёжзийклмнопрстуфхцчшщъыьэю
АБВГДЕЁЖЗИЙКЛМНОПРСТУФХЦЧШЩЪЫЬЭЮ
абвгдеёжзийклмнопрстуфхцчшщъыьэю
АБВГДЕЁЖЗИЙКЛМНОПРСТУФХЦЧШЩЪЫЬЭЮ
абвгдеёжзийклмнопрстуфхцчшщъыьэю
АБВГДЕЁЖЗИЙКЛМНОПРСТУФХЦЧШЩЪЫЬЭЮ
абвгдеёжзийклмнопрстуфхцчшщъыьэю
АБВГДЕЁЖЗИЙКЛМНОПРСТУФХЦЧШЩЪЫЬЭЮ
абвгдеёжзийклмнопрстуфхцчшщъыьэю
АБВГДЕЁЖЗИЙКЛМНОПРСТУФХЦЧШЩЪЫЬЭЮ
абвгдеёжзийклмнопрстуфхцчшщъыьэю

Daxline Cyrillic: Black/Extra Bold/Bold/Medium/Regular/Light/
Thin //SC/LF/TF

АБВГДЕЁЖЗИЙКЛМНОПРСТУФХЦЧШЩЪЫЬЭЮ
абвгдеёжзийклмнопрстуфхцчшщъыьэю
АБВГДЕЁЖЗИЙКЛМНОПРСТУФХЦЧШЩЪЫЬЭЮ
авгеёжзийклмнопрстуфхцчшщъыьэю
АБВГДЕЁЖЗИЙКЛМНОПРСТУФХЦЧШЩЪЫЬЭЮ
абвгдеёжзийклмнопрстуфхцчшщъыьэю
АБВГДЕЁЖЗИЙКЛМНОПРСТУФХЦЧШЩЪЫЬЭЮ
авгеёжзийклмнопрстуфхцчшщъыьэю

Tarquinius Cyrillic: Bold/Bold Italic/Book/Italic

АБВГДЕЁЖЗИЙКЛМНОПРСТУФХЦЧШЩЪЫЬЭЮ
абвгдеёжзийклмнопрстуфхцчшщъыьэю
АБВГДЕЁЖЗИЙКЛМНОПРСТУФХЦЧШЩЪЫЬЭЮ
абвгдеёжзийклмнопрстуфхцчшщъыьэю
АБВГДЕЁЖЗИЙКЛМНОПРСТУФХЦЧШЩЪЫЬЭЮ
абвгдеёжзийклмнопрстуфхцчшщъыьэю
АБВГДЕЁЖЗИЙКЛМНОПРСТУФХЦЧШЩЪЫЬЭЮ
абвгдеёжзийклмнопрстуфхцчшщъыьэю

Maiola Cyrillic: Bold/BoldItalic/Regular/Italic//LF/TF

АБВГДЕЁЖЗИЙКЛМНОПРСТУФХЦЧШЩЪЫЬЭЮ
абвгдеёжзийклмнопрстуфхцчшщъыьэю
АБВГДЕЁЖЗИЙКЛМНОПРСТУФХЦЧШЩЪЫЬЭЮ
абвгдеёжзийклмнопрстуфхцчшщъыьэю
АБВГДЕЁЖЗИЙКЛМНОПРСТУФХЦЧШЩЪЫЬЭЮ
абвгдеёжзийклмнопрстуфхцчшщъыьэю
АБВГДЕЁЖЗИЙКЛМНОПРСТУФХЦЧШЩЪЫЬЭЮ
абвгдеёжзийклмнопрстуфхцчшщъыьэю

Din Cyrillic: Black/Bold/Medium/Regular/
Light//Alternate

Ђ

original graphics by el lissitzky, 1922

Я

АБВГДЕЁЖЗИЙКЛМНОПРСТУФХЦЧШЩЪЫЬЭЮ
абвгдеёжзийклмнопрстуфхцчшщъыьэю
АБВГДЕЁЖЗИЙКЛМНОПРСТУФХЦЧШЩЪЫЬЭЮ
абвгдеёжзийклмнопрстуфхцчшщъыьэю
АБВГДЕЁЖЗИЙКЛМНОПРСТУФХЦЧШЩЪЫЬЭЮ
АБВГДЕЁЖЗИЙКЛМНОПРСТУФХЦЧШЩЪЫЬЭЮ
АБВГДЕЁЖЗИЙКЛМНОПРСТУФХЦЧШЩЪЫЬЭЮ
АБВГДЕЁЖЗИЙКЛМНОПРСТУФХЦЧШЩЪЫЬЭЮ

АБВГДЕЁЖЗИЙКЛМНОПРСТУФХЦЧШЩЪЫЬЭЮ
абвгдеёжзийклмнопрстуфхцчшщъыьэю
АБВГДЕЁЖЗИЙКЛМНОПРСТУФХЦЧШЩЪЫЬЭЮ
абвгдеёжзийклмнопрстуфхцчшщъыьэю
АБВГДЕЁЖЗИЙКЛМНОПРСТУФХЦЧШЩЪЫЬЭЮ
АБВГДЕЁЖЗИЙКЛМНОПРСТУФХЦЧШЩЪЫЬЭЮ
АБВГДЕЁЖЗИЙКЛМНОПРСТУФХЦЧШЩЪЫЬЭЮ
АБВГДЕЁЖЗИЙКЛМНОПРСТУФХЦЧШЩЪЫЬЭЮ

АБВГДЕЁЖЗИЙКЛМНОПРСТУФХЦЧШЩЪЫЬЭЮ
абвгдеёжзийклмнопрстуфхцчшщъыьэю
АБВГДЕЁЖЗИЙКЛМНОПРСТУФХЦЧШЩЪЫЬЭЮ
абвгдеёжзийклмнопрстуфхцчшщъыьэю
АБВГДЕЁЖЗИЙКЛМНОПРСТУФХЦЧШЩЪЫЬЭЮ
АБВГДЕЁЖЗИЙКЛМНОПРСТУФХЦЧШЩЪЫЬЭЮ
АБВГДЕЁЖЗИЙКЛМНОПРСТУФХЦЧШЩЪЫЬЭЮ
абвгдеёжзийклмнопрстуфхцчшщъыьэю

АБВГДЕЁЖЗИЙКЛМНОПРСТУФХЦЧШЩЪЫЬЭЮ
абвгдеёжзийклмнопрстуфхцчшщъыьэю
АБВГДЕЁЖЗИЙКЛМНОПРСТУФХЦЧШЩЪЫЬЭЮ
абвгдеёжзийклмнопрстуфхцчшщъыьэю
АБВГДЕЁЖЗИЙКЛМНОПРСТУФХЦЧШЩЪЫЬЭЮ
АБВГДЕЁЖЗИЙКЛМНОПРСТУФХЦЧШЩЪЫЬЭЮ
АБВГДЕЁЖЗИЙКЛМНОПРСТУФХЦЧШЩЪЫЬЭЮ
АБВГДЕЁЖЗИЙКЛМНОПРСТУФХЦЧШЩЪЫЬЭЮ

Meta Cyrillic: Black/Medium/Book/Normal//Italics/
SC/Expert//LF/TF/OSF

лорем ипсум

■ лорем ипсум

лорем ипсум

лорем ипсум

лорем ипсум

лорем ипсум

лорем ипсум

лорем ипсум

лорем ипсум

■ *лорем ипсум*

лорем ипсум

лорем ипсум

*лорем ипсум**

АБВГДЕЁЖЗИЙКЛМНОПРСТУФХЦЧШЩЪЫЬЭЮ
абвгдеёжзийклмнопрстуфхцчшщъыьэю
АБВГДЕЁЖЗИЙКЛМНОПРСТУФХЦЧШЩЪЫЬЭЮ
абвгдеёжзийклмнопрстуфхцчшщъыьэю
АБВГДЕЁЖЗИЙКЛМНОПРСТУФХЦЧШЩЪЫЬЭЮ
абвгдеёжзийклмнопрстуфхцчшщъыьэю
АБВГДЕЁЖЗИЙКЛМНОПРСТУФХЦЧШЩЪЫЬЭЮ
абвгдеёжзийклмнопрстуфхцчшщъыьэю
АБВГДЕЁЖЗИЙКЛМНОПРСТУФХЦЧШЩЪЫЬЭЮ
АБВГДЕЁЖЗИЙКЛМНОПРСТУФХЦЧШЩЪЫЬЭЮ
АБВГДЕЁЖЗИЙКЛМНОПРСТУФХЦЧШЩЪЫЬЭЮ

Elementa Cyrillic: Bold/Bold Italic/Regular/
Italic//SC/Symbol/Expert

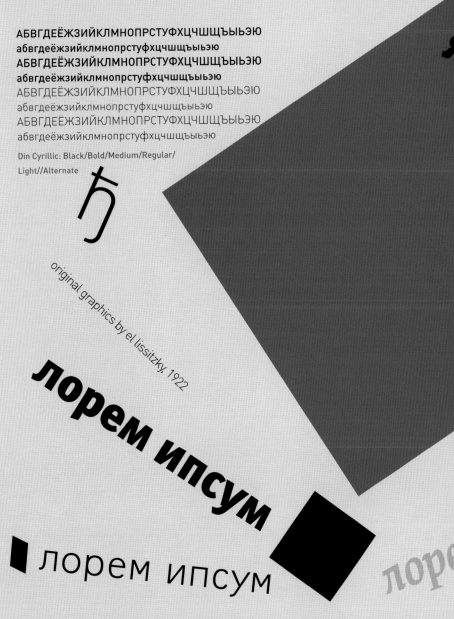

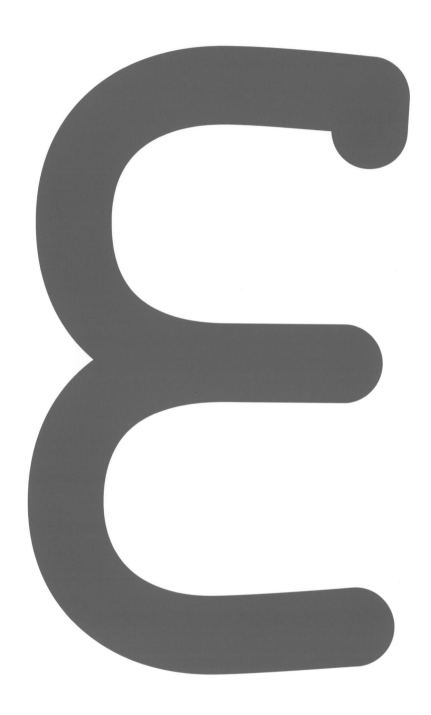

Round, open, friendly, unconventional but quite readable indeed. Five weights, *true italics*, lining figures, old style figures, expert sets & TRUE SMALL CAPS for all fonts → Enough scope to cater to any typographic need, *here is*

→ FF Roice!

FF ROICE is more an investigation than it is a type design. The original idea was not to create yet another good looking or cool or historically correct or commercially viable typeface, but to explore new ways of designing type, no matter what the outcome might be. Basic principles → no contrast, simplicity, readability, personality and accessability. 'It was clear from the beginning that too much respect for historical and stylistic conventions would result in a type design that would add very little to what's already available...'

The Novel and Other Prose
Roice Light 24p +1 em
Bernardim Ribeiro (1482~1552), whose five
eclogues introduced pastoral poetry to
Portugal, was equally an innovator in the
pastoral novel with his Saudàdès, better
known by its opening words Menina & moca
(published 1534~57). ¡This tale of rustic love and
melancholy, Chivalresque Elements mingling
with the pastoral and lyric songs with the
prose, transferred 60% themes and 3 Emotions
previously held the preserve of poetry to a
new medium and explored them with scant
concern for plot! 'From it Jorge de Montemor'
(Ontemayor) drew. Some part of his inspiration
for the Diana which, written in Spanish,
started a 3rd fashion subscribed to by
Cervantes and 'Lopess de Wega' Among many
Others and represents one of the outstanding
contributions of Portugal to the neighbouring
literature (¶45§12). Both countries shared in
the new enthusiasm of the 16th century — for
the romance of chivalry, in an age m3 when
imperial — enterprise to east and west was
such as to blur the dividing line between fact
antd the most improbable improbable flights
of the imagination. ¿The first?

abcdefghijklmnop

qrstuvwxyz@{[()]}

Roice's main characteristics: no contrast (no thick or thin parts), rounded end caps, unusual character shapes, small, serif like

.,.:;?! ABCDEFGHIJK

bulgettes at end caps to enhance reading, and round and open character shapes. The lack of contrast reduces vertical stress that

LMNOPQRSTUVWX

typically makes sans serif type less than easy to read. Roice is devised as a no nonsense type face but it's also quite playful,

YZ''""'''-ABCDEFGHI-

frivolous almost. Inspirations were Gill Sans, Courier and the VAG Volkswagen type face. It's named after Sir Henry Royce, one of the

JKLMNOPQRSTVWXY

greatest motoring engineers of the 20th century.

Z→%&*↓↑ABCDEFG

HIJKLMNOPQRSTUVWX

YZ⒜®©$ƒ£¥01234

56789012345678 ←

abcdefghijklmnop

Roice's main characteristics: no contrast (no thick or thin parts), rounded end caps, unusual

qrstuvwxyz@{[()]}

character shapes, small, serif like bulgettes at end caps to enhance reading and round and open

.,.;?! ABCDEFGHIJK

character shapes. The lack of contrast reduces vertical stress that typically makes sans serif type less

LMNOPQRSTUVWX

than easy to read. Roice is devised as a no nonsense type face but it's also quite playful, frivolous

YZ'""''-ABCDEFGHI–

almost. Inspirations were Gill Sans, Courier and the VAG Volkswagen type face. It's named after Sir

JKLMNOPQRSTVWXY

Henry Royce, one of the greatest motoring engineers of the 20th century.

Z→%&*↓↑ABCDEFG

HIJKLMNOPQRSTUVWX

YZ@®©$ƒ₤¥01234

56789012345678 9←

Flower of Joao de Barros, historian of empire,

Roice Medium
Roice Medium Small & Medium Caps

was in fact his Histo'ria do Imperador Larimundoz (1520), written purposely to develop his style for more serious tasks and serving,

Roice Medium Italic

through the adventures of this fictitious progenitor of the kings of Portugal™, his consistent aim of glori-fying his najtive land? In the Halmeirim de In-glaterra (1544) Francisco de Morais naturalized one son cœur branch of the Spanish descent of 2381 Amadis with an imaginative luxuriance and a purity of style which caused Cervantes to bracket it with the works of! Hoomer. It's own Portuguese progeny, the Dom Duardos [1587] of Diogo Fernandes and Baltasar Goncalves Lobato's Oom Clarisol de Bretanha (1602), were of an

Roice Bold

inferior order. The dramatist Ferreira de Vasconcelos kept alive memories of the Marthurian cycle with his Sagramor or

lining figures

Memorial da Segunda Tavolad–Edonda (1567). A

Roice Bold Small & Medium Caps

very different Type of Fiction en-tered €25,75 with the Contos de proveito e exemplo of Fernandes Trancoso, containing 38 tales

Roice Bold Italic Small & Medium Caps

Derived from Tradition Or Imitated from Boccaccio–straße and others which won and held favour for over a century.

FF Fago by Ole Schäfer 🖉 Martin Kahrmann

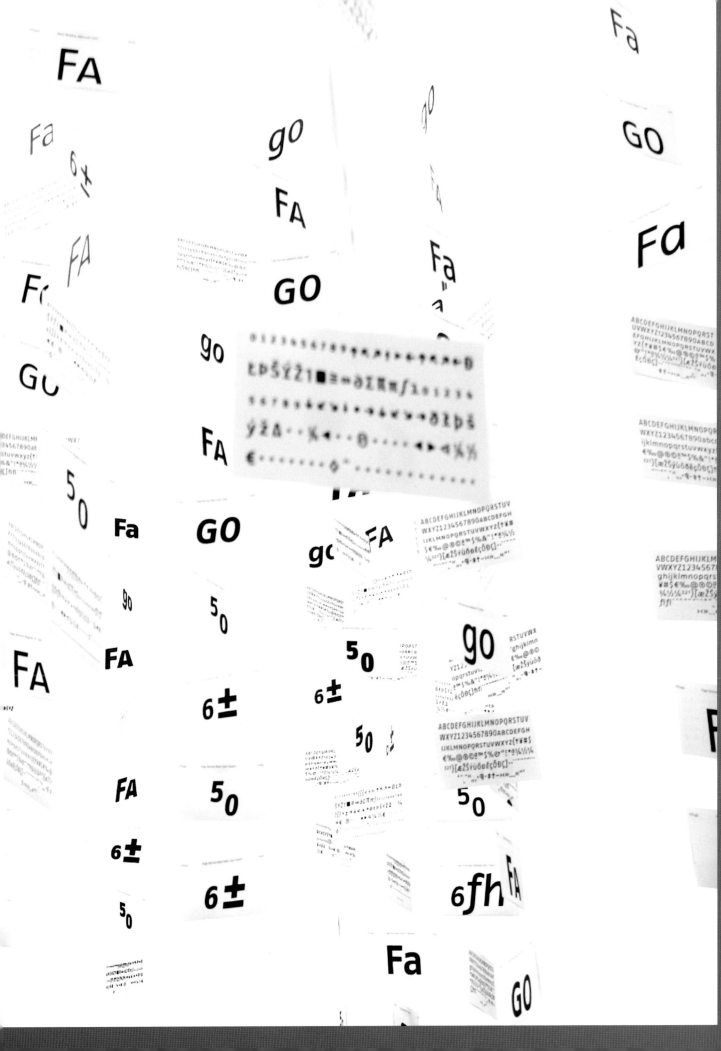

Arnhemsche Courant

LETTERGAZETTE

[QUADRAAT DISPLAY BOLD ITALIC 54 PT]   [QUADRAAT SANS DISPLAY BLACK 18 PT]

a a a a a a

AT ARNHEIM we come to a totally new Holland. The Maliebaan and the park at Utrecht, with their spacious residences, had prepared us a little for Arnheim's wooded retirement; *but not completely.* [QUADRAAT CAPS + REGULAR + ITALIC 14/18]

ARNHEIM THE JOYOUS

Rotterdam is given to shipping; The Hague makes laws and fashions; Leyden and Utrecht teach; Amsterdam makes money. It is at Arnheim that the retired merchant and the returned colonist set up their home. It is the richest residential city in the country. Arnheim the Joyous was its old name. *Arnheim the Comfortable it might now be styled.* [9/13]

It is the least Dutch of Dutch towns: the Rhine brings a bosky beauty to it, German in character and untamed by Dutch restraining hands. The *Dutch Switzerland* the country hereabout is called. Arnheim recalls Richmond too, for it has a *Richmond Hill* – a terrace-road above a shaggy precipice overlooking the river.

[QUADRAAT BOLD 8/13]

I walked in the early morning to Klarenbeck, up and down in a vast wood, and at a point of vantage called the Steenen Tafel looked down on the Rhine valley. Nothing could be less like

the Holland of the earlier days of my wanderings—nothing, that is, that was around me, but with the farther bank of the river the flatness instantly begins and continues as far as one can see in the north.

It was a very beautiful morning in May, and as I rested now and then among the resinous pines I was conscious of being traitorous to England in wandering here at all. No one ought to be out of England in April and May. At one point I met a squirrel—just such a nimble short-tempered squirrel as those which scold and hide in the top branches of the fir trees near my own home in Kent—and my sense of guilt increased; but when, on my way back, in a garden near Arnheim I heard a nightingale, the treachery was complete.

[QUADRAAT ITALIC 9/13]

And this reminds me that the best poem of the most charming figure in Dutch literature—Tesselschade Visscher—is about the nightingale. The story of this poetess and her friends belongs more properly to Amsterdam, or to Alkmaar, but it may as well be told here while the Arnheim nightingale—the only nightingale that I heard in Holland—is plaining and exulting.

TETTERGAZELLE

[QUADRAAT BOLD ITALIC CAPS 12 PT]

★

Tesselschade Visscher and the Chambers of Rhetoric
Tesselschade was the daughter of the poet and rhetorician Roemer Visscher. She was born on 25th March, 1594, and earned her curious name from the circumstance that on the same day her father was wrecked off Texel. In honour of his rescue he named his daughter Tesselschade, or Texel wreck, thereby, I think, eternally impairing his right to be considered a true poet. As a matter of fact he was rather an epigrammatist than a poet, his ambition being to be known as the Dutch Martial. Here is a taste of his Martial manner: [QUADRAAT BOLD + REGULAR 8/13]

Jan sorrows—sorrows far too much: 'tis true
A sad affliction hath distressed his life;—
Mourns he that death hath ta'en his children two?
O no! he mourns that death hath left his wife.

[QUADRAAT BOLD ITALIC 8/13]

I have said that Visscher was a rhetorician. The word perhaps needs a little explanation, for it means more than would appear. In those days rhetoric was a living cult in the Netherlands: Dutchmen and Flemings played at rhetoric with some of the enthusiasm that we keep for cricket and sport. Every town of any importance had its Chamber of Rhetoric. 'These Chambers,' says Longfellow in his *Poets and Poetry of Europe*, 'were to Holland, in the fifteenth century, what the Guilds of the Meistersingers were to Germany, and were numerous throughout the Netherlands. Brussels could boast of five; Antwerp of four; Louvain of three; and Ghent, Bruges, Malines, Middelburg, Gouda, Haarlem, and Amsterdam of at least one. Each Chamber had its coat of arms and its standard,

FF Quadraat

1 regular &
SMALL CAPS

2 italic &
ITALIC CAPS

3 bold &
BOLD CAPS

4 bold italic &
BOLD ITALIC
CAPS

1	2	3	4
abcdefghijklmnopqrst uvwxyz ABCDEFGHIJK LMNOPQRSTUVWXYZ [0123456789] ★ (@&§¶!$€£?) ABCDEFGHIJKLM NOPQRSTUVWXYZ [0123456789]	*abcdefghijklmnopqrstu vwxyz ABCDEFGHIJKL MNOPQRSTUVWXYZ [0123456789]★ (@&§¶!$€£?) ABCDEFGHIJKL NOPQRSTUVWXYZ [0123456789]*	**abcdefghijklmnopqrst uvwxyz ABCDEFGHIJK LMNOPQRSTUVWXYZ [0123456789]★ (@&§¶!$€£?) ABCDEFGHIJKLM NOPQRSTUVWXYZ [0123456789]**	***abcdefghijklmnopqrstuv wxyz ABCDEFGHIJKL MNOPQRSTUVWXYZ [0123456789] ★ (@&§¶!$€£%?) ABCDEFGHIJKLM NOPQRSTUVWXYZ [0123456789]***

headhunters **g** zine

i

bosky beauty

TOTALLY NEW HOLLAND

Klarenbeck

IZAAK WALTON

Tesselschade

*shipping?*ahoy!

short-tempered Dutchmen

MEISTERSINGER

PLAY HOUSE

Vondel

HOOFT

ZINNEPOPPEN

m

W

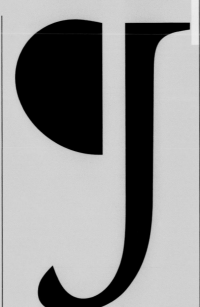

FF Quadraat
Sans Mono-
spaced
regular
italic
bold
bold italic

FF Quadraat
Display
italic
bold italic

FF Quadraat
Sans Display
semibold
black

FF Quadraat
Headliner
light
light italic
bold
bold italic

FLOWLANDS

forme

Galerie d' ART
typographique

moderne

* ⸮

{ ⟍ıꞁ

1230
156 }

f

R
A
+

& ⟍

ff Quadraat
family revue:
an easy-going
hard working
family man
shows articulate
points of view
in bigger sizes

P . 0 k

VELUWS POPNIEUWS

[QUADRAAT SANS DISPLAY BLACK 54 PT]

[QUADRAAT DISPLAY BOLD ITALIC 18 PT]

newsletter for the better new letter

ARNHEIM

Among the Dutch pictures at the Louvre is an anonymous work representing the Committee of a Chamber of Rhetoric.

[QUADRAAT SANS SMALL CAPS & ITALIC 18/26]

Roemer Visscher, the father of the poetess, was a leading rhetorician at Amsterdam, and the president of the *Eglantine Chamber of the Brother's Blossoming in Love* (as he and his fellow-rhetoricians called themselves). None the less, he was a sensible and clever man, and he brought up his three daughters very wisely. He did not make them blue stockings, but saw that they acquired comely and useful arts and crafts, and he rendered them unique by teaching them to swim in the canal that ran through his garden. He also was enabled to ensure for them the company of the best poetical intellects of the time—Vondel and Brederoo, Spiegel, Hooft and Huyghens.

[QUADRAAT SANS REGULAR, BOLD & ITALIC 9/13]

Of these the greatest was **Joost van den Vondel**, a neighbour of Visscher's in Amsterdam, the author of *Lucifer*, a poem from which it has been suggested that Milton borrowed. Like Izaak Walton Vondel combined haberdashery with literature. Spiegel was a wealthy patron of the arts, and a president, with Visscher, of the Eglantine Chamber with the painfully sentimental name. Constantin Huyghens wrote light verse with intricate metres, and an occasional epigram. Here is one:

[QUADRAAT SANS CONDENSED REGULAR, BOLD & ITALIC 9/13]

ON PETER'S POETRY.

When Peter condescends to write,
His verse deserves to see the light.
If any further you inquire,
I mean—the candle or the fire.

[QUADRAAT SANS SMALL CAPS & ITALIC 11/15]

Also a practical statesman, it was to Huyghens that Holland owes the beautiful old road from The Hague to Scheveningen in which Jacob Cats built his house. Among these friends Anna and Tesselschade grew into cultured women of quick and sympathetic intellect. Both wrote poetry, but Tesselschade's is superior to her sister's. Among Anna's early work were some additions to a new edition of her father's *Zinne-Poppen*, one of her poems running thus in the translation by Mr, Edmund Gosse in the very pleasant essay on Tesselschade in his *Studies in the Literature of Northern Europe:*

[QUADRAAT SANS REGULAR, BOLD & ITALIC 8/11]

1

A wife that sings and pipes all day,
And never puts her lute away,
No service to her hand finds she;
Fie, fie! for this is vanity!

2

But is it not a heavenly sight
To see a woman take delight
With song or string her husband dear,
When daily work is done, to cheer?

3

Misuse may turn the sweetest sweet
To loathsome wormwood, I repeat;
Yea, wholesome medicine, full of grace,
May prove a poison—out of place.

4

They who on thoughts eternal rest,
With earthly pleasures may be blest;
Since they know well these shadows gay,
Like wind and smoke, will pass away.

[QUADRAAT SANS CONDENSED FOUR WEIGHTS 9/13]

Tesselschade, who was much loved by her poet friends, disappointed them all by marrying a dull sailor of Alkmaar named Albert Krombalgh. Settling down at Alkmaar, she continued her intercourse with her old companions, and some new ones, by letter. Among her new friends were Barlaeus, or Van Baerle, the first Latinist of the day, and Jacob Cats.

[QUADRAAT SANS BOLD 8/13]

g g

g g

G

Most text on these pages was sampled from the Project Gutenberg EBook of *A Wanderer in Holland*, by E V Lucas 8th edition, New York 1908
> www.gutenberg.org

[QUADRAAT SANS REGULAR & ITALIC 7/12]

FF Quadraat
Sans
regular
SMALL CAPS
italic **bold**
FF Quadraat
Sans Condensed
regular
italic
bold
bold italic

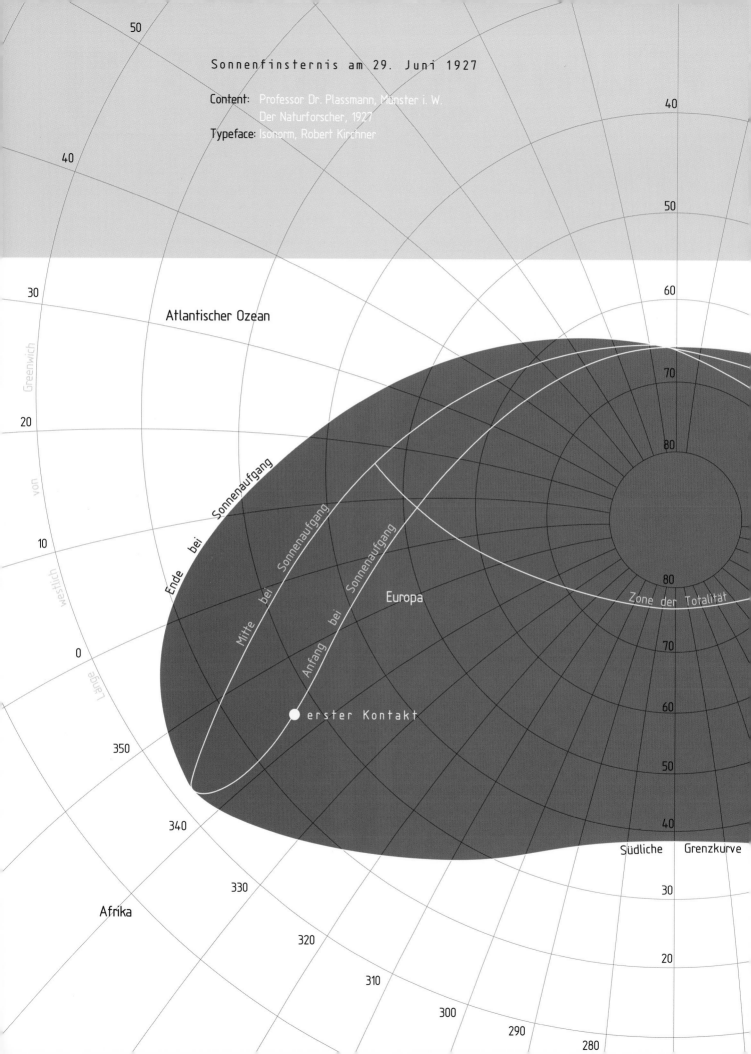

Sonnenfinsternis am 29. Juni 1927

Content: Professor Dr. Plassmann, Münster i. W.
           Der Naturforscher, 1927
Typeface: Isonorm, Robert Kirchner

Atlantischer Ozean

Greenwich

von

westlich

Länge

Ende bei Sonnenaufgang

Mitte bei Sonnenaufgang

Anfang bei Sonnenaufgang

erster Kontakt

Europa

Zone der Totalität

Südliche Grenzkurve

Afrika

50
40
30
20
10
0
350
340
330
320
310
300
290
280

40
50
60
70
80
80
70
60
50
40
30
20

Isonorm

Stiller Ozean

Nord Amerika

Anfang bei Sonnenuntergang

Mitte bei Sonnenuntergang

Ende bei Sonnenuntergang

letzter Kontakt

Asien

Isonorm Regular

ABCDEFGHIJKLMNOPQRSTUVWXYZÁÀÂÄÃÅÇÉÈÊËÜÛÙÚÑÓÒÔ
ÖÕŒÆÝŽabcdefghijklmnopqrstuvwxyzáàâäãåçéèêëüûùúñóòô
öõœæýž
1234567890.,:;--_+*'#!"§$%&/()=?E€

Isonorm Italic

ABCDEFGHIJKLMNOPQRSTUVWXYZÁÀÂÄÃÅÇÉÈÊËÜÛÙÚÑÓÒ
ÔÖÕŒÆÝŽabcdefghijklmnopqrstuvwxyzáàâäãåçéèêëüûùúñóò
ôöõœæýž
1234567890.,:;--_+'#!"§$%&/()=?E€*

Isonorm Monospaced

ABCDEFGHIJKLMNOPQRSTUVWXYZÁÀÂÄÃÅÇÉÈÊËÜÛÙ
ÚÑÓÒÔÖÕŒÆÝŽabcdefghijklmnopqrstuvwxyzáàâ
äãåçéèêëüûùúñóòôöõœæýž
1234567890.,:;--_+*'#!"§$%&/()=?E€

Isonorm Italic Monospaced

ABCDEFGHIJKLMNOPQRSTUVWXYZÁÀÂÄÃÅÇÉÈÊËÜÛÙÚ
ÑÓÒÔÖÕŒÆÝŽabcdefghijklmnopqrstuvwxyzáàâ
äãåçéèêëüûùúñóòôöõœæýž
1234567890.,:;--_+'#!"§$%&/()=?E€*

Certificated Quality System

ISO
ff 15

FF

FFUnit
by Erik Spiekermann

48/48 Unit Ultra Alt.

The Awful German Language '?¿!*;

Text by
MARK TWAIN (1835–1910)

18/20 Unit Bold Alt.

I went often to look at the collection of curiosities in Heidelberg Castle, and one day I surprised the keeper of it with my German. I spoke entirely in that language. He was greatly interested; and after I had talked a while he said my German was very rare, possibly a "unique"; and wanted to add it to his museum.

12/14 Unit Regular

If he had known what it had cost me to acquire my art, he would also have known that it would break any collector to buy it. Harris and I had been hard at work on our German during several weeks at that time, and although we had made good progress, it had been accomplished under great difficulty, and annoyance, for three of our teachers had died in the mean time. A person who has not studied German can form no idea of what a perplexing language it is.

12/20 Unit Bold

Surely there is not another language that is so slipshod and systemless, and so slippery and elusive to the grasp.

16/20 Unit Medium

One is washed about in it, hither and thither, in the most helpless way; and when at last he thinks he has captured a rule which offers firm ground to take a rest on amid the general rage and turmoil of the ten parts of speech, he turns over the page and reads, "Let the pupil make careful note of the following exceptions." He runs his eye down and finds that there are more exceptions to the rule than instances of it. So overboard he goes again, to hunt for another Ararat and find another quicksand. Such has been, and continues to be, my experience.

10/14 Unit Regular

Every time I think I have got one of these four confusing "cases" where I am master of it, a seemingly insignificant preposition intrudes itself into my sentence, clothed with an awful and unsuspected power, and crumbles the ground from under me.

FF Unit by Erik Spiekermann ✎ Susanna Dulkinys

16/20 Unit Regular

For instance, my book inquires after a certain bird – (it is always inquiring after things which are of no sort of consequence to anybody): "Where is the bird?" Now the answer to this question – according to the book – is that the bird is waiting in the blacksmith shop on account of the rain. Of course no bird would do that, but then you must stick to the book. Very well, I begin to cipher out the German for that answer. I begin at the wrong end, necessarily, for that is the German idea.

8/12 Unit Regular

making pens within pens: finally, all these parentheses and reparentheses are massed together between a couple of king-parentheses, one of which is placed in the first line of the majestic sentence and the other in the middle of the last line of it – after which comes the verb, and you find out for the first time what the man has been talking about; and after the verb – merely by way of ornament, as far as I can make out – the writer shovels in "haben sind gewesen gehabt haben geworden sein," or words to that effect, and the monument is finished. I suppose that this closing hurrah is in the nature of the flourish to a man's signature – not necessary, but pretty. German books are easy enough to read when you hold them before the lookingglass or stand on your head – so as to reverse the construction – but I think that to learn to read and understand a German newspaper is a thing which always remains an impossibility to a foreigner.

16/20 Unit Regular

I say to myself, "Regen (rain) is masculine – or maybe it is feminine – or possibly neuter – it is too much trouble to look now. Therefore, it is either der (the) Regen, or die (the) Regen, or das (the) Regen, according to which gender it may turn out to be when I look. In the interest of science, I will cipher it out on the hypothesis that it is masculine. Very well – then the rain is der Regen, if it is simply in the quiescent state of being mentioned, without enlargement or discussion – Nominative case; but if this rain is lying around, in a kind of a general way on the ground, it is then definitely located, it is doing something – that is, resting (which is one of the German grammar's ideas of doing something), and this throws the rain into the Dative case, and makes it dem Regen. However, this rain is not resting, but is doing something actively – it is falling – to interfere with the bird, likely and this indicates movement, which has the effect of sliding it into the Accusative case and changing dem Regen into den Regen."

12/16 Unit Black

Having completed the grammatical horoscope of this matter, I answer up confidently and state in German that the bird is staying in the blacksmith shop "wegen (on account of) den Regen." Then the teacher lets me softly down with the remark that whenever the word "wegen" drops into a sentence, it always throws that subject into the Genitive case, regardless of consequences –and that therefore this bird stayed in the blacksmith shop "wegen des Regens."
n. b. – I was informed, later, by a higher authority, that there was an "exception" which permits one to say "wegen den Regen" in certain peculiar and complex circumstances, but that this exception is not extended to anything but rain.

10/15 Unit Regular

– six or seven words compaced into one, without joint or seam – that is, without hyphens; it treats of fourteen or fifteen different subjects, each inclosed in a parenthesis of its own, with here and there extra parentheses which reinclose three or four of the minor parentheses,

FFUnit

by Erik Spiekermann

F Unit Thin, *FF Unit Thin Italic*, FF Unit Thin Alternative, *FF Unit Thin Alternative Italic*

Aaɑ Bb Cc Dd Ee Ff Ggg Hh Ilii Jjj Kk Lll Mm Nn Oo Pp
Qq Rr Ss Tt UUu Vv Ww Xx Yy Zz 1 2 3 4 5 6 7 8 9 0 *Aa*
3b Cc Dd Ee Ff Gg Hh Ilii Jjj Kk Lll Mm Nn Oo Pp Qq
Rr Ss Tt UUu Vv Ww Xx Yy Zz 1 2 3 4 5 6 7 8 9 0

F Unit Light, *FF Unit Light Italic*, FF Unit Light Alternative, *FF Unit Light Alternative Italic*

Aaɑ Bb Cc Dd Ee Ff Ggg Hh Ilii Jjj Kk Lll Mm Nn Oo Pp
Qq Rr Ss Tt UUu Vv Ww Xx Yy Zz 1 2 3 4 5 6 7 8 9 0 *Aa*
Bb Cc Dd Ee Ff Gg Hh Ilii Jjj Kk Lll Mm Nn Oo Pp Qq
Rr Ss Tt UUu Vv Ww Xx Yy Zz 1 2 3 4 5 6 7 8 9 0

FF Unit Medium, ***FF Unit Medium Italic***, **FF Unit Medium Alternative**, ***FF Unit Medium Alternative Italic***

Aaɑ Bb Cc Dd Ee Ff Ggg Hh Ilii Jjj Kk Lll Mm Nn Oo Pp
Qq Rr Ss Tt UUu Vv Ww Xx Yy Zz 1 2 3 4 5 6 7 8 9 0 *Aa*
Bb Cc Dd Ee Ff Gg Hh Ilii Jjj Kk Lll Mm Nn Oo Pp Qq
Rr Ss Tt UUu Vv Ww Xx Yy Zz 1 2 3 4 5 6 7 8 9 0

Unit Bold, *FF Unit Bold Italic*, FF Unit Bold Alternative, *FF Unit Bold Alternative Italic*

a a Bb Cc Dd Ee Ff Ggg Hh I l ii Jjj Kk Lll Mm Nn Oo
q Rr Ss Tt UUu Vv Ww Xx Yy Zz 1 2 3 4 5 6 7 8 9
b Cc Dd Ee Ff Gg Hh I l ii Jjj Kk Lll Mm Nn Oo Pp
r Ss Tt UUu Vv Ww Xx Yy Zz 1 2 3 4 5 6 7 8 9 0

Unit Black, *FF Unit Black Italic*, FF Unit Black Alternative, *FF Unit Black Alternative Italic*

a a Bb Cc Dd Ee Ff Ggg Hh I l ii Jjj Kk Lll Mm Nn Oo
q Rr Ss Tt UUu Vv Ww Xx Yy Zz 1 2 3 4 5 6 7 8 9
b Cc Dd Ee Ff Gg Hh I l ii Jjj Kk Lll Mm Nn Oo Pp
r Ss Tt UUu Vv Ww Xx Yy Zz 1 2 3 4 5 6 7 8 9 0

Unit Ultra, *FF Unit Ultra Italic*, FF Unit Ultra Alternative, *FF Unit Ultra Alternative Italic*

a a Bb Cc Dd Ee Ff Ggg Hh I l ii Jjj Kk Lll Mm Nn Oo
q Rr Ss Tt UUu Vv Ww Xx Yy Zz 1 2 3 4 5 6 7 8 9
b Cc Dd Ee Ff Gg Hh I l ii Jjj Kk Lll Mm Nn Oo Pp
r Ss Tt UUu Vv Ww Xx Yy Zz 1 2 3 4 5 6 7 8 9 0

For some reasons
& other reputably
legible **ideas**, we are
now dressed in a
leaf *of*
Acantus
Italic & **Bold**
COVERING OUR CAPS
Open **and** Expert
in a serious attempt
to make our *figures*
more **efficient**

Regular

ABCDEFGHIJKLMNOPQRSTUVWXYZ

0, 1, 2, 3, 4, 5, 6, 7, 8 & 9.

abcdefghijklmnopqrstuvwxyzßüäö@(¤$¢£ƒ)*

«««« MANIFESTO DEL FUTURISMO »»»»

Filippo Tommaso Marinetti

*** *Le Figaro,* 20 Febbraio 1909 ***

– 1 –_____ – 2 – Il coraggio, l'audacia, la ribellione, saranno elementi essenziali della nostra poesia. – 3 – La letteratura esaltò fino ad oggi l'immobilità penosa, l'estasi ed il sonno. Noi vogliamo esaltare il movimento aggressivo, l'insonnia febbrile, il passo di corsa, il salto mortale, lo schiaffo ed il pugno. – 4 – Noi affermiamo che la magnificenza del mondo si è arricchita di una bellezza nuova: la bellezza della velocità. – 5 – Noi vogliamo inneggiare all'uomo che tiene il volante, la cui asta attraversa la Terra, lanciata a corsa, essa pure, sul circuito della sua orbita. – 6 – Bisogna che il poeta si prodichi con ardore, sfarzo e magnificenza, per aumentare l'entusiastico fervore degli elementi primordiali. – 7 – Non vi è più bellezza se non nella lotta. Nessuna opera che non abbia un carattere aggressivo può essere un capolavoro. – 8 – Noi siamo sul patrimonio estremo dei secoli! poichè abbiamo già creata l'eterna velocità onnipresente. – 9 – Noi vogliamo glorificare la guerra-sola igene del mondo-il militarismo, il patriottismo, il gesto distruttore – 10 – Noi vogliamo distruggere i musei, le biblioteche, le accademie d'ogni specie e combattere contro il moralismo, il femminismo e contro ogni viltà opportunistica o utilitaria – 11 – Noi canteremo le locomotive dall'ampio petto, il volo scivolante degli areoplani. È dall'Italia che lanciamo questo manifesto di violenza travolgente e incendiaria col quale fondiamo oggi

il Futurismo!

Acantus Text

Italic

ABCDEFGHIJKLMNOPQRSTUVWXYZ

0, 1, 2, 3, 4, 5, 6, 7, 8 & 9.

*abcdefghijklmnopqrstuvwxyzßüäö@(¤$¢£ƒ)**

ff **Cellini**

Benvenuto
Cellini
Titling

Questa mia Vita travagliata io scrivo per ringraziar lo Dio della natura che mi diè l'alma e poi ne ha 'uto cura, alte diverse 'mprese ho fatte e vivo. Quel mio crudel Destin, d'offes'ha privo vita, or, gloria e virtù più che misura, grazia, valor, beltà, cotal figura che molti io passo, e chi mi passa arrivo. Sol mi duol grandemente or ch'io cognosco quel caro tempo in vanità perduto: nostri fragil pensier senporta 'l vento. Poi che 'l pentir non val, starò contento salendo qual'io scesi il Benvenuto nel fior di questo degno terren tosco. Io avevo cominciato a scrivere di mia mano questa mia Vita, come si può vedere in certe carte rappiccate, ma considerando che io perdevo troppo tempo e parendomi una smisurata vanità, mi capitò inanzi un figliuolo di Michele di Goro dalla Pieve a Groppine, fanciullino di età di anni XIII incirca ed era ammalatuccio. Io lo cominciai a fare scrivere e in mentre che io lavoravo, gli dittavo la Vita mia; e perché ne pigliavo qualche piacere, lavoravo molto più assiduo e facevo assai più opera. Così lasciai al ditto tal carica, quale spero di continuare tanto innanzi quanto mi ricorderò.

LIBRO PRIMO

Tutti gli uomini d'ogni sorte, che hanno fatto qualche cosa che sia virtuosa, o sí veramente che le virtú somigli, doverieno, essendo veritieri e da bene, di lor propia mano descrivere la loro vita; ma non si doverrebbe cominciare una tal bella impresa prima che passato l'età de' quarant'anni. Avvedutomi d'una tal cosa, ora che io cammino sopra la mia età de' cinquantotto anni finiti, e sendo in Fiorenze patria mia,

Spot the *differences!*
Strong serif in small sizes, *gentle* ones when big on the page.

anna

Cellini
Regular *& Italic*

Questa mia Vita travagliata io scrivo per ringraziar lo Dio della natura che mi diè l'alma e poi ne ha 'uto cura, alte diverse 'mprese ho fatte e vivo. *Quel mio crudel Destin, d'offes'ha privo vita, or, gloria e virtú piú che misura, grazia, valor, beltà, cotal figura che molti io passo, e chi mi passa arrivo.* Sol mi duol grandemente or ch'io cognosco quel caro tempo in vanità perduto: nostri fragil pensier senporta 'l vento. Poi che 'lpentir non val, starò contento salendo qual'io scesi il Benvenuto nel fior di questo degno terren tosco. Io avevo cominciato a scrivere di mia mano questa mia

Cellini Titling
Regular *& Italic*

Questa mia Vita travagliata io scrivo per ringraziar lo Dio della natura che mi diè l'alma e poi ne ha 'uto cura, alte diverse 'mprese ho fatte e vivo. *Quel mio crudel Destin, d'offes'ha privo vita, or, gloria e virtú piú che misura, grazia, valor, beltà, cotal figura che molti io passo, e chi mi passa arrivo.* Sol mi duol grandemente or ch'io cognosco quel caro tempo in vanità perduto: nostri fragil pensier senporta 'l vento. Poi che 'lpentir non val, starò contento salendo qual'io scesi il Benvenuto nel fior di questo degno terren tosco. Io avevo cominciato a scrivere di mia mano questa mia

anna

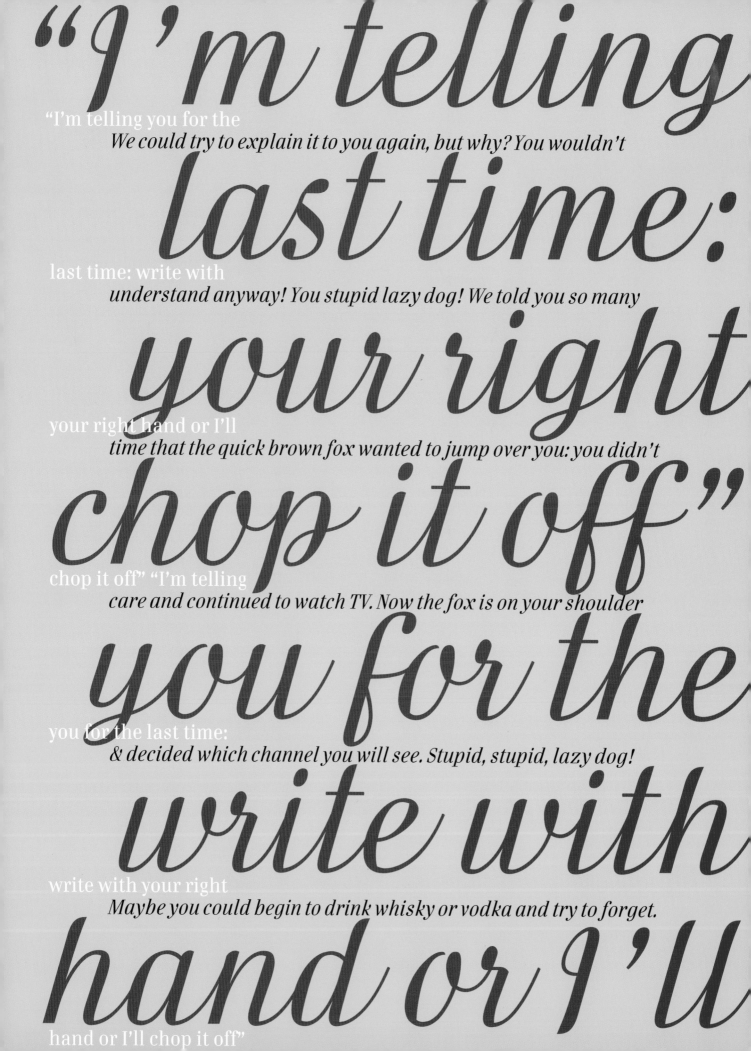

"I'm telling last time: your right chop it off" you for the write with hand or I'll

"I'm telling you for the

We could try to explain it to you again, but why? You wouldn't

last time: write with

understand anyway! You stupid lazy dog! We told you so many

your right hand or I'll

time that the quick brown fox wanted to jump over you: you didn't

chop it off" "I'm telling

care and continued to watch TV. Now the fox is on your shoulder

you for the last time:

& decided which channel you will see. Stupid, stupid, lazy dog!

write with your right

Maybe you could begin to drink whisky or vodka and try to forget.

hand or I'll chop it off"

Danubia

Brot & Schmalz

Danubia

* * * Type *out* of time * * *

from Wikipedia.org

Although the headwaters of the Danube are relatively small today, geologically, the *Danube* is much older than the Rhine, with which its catchment area competes in today's southern Germany. This has a few interesting geological complications. Since the Rhine is the only river rising in the Alps mountains which flows north towards the **North Sea**, an invisible line divides large parts of southern Germany, which is sometimes referred to as the European Watershed.

However, before the last ice age in the Pleistocene, the Rhine started at the southwestern tip of the **Black Forest**, while the waters from the Alps that today feed the Rhine were carried east by the so–called Urdonau (original *Danube*). Parts of this ancient river's bed, which was much larger than today's *Danube*, can still be seen in (now waterless) canyons in today's landscape of the **Swabian Alb**. After the

Upper Rhine Valley had been eroded, most waters from the **Alps** changed their direction and began feeding the Rhine. Today's upper *Danube* is but a meek reflection of the ancient one.

Since the Swabian Alb is largely shaped of porous limestone, and since the Rhine's level is much lower than the *Danube's*, today subsurface rivers carry much water from the Danube to the Rhine. On many days in the summer, when the *Danube* carries little water, it completely oozes away noisily into these underground channels at two locations in the Swabian Alp, which are referred to as the Donauversickerung *(Danube Sink)*. Most of this water resurfaces only 12 km south at the Aachtopf, Germany's wellspring with the highest flow, an average of 8,000 liters per second, north of Lake Constance – thus feeding the Rhine. The European Water Divide thus in fact only applies for those

BIER!

ANZEIGE ACHTUNG ACHTUNG

Wirkt gegen alles: Gegen *Krankheit* gegen Depression gegen fast alles . Garanti oder zurück. Alles.

+SCHNELL +ALLE MITMACHEN +SCHNELL +ALLE MITMACHEN +SCHNELL

NEID: ZUVIEL VIEL ZUVIEL!
ALLE UNTER EINER DECKE

UNVERSTÄNDLICH ÜBERRASCHEND PLÖTZLICH WENDUNG DIE VOLLE HÄRTE UNVERSTÄNDLICH ÜBERRASCHEND PLÖTZLICH WENDUNG DIE VOLLE HÄRTE UNVERSTÄNDLICH ÜBERRASCHEND PLÖTZLICH WENDUNG DIE VOLLE HÄRTE UNVERSTÄNDLICH ÜBERRASCHEND PLÖTZLICH WENDUNG DIE VOLLE HÄRTE

BRÜLL (43)

BRUTAL WAHNSINN! GEMEIN!

UNVERSTÄNDLICH ÜBERRASCHEND PLÖTZLICH WENDUNG DIE VOLLE HÄRTE

> EXKLUSIV!!
UND JETZT ALLE
UNFASSBAR

UNVERSTÄNDLICH ÜBERRASCHEND PLÖTZLICH WENDUNG DIE VOLLE HÄRTE

GEWINN

GANZ VIEL GANZ VIEL GANZ GANZ VIEL!!!!!

> SCHICKSAL:
KEINER WILL
KEINER HILFT

ÜBERRASCHEND PLÖTZLICH DA ABER WENDUNG DIE VOLLE HÄRTE

FF Balance by Evert Bloemsma · Lukas Kircher

Maiola

Designed by Veronika Burian

FONTSHOP PUBLISHED MAIOLA in July 2005 as a four-weight family with some typographical particularities, such as small caps, lining and old-style figures, fractions and ligatures. It is part of the touring exhibition e-a-t and was selected in the Type Design competition of Creative Review 2005, it was also awarded the TDC Certificate of Excellence in Type Design in 2004.   28 pt

FONTSHOP VYDAL V ČERVENCI 2005 čtyřřezovou rodinu Maiola s typografickými zvláštnostmi jako skákavé a verzálkové čislice, pravé kapitálky, zlomky a ligatury. Písmo se zúčastni putovní výstavy e-a-t a bylo zvoleno v soutěže pořádané Creative Review 2005. Bylo taky odměněno TDC certifikátem výmečné kvality písma 2004.   18 pt

FONTSHOP HAT IM JULI 2005 MAIOLA als vier-köpfige Schriftfamilie mit einigen typografischen Besonderheiten, wie Tabellenziffern, Mediävalziffern, Kapitälchen, Brüchen und Ligaturen, herausgebracht. Sie ist Teil der Wanderausstellung e-a-t und wurde bei dem Schriftwettbewerb von Creative Review in 2005 ausgewählt. Ferner wurde sie auch mit dem TDC Zertifikat für hervoragende Leistung in Schriftgestaltung in 2004 ausgezeichnet.   14 pt

EM JUNHO DE 2005, a FontShop publicou Maiola, uma família tipográfica com quatro variantes contendo vários extras, tais como algarismos alinhados e desalinhados (old-style), versaletes, fracções e ligaturas. Maiola é parte integrante da exposição itinerante e-a-t, foi seleccionada na competição de Type Design da Creative Review 2005, e em 2004 recebeu do TDC o certificado de Excelência em Type Design.   10 pt

FULL CHARACTER SET

UPPERCASE

ABCDEFGHIJKLMNOPQRSTUVWZYZ

LOWERCASE

abcdefghijklmnopqrstuvwxyz

SMALL CAPS

ABCDEFGHIJKLMNOPQRSTUVWXYZ

LIGATURES

ßfiflffffffifflssFIFLFFFFIFFL

DIACRITICS

ÀÁÂÃÄÅĀĂĄÅÆÆÇĆĈĊČĎĐÈÉÊËĒĔ
ĖĘĚĜĞĠĢĤĦÌÍÎÏĨĪĮİIJĴĶĹĻĽĿŁŃŅÑŇ
ŊÒÓÔÕÖŌŎŐŒØŔŖŘŚŜŞŠŢŤŦÙÚÛÜ
ŨŪŬŮŰŲŴÝŶŸŹŻŽÞ

àáâãäåāăąåæǽçćĉċčďđèéêëēĕėęěĝğġģĥħìíîïĩī
ĭįıijĵķĸĺļľŀłńņňⁿñŋòóôõöōŏőœøŕŗřśŝşšţťŧùúû
üũūŭůűųŵÿýŷźżžſþĸ

ÀÁÂÃÄÅĀĂĄÅÆÆÇĆĈĊČĎĐÈÉÊËĒĔĖĘĚĜĞĠ
ĢĤĦÌÍÎÏĨĪĮİIJĴĶĹĻĽĿŁŃŅŇŃÑŊÒÓÔÕÖŌŎŐŒ
ØŔŖŘŚŜŞŠŢŤŦÙÚÛÜŨŪŬŮŰŲŴÝŶŸŹŻŽÞ

CYRILLIC

АБВГДЕЖЗИЙКЛМНОПРСТУФХЦЧШЩЪЫЬЭЮЯ

абвгдежзийклмнопрстуфхцчшщъыьэюя

ЂЃҐЄЇЈЉЊЎЏЋЌЁSЈ ђѓґєїјљњўџћќёѕј

GREEK

ΑΒΓΔΕΖΗΘΙΚΛΜΝΞΟΠΡΣΤΥΦΧΨΩ

αβγδεζηθικλμνξοπρστυφχψως

ΆΈΉΊΌΎΏΪΫάέήίόύώϊϋΐΰ

FIGURES &
CURRENCY

0123456789€$¢£f¥¤ 0123456789€$¢£f¥

0123456789€$¢£f¥ 0123456789€$¢£f¥

%‰ %‰ %‰ %‰ ½¹⁄₂¹⁄₃²⁄₃¹⁄₄³⁄₄¹⁄₈³⁄₈⁵⁄₈⁷⁄₈ Nº№℮
1234567890 1234567890 1234567890
   1234567890   1234567890
            1234567890

MATHEMATICAL

+−±×÷=≠≈<>≤≥¬/|− — _^~¦\∂ΩΔΠΣ√∫◊∞

ACCENTS,
PUNCTUATION
& OTHER

ˇˆˇ˜¯˘˙˚˝`´

‚‛

,,;:....-!¡!¿?¿í""""„,,'''<>«»

&&·•·()[]{}*†‡§¶@©®™#ªºᴬᴼ

5

Made with FontFont

Font descriptions and samples of fonts in use from real and virtual worlds

FF ABSARA Xavier Dupré, 2004

FF Absara is a typeface of French proportions, but its shapes take their cues from the Dutch style: less polished, more direct. Their casualness refers to humanist handwriting. The roughly cut letterforms make for an interesting display typeface; but thanks to its generous proportions and firm serifs, FF Absara works equally well at text sizes. The idiosyncratic Italic creates a strong contrast against the Roman. FF Absara is functional and expressive, and lends a humanistic colour to both editorial and advertising design.

FF ACANTHUS Akira Kobayashi, 1998–2000

FF Acanthus was conceived as a 'modern' Roman with a lower-contrast appearance than the well-known Didot or Bodoni types in that category. FF Acanthus Regular was inspired by Henri Didot's typeface used in *De Imitatione Christi* (1788) but with more warmth and subtlety. FF Acanthus Text, made for smaller sizes, has slightly emphasized serifs, making it an excellent choice for body text. A set of ornaments and borders completes the FF Acanthus family.

FF ADVERT | FF ADVERT ROUGH Just van Rossum, 1991–1992

FF Advert is a good-natured text face drawn by Just van Rossum and is much appreciated by graphic designers for its unique lowercase 'a': there are single and two-story versions included in each font. FF Advert Rough consists of five roughened versions of Advert Bold, in progressive degrees of thickness. Each version of Advert Rough occupies the same set widths so they can be layered on top of each other as though they formed a colourful, mind-expanding cake.

FF AIRPORT Stephan Müller | Cornel Windlin, 1997

After FF Dot Matrix and FF Screen Matrix, FF Airport was the third technoid minimalist typeface by the Swiss studio Lineto. This time Pronto and Cornel succumbed to the typographical charm of LCD displays, freight waybills and boarding passes. The mixture of mobility and speed has produced primitive raster systems and brutally simplistic typographic tools. FF Airport consists of the FF Gateway and Luggagetag sub-families.

↑

Schein Berlin is a collaboration between German graphic designers Jan Hülpüsch and Henning Brehm, and photographer Daniel Porsdorf. Their specialty: creating plausible brands and publications specially made for appearance on tv and in films. In German government-funded media, any form of product placement is strictly forbidden; therefore locally-made series and films can only use 'virtual' products. Schein Berlin are masters at creating fictitious brands; and one of their secret weapons is the FontFont library. More of their packaging and products created with FontFonts can be found elsewhere in this section.

····›

Schein Berlin, lemonade label made with FF Amoeba and FF Danubia Script.

FF ALEGA | FF ALEGA SERIF Siegfried Rückel, 2002

FF Alega is an unusual sort of geometric face. Although it is based on a strict grid employing a limited number of angles, FF Alega is easy to read, even at relatively small sizes. It is a unique hybrid that is eminently readable in spite of its novel construction. Alega Serif is an extension of the original concept of Alega Sans. Again, a face with a technical look that is very readable; perhaps, because of the serifs, its feel is slightly more traditional.

FF ALESSIO Alessio Leonardi, 1994

Following the charming FF Priska, FF Alessio is a package of diverse display fonts partly made by hand (FF Forchetta was cut out of paper with scissors), partly designed digitally. Translated, the names of the fonts are knife, fork, cauliflower and Moulinex (a French kitchen appliance).

FF AMOEBA Peter G. Warren, 1995

Peter Warren designed Amoeba as a reaction against the geometric brutality of many of today's typefaces. He wanted to challenge traditional conventions of typeface design by adopting policies which included non-adherence to: the baseline, the x-height, and the division between upper and lower case. He strived to remain faithful to his original ideal that FF Amoeba should have no sharp corners or straight lines. Above all, he wanted FF Amoeba to be fun and pleasing to read.

FF ANGIE Jean-Fançois Porchez, 1995

FF Angie has a humanistic touch. Its roots are in cuneiform writing: the symmetric serifs remind us of triangular letterforms engraved in tablets. Legibility is improved by keeping letter shapes open and quite distinct from one to another. The Italics are lighter, narrower and more elegant than the romans. Each weight is complete with hanging and lining figures, all designed with the same width. Ornaments and black open caps for headlines complete the FF Angie family. Angie won the Brattinga prize at the 1990 Morisawa Awards in Japan.

FF ANGKOON Xavier Dupré, 2003

FF Angkoon is part of the French tradition of personal, idiosyncratic type design that is exemplified by faces like Vendôme by Excoffon/Ganeau or Eras by Albert Boton. Yet there is also a non-Western influence at work – Dupré designed FF Angkoon while living and working in Cambodia. Although it was not his intention to literally capture elements of Khmer writing or architecture in his typeface, FF Angkoon does have an uncommon sophistication that recalls that of the Angkor temples.

FF ARCHIAN György Szönyei, 1999

FF Archian by the Hungarian György Szönyei is a font composed of straight lines. But, instead of striving for simplicity, it uses geometric forms to create decorative, almost ornamental characters. FF Archian Normal was the first of the family. The other weights followed as variations on a theme, each inspired by a different discipline: architecture, painting and the fine arts.

arsinkey / belooussov / belyaev-gintovt / bendikov

MOSCOW

chayka / escape program / gurovich / iced architects

style /

nash / naumova / nina donis / ostengruppe / ostretsov

МОСКОВСКИЙ

project group savinkin/kuzmin / project meganom

simachev / soldatova / supremus / tishkov / vasiliev

СТИЛЬ /

v. tsesler & s. voichenko.

↑
Moscow Style, published in 2005 by Booth Clibborn Editions, an overview of contemporary Russian design compiled and designed by Conny Freyer and Eva Rucki at Troika (London). Typeface: FF Gateway, part of the FF Airport package.

⇢
Bubblegum Greeting Cards made (by an unknown designer) with FF Amoeba. Distributed by Clinton Cards.

FF ATLANTA Peter Bil'ak, 1995
FF Atlanta uses a vocabulary of forms and shapes formally related to the 1970s, playing with and re-inventing them in different ways. It parodies a period when style and form predominated over solutions. FF Atlanta is a family of three weights. Extra Light and Extra Bold push the typeface in opposite directions, giving it a natural, organic look.

FF ATMA Alan Greene, 2001
FF Atma is a text family with vertical stress, but with less contrast and greater legibility than most 'modern' typefaces. The name Atma is Kahouli for 'mental clarity'. The family is unique in that it offers three sizes of small caps, which may be serviceable in different ways.

FF AUTOTRACE Neville Brody, 1994
Following FF Blur, FF Autotrace was the second Brody typeface to be named after a digital alienation effect. Autotrace is a function which traces the bitmaps of a scanned image to produce contours, causing irregularities in the outlines as the resolution of the bitmaps is increased. This effect of distortion is the aesthetic basis for FF Autotrace. Just like with FF Blur, the font was named after the generic computer term to underline that the designer understands his typeface to be the definitive face to represent this effect.

FF AVANCE Evert Bloemsma, 2000
The most striking characteristic of FF Avance is the use of asymmetrical serifs in the Roman weights. Both upper- and lowercase letters have serifs in the upper left and lower right corners – remnants, as it were, of the connection between hand-written letters. With FF Avance, Evert Bloemsma rediscovered the possibilities of the serif as a means to enhance both the legibility and the expressive qualities of a text typeface.

FF BACKBONE Donald Beekman, 1999
The package FF Backbone is a collection of six display fonts by the Dutch type designer and musician Donald Beekman, originally drawn as display alphabets for music companies, album covers, group logos, posters and packaging for a 'smart drugs' distributor.

FF BACKSTAGE Stephan Müller | Cornel Windlin, 1999
FF Backstage is a package of fonts inspired by stencils, templates and other primitive signage devices. A newspaper clipping of the Chernobyl nuclear power station provided the starting point for FF Chernobyl. The FF WaterTower fonts are based on standard American cardboard stencil sets typically found in art supply shops.

FF BALANCE Evert Bloemsma, 1993
Developed over a period of ten years, FF Balance is an experimental sans-serif which subverts the conventions of the genre. Its horizontal strokes are heavier than the verticals and it appears slightly heavier at the top than at the bottom. All four weights have equal set widths: when formatting text with another weight, it will maintain the same length.

FF BASTILLE DISPLAY Albert Boton, 2002
A package of display fonts rooted in Albert Boton's previous work in advertising and package design. Bastille Display consists of FF District (which was later expanded into a larger family), FF Aircraft, FF Studio and FF Zan.

FF BAU Christian Schwartz, 2002
The workhorse type of the Bauhaus printing shop in Dessau was a typeface simply called Grotesk, introduced by the Schelter & Giesecke foundry in nearby Leipzig around 1880. This Grotesk can be regarded as a prototype for the ever-popular Helvetica of 1957. In 1999 Erik Spiekermann asked type designer Christian Schwartz to draw a revival of S&G's Grotesk, updating the family for contemporary typographic needs without rationalizing away the spirit and warmth of the original.

FF BAUKASTEN Alessio Leonardi, 1995
Baukasten means 'construction kit', and that is what this font family is: a set of possibilities for the user to build multicoloured typographic constructions. Leonardi described the typeface as 'an earthquaked bitmap font'. The six shaky alphabets work well together when layering the 'outline' variants over the 'filled' ones.

FF BEADMAP Ian Wright | David Crow, 2002
FF Beadmap began life as a bit of fun with plastic Hama beads from Denmark, which Ian's children received for Christmas. Ian used them to make little heads and type pictures based on embroidered samplers. He sent David one of these as a wedding present. Crow liked the idea of making it a workable font, and digitized it.

FF BEEKMAN Donald Beekman, 1999
FF Beekman is a family of geometric display fonts originally designed for the logo and headlines of 10Dance Magazine. It was constructed to allow horizontal and vertical stretching without losing its integrity.

FF BEOWOLF Just van Rossum | Erik van Blokland, 1990
FF BEOSANS Just van Rossum, 1992
Beowolf was created by 'hacking' the PostScript page description language and instruct the printer to mess up each character's curves. In 1992 Just van Rossum made BeoSans, a sans-serif based on the same principles. When used in its normal Type 1 mode, the Soft version can be used as a lively text typeface. With today's system software, the Beowolf randomizer no longer works, and is being replaced with OpenType functionality.

FF BERLINSANS David Berlow, 1992
FF BerlinSans is based on Lucian Bernhard's brilliant sans-serif from the late twenties. Assisted by Matthew Butterick, David Berlow expanded this single font into a series of four weights, all four complete with Alternates plus one Dingbat font.

FF BLOCKER Hannes Famira, 1998
Hannes Famira: 'FF Blocker is an inflated, arrogant face, strictly limited to the aesthetics of the cheap and fantastic. Horror monster, martial arts and action movies come to mind.'

FF BLUR Neville Brody, 1991
FF Blur was created by blurring a grayscale image of an existing grotesque and creating vectors from the results. Being deceptively simple, the process was often poorly imitated. Blur became one of the quintessential typefaces of the early and mid-1990s and has remained popular to date.

CANADIAN PACIFIC RAILWAY
Good for accomodation indicated below
for this date and car only
NOT TRANSFERABLE

From..

WINNIPEG

To...

DATE..

TOURIST CAR NO....................	Lower Depth	X
	Lower Depth	
	Single Occupancy Section	
....................M. TRAIN	Double Occupancy Section	

MILITARY | Amt. Collected ....
CAR CONDUCTOR'S PORTION

| Nr. of passangers | 1 | 2 | 3 | 4 | 5 | 6 |

Form. T. C. 1   No. **43600**

MAZZO'S INDIAN SUMMER

SEPTEMBER 1996
WARM GLOBAL GROOVES
EVERY FRIDAY IN MAZZO

MAZZO   ROZENGRACHT 114 | AMSTERDAM
T 020.6267500 | F 020.6263382
OPEN 23:00 - 05:00 HRS | TICKETS FL.15

GRAPHIC ARTS MESSAGE '92 TOKYO

THANKS FOR 73 YEARS CAMPAIGN

↖ ↖
Pentagram New York used FF Balance in its timeless identity for the Noguchi Museum, Long Island City, NY, which reopened in 2004.
Photo © jamesshanks.com.

FF Atlanta FontCard designed by Peter Biľak, 1995.

←
Hannes Famira designed this hoody sweater for his wife, New York civil rights attorney Veronica Eady, with his typeface FF Blocker, 2005

↖
Neville Brody, poster for Graphic Arts Message, .Too Corporation, Tokyo 1992. Typeface: FF Blur.

⇑ ⇑
Imaginary ticket made with FF Watertower. JS

⇑
Handout by Donald Beekman for an Amsterdam club, 1996. The origin of FF Totem, part of the FF Backbone series.

Child's play Age five
Child's play Age Six
Child's play Age Seven
Child's play Age Eight
Child'splay Age Nine
Child'splay Age Ten

Plausible dried meat packaging designed for German tv by Schein Berlin. FF Brokenscript, FF Fago and FF Danubia Script.

Leaflet published by FSI at the release of FF Care Pack, the library's first set of functional pictograms.

FF ChildsPlay was based on the handwritings of children of different ages.

FontCard for FF Bull. John Critchley.

FontCard by FF Burokrat designer Matthias Rawald.

FontCard for FF Bokka, FSI, 1995.

Exhibition panel about FF Bradlo for e-a-t (experiment and typography), an exhibition of typographic work by designers from the Czech and Slovak Republics, curated in 2004 by Alan Záruba (CZ) and Johanna Balušíková (SK).

FF BOKKA Critchley | Raven, 1997
London designer John Critchley invited illustrator Darren Raven to jointly design a font family based on Darren's spontaneous, symbolic, comic-like illustrations. The resulting family FF Bokka has four variations: Solid, Outline, Three-D and Shadow. These versions can be layered on top of each other and combined with no less than three fonts of drawings. Fun for all ages!

FF BRADLO Andrej Krátky, 1995
FF Bradlo was the first typeface published by Slovak designer Andrej Krátky. Originally designed for a bank, it is both dynamic and mediaeval; even after digitization it has retained its original chiselled appearance. Its asymmetric serifs and unusual details like ink traps, a relic from the early days of printing, set it apart from other similar typefaces.

FF BROKENSCRIPT Just van Rossum, 1991
A study in German broken fraktur typefaces. There is a peace symbol under shift-option-k on US mac keyboard.

FF BULL John Critchley, 1995
According to designer John Critchley, FF Bull is an authentic reproduction of old John Bull rubber stamp type sets, inked to varying degrees to produce six distinctive 'weights'. These are fully interchangeable and can be combined or overlaid to provide even more variations. Some of these weights contain special 'dirt-keys' which can be used to customize them still further.

FF BUROKRAT Matthias Rawald, 1996
FF Burokrat is Matthias Rawald's first published typeface. His inspiration for the ragged, upper-case only letters came via weekly account statements from the German Postbank. The high-volume printers of this bureaucracy 'par excellence' spit out hundreds of thousands of statements every day. The letters, based on OCR B with numbers from OCR A, vary significantly in weight from one form to another. This variation inspired the three versions of the family, FF Burokrat One, Two and Three.

FF CALL Scheuerhorst | Kisters | Ignaszak, 2000
For their work in cell phone advertising, the three designers were constantly in need of display type for phones from Nokia, Motorola, Siemens, etc. The result is FF Call, a package of over 70 fonts from a dozen brands of cellular phones.

FF CARE PACK Johannes Erler, 1992
FF Care Pack was the first of FontFont's many pictogram and illustration fonts. Contemporary and professional, it is a handsome and useful collection of warning signs and symbols for packaging and more.

FF CARTONNAGE Yanek Iontef, 2003
Yanek Iontef collected empty cardboard boxes from imported goods for years. To make space in his office, he opted to transform the visual language on the boxes into a font with universal appeal (then, presumably, donated the cardboard collection to his local recycling facility). FF Cartonnage is available in three weights, one of which is based on informational pictograms. The fonts imitate the imperfections of print on carton material and the wear-and-tear of travel.

FF CELESTE Christopher Burke, 1994
Designer Christopher Burke classifies FF Celeste as a modern humanistic face. The stroke contrast is less pronounced than in traditional models such as Walbaum, making FF Celeste more suitable for current digital typesetting and offset printing techniques. The letterforms are inspired by old-style letterforms with some vestige of a calligraphic influence to provide greater legibility. FF Celeste Small Text (1999) is a sturdier, slightly wider version specially designed for footnotes and other texts in small point sizes.

FF CELESTE SANS Christopher Burke, 2004
Like its serif companion, FF Celeste, FF Celeste Sans has a hybrid character. In Celeste Sans, Chris Burke tried to make a contemporary Grotesque, tempered by the dynamics of a humanist sans. Celeste Sans employs low contrasts between its thick and thin strokes, and so creates quite a different colour than Celeste Serif while maintaining the family's resemblance. This proves useful on occasions where a distinct yet harmonious contrast between serif and sans serif is required.

FF CELLINI Albert Boton, 2003
Designed in 1974 for the Hollenstein collection, these particular 'Bodoni' typefaces had existed only for photosetting. Albert Boton made the digital Regular in the '90s. In 2002 he added the Italic. For the release of FF Cellini, Boton completed the family with Regular SC, Titling versions, and a Medium and Bold. The structure of FF Cellini is similar to other Bodonis, but it differs in the details – a distinctive chracteristic being, for instance, the lengthening of the round points into drops in 'a', 'f', 'j', etc.

FF CHELSEA Frank Heine, 1994
FF Chelsea is one of those unusual alphabets with which the FontFont library quickly gained fame in the early years. The small caps font was designed by the young Stuttgart designer Frank Heine, whose 1992 typeface Remedy has become popular internationally. FF Chelsea is a 'chiselled' face with wedge-shaped strokes. Like other typefaces by Heine, the letterforms are influenced by handwriting and calligraphy. Especially attractive is the large range of ligatures and alternate characters which can be used to create interesting logos and headlines.

FF CHILD'S PLAY John Critchley, 1993
A collection of unique alphabets frozen in time, based on the handwriting of children aged 5 to 10 years. It contains a special dingbat font composed entirely of children's drawings. It enables the user to rediscover their first tentative scribbles and progress to more deliberate letterforms. For extra authenticity, the lower age groups include reverse letter option keys for deliberate misspellings!

FF CST EAST-WEST Ole Schäfer | Verena Gerlach, 2000
For several decades, two different signage systems divided East and West Berlin. The West used a sans serif dating back to the 1930s, while the East preferred a technical-looking sans face from the 1950s. Ole Schäfer and Verena Gerlach based their designs on the signs themselves rather than the drawings from which they were made. Cleaned-up versions of both alphabets were designed in three weights to be used as text fonts.

FF Burokrat / 3 weights / monospaced / layer it !

FF bokka

Andrej Krátky, 1994–1995

Bradlo

Písmo navrhnuté exkluzívne pre konkrétnu slovenskú banku, malo spĺňať požiadavky čitateľnosti, jedinečnosti, súčasného vzhľadu ako aj kompatibility s novými technológiami. **Tieto kritériá ako aj analýza existujúcich abecied viedli k novému typu lineárneho dynamického písma so serifmi aj bez serifov.** V serifovej variácii Bradlo Slab určujú jednostranne smerované serify celkový charakter písma a uľahčujú čitateľnosť v menších veľkostiach. Bradlo Slab a Bradlo Sans majú relatívne vysoké minusky umožňujúce sádzať text ekonomickejšie a dodávajú písmu modernejší tón. Šírka jednotlivých znakov a naklonená os tieňovania ťahov boli stanovené podľa princípov humanistickej konštrukcie písma. Bradlo využíva negatívne výrezy proti zalievaniu v tlači aj ako estetický detail. Pre finančné účely banky boli prispôsobené tabulátorové číslice, avšak písmo sa svojho pôvodného účelu nedočkalo. **V roku 1995 ho publikoval FontShop.**

Bradlo Sans Regular
!#$%&()*+,-./0123456789:;<>?@ABCDEFGHIJK
LMNOPQRSTUVWXYZ[\]^_abcdefghijklmnopqrstu
vwxyz(|)ÀÁÇÈ—ÔÛàáâãäçéêëèíìïîñóôõòøùúûü
¶§¶®©™ÆØVμ°™æø¿¡ƒÅÅÒŒ«»‹
›ÿŸñ±‰ÆÈÀËÈIÍIÒÓ ÒÓÚ

Bradlo Sans Bold
!#$%&()*+,-./0123456789:;<>?@ABCDEFGHIJK
LMNOPQRSTUVWXYZ[\]^_abcdefghijklmnopqr
stuvwxyz(|)ÀÁÇÈ—ÔÛàáâãäçéêëèíìïîñóôõòøùúû
ü¶†¢$§¶®©™ÆØVμ°™æø¿¡ƒÅÅÒŒ«»‹
›ÿŸñ±‰ÆÈÀËÈIÍIÒÓ ÒÓÚ

Bradlo Slab Regular
!#$%&()*+,-./0123456789:;<>?@ABCDEFGHIJK
LMNOPQRSTUVWXYZ[\]^_abcdefghijklmnopqrs
tuvwxyz(|)ÀÁÇÈ—ÔÛàáâãäçéêëèíìïîñóôõòøùúûü
¶†¢$§¶®©™ÆØVμ°™æø¿¡ƒÅÅÒŒ«»‹
›ÿŸñ±‰ÆÈÀËÈIÍIÒÓ ÒÓÚ

Bradlo Slab Bold
!#$%&()*+,-./0123456789:;<>?@ABCDEFGHIJ
KLMNOPQRSTUVWXYZ[\]^_abcdefghijklmno
pqrstuvwxyz(|)ÀÁÇÈ—ÔÛàáâãäçéêëèíìïîñóôõ
òøùúûü¶†¢$§¶®©™ÆØVμ°™æø¿¡ƒÅÅÒŒ«»
‹›ÿŸñ±‰ÆÈÀËÈIÍIÒÓ ÒÓÚ

The Bradlo font family was designed exclusively for a Slovak bank, with the goals of legibility, originality, contemporary appearance, and compatibility with current technology. A predominant feature of Bradlo Slab is the one-sided serifs which give characters legibility in small sizes. Bradlo Slab and Bradlo Sans have a relatively high x-height, resulting in compact setting and a contemporary look. The character widths and diagonal stress are rooted in the dynamic principles of humanistic typeforms. Bradlo takes advantage of technical details like ink traps not only to prevent clogging of small types, but also to create a stylish feature of larger sizes. Although Bradlo was first tuned to address the bank's financial purposes, including the design of tabular figures, the font family has never been used by the intended institution. Instead, it was published by FontShop in 1995 and is available to designers everywhere.

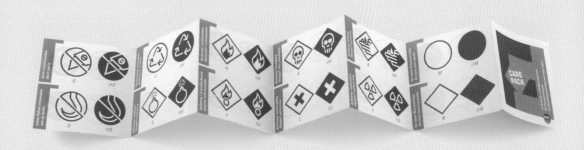

Kartonnen dozen ('Cardboard boxes'), an acclaimed novel by Flemish author Tom Lanoye. Jan Willem Stas used FF Cocon because 'it works so well in a sequence of positive and negative shapes, and because of its splendid counters'. Prometheus publishers, 2002.

Promotional poster for FF Crash Bang Wallop, Rian Hughes, 1994.

The ultimate offer. Ad for Druk magazine, FontShop Benelux, 2002. Typeface: FF Danubia. JM

Poster for the Cultural Year 2004 event, The Hague (Netherlands), designed by NLXL with FF DIN.

FF Double Digits

Reyman Studio in New York chose FF Dax for their redesign of the Bloomberg Personal Finance magazine logo and cover template, James Reyman: 'As this was a redesign for a prominent financial news media company, the new typeface had to be authoritative and clean; functional and versatile.'

FF CLAIR Ingrid Liche, 1995

For decades, Ingrid Liche has worked as a designer of advertising and packaging for natural medicines and cosmetics. As part of this work she developed several alphabets, most of which express an anthroposophic, Rudolf Steiner-inspired style. FF Clair is based on an alphabet drawn for a new private clinic in Switzerland.

FF CLIFFORD Akira Kobayashi, 1999

FF Clifford is a beautifully drawn traditional Roman from Akira Kobayashi. FF Clifford was based on 18th century English typefaces, but was never intended to be a faithful reproduction. Just like hand-made metal type, Clifford has different proportions for small, medium and large point sizes. Thus, it allows for subtle and sophisticated typography.

FF COCON Bloemsma 1998–2001

In FF Cocon, Dutch designer Evert Bloemsma wanted to do away with the small spurs of lowercase letters like 'a', 'b', 'd', 'h', 'm', 'n', 'p', 'r' and 'u' – the relics of the handwritten word. He set out to design an utterly contemporary alphabet and arrived at a surprisingly poetic solution by drawing a family of rounded and asymmetrical forms with details reminiscent of brush-strokes. The original Cocon had two widths – regular and narrow. Later, a compressed version was introduced.

FF CRAFT Peter Biľak, 1994

FF Craft was the first digital typeface made by Slovak designer Peter Biľak, who went on to become a well-known designer, organiser, editor, writer and type publisher. FF Craft was inspired by woodcuts; Biľak provided the user with ten different word spaces to create the natural rhythm inherent in their technique.

FF CRASHBANGWALLOP Rian Hughes, 1994

Rian Hughes' typefaces display his love for the world of comic books. FF CrashBangWallop was drawn in 1990 for SpeakEasy comics. The font comes with a small set of illustrations and symbols.

FF DANUBIA Viktor Solt-Bittner, 2002

The 18th century classicist typefaces with their abrupt transition from hairlines to stems and their vertical stress formed the starting point for FF Danubia. In drawing and redrawing FF Danubia, Vienna designer Viktor Solt-Bittner departed from this model, arriving at a highly personal interpretation. The delightful Danubia Script is also based on 18th century letterforms.

FF DAX Hans Reichel, 1996–2004

FF Dax Condensed was the first version of Dax, one of the most popular FontFont families. Reichel drew it to be a blend of his own Barmeno from 1983 and Futura Condensed. He wanted it to be 'relatively slim and clear. Not trendy.' Very few contemporary sans-serifs have managed to unite originality and experiment with usability and friendliness with this much ease. Later, the Dax family was completed with Normal and Wide widths, as well as Italics.

FF DAX COMPACT Hans Reichel, 2004

FF Dax Compact is a useful extension to the Dax family. The main difference from the standard versions is that the letters have relatively small ascenders and descenders and the upper case letters have the same height as the tall lower case letters. That makes the typeface larger yet more compact – which is what we usually want headlines to be.

FF DAXLINE Hans Reichel, 2005

Contrary to FF Dax, FF Daxline has optically equal weights — thus being a real grotesque face without abandoning the character of Dax. The aim with this variation was to balance the contrast so that it works well in long texts with small point sizes. Daxline is much wider than Dax, and the capitals are larger. There is even a lighter version than Light: Thin.

FF DIG, DOG, HIP Paul Sych, 1991

Three geometrically constructed fonts from the Toronto designer Paul Sych. FF Dig came about while experimenting with ovals as a motif. Hip employs bold horizontal widths and sharp angles and is intended to create an irregularity and imbalance of form. FF Dog is Sych's interpretation of early English manuscript text: the angularity of Old English textura combined with a compressed sans-serif.

FF DIN Albert-Jan Pool, 1995–2006

In response to the popularity of technical alphabets with a 'non-designed' look, FontShop planned a series of usable text faces based on these alphabets. Following FF OCR-F, the German-based Dutch designer Albert-Jan Pool began working on the famous DIN-Mittelschrift, popular for its technical look and straightforwardness. Pool considers this 'Autobahn' face to be 'probably the most non-designed typeface ever made.' He subtly improved the legibility by smoothing its joints and curves, and by expanding it into a family of five weights.

FontFont Library
Het ultieme aanbod

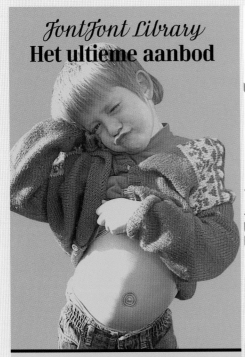

Eenmalige korting. Beslis nu!
Full Library. Halve prijs.
De volledige FontFont bibliotheek
van 26.900 € voor 13.450 €
»Slechts geldig tot 31 december 2002«

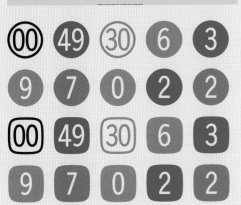

design → www.nlxl.com

Den Haag 2004 puur cultuur

OPENING CULTUURJAAR 3 JANUARI 2004

Vanaf 12.00 uur,
op verschillende lokaties in centrum Den Haag

100 slagwerkers trommelen Den Haag op!

Slotmanifestatie o.l.v. Cesar Zuiderwijk
en Percossa Percussion
Vanaf 17.00 uur, Atrium Stadhuis

www.denhaag2004.nl

Den Haag 2004
puur cultuur

FF Craft comes with several different word spaces

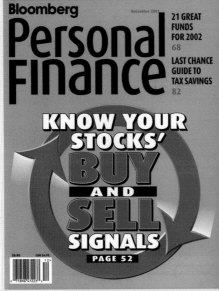

SPECIAL REPORT: WHAT'S AHEAD FOR THE MARKETS • 17

Bloomberg
Personal FINANCE

December 2001

21 GREAT
FUNDS
FOR 2002
68

LAST CHANCE
GUIDE TO
TAX SAVINGS
82

KNOW YOUR STOCKS'
BUY AND SELL
SIGNALS
PAGE 52

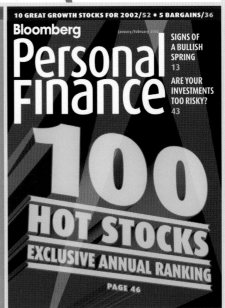

10 GREAT GROWTH STOCKS FOR 2002/52 • 5 BARGAINS/36

Bloomberg
Personal FINANCE

January/February 2002

SIGNS OF
A BULLISH
SPRING
13

ARE YOUR
INVESTMENTS
TOO RISKY?
43

100
HOT STOCKS
EXCLUSIVE ANNUAL RANKING
PAGE 46

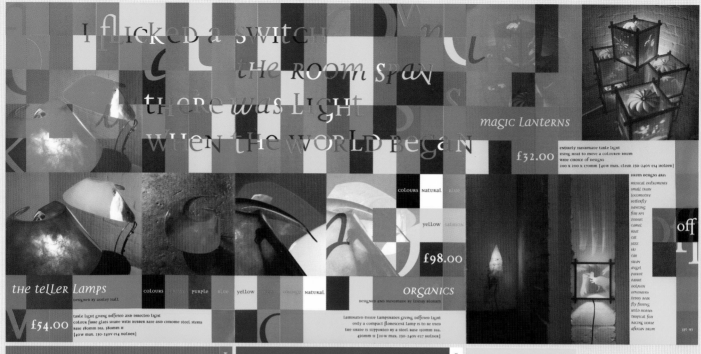

jə · gi naar pagina 73, cijfer 6

45

meə · ga naar pagina 74, cijfer 23

heeft u
uw hart
op de
juiste
plek?

waar zit
u met uw
hoofd?

2 ZANO əiq · ga naar pagina

53

bij uwe liefdaeer · ga naar pagina 74, cijfer 26

↑
Shiu-Kay Kan, a London
manufacturer of lamps
and lighting systems, used
FF Disturbance for their
1993 brochure, designed
in-house.

←
Two pages from the Annual
Report 1998-1999 of the
ONVZ Health Insurance
Company (the Netherlands).
Designers Dietwee and SYB
used two characters from
FF Dingbats, one with the
head chopped off. The copy
reads: (male) 'Is your heart
in the right place?' and
(female) 'Where are you with
your head?' (i.e. What are
you brooding about?).

→
Promotional posters for
FF Dirty Faces, designed by
Neville Brody, 1994-96.

FF DINGBATS Johannes Erler | Olaf Stein, 1993
While others are scanning their dingbat collections
hoping to stumble across a car-telephone or fax-
machine symbol, FontShop have the ultimate pi font
that should cater for your needs well into the next
millenium: some 800 symbols and icons from the
world of modern communication: faxes, ISDN, disks,
keyboards... all absolutely usable.

FF DIRTY FACES 1994–1996
FF Dirty Faces is a series of 'destructive' packages
compiled by Neville Brody. Between 1994 and 1996,
six packages of Dirty Faces were released. The FF
Dirty Faces packages contained fonts by Peter Biľak,
Neville Brody, chester, James Closs, Hannes Famira,
Luc(as) de Groot, Stefan Hägerling, Markus Hanzer,
Jürgen Huber, Manfred Klein, Klaus Dieter Lettau,
Fabian Rottke, Fabrizio Schiavi, Simone Schöpp,
John Siddle and Eva Walter.

FF DISTRICT Albert Boton, 2004
Albert Boton's expansion of his FF District Bold face
which was released in 2002 as part of ff Bastille
Display.

FF DISTURBANCE Jeremy Tankard, 1993
Jeremy Tankard's take on the 'single-case alphabet':
a font which combines the structure of the Roman
upper case and mediaeval lower case. The idea was
to select the most extreme letter shapes, the best
of both worlds, and put them into one alphabet for
maximum legibility.

FF DOLORES Tobias Frere-Jones, 1991
The first published typeface by Tobias Frere-Jones,
who has gone on to become a senior type designer
at the Font Bureau and a partner in Hoefler & Frere-
Jones. Dolores was inspired by the erratic energy of
children's handwriting.

FF DOME Neville Brody, 1993
FF Dome is part of a series of fonts based on a Brody
poster design from 1988. See also FF World and FF
Tokyo.

FF DOT MATRIX Cornel Windlin | Stephan Müller, 1994
'While some are busy with the quest for the perfect
typeface, we are quite happy to wallow in the
nether regions of typographical perversity. FF Dot
Matrix is a direct result of this fascination with the
shortcomings of technology's promise of purity and
perfection and their impact on typography. Welcome
to the age of junk!'

FF DOUBLE DIGITS Klein | van Rossum, 1992
FF Double Digits is a practical Pi font enabling the
user to create various kinds of frames with numbers
from 1 to 99.

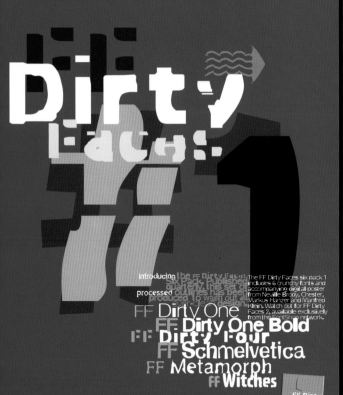

Dirty Faces 1

Introducing the FF Dirty Faces. Published quarterly, this processed outlines has been produced to wash out...

The FF Dirty Faces six pack 1 includes 6 crunchy fonts and accompanying digital poster from Neville Brody, Chester, Markus Hanzer and Manfred Klein. Watch out for FF Dirty Faces 2, available exclusively from the FontShop network.

FF Dirty One
FF Dirty One Bold
FF Dirty Four
FF Schmelvetica
FF Metamorph
FF Witches

FF Dirty Faces 1

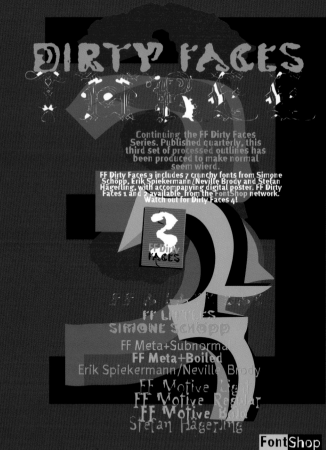

DIRTY FACES 3

Continuing the FF Dirty Faces Series. Published quarterly, this third set of processed outlines has been produced to make normal seem wierd.

FF Dirty Faces 3 includes 7 crunchy fonts from Simone Schopp, Erik Spiekermann/Neville Brody and Stefan Hagerling, with accompanying digital poster. FF Dirty Faces 1 and 2 available from the FontShop network. Watch out for Dirty Faces 4!

FF Lithos
SIMONE SCHOPP

FF Meta+Subnormal
FF Meta+Boiled
Erik Spiekermann/Neville Brody

FF Motive Light
FF Motive Regular
FF Motive Bold
Stefan Hagerling

Dirty Faces Four

Continuing the FF Dirty Faces Six Pack. Published quarterly, this fourth set of processed outlines has been produced to make normal seem wierd.

Dirty Faces 4 includes 6 crunchy fonts and their accompanying digital posters from: Fabrizio Schiavi, Hannes Famira & Klaus Dieter Lettau. Dirty Faces 1, 2 and 3 are available and watch out for Dirty Faces 5, available exclusively from the FontShop network.

9600

4 Dirty Faces

Voodoo Child
Voodoo Regular
MUTILATED FAT
MUTILATED CAPS

DIRTY FACES 5

Dirty Fat Normal
Boomshanker Light
Boomshanker Solid

Continuing the FF dirty faces Pack. Published quarterly, this fifth set of processed outlines has been produced to make normal seem wierd!

FF dirty 5

FF DOUBLE DUTCH Marianne van Ham, 1992
Each glyph of FF Double Dutch consists of two
overlaid, slightly different version of a Bodoni-like
character. A typical product of the early nineties,
when type became an experimental art form.

FF DUBRUSH Dung van Meerbeeck, 1992–1994
The Saigon-born Belgian designer Dung van Meerbeeck has a natural flair for drawing highly original,
spontaneous letterforms. Published between 1992
and 1994, his FontFonts form a versatile collection
of scripts, designed as though they might have
been written with a flexible pen or pointed brush.

FF EBOY Steffen Sauerteig | Kai Vermehr, 1998
The FF Eboy family is based on the geometry of pixel
fonts for the screen, and was created especially
for use on screen and the web. However, intrepid
designers won't shy away from using the face in
print as well. The package also includes FF Xcreen,
a screen font with reduced height.

FF EDDIE Eddie Baret, 2001
French designer Eddie Baret based this font on the
writing in a sketch book of his younger brother's.
It's the writing of a 5 or 6-year-old kid at the
moment in which he learns to read and write. At
first, the boy was really amazed and proud to see
his writing on the screen. Later, he aknowledged it
was 'badly written' and that his writing had become
a lot better in the mean time.

FF EKTTOR Fabian Rottke, 1994
Fabian Rottke: 'I drew the letters for FF Ekttor
using an elderberry branch and ink and then
digitized them. The result was a very irregular set
of characters, from which I chose letters for each
of the Light and Bold weights. The mixed weight is
a combination of the Light and Bold, spread over
the upper and lower case letter positions. They are
distributed in such a way that the irregularities and
diversity found within the original face are visibly
apparent.'

FF ELEGIE Albert Boton, 2002
Élégie: tender and sad poetry. Albert Boton's
typeface of that name is based on the calligraphy
and lettering of artists such as Auriol, Benjamin
Rabié, Mucha and Lautrec at the end of the 19th and
beginning of the 20th century. Boton made his

original drawings in 1993 with a Brause ink pen.
The result is a lively handwritten typeface family with
Roman, Italic, Swash and Ornament variants.

FF ELEMENTA Mindaugas Strockis, 1998–2002
FF Elementa is a complete family, a rarity in the world
of digitized typewriter faces. Strockis: 'It came out
of a dream of a perfect typewriter – the one which is
always tidy, clean and sharp, with all sorts of dia-
criticals and special symbols, Bolds and Italics, but
nevertheless an earnest old-fashioned typewriter.'
In true Magda-and-Trixie spirit, Strockis later added
FF Elementa Rough.

FF ELEMENTARY Nicole Kapitza, 1995
Nicole Kapitza's personal comments about FF
Elementary: 'Drawings, symbols and ideograms have
always fascinated me. There are symbols for almost
every facet of life. FF Elementary depicts themes that
usually are not found in most pi and symbol fonts:
nature, outer space, the environment, sex, violence,
various fears, sexual orientation,... Themes that
surround and affect our daily lives.'

FF ENGINE Alex Scholing, 1995–1996
According to Scholing 'FF Engine was an attempt to
make a good, solid, general- purpose typeface with
as little effort as possible. The first thing I did to
reduce complications was do away with the contrast
in the letters, which means FF Engine is a so-called
monolinear typeface (well, almost; try to find how
I cheated...). To enhance legibility I added small
serif-like bulges at the ends of the stems.' Scholing
later decided that his first typeface was rather
immature. For years he worked on a more sophisticated typeface based on the same idea. This became
FF Roice (2003).

↑
The original model for
FF Eddie was a page from a
notebook belonging to the
little brother of designer
Eddie Baret.

←
Imaginary ticket made with
FF Dot Matrix. JS

↓
FF Elegie on a t-shirt.
MvB for FSI.

↗
FF Ekttor by Fabian Rottke.

⋯→
Honey label for Bienen-
wirtschaft Meissen, one of
Germany's leading honey
manufacturers. 2004, Büro
Wilhelm, Amberg.

Masthead of the French
film magazine *Ciné Live*
using FF DuMifu from the
FF DuBrush series.

⋯→ ⋯→
FontCard for FF Elementary
designed by Nicole Kapitza.
FSI, 1995.

FF
Double
Dutch
Double
Dutch

---->
Cover for *From Brooklyn to Breukelen*, a book on twenty years of hip-hop in the Netherlands. Design: Donald Beekman with FF Flava and FF Beekman, 2002.

FontCard for FF Extra, designed by Paul H. Neville for FSI, 1995

Packaging made by Schein Berlin using FF Fontesque.

FF EUREKA Peter Biľak, 1998
Peter Biľak originally drew FF Eureka in 1995 for use in a self-published booklet set in Slovak, his native language, and English. In order to accommodate the many diacritics used in Slovak, Biľak gave Eureka long ascenders and descenders. The Eureka family was gradually extended, adding sans, condensed and monospaced variants.

FF EUREKA SANS Peter Biľak, 2000–2001
FF Eureka Sans was developed over a period of several years. Completed after the Serif version was finished, the Sans was continually re-examined and updated as it was used for books, magazines, brochures, posters, TV and even postage stamps. With letterforms ten percent narrower than comparable text faces, the proportions of Eureka are quite economic. This economy frees the user to space the letters more generously, an important advantage for, as Biľak says, 'looser spacing helps to avoid the typographic noise inside a text, and retains the individuality of letters.'

FF EXTRA Paul H. Neville, 1995
At some point in his *Essay on Typography*, Eric Gill illustrates how not to design type, showing – among other things – a very thick capital 'A' with a very small counter. This inspired Paul Neville: 'It was labelled "Hardly Recognisable" and I immediately knew that it was a great inspiration to base a font on. As I worked on the characters, I really tried to break them down into their simplest forms. My aim was to develop an incredibly thick display face, while still retaining a high degree of legibility (you can be the judge on that one).'

FF FAGO Ole Schäfer, 2000
FF Fago is a true corporate typeface, the result of many years of experience with the challenges and requirements of complex corporate design projects. FF Fago offers a series of five finely balanced weights in three widths each, enough for every conceivable application. The various widths were carefully drawn to complement each other. FF Fago Mono is a monospaced, typewriter-like addition to the family, perfect for technical texts. Or just for fun: FF Fago isn't just for corporate design.

FF FANCYWRITING Timothy Donaldson, 1996
According to its designer, 'the impetus for FF FancyWriting came from a desire to create handwritten letterforms in a digital manner. Using a Wacom tablet and Painter I dashed off a number of versions of each letter. I then went off for a cup of tea and completely forgot about the idea until I came across it, a few days later, lurking in the depths of my hard disk. I picked out the best letters and autotraced and tweaked them, then made the thin and fat versions (micro and mega).'

FF FLAVA Donald Beekman, 2003
As an active member of the Dutch music scene, Donald Beekman was often asked to design record covers and handouts. As Aachen Bold was a much appreciated headline face in these circles, Beekman decided to design a more personal, outspoken alternative with a contemporary feel. FF Flava comes in 4 versions: the two variations with rounded top or bottom can be combined to form instant logotypes.

FF FLÈCHES Pierre di Sciullo, 1993
FF Flèches is a symbol typeface designed by the French conceptualist typographer Pierre di Sciullo. A fun package of crazy arrows, one font with horizontal pointers, and its counterpart with verticals. When it comes to giving directions, FF Flèches is the way to go.

FF FOLK Maurizio Osti | Jane Patterson, 2003
FF Folk is based on the lettering used by Lithuanian-American artist Ben Shahn in his paintings, lithographs book cover designs. Designed in 1940, the alphabet was reconstructed and redesigned by

Osti and Jane Patterson in 1995 with the consent and approval of Mrs. Bernarda Shahn and the Estate of Ben Shahn (VAGA New York). Maurizio Osti drew two character shapes for each letter to best capture the vibrant variety present in the original art.

FF FONTESQUE Nick Shinn, 1994
A good casual setting of type has a distinctive quality all its own, quite unlike hand-lettering. But it's a lot of work. Letter by letter one has to improvise. Fontesque solves the problem. It provides casual setting right from the keyboard, yet with proper typographic colour, even at text sizes. FF Fontesque, Nick Shinn adds, 'is an argument against conformity and perfection, a plea for the virtues of individuality and idiosyncrasy.'

FF FONTESQUE SANS Nick Shinn, 2001
Introducing the typeface that belongs in every food cupboard, uh, fonts folder, Nick Shinn took his popular FF Fontesque, peeled off the serifs, threw it in a pot with some Helvetica, added a dash of Swiss, and cooked to perfection. Mmm, enjoy!

FF FONTSOUP Joan Carles Casasín | Andreu Balius, 1997
Alphabet soup is widely spread in the western world and the letterforms vary from country to country. A Catalan version was digitized by Casasín and Balius of Typeware back in 1993 and became perhaps the first printable pasta. Three years later FontShop asked Typeware to digitize a German version; the result is an intercultural family of floating fonts.

FF FRIDAY, SATURDAY, SUNDAY Jan Jedding, 1994
The designer's personal comments about FF Friday, Saturday, Sunday: 'I simply wanted to try out a new program. I scanned in my own handwriting, distributed the characters over the keyboard and then ironed out the small details here and there… and then a bit more… and then… one Friday, they were finished!'

FF Elementa

A Dream of the Perfect Typewriter.

Vita
currentes
imitatur
undas

Normal
Bold
Italic
Bold Italic

Der Traum von einer idealen Schreibmaschine.

LÉONARD·DE·VINCI

OPÉRA·DE·ROUEN

de.la.danse

W.Forsythe   M.Cunningham
Rosas   K.Kvarnström
T.Brow   S.Waltz   M.Sa
rukkaï   Y.Oïda

Friday, **Saturday, Sunday**

↑↑
The dream of the perfect typewriter as staged by Mindaugas Strockis using FF Elementa. FSI, 1999.

┄┄►
FontCard by FontSoup designers Joan Carles Casasín and Andreu Balius (Typerware), FSI FontShop International, 1997.

♫
Poster proposal for the Rouen Opera (France), designed by Johanna Balušíková. Typeface: FF Eureka Mono.

┄┄►
Poster designed by Maurizio Osti with FF Folk.

⚓
James Reyman, New York: graphic bug for the 2004 election campaign, commissioned by the *New York Times*. Typeface: FF Fago.

FONTSHOP INTERNATIONAL Presents: **THE FF FONTSOUP FAMILY**
available in two flavours:
Catalan & German
and three weights:
Regular, Boiled & ExtraBoiled

Mmmm, I Like FF FontSoup!
Feed your designs with the vitaminic typefaces

by Typerware®

Oh, that's how they are inside the pack, in the supermarket.
I like it mum. They're so tasty...   Uh, muuuum. I think you forgot they started boiling one hour ago

LET YOUR COMPUTER TASTE THEM!

CNA

Roma   Auditorium del Massimo

CNA

CONVENTION 1999

ALL'ALTEZZA

DEL CAMBIAMENTO

venerdì 22
sabato 23
domenica 24
ottobre 1999

CAMPAIGN · THE BIG ISSUES · 2004

moonbase alpha '95

Governor *diagonal*
outward for endive

FF Ginger Light, Light Italic, Light Flamboyant, Regular, Reg Italic, Reg Flamboyant

ABCDEFGHIJKLMNOPQRSTU
VWXYZ abcdefghijklmnop
qrstuvwxyz 0123456789 &!

ABCDEFGHIJKLMNOPQRSTU
VWXYZ abcdefghijklmnop
qrstuvwxyz 0123456789 &!

Balcony register frontal *marmalade enters*
nimble consortium relish backward foxing
diversion abundant Myopic genesis quilts
FF Ginger Light, Light Italic

Cramping style to process made possible
***rather tempting* forgivable knife derelict**
since like birdhouse *developers question*
FF Ginger Regular, Regular Italic

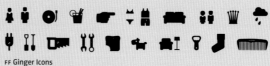

FF Ginger Icons

←⋯
FontCard by FF Moonbase
Alpha designer Cornel
Windlin, FSI FontShop
International, 1995.

FF Ginger specimen. MvB

⋯→
Double-page spreads
from the children's book
*Maanprinses zoekt haar
muiltjes* (2004) by
Marlies Visser,
Netherlands.
Made with FF Handwriter.

↘
FUSE Classics: YouCan
(Read Me) by Phil Baines.
GP

FF FUDONI Max Kisman, 1991
FF Fudoni was probably the world's first cut-and-paste typeface: an irreverent monster created by welding together parts of two of the most used typefaces in the world, Bodoni and Futura.

FF FUSE CLASSICS Cornel Windlin | Pierre di Sciullo | Malcolm Garrett | Phil Baines
FUSE was a quarterly disk and poster publication dedicated to experimental type. FF FUSE Classics is a collection of the most successful FUSE typefaces, redesigned and with complete character sets: FF Moonbase Alpha by Cornel Windlin (from FUSE 3: Disinformation); Pierre di Sciullo's FF Scratched Out (FUSE 5: Virtual); FF Stealth by Malcolm Garrett (FUSE 1: Invention). FF YouCan (Read Me) is Phil Baines's 1995 version of F Can You (Read Me)?, designed in 1991 for FUSE 1: Invention.

FF GINGER Jürgen Huber, 2002
FF Ginger is an alternative to the widely-used Crillee and Serpentine faces, which are especially popular in Bold-Italic. They express speed and dynamism and are excellent choices for internet providers, couriers, service bureaus, etc. Ginger's Light version and matching Icons extend its typographic scope, and the Flamboyant versions add a spark to individual letters and initial caps.

FF GOTHIC Neville Brody, 1992
Based on a grid of squares and triangles, FF Gothic is probably Neville Brody's most rigid and strictly geometric type family. Its many variations allow for play and variety in spite of the simplicity of the basic forms.

FF GOVAN Ole Schäfer | Erik Spiekermann 2000
When Glasgow 1999 City of Architecture and Design wanted a typeface to represent the city, Meta Design won the competition with a font that is sturdy, friendly and contemporary, while subtly referring to the lettering of Ronnie Mackintosh, Glasgow's most famous designer. The strength of the family lies in the innovative manner in which the three widths, two ascender heights, two descender lengths and dingbats can be combined. The results are striking and offer a unique possibility to create sculptures with type and play with language, as Glaswegians tend to do.

FF GRAFFIO Alessio Leonardi, 1995
'FF Graffio is a nervous typeface: I did it after I went to the cinema to see Natural Born Killers... I love cats, but I'm allergic to them.'

FF HANDWRITER Leonardi, 1997
Alessio Leonardi: 'FF Handwriter is the only truly portable typewriter typeface and looks great to boot. It guarantees success if used for love letters and shows a lot of character when used for filling in official forms. Especially handy are the many symbols for office and interpersonal communication.'

FF HANDS Just van Rossum | Erik van Blokland, 1990
Probably the world's first digital handwriting font, based on the handwriting of designers Erik van Blokland and Just van Rossum of LettError. Educated in an environment where handwritten letterforms were considered to be the origin of all typography (the Royal Academy in The Hague, Holland), it was a natural step for them to derive a typographically sound font from their own hands.

FF HARDCASE Dmitri Lavrow, 1996
Dmitri Lavrow from Russia designed HardCase 45 for use on his own letterhead. He wanted a monolinear, monospaced typeface that would be modest yet slightly bizarre. The result is a design that manages to avoid the homogeneity most fall victim to. At FontShop's request, Dmitri expanded the family to a total of five weights.

FF HARLEM Neville Brody, 1993
A grotesque with soul, sporting counters that move about. As used in Brody's poster for the movie *A Rage in Harlem.*

FF HEADZ Florian Zietz, 2005
The concept for FF Headz is similar to the idea found in certain children's books, where pages are split into sections that can be grouped in unusual and humorous combinations. For example, a crocodile head from one page might be paired with an elephant body from another page to form a 'crocophant'. One rainy afternoon, Zietz began drawing heads with his niece Sophie (11) and nephew Jakob (9). Using a Euro coin as a template, the creative team drew hundreds of heads in a couple of days.

FF HYDRA | FF HYDRA TEXT Silvio Napoleone, 2002–2004
The inspiration for the FF Hydra font family came mostly from the unique lettering of French poster art of the 19th and early 20th centuries. Toronto designer Silvio Napoleone found that the lettering of this period combined elements that are quite relevant to today's modern design aesthetic. FF Hydra was designed as a versatile text and headline font. In 2004 the Text version was introduced.

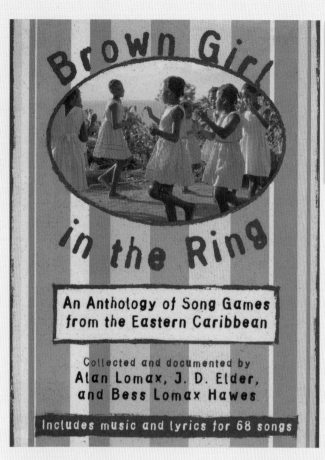

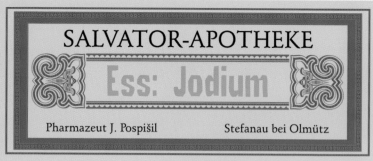

FF Irregular

Light *Italic* CAPITALS **Bold** Black Inline

FF IDENTIFICATION Rian Hughes, 1993
We hope you don't want us to tell you what this typeface is good for. Just be on the lookout for this multi-code alphabet on record sleeves, stickers, posters and magazines: Morse, character Frequency, Semaphor and Alphabet are the different styles in this typographic potpourri.

FF IMPERIAL Donald Beekman, 2001
FF Imperial Spike was originally developed as a logo for Imperial Recordings, a Dutch techno/trance label. It is an alphabet with a fantasy, Tolkien-inspired look. Imperial Bone has rounder forms, reminding of, well, bones. Although Beekman never intended the Imperial family to be a heavy metal typeface, that is what many people see it to be.

FF INFO Erik Spiekermann | Ole Schäfer, 1996–2000
When the Düsseldorf Airport was partly destroyed by a fire in April 1996, things had to be fixed up quickly. By the start of the summer season, a temporary signage system had to be put in place. MetaDesign did the job in a mere six weeks. A new typeface was developed on the spot, taking an existing Spiekermann concept as its point of departure. The FF Info family was later completed with a special version for long texts: FF Info Text.

FF INFO OFFICE Erik Spiekermann | Ole Schäfer, 1998
Since every PC owner can now print out his or her correspondence with Times New Roman or Helvetica/Arial, real typefaces are no longer a novelty. Yet, the typewriter face still exists in the collective imagination as the epitome of office communication. FF Info Office combines the advantages of a typesetting face with the merits of a typewriter face.

FF INKLING Joel Decker, 1997
Inkling was born out of the question 'How can one communicate through the digital realm using voices closer to their original sources, yet at the same time being true to their technology?' Two inspirations that helped lead to the final draft of Inkling are the early stages of children's cursive writing and Joel Decker's experiments of faxing cursive writing over and over, pushing legibility and idiosyncrasy to the extreme, and then cleaning it up to arrive at a kind of primitive-digital hybrid.

FF INSTANT TYPES Just van Rossum, 1992
In the same spirit as Erik van Blokland's typewriter font Trixie, Just van Rossum made FF Instant Types, digitizing found letters from packaging and flight cases, as well as alphabets from a children's stamp box and Dymo lettering punchers. Instant Types are: FF Confidential, Dynamoe, Flightcase, Karton and Stamp Gothic.

FF INSTANTER Frank Heine, 1994
Inspired by the 'Grotesk' faces of the 1920's, most directly by Erbar, FF Instanter was designed to be a dynamic Grotesque. In spite of its liveliness and similarity to handwriting, FF Instanter is extremely legible even in very small point sizes.

FF IODINE Stephan Müller, 1995
FF Iodine is the digital version of an alphabet originally created for labels and signs in drugstores by the Moravian pharmacist J. Pospisil. He created the individual letters by layering horizontal handwritten and vertical stencil elements. The end results were re-drawn with pen and ink. Stephan 'Pronto' Müller extended and modified these original drawings to fit today's typographic standards.

FF IRREGULAR Markus Hanzer, 1994
'The traditional problem with computer graphics has always been its sterility,' says designer Markus Hanzer. 'People have tried over and over again to simulate the dirtiness, spontaneity and complexity of handmade art. FF Irregular is an attempt to let a font develop "randomly". It was the result of a series of attempts to change and develop characters electronically. Much like a human hand, the computer program introduced unpredictable changes and found a form of its own.'

FF ISONORM Robert Kirchner, 1993
Even before AutoCAD decided to acknowledge the existence of PostScript, artists and designers have been asking for a PostScript version of the Isonorm draughtsman's face. A lot of creative people have been eagerly waiting to misuse this geometrically-constructed standard letterform for their free-wheeling design. So now, at last, you can have some fun.

FF JACKIE Dario Muhafara, 2003
This font is inspired by the type on Jack Daniel's whisky labels. Starting from there, Dario Muhafara made some changes to design a font with a contemporary look between a retro design and a serious script font.

FF JACQUE Max Kisman, 1991
When Max Kisman was asked by a Dutch magazine what his favourite typeface was, he could not think of one. His friend Chris Vermaas said, 'Well then, make it!' Kisman sat down at his Mac and drew FF Jacque directly on-screen.

CITIZEN

author PENELOPE REEMES

>FF Inkling-Regular
>FF Inkling-Bold

Inkling
(58pt
x
·-@

technology *in the soil*

We scribbled:

A vial of ink in one hand *a microchip*

hovering above the other...

Stay Tuned
Stay Tuned
Stay Tuned
Stay Tuned

₪	18.50	TRICASE	10.55	₪
₪	19.10	Santa Maria di Leuca	10.35	₪
₪	19.30	Ugento	10.15	₪
₪	19.45	Casarano	10.00	₪
₪	19.50	Matino	9.55	₪
₪	19.55	Parabita	9.50	₪
₪	20.05	Collepasso	9.40	₪
₪	20.45	Galatina	9.25	₪
₪	20.50	LECCE V. Le Foscolo 41	8.30	₪
20.00	₪	OTRANTO	₪	9.40
20.20	₪	Maglie	₪	9.20
20.50	₪	LECCE V. Le Foscolo 41	₪	8.50
₪	20.30	GALLIPOLI	9.30	₪
₪	20.50	Gallipoli	9.10	₪
₪	21.00	Nardo	9.00	₪
₪	21.10	Copertino	8.50	₪
₪	21.30	LECCE V. Le Foscolo 41	8.30	₪
₪	21.30	LECCE V. Le Foscolo 41	8.30	₪
₪	22.00	Brindisi	8.00	₪
₪	22.30	Mesagne	7.50	₪
₪	22.45	San Vito dei Normanni	7.45	₪
₪	22.50	Carovigno	7.40	₪
₪	23.00	Ostuni	7.00	₪
₪	23.10	Rosa Marina	6.50	₪
₪	23.35	Fasano	6.25	₪
₪	23.45	Monopoli	6.00	₪
₪	23.55	Polignano a Mare	6.00	₪
₪	0.00	Mola di Bari	5.50	₪
₪	!	BARI - Via Capruzzi	5.50	₪
₪	0.40	BARI - Piazza Moro	!	₪
₪	!	Candela	4.00	₪
₪	!	Lacedonia	!	₪
₪	3.15	Grottaminarda	3.15	₪
₪	!	Benevento	!	₪
₪	3.45	Avellino Ovest	2.45	₪
₪	5.30	ROMA - Staz. Tiburtna	0.45	₪

Costo Biglietto per Roma Itl. 62.000 + Itl. 3.000
(Prenotazione) = Itl. 65.000 (33.57 EURO). Jigger

Ak ↑-apn dent
m'a souhaité
une bonne année

←·· ←···
There's a Brown Girl in the Ring by Alan Lomax, J.D. Elder and Bess Lomax Hawe, Random House, New York, 1997. Cover (designer unknown) made with FF Stamp Gothic.

FontCard by FF Iodine designer Stephan Müller, 1995.

←···
Ficticious book cover made with FF Info. MvB for FSI.

FontCard for FF Inkling by Joel Decker, 1997.

↖
Poster designed by Max Kisman to show off FF Fudoni and FF Jacque, ca. 1991

←···
Imaginary time table made with FF Jigger. JS.

↓
New Year's badge for a Belgian theatre group. Dorp & Dal with FF Instanter, 1997

FF JAMBONO Xavier Dupré, 2002
Xavier Dupré: 'I designed Tartine and Jambono in
2000-2001 when I worked as type designer in a
packaging design agency in Paris. I just wanted to
have a complete font up my sleeve when I need to
design a logo for someone. Jambono is a display
type for packaging but can also be used in text
thanks to the several weights I have drawn. It's a
dynamic face with a soft and playful look.'

FF JIGGER Steffen Sauerteig, 2000
FF Jigger is an adaptation of the heavily shadowed
type seen on television whose purpose is to differentiate text from moving backgrounds. The fonts
are intended for headline use and work best as a mix
of upper and lower case. FF Jigger comes in a round
and a square version, both of which are available as
shadowed fonts or with separate fore- and backgrounds which can be coloured independently.

FF KARBID Verena Gerlach, 1999
The inspiration for FF Karbid came from 1930s German storefront lettering, the peculiarities of which
are still visible in the Display version (see the letter
'g', for instance). With this as a starting point Verena
Gerlach then produced a family of well-behaved but
energetic text faces.

FF KARO Martin L'Allier, 2005
A quote from Matthew Carter was the inspiration for
L'Allier's project: 'Blackletter is technically the perfect digital typeface. It decomposes perfectly into
a mosaic on a computer screen. There are beautiful
bitmaps. It's even self-hinting. It's so perfect for the
digital medium, why has it not supplanted roman in
our current all-digital typography?' (Peter Wildbur,
Information graphics, 1989). L'Allier initially set out
to create a bitmap Fraktur, but saw that the field was
already well-covered, and that Bézier curves offered
a great deal more flexibility. After extensively
researching Fraktur typefaces, he produced a font
family that combines the calligraphic heritage of
Fraktur fonts with the rational and optical dynamics
of the grid.

FF KATH Condensed Paul H. Neville, 1992
FF Kath Condensed is an early, historically inspired
FontFont for headlines.

FF KIEVIT Mike Abbink, 2001
With FF Kievit Mike Abbink of San Francisco wanted
to design 'a sans-serif that has the purity and
simplicity of a great modernist typeface like Frutiger,
but maintains enough of the humanist aspects
that you find in an oldstyle serif like Garamond for
the legibility and fluidity.' Apart from being utterly
readable, FF Kievit is also a very neutral face, neither
bookish nor exaggeratedly 'cold'.

FF KIPP Claudia Kipp, 1993
FF Kipp is based on a 1930s wood type alphabet that
Claudia Kipp discovered in Leipzig. The face has
been broken into different levels of wear and tear,
which can be layered to evoke the printing made
with letterpressed wood typefaces.

FF KATH CONDENSED

← FF Kath designer
Paul Neville calls
this mini-specimen
a 'gravestone'.

⋯→
Poster for a show by
the Barcelona 'techno
performer' Marcel·lí
Antunez Roca. Designed
by Laura Meseguer at
Cosmic, Barcelona, 2000.
Typeface: FF Kipp

⋯→ ⋯→
FontCard by FF Koko de-
signer Kai Zimmermann,
1998.

↘ ↘
Pocket-watch design with
FF Bagel digits (part of the
FF Levant package). MvB

FF KISMAN Max Kisman, 1991
FF Kisman is a collection of display fonts originally
made for various magazines art-directed by Kisman:
FF Scratch was hand-cut from ulano masking film
and FF Cutout was made with scissors. FF Network,
like FF Rosetta, was a very early Macintosh font
designed for Kisman's own use. All were completed
in 1990-1991 at the request of FontShop.

FF KLUNDER SCRIPT Barbara Klunder, 1994
Based on the hand-lettering of Barbara Klunder, an
award-winning, internationally known Canadian
illustrator and graphic designer. To quote Barbara
on the typeface: 'I think the best use of this font is as
body copy – it turns a sentence into a dance.'

FF KNOBCHEESE Rian Hughes, 1994
Rian Hughes' typefaces display his love for the
world of comic books. FF Knobcheese, with its
circular, internal spaces, is an unusual typeface
reminiscent of... chunks of Swiss cheese.

FF KOKO Kai Zimmermann, 1998
Zimmermann has this to say about his typeface:
'Koko combines blue-collar, utilitarian simplicity and
soft playfulness.'

FF KOSMIK Erik van Blokland, 1993
Like the groundbreaking FF Beowolf, FF Kosmik
endeavors to break the monotony of conventional
typography by providing different variants for each
character. While in Beowolf the shapes are drawn
randomly while printing, Kosmik has three pre-
drawn alphabets. A secret digital technique imple-
ments these variants in succession. The letterforms
are based on van Blokland's handwriting as seen in
his comics.

FF KURT Vivien Palloks, 1998
'Kurt is from Berlin, that's obvious,' says Palloks
about her first published typeface. FF Kurt originated as hand-cut stamp forms. The design was
meant to represent a very eclectic area of Berlin
where everything is an original. And indeed so is
the typeface, each letter is an individual and yet
together they form a harmonious whole.

FF LANCÉ CONDENSED Joachim Müller-Lancé, 1997
Work on FF Lancé began in 1983 at design school.
Back from an inspiring vacation in Brittany, France,
Joachim Müller-Lancé drew the first characters by
hand in type class, for a photography project with
pictures from this travel. Ten years later, Lancé
completed the alphabet as a three-weight family.
Lancé was the first typeface he ever digitized, so
it was a huge surprise when he won the Morisawa
Prize for it.

FF LAYOUT Gerd Wippich, 1996
FF Layout is intended to be used for planning complex layouts. It contains a block-letter, hand-written
face in four weights, plus the Oxmox font in Regular
and Bold, where all letters are replaced with either x,
m, or o, and the 'greeked' text Tramline that displays
the text as solid grey lines. While the comic-like
Layout can be used well any number of ways, the
other fonts only really make sense for actual layout
work. Says Wippich: 'With my family of fonts the
graphic designer is able to reclaim a lost element of
the design process, the layout stage.'

TORNA A BARCELONA

MARCEL·LI ANTUNEZ ROCA

AFASIA

del 4 al 15 d'Octubre

CCCB

WWW. MARCEL·LI. COM

ACCIÓ·ELECTRÒNICA
VISUAL·SONORA
ROBÒTICA

TICKETS
TEL·ENTRADA
902 10 12 12
CAIXA CATALUNYA

iNFO al CCCB
Tel. 933 064 100

Centre de Cultura Contemporània de Barcelona

Produït per el TNC-Teatre Nacional de Catalunya, MECAD \ Media Centre d'Art i Disseny (Sabadell-Barcelona), el Festival de Teatre Visual i de Titelles de Barcelona i el Institut del Teatre de la Diputació de Barcelona. Projecte inclòs en el *Programa de Desarrollo de Nuevas Tecnologías* de la Societat General d'Autors i Editors i la Fundació Autor, així com en el *Proyecto Arte y Tecnología* per a la Fundación Telefónica. Col·laboren: CCCB, Advanced Applications Pro Arts i ICUB de l'Ajuntament de Barcelona

KO LO
KO VE
SY AL
OU L
VE MU
RY CH

Ein neuer Anfang

CDU

One of the surprises of the 2005 German elections was the choice of typefaces used during the election campaign: about 80% of the parties used FontFonts. FF Kievit assisted Angela Merkel in becoming the first female Chancellor.
Photo: Jürgen Siebert.

FontCard by FF Kurt designer Vivien Palloks, 1998.

FF LEGATO Evert Bloemsma, 2004
'Legato' means: to play the notes of music in a 'connected' manner. The idea of connecting separate units to enhance the overall expression can be applied to type as well. FF Legato is a sans-serif typeface designed to build better word images by means of diagonal stress. The 'contrast' between thick and thin parts leads the reader's eye from one character to the next and thus improves legibility.

FF LETTER GOTHIC TEXT | LETTER GOTHIC Albert Pinggera, 1996–1998
FF Letter Gothic Text was FontShop's third 'untypographic' typeface. As in the case of the DIN and OCR typefaces, both of which were originally designed for industrial use, the monospaced typewriter font Letter Gothic is experiencing something of a renaissance. As the name FF Letter Gothic Text suggests, Albert Pinggera's version of the classic face is not monospaced. This disappointed some early users. A three-weight monospaced version simply called FF Letter Gothic was published in 1998.

FF LETTER GOTHIC SLANG Susanna Dulkinys, 1999
This reworking of Letter Gothic was born of a need for the perfect typeface for the Wired book *Jargon Watch, a pocket dictionary for the digerati.* Susanna Dulkinys: 'Jargon is a jumbled form of ephemeral language filled with metaphor. Words are transposed to create another meaning. FF Letter Gothic Slang does the same on the character level. Transposing, flipping and turning letterforms until they appear to be other characters altogether.'

FF LETTERINE Alessio Leonardi, 1995
'I love the Archetipetti (little archetypes) and I think they love me too. I invented FF Letterine in order to be able to communicate with those tiny creatures. Archetipetti are really polite and politically correct, even if they sometimes don't look so. FF Letterine Esagerate was not my work: the Archetipetti did it. They thought that sometimes you need to exaggerate things and feelings.'

FF LEVANT Per Baasch Jørgensen, 2002
The idea for FF Falafel, the 'Arabic' typeface of the FF Levant package, came from looking at Arabic lettering and seeing shapes that resembled Latin letters. Would it be possible to create an entire Latin alphabet by extracting shapes from Arabic? Eventually the intricate and often overlapping letterforms necessitated some 40 ligatures in a separate font. FF Bagel, based on Hebrew, was made with the same principle of first giving an impression of a foreign writing, and only then revealing itself as legible to Western readers.

FF LIANT Ingrid Liche, 1995
For decades, Ingrid Liche has worked as a designer of advertising and packaging for natural medicines and cosmetics. As part of this work she developed several alphabets, most of which express an anthroposophic, Rudolf Steiner-inspired style. Liant Medium was originally developed for the corporate identity of the natural cosmetic company Weleda.

FF LOCALIZER Critzler, 1996
First used in the books on (and by) the German techno scene, and techno design specifically, Localizer is at the same time a nostalgic '70s and a '90s typeface. Along the lines of 'we thought this would

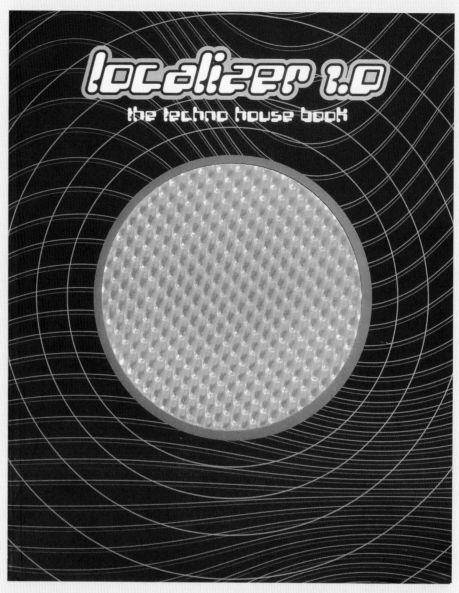

be the future, then it wasn't, but it didn't matter after all, so here it is'.

FF LOCALIZER CLONES Critzler, 1997
Critzler's personal update of his FF Localizer Sans. FF Localizer Clones consists of two sub-families, FF Bionic and FF Chemo, which can be combined by overlaying (e. g. Chemo-Bubble in black plus Chemo-Dot in orange plus Chemo-Stroke in blue result in letters consisting of different colors). Although the principle of layering has led to rather bizarre and unusual lettershapes, these are all based on the Localizer Sans grid and therefore continue its character, allowing several fonts to combine in one line.

FF MAGDA Cornel Windlin, 1995
FF MAGDA CLEAN Critzler | Henning Krause, 1998
Intended as a sister font to the inescapable FF Trixie, FF Magda offers a less nostalgic, more modern and fuzzy typewriter face to designers with an appetite for banal everyday typography. A clean version, appropriately called FF Magda Clean, was later made by Critzler and Henning Krause.

FF MAIOLA Veronika Burian, 2005
FF Maiola started as part of Veronika Burian's MA in Typeface Design at the University of Reading in 2002/2003. Maiola, although a contemporary typeface, retains strong links to historical models. Sources of inspiration include Czech type designers Oldrich Menhart and Vojtech Preissig, whose works display vigour and elegance married to expressive and individual character. However, the intention was to give a personal interpretation of their ideas, imparting their concepts of irregularity and angularity in an inconspicuous way. In 2004 Maiola received the 'Certificate of Excellence in Type Design' award from the Type Director's Club (TDC).

FF MAMBO Val Fullard, 1992
A happy, dance-like display face based on hand-lettering.

FF MANGA Donald Beekman, 2001
Amsterdam designer Donald Beekman got the idea for FF Manga Steel and FF Manga Stone while reading the book *Sun and Steel* by Yukio Mishima. The two headline faces are constructed with elements from Japanese scripting and work equally well set horizontally or vertically.

FF Liant
Regular Medium **Bold**

SENSE PAPERS

CATORZE HISTÒRIES PERSONALS

PRÒLEG DE SOS RACISME

ISAAC FERNÁNDEZ SANVISENS
CATALINA GAYÀ MORLÀ

mina

Из-за непрекращающихся

песчаных бурь

вы никогда не

увидите солнца

н е б е в

A typeface in the Swiss
(cheese) tradition.
With knobs on.

FF Knobcheese
FF Knobcheese Outline
FF KNOBCHEESE INITIALS

Designed by Rian Hughes ©1992. Available from Fontshop 1994. Best used with a cheap Burgundy.

DER OXMOXSPIEGEL
★★★★★

Berlin, Dienstag, 20. Februar 1996 / 52. Jahrgang / Nr. 15543 *   1 DM / A6622

Wirtschaft	Berlin	Kultur	Secrets of the little grey cells

Grausam: Worthülsen statt Inhalte

Xixio Omnio foxoi »Ximo Oxomoxo«

Ion Xoxoxoxoa Ooro omxio Xinonoxmoxhoxx
Xolxoxoxi rolxxi xoxoxoxoo xixoxx Xoxan

»La Fontaine aux Lettres«

Xixio XXI Xnxixomoxhx

Xixio Oonxomxxox mxo Xnx omxnx

Critzler was one of the co-designers of *Localizer*, a 1995 bible of techno published by Die Gestalten. The FF Localizer font was first seen on the cover of this book.

Cover for the Catalan book *Sense papers* ('Without ID') designed with FF Magda Clean by the Barcelona studio Enric Jardí, 2005.

Poster for FF Knobcheese; Rian Hughes, 1994.

FF Marten was one of the first FontFonts for which a Cyrillic character set was designed. In the early '90s it was immediately picked up by young Russian life-style and music magazines.

FontCard for FF Layout by Jürgen Siebert, showing how to use the typeface for mock-ups. 1996.

← — —
FontCard for FF Merlin by
Nick Shinn, FSI 1997.

FontCard by FF Localizer
designer Critzler,
FSI 1997.

↖
FF Mambo on a fast-food
restaurant handout.

FF MARKET H.A.Simon, 1996
H.A. Simon, a veteran of the German typesetting
and advertising world, first drew FF Market for use
in promotional material for a few of his jobs. As the
name suggests, the typeface lends itself for use in
the marketplace: advertisements, posters, stickers,
packaging, point-of-sale promotions, etc.

FF MARTEN Martin Wenzel, 1991
The first design by Martin Wenzel was geometrically
constructed, yet manages to maintain a character
of iets own. It was one of the first FontFont display
typefaces to come with a Cyrillic version.

FF MASTERPIECE Peter Bil'ak, 1996
Peter Bil'ak drew FF Masterpiece as a parody of
calligraphy and as a reaction of two years of training
in formal writing with the broad-nibbed pen. He
also enjoyed the irony of creating an expert set for
a family where one would least expect it, and then
couldn't leave it without a set of initials.

FF MATTO Alessio Leonardi, 1996
'FF Matto is a really classic typeface with all the
letters you need to write all the things you mean. If
it looks irregular it's only because the computer
is less perfect than my right hand. "Matto" means
"crazy" in Italian,' says Alessio. What he doesn't
mention is that 'porco' means 'pig', and such is the
name of the expert set for the rest of us - fonts with a
halo of dirt bits that infect neighbouring letters.

FF MAVERICK Christoph Kalscheuer, 1995
Christoph Kalscheuer's first typeface FF Maverick
is a quirky semisans with a strong vertical contrast.
It was originally designed for cultural events and
packaging projects.

FF MAX Morten Rostgaard Olsen, 2003
Max is a Danish sans serif face, inspired by
Novarese's Eurostile (1962). The letter shapes in
FF Max have a rounder, friendlier form than Eurostile,
giving the whole typeface a certain human touch.
FF Max works well as a headline face for magazines
and newspapers, but does a fine job at small point
sizes, too.

FF MEGANO Xavier Dupré, 2005
With FF Megano, Xavier Dupré set out to make a 'fun
sans'. The roundness of the diagonals is evocative
of feminine curves, making the typeface a favourite
for cosmetics packaging. As with most of Dupré's
typefaces, FF Megano is 'a mixture of sweet and
aggressive shapes'. Dupré says he 'tried to combine
the things I like in typography – humanistic oblique
axis, high readability, and a touch of fun.'

FF MERLIN Nick Shinn, 1997
Nick Shinn: 'A gothic fantasy of mystery, malice
and antiquity, shaped in the image of the hooked
beak, the talon, the thorn, the barb and the blade.
Crooked, scarred and defiant, the humanist alphabet wears a jagged mantle of blackletter texture.'
FF Merlin is excellent for film posters, book jackets,
games… whenever some edginess is required.

FF META Erik Spiekermann, 1991–2003
FF META CONDENSED Spiekermann | Schäfer, 1998
FF META HEADLINE Spiekermann | Schwartz, 2005
FF Meta was conceived in 1985 as a typeface for use
at small point sizes. Published as one of the first
FontFonts, FF Meta very quickly became one of the
most popular typefaces of the digital era, and has
been referred to as 'the Helvetica of the 90s' (not
necessarily a compliment!). Originally conceived as
a typeface for use in small point sizes, FF Meta very
quickly became popular as a headline face as well.
It is especially for this use that a condensed and
recently a headline version were developed.

FF MINIMUM Pierre di Sciullo, 1993
Pierre di Sciullo of France is a philosopher and
writer as well as a designer. FF Minimum is a series
of speculations about the possibility of an entirely
simple alphabet. It is philosophical and playful at
the same time, suggesting forms which sit on the
floor, hang on the ceiling, or drunkenly stumble
about.

FF MODERNE GOTHICS Jim Parkinson, 1996
Jim Parkinson is one of America's most outstanding
lettering artists, whose clients include Newsweek,
Rolling Stone and many daily newspapers. The three
designs that make up FF Moderne Gothics (FF Golden
Gate, FF Matinee and FF Motel) are variations of a
mid-twentieth century lettering style of uppercase
letters with alternative characters that was popular
for signs and print. Of particular interest are the
'catchwords' in several languages that contrast
beautifully with the three styles.

FF MOTTER FESTIVAL Othmar Motter, 2000
FF Motter Festival is proof that Othmar Motter,
designer of spectacular 1970s display faces, is still
producing interesting work. FF Motter Festival is an
almost monolinear sans-serif with forms borrowed
from the traditional seriffed roman, with a touch of
blackletter. An alternation of arches and pointed
endings gives the three weights of the typeface its
characteristic, idiosyncratic rhythm.

FF MURPHY Fedor Hüneke | Rainer Stolle, 1995
Fedor Hüneke & Rainer Stolle, based in Duisburg,
Germany, work on multimedia projects (conception,
screen-design, interface-design, software development). Murphy was developed alongside a TV
project – a pseudo-scientific satirical program about
Murphy's Law. Hüneke and Stolle worked together
conceptualizing the font.

FF NELIO Sami Kortemäki, 2001
FF Nelio is a reaction to cell phone culture. Although
bitmaps and pixels are still experienced as high-
tech features, technology is there to make people's
life more comfortable. So why not make a cosy
bitmap script with a nostalgic touch of old cross
stitchings?

FF Megano

Light *Italic* CAPS
Regular *Italic* CAPS
Medium *Italic* CAPS
Demibold *Italic* CAPS
Bold *Italic* CAPS
Black CAPS

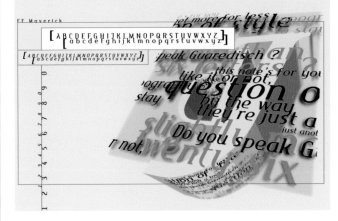

↑↑
Graphics and signage for
the Centre National de la
Danse in Pantin, France,
designed by Pierre di
Sciullo using variations
and 3D adaptations of his
FF Minimum series. Archi-
tecture: Antoinette Robain
and Claire Guieyse.
Photos © Pierre di Sciullo.

←···
'Open day': poster
designed by Robert Jan
van Noort for the Royal
Academy of Arts in The
Hague, 2002. Typefaces:
FF Moderne Gothics
(FF Golden Gate,
FF Matinee and FF Motel).

↑
FontCard for FF Maverick.
Designed by Christoph
Kalscheuer, FSI 1995.

↘
Logo for Goya, a (short-
lived) Berlin night club,
2005. United Designers
Network used FF Bau
Super for the name, set
against an ornament from
FF Masterpiece.

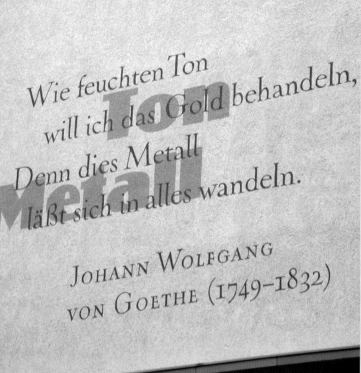

Wie feuchten Ton
will ich das Gold behandeln,
Denn dies Metall
läßt sich in alles wandeln.

JOHANN WOLFGANG
VON GOETHE (1749–1832)

Mark Thomson rebranded
the established British
publisher Collins using
FF Nexus as the principal
typeface, 2003–2004.

The 2001 *Words on the
Wall* project in Weimar,
Germany, was conceived
by Jay Rutherford of the
Bauhaus University.
Quotations chosen to
reflect the locations were
implemented on the
façades of 14 buildings.
FF Oneleigh was used
throughout, alongside
Jakob Erbar's Koloss.

Donald Beekman used
FF Noni for the window
design of this Amsterdam
headshop.

Advertisement for
FF Offline, commissioned
by FontShop Benelux.
Roelof Mulder, 1998.

FF NEWBERLIN Peter Verheul, 1991

FF Newberlin was originally published as part of
FontShop International's Five Dutch Designers
release. Verheul, a former student at the Royal Academy in The Hague, created these alphabets to give a
personal touch to correspondence. FF Newberlin is
a script-like typeface constructed exclusively from
straight lines.

FF NEXUS Martin Majoor, 2004

FF Nexus is Martin Majoor's third FontFont family,
after the best-selling Scala and Seria. The idea
behind FF Scala was to design a serif, humanistic
typeface from which a sans serif version would
be derived. The FF Nexus family is three typefaces
based on one principle. FF Nexus borrows some of
its structure from FF Scala, but adds the slab-like
FF Nexus Mix and monospaced FF Nexus Typewriter
to the set. Its OpenType features, such as built-in
Small Caps, alternate glyphs, and optional swash
glyphs make it an extremely versatile type system.

FF NONI Donald Beekman, 2000

A vacation to Thailand served as inspiration for the
FF Noni family – a combination of a Thai look with
a techno feel. The first opportunity to use the font
came with the design for Noni, a Hawaiian herbal
energy powder made by smart drug producers
Conscious Dreams. While working on Noni Wan
Beekman found that he was constantly in need of
alternative characters with longer tails and pointier
serifs. The result was Noni Too which works as a
stand-alone font but also can be used to add a bit of
spice to Noni Wan.

FF OCR-F Albert-Jan Pool, 1995

FF OCR-F was the first in a series of fonts based on
popular industrial alphabets. It is a subtle reworking
of OCR-B, with two completely new weights, Light
and Bold, and oldstyle figures for all three weights:
a true non-monospaced, yet not a proportionally
spaced family with moderate kerning pairs.

FF OFFLINE Roelof Mulder, 1996

An early version of FF Offline Regular was made in
1993 for an art catalogue titled *Oceaan Coalities*.
The stencil alphabet recalls the lettering on trans-
port boxes, evoking travel and ocean liners.
It took considerable time to complete the family.
As Mulder says, ironically: 'Speed is what you need'.

FF OLSEN Morten Rostgaard Olsen, 2001

FF Olsen is a sturdy text face specially designed for
maximum readability at small sizes. The typeface
combines details from sans and serif faces to place
the best of two worlds in one font. In its original
version, FF Olsen is used by the Danish Ministry of
Education.

FF ONELEIGH Nick Shinn, 1999

Nick Shinn is known for his provocative view on
typographic history. In designing FF Oneleigh, he
had a look at the radical serif faces of the early 20th
century, like Goudy's Kennerly and Koch's Antiqua.
'I took a little inspiration from each of these, mixed
with some ideas of my own. The main goal was to
produce an "alternate history" 1920s typeface, with
lots of original letterforms and details.'

9/10
Julio
2004

V Festival de Música Étnica

ETNI
MÁ
LA
GA

Playa del Peñón del Cuervo

T|C TEATRO CERVANTES
organiza

mlga Ayuntamiento de Málaga

m80i

do the do

op pad

Tijdschrift voor actieve vakanties *februari 1995* beursnummer ƒ.12,50

Op Pad Beurs
4/5 februari '95

Test
Wandelschoenen
3-kilo-tenten
Fietstassen

Wandelen,
fietsen en
kanovaren
met kinderen

op pad

in:
Nederland
Frankrijk
Oostenrijk
Finland
Albanië
Zuid-Amerika

Actieve tochten
Alle mogelijkheden

ANWB media

nippon-jones
OFFWORLD COLONIST SERVICES

Poster for an ethnic
music festival in Malaga,
Spain, designed by the
Barcelona studio Cosmic
with FF OCR-F, 2004.

↑↑
Dutch artist Henk Tas
created a mosaic using a
hand-made variation on
FF Offline.

↑
Op Pad, the outdoors
magazine of the
Netherland's road users'
organisation ANWB.
Designed by Proforma,
Rotterdam (Pauline de
Rooij) with FF Newberlin.

←----
Promotional poster for
FF Outlander designed by
Rian Hughes, 1995.

FF OTTOFONT Barbara Klunder, 2001
Toronto illustrator Barbara Klunder: 'I approach
designing an alphabet as an opportunity to draw.
Ottofont us an urban, handmade font with some
"grit". The dingbats reflect what we might need in the
near future in our publications: images of cells, biol-
ogy, rats, death, but also images of hope – leaves,
babies, food, music.'

FF OUTLANDER Rian Hughes, 1995
FF Outlander was announced as being 'the corporate
typeface of Nippon-Jones Offworld Colonist Services,
a division of TranseurochineConurb Infrasystems®.
The four basic weights (Light, Medium, Bold, Black)
are stringently applied across the ten subsectors
that comprise the main organisation and are
covered in detail in Paragraphs 3544-3998 of the
TCI Design for Exploitation CD-ROM.'

FF OXIDE Christian Schwartz, 2005
Named for the chemical composition of rust,
FF Oxide has an unvarnished industrial aesthetic.
In 1999, designer Christian Schwartz was asked
to draw a stencil typeface for a Pittsburgh-based
clothing label. He found his inspiration at a
hardware store down the street, purchasing a set
of 1.5" stencils with a bare minimum number of
'breaks' in the characters, making for an unusually
subtle stencil effect. FF Oxide debuted on a line of
t-shirts and sat forgotten until 2005, when Schwartz
completed the family with additional weights and
stencil treatments.

FF PAGE Albert Boton, 2003
Albert Boton started with Page during studies for the
Yellow Pages of a telephone directory. Later on, he
just continued on his own, made a Sans version and
added Small Caps. He took special care of the form
of the inner curves of certain letters which give the
typeface a vigorous, strong character.

FF PAPERTAPE Matthias Jordan, 2000
The German Bundeswehr (army) uses high
frequency radio teletype machines with built-in
papertape writers and readers. With FF Papertape
Dots this code has been converted to Type 1
outlines; letters of a sort, but still not readable for
most non-machines. However, while completing

his military duty, Matthias Jordan designed a truly
legible variation: FF Papertape Letters.

FF PARABLE Christopher Burke, 2002
Parable is a robust roman designed for small text
sizes, between 6 and 10 points, making it an ideal
face for setting a dictionary or a bible. In fact, it
has recently been chosen as the main text font for
the Concise Oxford English Dictionary. At larger
sizes, some of FF Parable's features which were
engineered for small-scale functionality become
interesting details. Parable Sans is currently in
development.

FF PARANGO Xavier Dupré, 2001
FF Parango was based on a typeface that Dupré
designed during his studies at the Scriptorium
of Toulouse. Vaguely based on the proportions
of the greatest of French oldstyles, the typefaces
cut by Claude Garamond, it is Dupré's personal
interpretation of the French typographic style 'with
its alternating narrow and wide letters.' With its
soft angles and low contrast between thick and thin
strokes, it evokes the feel of ancient printed pages;
yet its crisp look makes it distinctly contemporary.

FF PEECOL Steffen Sauerteig | Kai Vermehr, 1998
The idea for FF Peecol was born from the need for
small, quickly downloadable files on the web. E-boy
found that consistently using 36 x 36 pixel images
significantly reduced the overall load-time. In no
time at all they had developed a series of upper and
lower bodies, text balloons and accessories – a
building block set of Frankensteinian proportions.
It seemed a logical step to then make a font of the
various components. The wish now is to share the
Peecol idea and hope that other designers will
follow suit, creating new designs of standard size
and raster that can be freely mixed and matched.

FF PENGUIN Nick Cooke, 1995
Nick Cooke: 'A couple of years ago whilst leafing
through a typographic magazine a Japanese
typeface jumped out and hit me in the face! This
brute of a design was to be the inspiration for
FF Penguin. I believe it was cut out of paper - it
was crude and simple yet sophisticated, but very
beautiful. I wondered if I could utilise the basic

shapes it used; very rounded convex curves and
straight lines. After many drawings I finally refined
it to its present state. The Deco version was based
upon a piece of personal artwork. Use all versions
as LARGE AS POSSIBLE.'

FF PEPE Pepe Gimeno, 2003
Pepe Gimeno of Valencia, Spain, is a well-known
designer of lively, colourful posters and publications. His script FF Pepe is at once informal and
painstakingly drawn. The capitals are deformed,
which gives them a strong personality. The more
uniform lower case letters create a good grey fabric
and a fine visual rhythm.

FF PLUS Jürgen Huber, 2003
FF Plus is a sans serif typeface without frills, good for
many typographic challenges. Each of four weights
includes Regular, Italic, Small Caps and SC Italics.

FF POP Neville Brody, 1992
Built on a simple grid of horizontal and vertical lines,
FF Pop is Brody at his most minimalist. It comes in a
monoline and an LED version.

FF PRATER Wagenbreth | Sauerteig, 2000
Prater is a 'beer garden' in the Eastern part of Berlin
with a unique graphic identity, handmade by art-
ist-illustrator Henning Wagenbreth. The alphabets
created by Wagenbreth were the starting point for a
refreshing type family. To recreate the irregularity
of manual mark-making, each FF Prater alphabet
comes in two slightly different versions. FF Prater
has serif and sans serif fonts, as well as a cheeky
little script and a 3-D version, which can be layered.

FF PRIMARY Martin Wenzel, 1995
FF Primary is a condensed typeface with straight,
simple forms based on the principles of writing with
a broad-nibbed pen. FF Primary Round uses almost
the same shapes, but has much smoother details.
The most sensational font in the family is FF Primary
Stone, made to suggest volume. It is split into four
different styles: a left, right, top and a bottom part of
each letter. By layering the same character in each
font with different colours or grey hues, one can
control from which side the 'light' originates and
whether the letters have depth.

Stéphane De Schrevel, poster for a conference at Ghent University (Belgium), made with FF Profile.

FF Oxide by Christian Schwartz was originally created for a well-known fashion brand.

Front cover of the Austrian magazine *Miromente*, 2005. Designed by Clemens Schedler with FF Parable.

FF Peecol. Page designed in 2000 for *Druk* magazine by eBoy.

FF Penguin FontCard: an on-screen low-resolution rendition of the font.

Pandoera, cultural children's newspaper, Ghent, Belgium. Randoald Sabbe (design), Stief Desmet (illustrations). Typeface: FF Prater.

Poster by SignBox & Derks for the Hogeschool Gent (College of Business and Arts in Ghent, Belgium), 2005. Headline typeface: FF Prater.

FF PRISKA SERIF   Alessio Leonardi, 1993
FF Priska is a font family full of fun. The star is Little Creatures, of which each character is an assemblage of animal and human forms. The Book of Genesis should be reset in FF Priska Serif Little Creatures.

FF PROFILE   Martin Wenzel, 1999
Having made some highly original headline fonts, such as FF Primary and FF Rekord, Berliner Martin Wenzel decided he wanted to design a mature text typeface. In order to learn how to do this, he enrolled in the Royal Academy in The Hague (Holland), where many other FontFont designers were also educated. The result was FF Profile: a versatile extended family in the Dutch tradition of the 'humanist sans', combining classic proportions with contemporary details.

FF PROVIDENCE   Guy Jeffrey Nelson, 1994
Guy Jeffrey Nelson first drew the FF Providence family in 1987 for use in a comic book series: FF Providence Sans for the dialogue, and the serif variant for the running narrative. In 1994 FF Providence was completed with additional weights and dingbats.

FF PULLMAN   Factor Design, 1997
Inspired by the logo printed on the side of a cup from the erstwhile GDR dining car company Mitropa, Johannes Erler started work on FF Pullman in 1995. The original, somewhat stiff, basic font was joined by an elegant inline version. A layer font was added so that the inner and outer forms could be given different colours.

FF Q TYPE   Achaz Reuss, 2004
The idea behind FF QType was to design a typeface based on a square with a wide range of widths and weights. The family consists of five subfamilies (Compressed, Condensed, Semi-Extended, Extended and Square) with five weights each.

FF QUADRAAT   Fred Smeijers, 1992–1997
Fred Smeijers approaches type design from the point of view of a typographer. Quadraat grew from a need in his typographic work for a contemporary serifed roman that was heavier than Times but lighter than Plantin. FF Quadraat, of course, is much more than that. It combines Renaissance proportions with contemporary details and its Italic is highly original and economical as well. Even the earliest version of Quadraat had sophisticated typographic possibilities, such as a special small-caps set of numerals. Quadraat was subsequently developed into a large, versatile family with sans-serif, headline, display and monospaced versions.

FF QUADRAAT SANS   Fred Smeijers, 1997–1998
Like its seriffed companion, FF Quadraat Sans is a typeface with a rather strong character of its own. Designer Fred Smeijers had a hard time making his sans-serif into as strong a gesture as FF Quadraat, without neglecting traditional proportions. But he succeeded admirably, giving the sans version a lively and humane character. Quadraat Sans has display qualities but works well as a text face, too.

FF QUADRAAT DISPLAY | QUADRAAT HEADLINER
Fred Smeijers, 1998–2000
Fred Smeijers drew the display faces based on his FF Quadraat Display for personal use in faxes to friends and on posters from his design studio. The FF Quadraat Display fonts are powerful, but they aren't of the loud-mouthed, fun-font variety. They strive for a sort of noticeability we don't see much anymore.

FF QUILL   Manfred Klein, 1994
In music there are many different genres – from classic to punk – for a wide array of listeners. Manfred Klein believes that in typography this is also true. His script font FF Quill is the typographic equivalent of free jazz. He improvised the use of a graphic tray, working and re-working freely constructed elements of letters.

FF RATTLESCRIPT   Mårten Thavenius, 2000
For an informal script typeface, FF Rattlescript is remarkably legible; the structure of the family, with four weights, small caps, and two styles of numerals, is quite sophisticated. The name came to the designer during a trip to Death Valley, California when he ran across a rattlesnake. Thavenius was struck by the marks it made in the sand, which had the flow of handwritten text over paper.

FF READOUT   Steffen Sauerteig, 1999
Our world is increasingly computer-oriented, and we are surrounded by digital displays through which the machines talk to us. FF Readout is monospaced and all the characters are constructed from the same basic form. The Front and Back variations can be layered to form different colored foregrounds and backgrounds.

FF REKORD   Martin Wenzel, 1994
FF Rekord is a completely musical typeface, inspired by the abbreviations and symbols used on sound equipment. The symbol character set contains all the pictograms a designer needs for record covers, posters and calendars, or other musically-oriented printed matter. The three alphabets also have music in their veins and seem to have spent a night in front of the loudspeakers at a techno disco.

Page sans–Page

Albert Boton, postcard designed with his typeface FF Page.

Comic strip made by Gordon Protz using FF Providence Sans and FF Providence Dingbats.

Niederländische Kultur in Jena 1997 · Eröffnung 20. Juni, Theaterhaus Jena
Literatur · Ausstellungen · Musik · Theater · Kleinkunst · Film · Architektur ·
Wissenschaft · Technik · Schülerprojekte · Vorträge · Workshops

Nederland in Jena

Plakat Wim Westerveld, Foto Mathias Schormann

Inhalt

Die gleichen Ziele   Logo   Corporate Design   Kommunikationsberatung   Broschüren   Zeitschriften   Anzeigen   Öffentlichkeitsarbeit   Internet   Veranstaltungen   Netzwerk   Kontakt

Weasel.®

Kidwear®

Tiende Festival
De Beweeging
10   Een fysieke theatergebeurtenis
Antwerpen, 1-14 maart 1998

Tiende Festival
Over De Beweeging
Archief 1997
Links
Vraag informatie
English version
Virtual MOMI

THIS IS NOT A TYPEFACE!

⬆
FF Pullman, Factor
Design, 1997.

⬉
Poster for a presen-
tation of Dutch arts,
architecture, science
and literature in Jena,
Germany, 1997.
Design by Wim Wester-
veld, photo by Mathias
Schormann. Typeface:
FF Quadraat Sans.

⬅
Contents page from the
corporate brochure of
Atelier Schümann,
Hamburg (Germany),
designed with FF QType.

⬅
FF Rattlescript on an
anonymous label for
children's clothing.

Website for a dance
festival in Antwerp,
Belgium, made with
FF Rekord, JM 1998.

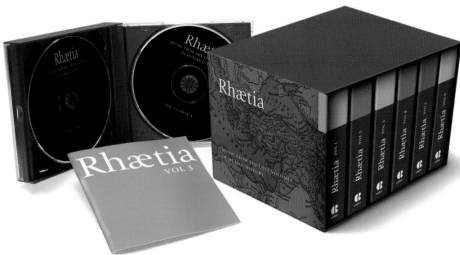

FF REMINGA Xavier Dupré, 2000
FF Reminga is a contemporary text face, rather sober and especially legible in 10-12 point size. The Titling versions are narrower and even more elegant and calligraphic.

FF REVOLVER Rian Hughes, 1993
Before starting his own foundry, Device Fonts, London designer Rian Hughes published several of his imaginative and witty typefaces in the FontFont library. Revolver from 1993 was one of the first. It helped define the 'ironic' category in the FontFont catalogues.

FF RIAN'S DINGBATS Rian Hughes, 1993
Hughes, who is an illustrator as well as a type designer, risked putting himself out of a job by publishing this extensive collection of wonderful dingbats and expressive graphic cartoons. Now everybody can make publications with real Rian Hughes drawings without even knowing his phone number.

FF ROICE Scholing, 2003
When Dutchman Alex Scholing designed his 1995 font FF Engine, he had no type designing experience whatsoever. He soon decided that he could do better than that. FF Roice – the name refers to the best engine in the world – is an informed redesign of FF Engine. The old FF Engine was conceived as a slightly strange, idiosyncratic but usable text face. The new FF Roice is all that, but it is also well-mannered and well balanced – it is simply more mature.

FF ROPSEN SCRIPT Jürgen Brinckmann, 2001
In Prenzlauer Berg, a section of erstwhile East Berlin and home to type designer Jürgen Brinckmann, there is a street named for the American singer Paul Robeson. The local population pronounce it 'ropsen': a fine name for a friendly face. FF Ropsen was created in 1999 from various handwriting samples, and early versions were used in school-books Brinckmann designed. Over several months the typeface was refined until Brinckmann's ideal was reached: a script face that works as a headline face as well as in a block of text.

FF ROSETTA Max Kisman, 1991
The making of FF Rosetta was closely linked to that of the fonts in the FF Kisman package: all are display fonts originally made for various magazines art-directed by Max Kisman, and designed on the earliest Apple Macintosh computers.

FF ROUTES Hans Reichel, 2001
Hans Reichel, designer of FF Dax, FF Schmalhans and FF Sari, is an inventor as well as a designer and a musician. For FF Routes he invented a system which allows the user to make a quick, colourful road diagram by simply typing the elements: streets, crossroads, bridges, tunnels and special signs as well as conventional icons.

FF SALE Tony Booth, 1996
FF Sale is a freestyle brush letter originally drawn by hand. While appropriate for use in many design situations, the typeface is most at home in the world of hard-sell ads and clearance sales. FF Sale Dingbats include readymade balloons, explosions, arrows, etc. with well-known ad slogans such as sale!, special!, big!, etc.

FF SARI Hans Reichel, 1999
The origins of FF Sari date back to 1983 when Hans Reichel made his first typeface for a well-known Berlin foundry, under the tutelage of the company's type director. That early work already betrayed the graphic sensibility and originality which would later guide Reichel in making the FF Dax family. FF Sari is based on the same ideas as the early typeface but is completely redrawn and extended.

FF SCALA Martin Majoor, 1990–1998
Martin Majoor designed Scala when working as a graphic designer for the Vredenburg Music Center in Utrecht for use in the venue's own printed matter, which was designed in-house on a Mac computer. He designed a family which included oldstyle (or lowercase) numerals and Small Caps, features that were lacking in the digital faces available at the time. In 1991 FF Scala was released on the FontFont label as its first serious text face and has remained one of its bestsellers to date.

FF SCALA SANS Martin Majoor, 1993–1999
The companion sans-serif to the successful FF Scala. Again it is its simplicity which makes FF Scala Sans so captivating, while at the same time its distinct character is immediately recognizable. As in FF Scala serif, lower-case or oldstyle figures are standard – a rare thing in a sans-serif. The family consists of six variants including an Italic Small Caps style.

FF SCALA JEWEL Martin Majoor, 1996
A tongue-in-cheek addition to the Scala family, FF Scala Jewel is a collection of decorated uppercase letters in four designs which are vaguely based on historical ornamented titling alphabets: Crystal, Diamond, Pearl and Saphyr.

FF SCHMALHANS Hans Reichel, 1997
FF Schmalhans has some features in common with Reichel's FF Dax, but its proportions and atmosphere are distinctly different. Schmalhans began life as an alphabet of capitals drawn in the 1970's for use on flyers and record sleeves. Only in 1996 did the current family take shape, with six weights and a lowercase. The term 'Schmalhans' derives from a German saying, *Schmalhans ist Küchenmeister*, or 'Skinny Hans is boss of the kitchen' – used when food is scarce.

FF SCHULBUCH Just van Rossum, 1991
A series of fonts commssioned for schoolbooks, based on the historical schoolbook types used in Northern and Southern Germany, and Bavaria.

FF SCHULSCHRIFT Just van Rossum, 1991
FF Schulschrift is based on three hand-lettering norms currently prescribed for German elementary schools by the Ministry of Culture and Education. FontShop collaborated closely with educational experts and school textbook publishers to develop the fonts according to official standards. To create a flowing connected script, Just van Rossum developed Scripter, a special application which automatically inserts correct connection points between the letters of a text once it is set.

Bordeaux bottle designed with Ropsen Script and Scala Sans. MvB

Design for a fictitious CD collection, using FF Reminga. MvB

The early versions of FF Schulschrift used Just van Rossum's Scripter program for connecting the letters. This task is now performed by the OpenType contextual features.

Poster for a concert at an Amsterdam church. Designed by Mark van Wageningen using FF Scala and FF Scala Sans.

FontCard by FF Sale designer Tony Booth, FSI 1996.

Promotional posters for FF Revolver and FF Rian's Dingbats by Rian Hughes, 1993.

This is FF Schulschrift, unconnected

This is FF Schulschrift, connected

FF SCREEN MATRIX Windlin | Müller, 1995
FF Screen Matrix was originally designed for the
Visualize The Future exhibition at the Parco Gallery
in Tokyo. The font was made to imitate an existing
lcd display and was subsequently redesigned and
extended by Stephan 'Pronto' Müller.

FF SCREENSTAR eBoy, 2003
eBoy: 'We needed a good type for our every-day
needs suitable for the screen. Most of the existing
fonts are vector derivates or are too well-known.
Scriptstar was added later. We had learned that
hand-edited script faces look good as screen fonts
and that there were no such fonts on the market.
Besides the use as screen fonts, Screenstar and
Scriptstar are also usable in print media, and we use
it every day in our eBoy stationary. Unobtrusive but
unique.'

FF SCRIBBLE Ole Schäfer, 1995
In the hot metal and photocomposition eras,
headlines in large point sizes were sketched with
hatched letterforms for presentation purposes or
as templates for typesetters. FF Scribble is a well
pronounced, compact Grotesque drawn in this
manner. It lends itself best to 24 point headlines.
The font also has a message: make a sketch of what
you would like to create before you even touch the
computer.

FF SCRIBE TYPE Manfred Klein
The earliest printing types did not look like the
romans we prefer today. They sought to imitate
the blackletter (or gothic) scripts which were used
by 15th century scribes for copying books by hand.
Some of the fonts in Manfred Klein's FF Scribe Type
package are based on early printing types, such
as the types of Gutenberg and Koberger. But like
his typefaces inspired by actual mediæval scripts,
these fonts evoke the soft scraping of the quill
rather than the pounding of the press.

FF SCRIBE TYPE 2 Jürgen Brinckmann, 1993
The second Scribe Type package features digital
versions of mediaeval and renaissance handwriting styles, such as the Carolingian and humanist
minuscules. The package consists of FF Humanist,
FF Lukrezia, FF Madonna and FF Ophelia.

FF SERIA | FF SERIA SANS Martin Majoor, 2000
As a book typographer, Martin Majoor was convinced that his FF Scala was inappropriate for fiction
and poetry because of the 'stubby' look caused by
its short ascenders and descenders.
As a result he drew FF Seria, a 'literary' type family
with extremely long ascenders and descenders and
very fine detailing. Majoor decided straight away to
make both a serif and sans version for the Seria family. Seria has a remarkable upright Italic: designed
with all the calligraphic references of a real Italic,
but with the slope reduced to a minimum.

FF SHERIFF Peter Verheul, 1996
FF Sheriff stands out as one of the most idiosyncratic
seriffed text faces in the FontFont library. At small
point sizes it is surprisingly readable, while as
a display font it has a character all of its own.
FF Sheriff is sturdy and space-saving, and possesses typographic individuality without being too
conspicuous.

FF SIGNA Ole Søndergaard, 2000
FF Signa is a classic sans serif face with a contemporary character. Simple letterforms and a minimum of
detail produce clear and harmonious word images.
Designed for the Danish Design Center, it is used
there for printed material and exhibitions as well as
the internal signage system. FF Signa is a typically
Danish typeface, rooted in architectural lettering
rather than book typography.

FF SINGER Matthias Thiesen | Stefan Hägerling, 1995
The designers' personal comments about FF Singer:
Legibility is a fluid process, dependent on use and
habit. FF Singer is one of the most legible typefaces
of the future - that is if you can crack the code!

FF SNAFU Jonathan Hitchen, 2002
FF Snafu is a soft stencil font. It started life as a
pixel-styled font called Fucking Good Stencil which
emerged out of an idea for a suite of fonts aimed
at lazy designers who could simply select 'fucking
good' from their font menu.

↑
Two imaginary beer
brands created by
Schein Berlin for
German television.
Zweimaster has FF Zine;
the Branzhofer logo was
made with FF Johannes
G (FF Scribe Type 1).

↑
Magazine design
with FF Signa by Ole
Søndergaard, Denmark.

↖
Virtual flyer made with
FF Snafu. MvB

↗
One-off newspaper
issue to promote the
Dutch design and
marketing agency
Bureau Stern. DHDV
Sternblad was entirely
set in FF Seria. 2002.

↖ ↖
Brochure for the Shenkar
College of engineering
and design (Israel),
made with FF Signa.
Art directed by Oded
Ezer. Designed by
Oded Ezer and Tatiana
Luxembourg.

DHDV STERNBLAD

STERNUM AD FUNDUM

ONAFHANKELIJKE COURANT OVER COMMUNICATIE VOOR KUNST EN CULTUUR / NUMMER 1 – 2002

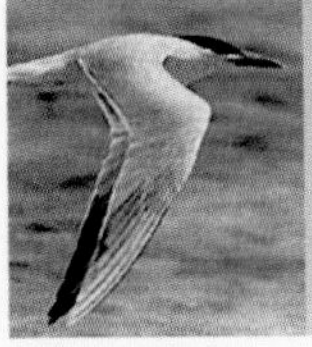

NATUURLIJK

Stern terug van weggeweest in Nederland

pagina 4

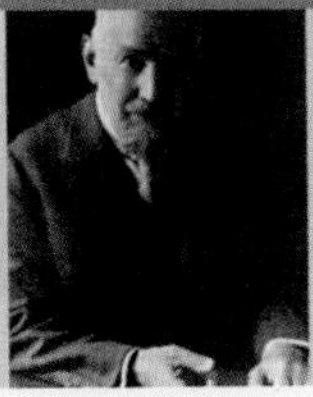

WILLIAM STERN

De uitvinder van het 'IQ'

pagina 6

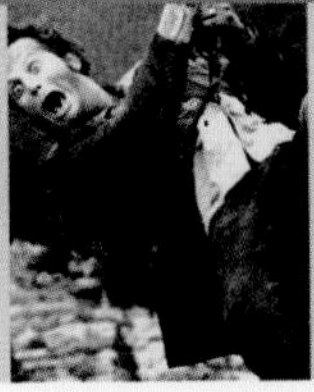

DANIËL STERN

De stem van The Wonder Years

pagina 3

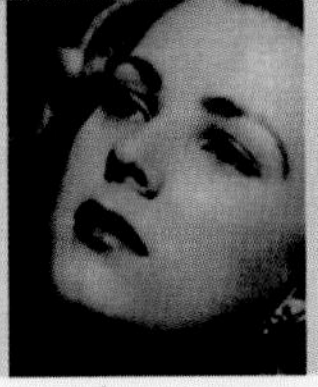

ACHTEROP

Miroslava Sternikova et cetera

pagina 8

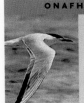

Nieuw: Stern / Den Hartog & De Vries

Sinds 1 september 2001 werken ontwerper Jan Willem den Hartog en auteur Alex de Vries samen in het bureau Stern. Het nieuwe bureau werkt vooral op het terrein van kunst en cultuur voor alle disciplines. Kenmerkend voor Stern is een heldere stijl en een directe en snelle manier van werken.

Den Hartog en De Vries hebben beiden een grote expertise in hun vakgebied. Zij werken voor overheden, het onderwijs, musea, schouwburgen, theatergroepen, kunstenaars, bedrijven en non-profit instellingen. Stern / Den Hartog & De Vries - Communicatie voor Kunst en Cultuur richt zich in de werkzaamheden op een breed terrein: boekuitgaven, catalogi, jaarverslagen, huisstijlen, rapporten, adviezen, affiches, uitnodigingen, folders, brochures. Ontwerp en tekst en/of redactie worden integraal door Stern verzorgd.

Aan het bureau zijn tevens verbonden Yvonne van Dongen en Trudie Lute. Daarnaast beschikt Stern over een uitstekend netwerk van professionele free lance ontwerpers, fotografen, tekstschrijvers, vertalers, redacteuren, drukkers, lithografen enzovoort.

Stern / Den Hartog & De Vries
COMMUNICATIE VOOR KUNST EN CULTUUR
Amsterdamseweg 21
6814 GA Arnhem
TELEFOON 026-351 15 46
FAX 026-351 32 97

Uitgeverij De Zwaluw

Een onderdeel van Stern is uitgeverij De Zwaluw die gespecialiseerd is in exclusieve publicaties op het gebied van kunst & cultuur.

Onlangs verscheen bij De Zwaluw een boekwerk over beeldend kunstenaar Jacobien de Rooij. Op pagina 5 leest u alles over dit fraaie boek.

Zie ook: pagina 5 en 7, zakelijke berichten, De Zwaluw fonds

Nieuwe krant: nieuwe letter

Dit eerste exemplaar van het DHDV-STERNBLAD is gezet uit een gloednieuwe letter, de Seria. Deze letter werd vorig jaar afgerond door de Arnhemse letterontwerper Martin Majoor. Hoewel de Seria voornamelijk werd getekend voor 'literaire' toepassingen komt deze veelzijdige letter ook heel goed tot zijn recht in deze krant. Op pagina 6 kunt u meer lezen over de letter en de ontwerper.

Meer exemplaren ontvangen?

Wanneer u meer exemplaren wenst te ontvangen van deze krant (bijvoorbeeld om uit te delen onder relaties, vrienden of bekenden) dan kunt u een verzoek per e-mail sturen naar **sternalex@planet.nl** of een fax naar **026 3513297**.

Vergeet niet uw naam en postadres te vermelden.

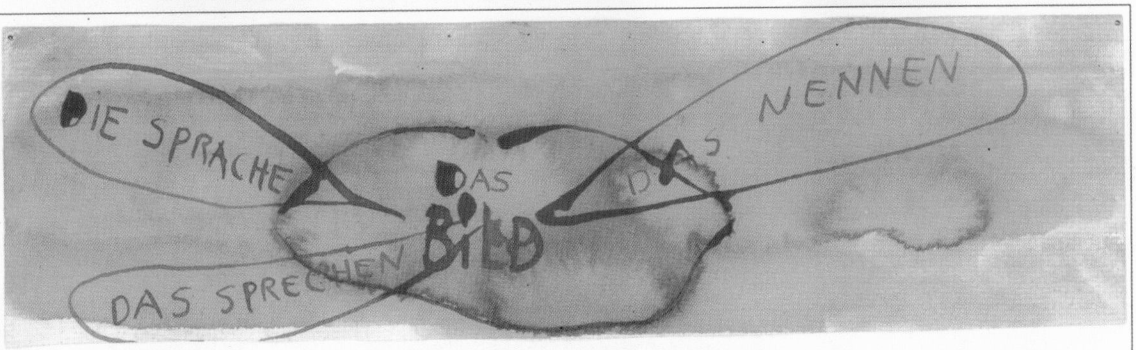

Een tekening van beeldend kunstenaar Mariette Linders. Deze siert -onder meer- het kantoor van het nieuwe bureau Stern te Arnhem en brengt (toevallig?) in kaart waar het in veel gevallen om gaat.

EEN SCHAAMTELOZE RECLAMETEKST

Bureau Stern maakt inhoud duidelijk

ARNHEM—Het nieuwe Communicatiebureau Stern / Den Hartog en De Vries heeft in de wereld van kunst en cultuur een vruchtbaar standpunt ingenomen. Betrouwbare bronnen melden dat het in Arnhem gevestigde bureau, waarin ook de kwaliteitsuitgeverij De Zwaluw een plaats heeft gekregen, een inhoudelijk analytische benadering koppelt aan uitvoerend pragmatisme.

Deze beproefde werkwijze is weliswaar een praktijk die ook elders kan worden gevonden, maar de benadering van Stern is enkel en alleen gericht op begrijpelijke en heldere overdracht van tekst en beeld. De herkenbare stijl van het bureau wordt daardoor nooit een brandmerk dat iedere willekeurige opdrachtgever wordt opgelegd. Bij Stern is geen enkele opdrachtgever willekeurig: de relatie tussen Stern en opdrachtgever is de logische consequentie van wederzijdse selectie op basis van kwaliteitscriteria en nuchtere overweging van zakelijke argumenten. Het is met name de combinatie van inhoudelijke duiding en duidelijke inhoud die de uiteindelijke vorm van de producten van Stern / Den Hartog & De Vries kenmerkt.

Het Arnhemse bureau gaat op het gebied van kunst en cultuur geen zee te hoog en geen brug te ver. De bureaunaam Stern is bewust gekozen vanwege de eigenschap dat deze zeezwaluw de grootste vliegafstanden aflegt op de trekroutes van broedplaats naar overwinteringsgebied. De Noordse Stern vliegt heen en weer tussen Noord- en Zuidpool en legt daarbij twee maal per jaar gemiddeld 16.000 kilometer af. Het enorme bereik van deze kleine vogel is een eigenschap die het communicatiebureau ook bezit. De kern van het bureau wordt gevormd door Jan Willem den Hartog en Alex de Vries, die beiden in hun vakgebied bekend staan als generalisten met een brede belangstelling, maar ook met specialistische kwaliteiten en kennis.

Den Hartog is als grafisch ontwerper een typograaf die een streng esthetische gevoel voor letters en leesbaarheid paart aan een aansprekende beeldende inventiviteit. Zijn specifieke interessegebieden zijn kunst, muziek, architectuur en literatuur. Het maken van boeken heeft zijn persoonlijke voorkeur, maar hij blinkt ook uit in communicatief drukwerk: affiches, flyers, folders en advertenties. Zijn stijl laat zich kenmerken als 'warmbloedige eenvoud': zijn ontwerpen hebben een direct informerende uitwerking en daaronder zindert een poëtische spanning. Als ontwerper beschikt hij over de kwaliteiten van een regisseur die niet enkel alle vormgevingsonderdelen de beste rol laat vervullen, maar die ook een uitstekend oog heeft voor casting: waar de inzet van fotografen, illustratoren, lithografen en drukkers is vereist, vormt hij hecht opererende teams waarvan de leden elkaar perfect aanvullen. Den Hartog voorziet iedere opdrachtgever van passend advies, helpt bij het uitzetten van een effectieve strategie en draagt zorg voor een vlekkeloos productieproces.

> ...meerwaarde voor iedere opdrachtgever ...

Auteur en adviseur Alex de Vries heeft zijn sporen zowel uitvoerend als bestuurlijk verdiend. Als publicist op het gebied van met name beeldende kunst en theater heeft hij meer dan 250 publicaties op zijn naam staan in tijdschriften, catalogi en boeken. In het kunstonderwijs en op culturele beleidsterreinen heeft hij als directeur, rapporteur, commissielid en -voorzitter in de meest uiteenlopende instellingen, stichtingen, verenigingen en overheidsorganen gefunctioneerd. Zijn teksten zijn de mensen en zaken die het betreft altijd 'op het lijf' geschreven. De Vries schrijft in zijn beschouwende teksten betrokken en bevlogen vanuit persoonlijke overtuiging en opvattingen. Hij beheerst echter ook als geen ander de afstandelijke analyse, efficiënt en betrouwbaar in het doeltreffend verwoorden van de boodschap die moet worden overgebracht. Hij is doorwrocht en eloquent waar nuances moeten worden aangebracht en bondig en goed gebekt waar eenduidigheid is vereist. Kortom, hij is zowel een eigenzinnige essayist als een doeltreffende copywriter.

In de combinatie van Jan Willem den Hartog en Alex de Vries is Stern een communicatiebureau waarin bijzondere eigenschappen worden verenigd die voor iedere opdrachtgever tot een meerwaarde leiden. Inhoudelijke doelstellingen krijgen effectief verwoord en inzichtelijk vormgegeven een aansprekende betekenis voor elke doelgroep.

Met wie ook wordt gecommuniceerd, Stern doet het op het gewenste niveau.

VREEMDE VOGEL IN HET COMMUNICATIEBEDRIJF

De naam van het bureau van Jan Willem den Hartog en Alex de Vries is onder meer afgeleid van de naam van de al langer bestaande uitgeverij 'De Zwaluw' van Jan Willem den Hartog waarin hij zelfstandige uitgaven onderbrengt. Maar waarom heeft Den Hartog in 1993 zijn kleine uitgeverij zo genoemd? Het eerste boek dat hij opnam in het fonds van de uitgeverij was 'Architectuur & Mimesis 1989-1992' van Han Janselijn. Deze kunstenaar had een fraai tekeningetje van een zwaluw gemaakt dat Den Hartog als logo wilde gebruiken. Janselijn gaf daarvoor toestemming, maar vreemd genoeg is het in die eerste uitgave niet terug te vinden, wel een zwaan en een merel. Het logo duikt voor het eerst op in de derde uitgave van De Zwaluw: 'Liederen uit Middeleeuwen en Renaissance' van Rudy Bremer uit 1997.

Toen in februari 2001 Den Hartog en De Vries besloten vanaf 1 september van dat jaar te gaan samenwerken was de bureaunaam meteen het onderwerp van een briefwisseling. Vrij associërend kwam Alex de Vries uit op een samentrekking van Ekster en Stern, om zo het bureau Ekstern te kunnen worden. Den Hartog maakte bezwaar, 'omdat de ekster een klotevogel is'. De Vries deelde die aversie niet, had wel sympathie voor het beestje, vooral vanwege de plot van het Kuifje-album 'De juwelen van Bianca Castafiore' uit 1963, waarin de hoofdpersonen naar aanleiding van de verdwijning van de juwelen van de legendarische zangeres de vreselijkste scenario's bedenken en er allerlei onzalige verwikkelingen zijn, met name ook door verkeerd doorverbonden telefoontjes van en met Slagerij Van Kampen en een kapotte traptrede in huize Moolensloot. Uiteindelijk vindt Kuifje de juwelen terug in het nest van een ekster, die al in het tweede plaatje van de strip te zien is.

Later bleek de kwalificatie 'klotevogel' toch passend, toen op Internet een vreemd bericht van 28 december 2000 werd ontdekt: 'Eerdere berichten op Eurobirdnet leerden ons dat er bij Den Oever vier zwarte sterns en twee witvleugelsterns overwinteren. Helaas is er gisteren (27 dec.) een zwarte stern naar het Rijk der Doden gepikt door een moordlustige ekster. De ongelukkige zwarte stern bleek al verzwakt en was niet opgewassen tegen het voortdurende gebeuk op zijn kop. De tragedie duurde ongeveer 10 minuten. Toen was het arme beest dood en de ekster gevlogen. Overigens, de adulte witvleugelstern was nog aanwezig en kwam om het kwartier even buurten in de haven. Van de andere sternoverwinteraars geen spoor.' Aldus Harvey van Diek, medewerker communicatie van Sovon Vogelonderzoek Nederland.

Daarop kwam van birdwatcher Rob Kloosterman de volgende reactie: 'Harvey van Diek schrijft in zijn bericht over een "vermoorde zwarte stern". "De stern is door een ekster vermoord", aldus luidt het ethisch oordeel. Het blijkt niet om een zwarte stern te gaan, maar dat is hier niet zo relevant. Het gaat mij om de op menselijk gedrag betrokken gedachte dat het hier een criminele daad van een vogel betreft, want dat willen wij zeggen met de term "moord".

Moord is bij ons moreel verwerpelijk, maar wij kunnen ons afvragen of dieren morele afwegingen maken. Maar ook indien dit bevestigend te beantwoorden is, dan zijn die afwegingen niet noodzakelijkerwijs zoals die van mensen. Vaak hebben mensen een probleem met predator gedrag. Maar dat is selectief. Van sommige dieren kunnen wij het accepteren, van andere niet. Zaagbekken, om maar wat te noemen in dit jaargetijde, blijven gespaard. Vermoorden die ook vissen? Bij de vogels moeten vooral kraai-achtigen het ontgelden. Mythevorming en verguizing volgt. Kijken wij ook naar de vos, wolf, jakhals en vele andere soorten. Een logische verklaring voor die selectiviteit, in dit geval van vogelaars, kan ik niet vinden...'

Vanwege Den Hartogs bezwaren tegen de ekster en het feit dat de Stern ook wel 'zeezwaluw' wordt genoemd, kiest het duo voor de bureaunaam Stern, een naam die nog niet door enig ander communicatiebureau wordt gebruikt. Onderzoek leert dat er wel een textielophaalorganisatie in Nijmegen onder de naam Stichting Stern werkt en dat de Stern Groep zich bezighoudt met autobedrijven, autodiensten en benzinestations (verwachte stijging per winstaandeel in 2001 5 tot 10 procent), dat zich in Epe het Restaurant Stern bevindt, dat in de zeilsport de Sternklasse een begrip is, dat tal van beroemdheden Stern als achternaam hebben (Isaac Stern, Howard Stern), dat er tijdens de Tweede Wereldoorlog een bedenkelijke zionistische organisatie onder de naam Stern Gang (naar de oprichter Yaïr Stern) opereerde, dat een Amerikaanse flipperautomatenproducent Stern Pinball Incorporate heet, dat de architect Robert Stern betrokken zou zijn bij een voorgenomen herinrichting van de Arnhemse binnenstad, dat in de Max Havelaar van Multatuli het Ernest Stern is, de zoon van Ludwig Stern een Hamburgse zakenrelatie van Droogstoppel, die het beroemde 'pak van Sjaalman' tot een boek zal bewerken en dat in de vogelfamilie Stern een echt vreemde vogel in de hoedanigheid van de Inca Stern voorkomt en dat de latijnse naam van de Koningsstern Sterna maxima is en natuurlijk dat een beroemd Duits weekblad Der Stern heet, maar de letterlijke vertaling daarvan is toch echt De Ster en niet De Stern.

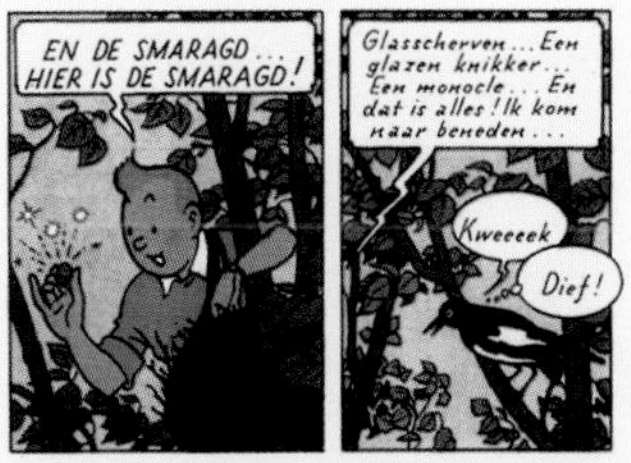

Uit: Hergé – Kuifje, De juwelen van Bianca Castafiore, uitg. Casterman

STERN DHDV

EEN ABONNEMENT IS VOORDELIGER

Het is misschien even wennen, maar ook voor alle diensten op het gebied van communicatie kunt u of uw organisatie een abonnement afsluiten. En dat is natuurlijk voordeliger dan het aanschaffen van losse nummers. Vul onderstaande bon in en u ontvangt vrijblijvend alle informatie inclusief de tarieven en voorwaarden.

Graag ontvang ik informatie over de mogelijkheden van een communicatie-abonnement bij Stern/Den Hartog & De Vries

NAAM ORGANISATIE ....

CONTACTPERSOON ....

STRAAT ....

POSTCODE .... PLAATS ....

TELEFOON .... E-MAIL ....

Stuur deze bon in een gesloten enveloppe naar:
Stern / Den Hartog & De Vries
Amsterdamseweg 21
6814 GA Arnhem

010920 016814

Inderdaad:

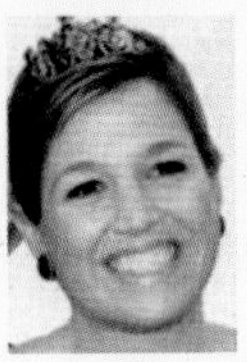

Sterna Maxima

OFWEL—DE KONINGSSTERN

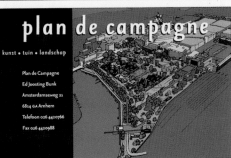

plan de campagne

kunst • tuin • landschap

Plan de Campagne
Ed Joosting Bunk
Amsterdamseweg 21
6814 GA Arnhem
Telefoon 026 4420766
Fax 026 4420988

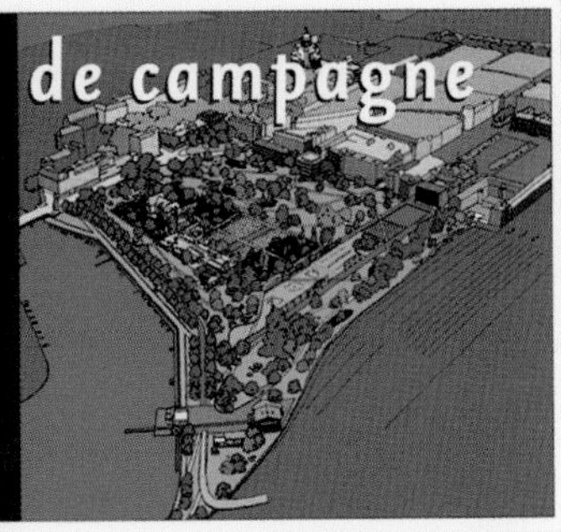

DOVER PUBLICATIONS

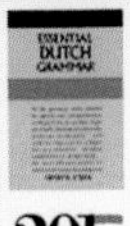

Essential Dutch Grammar
BY HENRY R. STERN
'A Great Buy'

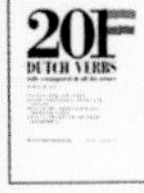

201 Dutch Verbs
BY HENRY R. STERN
Fully Conjugated in All the Tenses

SCHWALBE & CO
FILATELIE
ORGANISATIE VAN BESLOTEN VEILINGEN
FAX 026 3513297

FF SOUPBONE Bruce Alcock, 1993
FF Soupbone was originally designed on a Mac Classic, using a mouse to draw each letter-form in the original (regular) weight. Slowly. Although it was designed to look like handwriting done with a marker, Soupbone was entirely made in the computer. The Bold, Extra Bold, and most of the dingbats were made with a Wacom tablet. The whole process took about three years, amid other projects.

FF SPONTAN Manfred Klein, 1991
FF Spontan was one of the first handwriting fonts following the ground-breaking FF Hands package. Its style is completely different, and recalls ancient Greek inscriptions.

FF STEEL Fabrizio Schiavi, 1995
According to Schiavi FF Steel is 'a whole family of typefaces that arose from a study completed in April of 1993 about type and its application in context. In this study I tried to create a script that was compatible with a context of techno music. Originally I used an old brush and a strong sheet of paper to obtain very incised, trash-like lines. FF Steel String and FF Steel Mix come from this process. FF Steel Jones was born later, made to make evident the healthy structure, or better said, the 'steel construction' of this work of type.'

FF STONED Theo Nonnen, 1996
The modular type system FF Stoned is made up of 15 fonts: the basis font FF Stoned Normal, an overlay font FF Stoned Scratches, and 13 ornamental fonts. FF Stoned is a family to construct things with. Rules, borders and mosaics can be built using repetitive patterns of abstract characters. During the design of FF Stoned, Theo Nonnen was assisted by Barbara Schmitt, Caroline Berger and Susanne Curlott.

FF STRADA Albert Pinggera, 2002
As a designer specialised in complex typographic projects, Italian designer Albert Pinggera naturally opportunities of variation; the additional condensed version allows for economical typesetting without loss of legibility. FF Strada is well suited for setting bilingual text – especially forms – because of its legible, strong Italic, which can be used as a secondary text face.

FF SUBVARIO | FF SUBMONO Steffen Sauerteig | Kai Vermehr, 1998
Two more pixel-font packages from eBoy. FF SubVario and FF SubMono. Both are optimized for 24 pt at a resolution of 72 dpi. As with all PostScript fonts, the Sub families are fully scaleable on screen and in print.

FF SUPER GROTESK Svend Smital, 1999
Super Grotesk, a 1930s face by Arno Drescher, was the Futura of post-war East Germany. Based on showings in specimen books and East German printing, Svend Smital's FF Super Grotesk is a revival with a number of additions.Smital designed an alternative set, with a two-storey lowercase 'a' and 'g' and oldstyle figures. A third version includes a number of wonderfully crafted ligatures.

FF TAG TEAM (FF MARKER) Thomas Marecki, 1994
Thomas about FF Tag Team and graffiti art: 'The illegal typography on façades in big cities today is rarely given recognition, although it offers a

lot of creativity and playfulness with forms. The delinquency and petty damage associated with this form of expression gets in the way of appreciating its real value.'

FF TARQUINIUS Norbert Reiners, 1995–1997
The typeface family FF Tarquinius is based on a calligraphic alphabet drawn with a quill. In the digital font, the original style of writing has been maintained. Serifs appear only where there are connecting links between the letters in the original handwriting. FF Tarquinius Book is a slightly heavier and wider version made to set longer texts at small point sizes as well as at 12pt.

FF TARTINE Xavier Dupré, 2002
Xavier Dupré: 'I designed Tartine and Jambono in 2000-2001 when I worked as type designer in a packaging design agency in Paris. I just wanted to have a complete font up my sleeve when I need to design a logo for someone.'

FF TIBERE Albert Boton, 2003
The typeface Tibere is based on the Capitalis Monumentalis of the Roman empire, unique in its classical beauty and still the base of many of our Latin letters today.

FF TICKET Daniel Fritz, 2000
FF Ticket recreates the look of thermal printer type as found on tickets, luggage tags, forms, etc. The font is based on a modular system.

FF TOKYO Neville Brody, 1993
On March 20, 1988, Mike Tyson successfully defended his world championship title against Tony Tubbs. The poster for the event at the Tokyo Dome was designed by Neville Brody. The alphabets which Brody hand-drew for the poster were completed and digitized into ten fonts. All three typefaces have a number of alternate fonts, which can be mixed and (in Tokyo's case) layered.

FF TRADEMARKER Critzler, 1999
FF TradeMarker began as a 'remix' of Serpentine Bold. After much use on record sleeves, flyers and logos, and some test prints Critzler realized that words written in the face seemed to be instant logos, and this is what inspired the name. From the Bold weight he developed a Light version, no longer strictly oriented around Serpentine. The two weights differ in many ways but can be combined to great effect. Critzler's TradeMarker is a contemporary alternative to the much-used Serpentine.

FF TRANSIT MetaDesign | BVG, 1997
FF Transit was originally developed at MetaDesign for the Berlin public transport company BVG. Based on the Frutiger typeface, it is a freshly drawn, narrow version with many variants made for rigorous applications in a complex signage system. *Front* and *Back* are designed to compensate for the visual distortion that appears on illuminated signs which are either backlit or lit from the front. The typefaces also compensate for the text being displayed as negative text (white text on a dark background). The five *Transit Print* fonts were optimized for the design of printed matter.

Mm FF STONED SD.

↑
FontCard for FF Stoned, Theo Nonnen, FSI 1996.

FontCard for FF Steel, Fabrizio Schiavi, 1995.

KidsZone, a German children's magazine about games, headlines: FF Trademarker. Computec Media.

↗↗
The Barcelona design studio Enric Jardí used FF Super Grotesk in their cover designs for a series of literary paperbacks.

↗↗
Bookcover with FF Ticket. MvB

↗
Fictitious train ticket made with FF Ticket. JS

⟶
Invitation to an exhibition at the Pierre Léotard gallery in Paris, France. Designed by Pierre Léotard with FF Tibere.

Packaging made with FF Tartine, Black & Gold, Paris.

Forsythe evolution Fate of the individual

Fate of the individual
Helen Forsythe

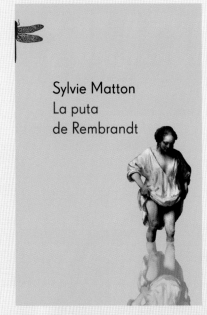

Sylvie Matton
La puta
de Rembrandt

Billet   PARIS GARE LYON ⇄ LYON PART DIEU
A composter avant l'acces au train   AUGENDRE/XA
01 ADULTE

Dep 11/06 à 09H00 de Paris Gare Lyon   Classe 2 VOIT 08:PLACE
Arr   à 10H55 à Lyon Part Dieu   N067
                                         01 ASSIS NON FUM
Periode normale   TGV 6675   DUPLEX:EN HAUT 01 COULOIR
Carte 12-35 A presenter

Dep   à   de***   Classe***
Arr   à   à

Pris per voyageur 27.00   Prix EUR   **27.00
                                              FRR   ** 177.11
CJ33 KM513   :DV 3890ßß2745
27.00   :CA   14758 1675
BD PN 4563890ßß2745   :500467   CVRI
                                         Dossier QQGHASK Page 1/1

JSYSMA45738920

Le Voyage à Belle-Isle

Photographies 1890-1907

Auray, Carnac, Quiberon, Belle-Isle-en-Mer, Houat, Hoëdic

Collection Yannick Guimond et Fonds Louis Lacombe

Louis Lacombe, Le Palais, Belle-Isle, le 25 juillet 1907

Exposition

du 20 au 31 mai 2003 du mardi au samedi inclus
de 15 h à 19 h, le mercredi jusqu'à 20 h.

ATELIER-GALERIE PIERRE LÉOTARD, 49 RUE DE LA FOLIE-MÉRICOURT, PARIS IIe

Personal gain foiled
after several mines
FF Turmino Medium, Extra Bold

ABCDEFGHIJKLMNOPQRSTUVWXYZ 0123456789 $¢£€
abcdefghijklmnopqrstuvwxyz 0123456789 (&?!@)

Flexible plowing jargon mag
existentially corpuscle mint
Spending shortfall reaches
plethora Chimney guffaw
My gourmet raisin bread
luxuriate timber stamps
FF Turmino Light, Normal, Medium, Bold, Extra Bold, Black

FF Scribble Regular
FF Scribble Scrawl
ff SCRIBBLE UNITED
FF Scribble Less One + Two

Liebig
Velouté
de Cèpes
A la Crème Fraîche
SANS COLORANT NI CONSERVATEUR

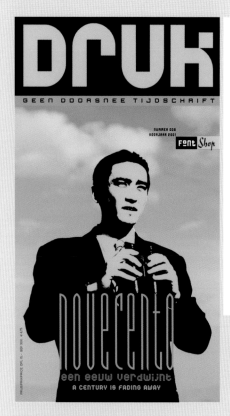

FF TRIXIE Erik van Blokland, 1991
Contrary to popular belief, Trixie was not the name of a typewriter but of the typewriter's owner, a friend's girlfriend in Berlin. To van Blokland, its letters represented the essence of seasoned typewriter type. He digitized its output in various grades of muckiness.

FF TROMBO Andreas Jung, 1995
FF Trombo was designed while the typographer Jonathan Barnbrook was a visiting professor at the Academy in Stuttgart. Barnbrook assigned Jung's class the project of designing 100 typefaces in one week. Jung produced one face, taking a longer period of time – that was FF Trombo. Its name comes from one of Jung's favorite hobbies: playing the trombone...

FF TRONIC Hyun Cho, 2003
The letterforms we take for granted as headers on faxes and on transmission verification reports served as inspiration for Hyun Cho's FF Tronic. Hyun Cho is an art director in Seoul, South Korea. He studied graphic design at the Yale University School of Art and obtained a BFA in visual communication design at the Kyung Won University. He has won several design awards in the US, Korea and Germany. The work on his first FontFont typeface FF Tronic was done together with his friend Min Choi, also a Korean graphic designer.

FF TURMINO Ole Schäfer, 2002
Created for magazine and newspaper headlines, FF Turmino is probably the first typeface that inverts the usual relation between weight and width. In other words: the heavier the font the more condensed it is. When using the family for newspapers or magazines it is now possible for the first time ever to set more text in Black than in Normal or Light. The result is a happy little family that helps to create a tasteful magazine spread as well as a loud front page.

FF TYPEFACE 4, 6 & 7 Neville Brody, 1991–1992
In the mid-1980s, Brody created around a dozen alphabets for use in his magazine and music designs. Typeface Four was drawn for The Face in 1985. Typeface Six and Seven were the light and bold version of a caps-only alphabet made in 1986. When completing these typefaces for inclusion in the FontFont series, Brody added a middle weight, Typeface Six-point-Five.

FF TYPESTAR Steffen Sauerteig, 1998
FF Typestar is a collection of five unaffected fonts for the working world - the classic typewriter meeting the demands of modern communication. The four basic weights offer everything necessary for office communication and the OCR variation is a monospaced alternative for more mechanical moments.

FF UNIT Erik Spiekermann | Christian Schwartz, 2003
FF Unit is the grown-up, no-nonsense sister of FF Meta. The puppy fat is gone, along with it went some curves, and the shapes are tighter. While FF Meta has always been a little out of line and not exactly an over-engineered typeface, FF Unit is less outspoken and more disciplined. FF Unit is not cold, just cool: no redundant ornaments, just a lot of character. The tighter shapes make it suitable for big headlines that can be set tight. Smaller sizes benefit from the increased contrast between vertical and horizontal strokes and open spacing.

FF WORLD Neville Brody, 1993
On March 20, 1988, Mike Tyson successfully defended his world championship title against Tony Tubb. The poster for the event at the Tokyo Dome was designed by Neville Brody. The alphabets which Brody hand-drew for the poster were completed and digitized into ten fonts. All three typefaces have a number of alternate fonts, which can be mixed and (in Tokyo's case) layered.

FF WUNDERLICH Martin Wunderlich, 1993
Designed by Martin Wunderlich from Kiel in Germany, FF Wunderlich is a text font similar in feel to Rotis, but which adds a dynamism based on the difference between the inner and outer outlines of each character.

FF YOKKMOKK Elke Herrnberger, 1993
The typefaces were made during the junior FUSE project at the FachHochschule Düsseldorf, Germany.

FF ZAPATA Erik van Blokland, 1997
Erik van Blokland is fascinated by nineteenth-century Americana. FF Zapata is based on various wide slab serifs from the era of metal and wood type. These 'Antiques' were widely used as display faces on posters, advertisements, even invoices. Every Antique was a new interpretation of an existing genre. And so is FF Zapata: an original, digital Antique that does not imitate a specific model.

FF ZINE Ole Schäfer, 2001
Berlin designer Ole Schäfer specialises in large families of business-like text faces. FF Zine is a case in point: three sub-families (Sans, Serif and Slab), five weights each, and two types of numerals. As the name indicates, FF Zine is meant for editorial design, mainly as a face for headlines and subheads. Art directors often have trouble finding matching fonts in different styles. A dedicated display font that offers three subtly different 'atmospheres' was called for.

FF ZWO Jörg Hemker, 2002.
FF Zwo is based on a constructivistic system which was abandoned over time in favour of functionality. The final result is a very legible and clear typeface. The family has 8 weights from Extra Light to Black, each with Plain, Italic, Small Caps and Small Caps Italic. Each font has lining figures and experts. There is also an Alternative version for each font with different figures, some optional lower case letters, and special characters. They are especially suitable for headlines and short texts. The main aim was to combine formal discretion and subtle irony.

Credits
MvB: Mark van Bronkhorst
GP: Gordon Protz
JS: Julia Sysmäläinen
JM: Jan Middendorp

KONTRAPUNKT
DIE ARCHITEKTUR VON DANIEL LIBESKIND
EINE AUSSTELLUNG IM JÜDISCHEN MUSEUM BERLIN

Jüdisches Museum Berlin

JOHN MILLHAUSER
ART DIRECTION

213.200.1792 · www.justmyname.com · john@justmyname.com

Cover of the '20th Century Issue' of *Druk*, FontShop Benelux's promotional magazine (2001). Apart from the word 'Shop' (Reiner Script) all typefaces used are FontFonts by Neville Brody: FF World, FF Gothic and FF Typeface Four. JM

Publications for Sennheiser sound equipment, designed by Gramm Werbeagentur GmbH, Düsseldorf (Germany) with a special version of FF Zwo. Sound of Silence: brochure for pilot's headphones which have special noise compensation for relaxed flying.

Poster for the Jewish Museum, Berlin, designed by Grappa-Blotto, 2003. Typeface: FF Typestar.

Poster for the Public Theater, New York, designed in 2000 by Paula Scher (Pentagram NY) with FF Typestar.

Card designed by Ian Lynam with FF Zapata.

Neville Brody typefaces based on his hand-rendered alpabets from the 1980s.

Reza Abedini is a leading figure of the current new wave in Iranian graphic design. Abedini is an award-winning poster designer, art director and set designer. He has been the managing director and editor-curator of several magazines and exhibitions on Iranian visual culture. He was a teacher at the Teheran Fine Arts School and Azad University. His 2006 book *New visual culture of modern Iran*, edited and designed in collaboration with Dutch designer Hans Wolbers, presents an overview of the graphic art and design scene in his country.
Reza Abedini designed the FF Magda and FF DuDuchamp specimens

Vincent van Baar is a design director at Studio Dumbar in Rotterdam, the Netherlands. He is a collector of typographic rarities, industrial catalogues and mechanical computing devices. He was art director of *Zeezucht*, the magazine created by Studio Dumbar for the Zeebelt theatre in The Hague; he is the driving force behind Zefir7, a long-standing series of monthly design lectures in that same theatre organized in cooperation with the BNO (Association of Dutch Designers). Vincent van Baar was co-editor of *Emigre* #25, the legendary Dutch issue of the magazine. One of his present tasks at Studio Dumbar is art directing the Dutch design magazine *Items*.
Vincent van Baar designed the FF Hydra specimen

Patrick Baglee is a copywriter and type enthusiast. He chaired the Typographic Circle for three years, edited its multi-award winning magazine *Circular*, and is the founder and chairperson of 4Designers, an annual student conference held in London and New York. His writing on design and typography has been published in *Eye, U&lc, Graphis, Blueprint, Etapes Graphiques, Design Week* and *Creative Review*. He has won Cannes, D&AD, Type Directors Club, Precision Marketing, Campaign Digital and Clio awards and has judged writing, interactive design and digital craft at D&AD. Patrick was a member of the MetaDesign team on the Glasgow project. He is the son of a compositor, and lives and works in London.
Patrick Baglee wrote the article about the design of FF Govan

Johanna Balušíková-Biľak is a designer based in the Netherlands since 1999. She is a partner at *Typotheque.com*, which published her debut typeface *Jigsaw* and a series of limited edition t-shirts. Currently focused on cultural collaborative projects, she is a co-author of the *e-a-t (experiment and typography)* exhibition and the publication *We Want You To Love Type*, both of which explore Czech and Slovak work since 1985.
Johanna Balušíková designed the FF Eureka specimen

John D. Berry is an editor/typographer who works both sides of the design/content divide. He is the former editor and publisher of *U&lc (Upper and lower case)* and of *U&lc Online*. He edited the book *Language Culture Type: international type design in the age of Unicode* (ATypl/Graphis, 2002), and he was both editor and designer of *U&lc: influencing design & typography* (Mark Batty Publisher, 2005) and *Contemporary Newspaper Design: Shaping the news in the digital age: typography & image on modern newsprint* (Mark

Batty Publisher, 2004). John has a deep and eclectic background in both writing/editing and typography; he has made a career for more than twenty-five years in Seattle, New York, and San Francisco as an editor and book designer. He writes and consults extensively on typography, and he has won numerous awards for his book designs. He lives in Seattle with the writer Eileen Gunn.
John D. Berry wrote the article about FF Profile

Peter Biľak was born in Czechoslovakia and now works in The Netherlands as a graphic designer and type designer. In 1999 he started his type foundry Typotheque. In 2000, he co-founded DOT DOT DOT magazine. Since 2004, he has created a number of performances with the dancer Lukas Timulak.
Peter Biľak designed the FF Masterpiece page

Evert Bloemsma
Dutch type designer Evert Bloemsma studied graphic design at the Arnhem Academy of Art and graduated in 1981. He spent three years in Hamburg working for URW, where he digitzed his first typeface, Balance, then moved to Venlo to work for the hardware manufacturer Océ. He returned to Arnhem, where he worked as an independent type designer, teacher, architectural photographer, typographer and writer. He designed four FontFont families: FF Balance, FF Avance, FF Cocon and FF Legato. Evert Bloemsma died in April, 2005.
Evert Bloemsma interviewed Hans Reichel, the designer of FF Dax, FF Schmalhans, FF Sari and FF Routes

Erik van Blokland studied Graphic and Typographic Design at the Royal Academy of Fine Arts (KABK) in The Hague, Holland. While working at MetaDesign Berlin, Erik struck up a collaboration with Just van Rossum under the name LettError. Having experimented with computer programming in connection to type design, they came up with Beowolf, the first typeface with a mind of its own. It was released by FontShop in July, 1990. After stints at several places in the world, including David Berlow's FontBureau, Erik van Blokland settled in The Hague as an independent designer, working together separately with Van Rossum. Their work now includes type design, illustration, magazines, corporate design, interactive design, animation, music, and websites. In collaboration with several colleagues and family members, they created two suites of programs and scripts for type design, RoboFog and RoboFab.
Erik van Blokland and Just van Rossum wrote 'Is best really better?';
Erik contributed new illustrations to Emily King's LettError article

Alexander Branczyk. For seven years, Alexander Branczyk worked at MetaDesign, where he was among the first users of the Meta typeface and designed the black-and-yellow FontShop identity with Erik Spiekermann. In 1994 he founded xplicit Gesellschaft für visuelle Kommunikation mbH (xplicit. de) with Thomas Nagel and Uwe Otto. He began designing type while working as art director of the music magazine *Frontpage* (1992–1997). Branczyk was one of the initiators of the experimental Type Collaboratorium Typeface2face.com and was co-editor of the book *Emotional–Digital* about the international type design scene. He designed

numerous corporate fonts for German firms and recently worked as a guest professor of Typography at the Bauhaus-Universität Weimar.
Alexander Branczyk art-directed the FF Meta specimen, a collective xplicit creation

Jon Coltz describes himself as 'an enthusiastic interloper in the field of typography'. He occasionally writes about type on his weblog, called daidala, and he serves on the Board of Directors of the Society of Typographic Aficionados. A lifelong resident of Minneapolis, Jon trained in neuroscience at the University of Minnesota and currently works as a statistician for a large food company. Jon is an unabashed fan of FontFonts, particularly FF Kievit.
Jon Coltz interviewed FF Alega designer Siegfried Rückel and FF Kievit designer Mike Abbink, and designed the FF Kievit specimens

Alan Daastrup was born in Denmark; his interest in calligraphy was sparked at the age of 15 by the vivid lettering and graphics of the 1980s heavy metal scene. Pursuing his interest in calligraphy he moved to England, where he later graduated from Roehampton Institute, London, with a BA Hons. in Calligraphy. Between 1999 and 2002 he lived in Barcelona, working mainly in areas of book design, as well as teaching typography and calligraphy. He was also the initiator and co-founder of the digital newsletter, TypoRed. He is currently working as a book designer, lettering artist and typographic consultant.
Allan Daastrup interviewed FF Celeste and FF Parable designer Christopher Burke

Antje Dohmann graduated in Applied Cultural Studies in Lüneburg. With short interruptions, caused by Jonathan (born in 1994), Julius (1997) and Erik (2004), she has worked for the German trade magazine *PAGE* since 1992, where her main job is to write and edit articles on type and typography.
Antje Dohmann wrote the articles about Ole Schäfer s typefaces FF Zine and FF Fago

Susanna Dulkinys is an interdisciplinary designer. 24 years of design experience have resulted in international work in corporate design, branding, publication design, motion graphics, packaging and most recently product design. Susanna is a partner of UDN | United Designers Network which she founded with Erik Spiekermann in 2001. UDN has offices in Berlin, San Francisco and London and works on large corporate design systems for clients like Bosch and DB, the German railway. Her work continues with building a luxury chocolate brand in San Francisco, California. Other recent projects include design concepts for CNN International's on-air graphics, a complete overhaul of the on-air graphics for Germany's n-tv, and a product line of clocks based on Buckminster Fuller's Dymaxion map. Susanna divides her time between Berlin and San Francisco.
Susanna Dulkinys designed the FF Unit specimen

eBoy are Steffen Sauerteig, Svend Smital and Kai Vermehr. The Berlin studio is specialized in pixel illustrations; apart from typefaces reflecting this low-res aesthetics, they created typographically sophisticated fonts such as FF Typestar and FF Super Grotesk.
Eboy created the eBoy pages

Yanek Iontef was born in the USSR and at the age of 16 moved to Israel, where he studied graphic design at Bezalel Academy of Art and Design, Jerusalem. He worked as a graphic designer in London and as a Senior Designer at Metamark International, Tel Aviv. Since 1995 he has taught typography and type design at the Bezalel Academy. He currently works in Tel Aviv as a freelance designer specializing in type design, corporate identity and editorial design. A TDC2 award-winning type designer, he also has his own type foundry, producing a range of Hebrew and Latin fonts.
Yanek Iontef designed the FF Cartonnage page

Verena Gerlach, art director and typographer, was born in Berlin. She was an instructor of photography at the Hochschule der Künste in Berlin in 1991 and spent 1992 doing a first-year course at Glasgow School of Art. From 1993 to 1998 she studied communication design at Kunsthochschule Berlin Weißensee and spent two terms as an exchange student at the London College of Printing. Since 1999 Verena Gerlach has been running her own studio for graphic design and typography in Berlin. She has worked as a lecturer in type design and typography at designakademie berlin since 2003.
Verena Gerlach designed the pages about her typefaces FF CST (designed with Ole Schäfer) and FF Karbid

Born in Valencia (Spain), **Pepe Gimeno** has been working as a graphic designer and communications designer for over 30 years. He is a member of the Type Directors Club of New York, and was the subject of an extensive monograph published by Experimenta Ediciones de Diseño and a 2004 exhibition at the IVAM, Valencian Institute of Modern Art.
Pepe Gimeno designed the page presenting his FF Pepe

Martin Kahrmann is an independent typographer and typesetter working in Berlin. Until his late twenties he tried many different jobs, from 2-star cuisine best boy to banana plantation worker. Having decided to switch to pre-print in the early 1990s, he trained as a professional typesetter and added a BA in Graphic Design at Central Saint Martin's in London. Since then he worked as a freelance designer for design and advertising companies in London, Hamburg, Munich and Berlin for a living; and beautiful but commercially useless visuals, furniture and pottery for the fun of it.
Martin Kahrmann designed the useless but beautiful FF Fago specimen

Lukas Kircher was born in Austria in 1971 and studied at the High School of Applied Arts in Vienna. He designed numerous newspapers and magazines in Germany, Austria and other European countries. His Berlin-based company KircherBurkhardt is specialized in editorial design and corporate publishing. Lukas Kircher is a member of the German Art Directors Club and the Lead Awards, and is still searching for a good Austrian café in Berlin.
Lukas Kircher designed the FF Balance specimen in the shape of a beer magazine frontpage

Emily King studied design history in London, first at the Royal College of Art and later at Kingston University. She wrote her MA thesis

on the design of film title sequences from the 1950s and 60s and her PhD on the design of type in the digital age. Recently she has divided her time between writing and curating. She edited the recent Peter Saville monograph and has just completed a biography of the influential graphic designer Robert Brownjohn. Her exhibitions include The Book Corner, an exhibition of book design curated for the British Council, and the graphic design sections of the London Design Museum's 2003 and 2005 European Design Shows. She is a regular contributor to international design magazines including *Print* and *Grafik* and is also the Design Editor of *Frieze* magazine.
Emily King wrote the articles about LettError and Max Kisman

Barbara Klunder is an internationally known illustrator and graphic designer from Canada. In her 25-year career of theatre, music and making posters for good causes, she's also designed and crafted carpets, jewellery and sweaters. When FSI approached her to digitise and create fonts based on her unique scripts style, she enlisted the help of PageActive, a creative integration service in Toronto.
Barbara Klunder designed the pages showing FF Klunder Script and FF Ottofont

Akira Kobayashi studied at Musashino Art University in Tokyo and later went to London to study calligraphy at London College of Printing. Between 1983 and 1997 he worked as a type designer at several Japanese companies. From 1997 until 1991 he was a freelance type designer and a teacher in Tokyo. In 2001 he was appointed Type Director at Linotype GmbH. Since then, Akira Kobayashi collaborated with Hermann Zapf and Adrian Frutiger in creating new versions of some of these designer's most classic typefaces.
Akira Kobayashi wrote the article about the making of FF Clifford

Dennis Koot is a designer working at Studio Dumbar since his graduation in 2000. He loves to work on a range of different kinds of projects. One of these projects is designing the Dutch bi-monthly design magazine *Items*. His designs for the magazine's covers won the team a Red Dot Award. Since september 2005 Dennis Koot has taught at the Willem de Kooning Academie in Rotterdam. He is also a member of dj-duo UNISECS. They play art-pop.
Dennis Koot designed the multi-specimen 'Jackie'

Alessio Leonardi is a communication designer, typographer, writer, publisher and father, as well as a cook and artist in his leisure time. He was one of the initiators of Leonardi. Wollein design agency and the founder of the typeface label and online shop BuyMyFonts.com. He recently founded the company Lion & Bee with his wife, fellow-designer Imme Leonardi. Having a natural penchant for reflection and philosophy, he has contributed to several international design magazines, and wrote, designed and published the ultimate history of the alphabet, *From the Cow to the Typewriter*. At the annual type conference TypoBerlin, he suceeded Erik Spiekermann in his role of MC.
Alessio Leonardi designed the pages about his own FontFonts, as well as the FF Acanthus, FF Cellini and FF Danubia specimens.

Yang Liu, born in Beijing, obtained a master graduate in Visual Communication at the University of the Arts, Berlin. Worked as a designer in London (Omnific/TM&Co), Berlin (TM&Co), and New York (Chermayeff & Geismar Inc). Won several awards for her poster designs: the Red Dot Award 2003, the Bronze Medal at the Poster Biennale in Warsaw, a Certificate of Excellence at the TDC, New York. In 2004 and 2005 she was a guest professor for Communications Design at the Central Academy of Fine Art in Beijing. Currently she lives and works in Berlin and Beijing.
Yang Liu designed the FF Trombo and FF Tronic specimens

Ellen Lupton is a writer, curator, and graphic designer. She is director of the MFA program in graphic design at Maryland Institute College of Art (MICA) in Baltimore. She also is curator of contemporary design at Cooper-Hewitt National Design Museum in New York City, where she has organized numerous exhibitions, each accompanied by a major publication, including the National Design Triennial series (2000 and 2003), Skin: Surface, Substance + Design (2002), Graphic Design in the Mechanical Age (1999), Mixing Messages (1996), and Mechanical Brides: Women and Machines from Home to Office (1993). With J. Abbott Miller she co-authored *Design Writing Research: Writing on Graphic Design* (1996). Her most recent book is *Thinking with Type: A Critical Guide for Designers, Writers, Editors and Students* (2004).
Ellen Lupton wrote and designed the FF Scala specimen

Ian Lynam, graphic designer and type designer, operates his own studio in Tokyo. Dividing his time between Japan and the United States, he has also worked as art director and senior designer for design and advertising companies in Portland, Oregon and in Southern California for clients such as Pony, NEC, Virgin, Adidas, Columbia Tristar, Portland Film Festival, MTV and Nike. In 2003 and 2004 he received Adobe Design Achievement Awards. He designed several custom type faces for corporate clients and produced a number of display fonts based on the work of 20th century designers such as Oz Cooper and Piet Zwart.
Ian Lynam interviewed FF Atma designer Alan Greene

Faten Mahmood, originally from Karachi, Pakistan, is a promising graphic design student at the American University in Dubai.
With her Indian fellow student Varsha as a model and Varsha's mother as a consultant, Faten made the photos for the sari demonstration in Laura Meseguer's FF Sari specimen.

Martin Majoor has been designing type since the mid-1980s. In 1988, when working as an in-house designer for the Vredenburg Music Centre in Utrecht, he designed the typeface Scala for use in their printed matter; two years later FSI published FF Scala as the first text face in the FontFont library. In 1994–95 he created the typeface Telefont for the Dutch telephone directories. Majoor's third major typefamily, FF Seria/Seria Sans (2000) won him Certificates of Excellence in the ISTD Awards 2001 and the ATypI-Bukva:raz! Type Design Competition. His recent FF Nexus family (2004) was the winner in the Text Families category of the 2006 Creative Review Type Design Awards. Majoor has taught at several design colleges and lectured at conferences across Europe and in the USA and has written numerous articles on typography. He now works as an independent graphic designer and type designer in both Holland and Poland; since February 2006 he has taught type design and typography at KTR, a private school in Warsaw.
Martin Majoor researched and wrote the article 'The Nexus principle'

Laura Meseguer is a graphic designer and type designer living and working in Barcelona. She was a partner in Cosmic design studio until 2005, when she opened her own studio. She is a member of Type-Ø-Tones, a Barcelona group of type designers which runs its own independent foundry. In 2003–2004, Laura Meseguer took a year off from her regular work to study type design at the post-graduate course 'Type]Media' of the Royal Academy of Arts in The Hague, the Netherlands. Rumba, the typeface she designed as part of this course, was selected in the TDC TypeDesign Competition 2005.
Laura Meseguer designed the FF Market/District, FF Minimum and FF Sari specimens

Jan Middendorp is a Dutch writer and designer. He was the founding editor and art director of the FontShop Benelux magazine *Druk* (1999-2002). His articles on design and typography have been published in *Items, Eye, Typographic, Revue Suisse de l'Imprimerie/TMb, Experimenta, TYPO, tipoGrafica* and *Etapes*. He wrote two historical overviews of Dutch graphic design and type: *'Ha, daar gaat er een van mij!'* ('Hey, there goes one of mine!', on graphic design in The Hague, 2002) and *Dutch Type* (2004). He wrote and designed the award-winning book *Lettered, the alphabets of Clotilde Olyff* (2000) and collaborated on publications about LettError and René Knip. He has designed catalogues for museums and art galleries in Belgium and Holland. He recently moved from Ghent, Belgium to Berlin, Germany.
Jan Middendorp edited this book and wrote several articles, as well as designing the FF Blur, FF Lancé and FF Parable specimens

François Moissette is a young graphic designer from France. He is currently director of graphic design at *Infinirouge,* a design company in Metz. In addition, he is part of a collective called *Images d écritures* and creates postcard ufos with *Lezorangesgivrées*. He recently drew a character for *Building letters* (Fleurons of Hope) and designed the 2005 FontFont calendar page dedicated to typefaces by *Xavier Dupré*, with whom he collaborates on a regular basis. His experimental font *The birth of a Nation* was one of the winners of the 2005 *Fuse Security* type design contest.
François Moissette designed the FF Absara and FF Angkoon specimens

Stephan Müller is a Swiss graphic designer living and working in Berlin. His typeface designs are mostly by-products of design projects. Müller has always been fascinated by applied typography in public spaces traffic signage, airport terminals or shopping centers. Together with Cornel Windlin he published various fonts based on LCD displays, dot matrix printers and car registration plates (FF Dot Matrix, FF Screen Matrix, FF Backstage, FE Mittelschrift). In 1999 Windlin and Müller founded their own font label, lineto.
Stephan Müller designed the pages about his FontFonts and their sources

Albert Pinggera comes from southern Tyrol (or Alto Adige), the German-speaking region in northern Italy. He apprenticed at the typesetting and graphic design department of a newspaper in Bolzano and in 1993 went to Munich where he worked with Gert Wiescher. A year later he moved on to MetaDesign Berlin to assist Luc(as) de Groot in the type department. In 1995 Albert moved to The Hague for the postgraduate course in type design and typography at the Royal Academy of Art. After graduating in 1997 he returned to Northern Italy, and founded the company design.buero in the mountain town of St. Leonhard in Passeier. FF Strada was a winning entry in TDC2 2003 – the Type Directors Club annual type design competition.
Albert Pinggera wrote and designed the FF Strada pages

Albert-Jan Pool studied at the Royal Academy of Arts in The Hague, the Netherlands. Having moved to Germany in 1987, he was Type Director at Scangraphic and manager of Type Design and Production at URW before opening his own studio in Hamburg. He designed two popular FontFont families based on one industrial sans-serifs: FF OCRF and FF DIN. In 1997 he designed his first corporate typeface Jet Set Sans for Jet/Conoco (with Syndicate Brand & Corporate). The next one was C&A Infotype (with Factor Design). During his partnerhip with FarbTon Konzept + Design (1999–2005) he designed a corporate typeface for Hein Gas, a German gas supplier. He co-wrote and designed the book *Branding with Type* (Adobe Press).
Albert-Jan Pool researched and wrote the article about the history of the DIN alphabets

Gordon Protz was born near Berlin. While at secondary school in the early 1990s, he published a secret (and therefore uncensored) satirical pupil's magazine using a Commodore 64, scissors, glue, and a copy shop. He had discovered his fascination for type at an earlier stage, when creating several bitmap fonts on the C64. After fulfilling his civilian service, he did several internships and an apprenticeship as a media designer, a job he is currently holding as a freelancer in Berlin.
Gordon Protz designed the illustrations of the FF Atma article and several other mini-specimens.

Just van Rossum studied Graphic and Typographic Design at the Royal Academy of Fine Arts (KABK) in The Hague, Holland. While working at MetaDesign Berlin, Just struck up a collaboration with Erik van Blokland under the name LetTerRor. Having experimented with computer programming in connection to type design, they came up with Beowolf, the first typeface with a mind of its own. It was released by FontShop in July, 1990. After stints at several places in the world, including David Berlow's FontBureau, but not Adobe, Just van Rossum settled in The Hague and later Haarlem as an independent designer, working together separately with Van Blokland. Their work now includes type design, illustration, magazines, corporate design, interactive design, animation, music, and websites. In collaboration with several

colleagues and family members, they created two suites of programs and scripts for type design, RoboFog and RoboFab.
Erik van Blokland and Just van Rossum wrote 'Is best really better?

Peter De Roy teaches graphic design in Ghent, Belgium. He lives and works near Brussels, where he operates the graphic design studio SignBox with his partner Betty Reyniers. From 2000 onwards, SignBox worked on many publications issued by FontShop Benelux; they art-directed and edited the FontShop magazines *UnderCover* and *96*.
Peter De Roy designed the FF Zine and FF Quadraat specimens

Alex Scholing is a graphic designer and co-founder of the design firm Eat in Amsterdam. His main activity is not making typefaces but doing communication design for clients. According to Scholing, FF Engine and FF Roice are private investigations that got out of hand.
Alex Scholing designed the FF Roice specimen

Piet Schreuders is a Dutch designer, type enthusiast and researcher. He is the founder, editor and designer of two of the Netherlands' best-loved underground magazines, *Furore* and *De Poezenkrant*. He was co-author of *The Beatles' London*, and author of *Paperbacks, U.S.A.*, as well as the controversial (and award-winning) book *Lay In Lay Out*. He is currently the art director of the weekly media guide of Holland's progressive tv and radio organisation VPRO. His most recent book is *The Paperback Art of James Avati*. He lives in Amsterdam.
Piet Schreuders designed the FF Clifford specimen

Christian Schwartz is a New York-based type designer and co-founder of Orange Italic. He has worked at MetaDesign in Berlin and at Font Bureau in Boston. Schwartz specializes in creating custom typefaces for publications and corporate design and has designed commercial typefaces for FontFont, Emigre, Font Bureau, and House Industries. His work has been honored by the New York Type Directors Club, D&AD, and the Smithsonian's Cooper Hewitt National Design Museum.
Christian Schwartz wrote the article about the making of FF Bau

Nick Shinn was born in London in 1952 and has a Dip.AD (Fine Art) from Leeds Polytechnic (1974); he has lived in Toronto since 1976. Initially an ad agency art director, he started a digital design studio in 1988 and launched ShinnType in 1999. Since 1980, he has designed over 20 typefaces. He teaches part time at York University, Toronto, writes frequently for design magazines, and is a director of SOTA, the Society of Typographic Aficionados.
Nick Shinn wrote and designed the FF Oneleigh specimen and the History of FF Fontesque

Jürgen Siebert was editor-in-chief of *Page* magazine and marketing director of FontShop International. He is now FontShop Germany's marketing director. Jürgen is co-author of FSI's type bible, the *FontBook*. He also edits the popular German-language fontblog.de.
Jürgen Siebert wrote the article on FF BerlinSans

Fred Smeijers is a type designer who specializes in typographic research and development for product manufacturers. Born in the Netherlands, Smeijers studied graphic design at the Academy of Art in Arnhem. His first published typeface, FF Quadraat, was launched by FSI in 1992. His work of the 1990s included the expansion of the Quadraat family, type and lettering jobs for Philips, the typefaces TEFF Renard and Romanee, and his book *Counterpunch*. With the award of the Gerrit Noordzij Prize in 2000, Smeijers's achievements in the field of practice, research and education were formally recognized. His book *Type now* was published as part of the award. That year also saw the launch of the label he co-runs: OurType. In 2004 Smeijers was appointed Professor of Digital Typography at the Hochschule für Grafik und Buchkunst, Leipzig.
Fred Smeijers wrote the FF Quadraat article

Viktor Solt-Bittner. After designing pictograms, signs and diagrams at Simlinger Information Design, Viktor Solt-Bittner became a freelance graphic designer in 1996. He designed typefaces for Adobe, ITC and Fontshop. In 2002, together with Petra Kohlmayr, he founded Bonsai Cuts, a studio specializing in animated short films. Viktor Solt-Bittner teaches at the FH Joanneum in Graz. He lives and works in Vienna.
Viktor Solt-Bittner illustrated the FF Danubia article

Erik Spiekermann, co-founder of the FontFont type library, is an information architect and type designer (FF Meta, ITC Officina, FF Info, FF Unit, LoType, Berliner Grotesk plus exclusive typefaces for Bosch, Deutsche Bahn, Nokia *et al*). He founded MetaDesign in 1979 and was Managing Director until he left the company in 2001. Erik holds a professorship at the University of the Arts in Bremen and was recently awarded an honorary doctorate from Art Center College of Design in Pasadena.
He was awarded the Gerrit Noordzij Prize in 2003. He is on the board of the German Design Council and the ATypl and is Past President of the International Institute of Information Design as well as the International Society of Typographic Designers.
Erik Spiekermann runs the United Designers Network in Berlin, London and San Francisco.
Erik Spiekermann co-edited and designed (and typeset!) this book and wrote articles about FF Meta and FF Info

Julia Sysmäläinen from Finland studied philology and graphic design in Helsinki. She is now working for the United Designers Network in Berlin and continuing her studies in the Master's programme of the University of Art and Design, Helsinki. She has worked for the Center of International Mobility CIMO, the City of Helsinki and different design companies in Finland before founding her own 'studio 03'. She won first prizes in the Finnish EU Presidency 2006 visual identity competition and the Finnish Design Year 2006 competition.
Julia Sysmäläinen designed the FF Parango, FF Isonorm, and Cyrillics specimens as well as a number of imaginary tickets

Born in Budapest, **György Szönyei** began his professional career as a window-dresser. From 1973 to 1978 he studied graphic design at the Hungarian Academy of Applied Arts; he has since worked as a typographer, graphic designer, type designer and artist. He writes about art for several periodicals, and teaches graphic design and typography at the Decorator Training College. As a typedesigner, he was awarded the Morisawa prize in the Kanji category of the 1996 Morisawa International Typeface Design Competition. In his spare time, Szönyei collects objects from the 1950s and 60s and plays the bass guitar in a jazz group.
György Szönyei designed the FF Archian pages

Mark Thomson is a British designer and typographer. In the 1990s he was Art Director of Taschen, introducing Scala Sans as the publisher's main typeface. From 1998 to 2003 he was principal of London-based International Design UK, designing and producing many award-winning books for publishers and clients around the world. In 2003 became Art Director of the established British publisher Collins, rebranding the company with Martin Majoor's Nexus as the principal typeface along with types by Fred Smeijers and Peter Bil'ak; in 2005 he also became Corporate Design Director of its parent company HarperCollins. He lives and works in London.
Mark Thomson edited and designed the FF Nexus specimen

Jaap van Triest completed his studies at the Arnhem Academy of Fine Arts in 1981 with a 320-page architecture reader and his publication *Auto* – a documentary / on the Citroëns DS and ID. In 1982 he set up a design practice in Amsterdam. Typefaces by his classmate, friend and teaching colleague Evert Bloemsma made early appearances throughout the 1980s in several publications designed in collaboration with Bloemsma. With Karel Martens he designed and edited two well-known graphic design monographies: *Karel Martens Drukwerk\Printed Matter*, 1996, a winner of Leipzig's Goldene Letter, and *Wim Crouwel – Mode en Module*, 1997. He also works as a teacher of design and typography at the Breda Art Academy and writes on graphic design and printing: in 1997 *Galeislaven en rekentuig*, with Sybrand Zijlstra, and in 2005 *Rollenrotatiedruk in Nederland 1950-2004*, a book on web-printing history and practice he co-published and designed.
Jaap van Triest edited and designed the FF Legato specimen

Tiffany Wardle is a graduate of the BFA Graphic Design program from Brigham Young University and is also a graduate of the MA Theory and History of Typography & Graphic Communication program at the University of Reading. Tiffany is a graphic designer and educator living near Salt Lake City, Utah. She is on the board of the Society of Typographic Aficionados and in her spare time is a moderator online at Typophile.
Tiffany Wardle designed the FF Maiola specimen

Having studied at Weissensee art college in (East) Berlin, **Henning Wagenbreth** is a poster designer and illustrator with a unique, unmistakable style, as well as an award-winning book designer. He is a professor of visual communication at the Berliner Hochschule der Künste. The alphabets he made for his hand-painted identity of the Prater beer garden and restaurant later became FF Prater.
Henning Wagenbreth designed the FF Prater pages

Martin Wenzel is a German-born type and graphic designer. He left Berlin in 1993 to study type and graphic design at the Royal Academy in the Hague. After his study, in 1998, he worked as a designer for Petr van Blokland + Claudia Mens in Delft. Concurrently he worked on freelance projects in corporate design, web interface design, production and typographic work. In 2005 he moved back to Berlin, where he runs his own studio for German and international clientele, MartinPlus.com.
Martin Wenzel designed the FF Profile specimen and wrote and designed the pages about his own typefaces

Wim Westerveld studied at the Arnhem Art Academy. From 1985–92 he worked as a designer for BRS Premsela Vonk – now Eden – and Total Design in Amsterdam, and as a teacher of Typography at the Utrecht Art Academy. In December 1992 he moved to Berlin, where he worked with Thomas Bauer and Max Mönnich (de blik), and Matthias Wittig (fernkopie). He was a guest lecturer on Typography at Art Academies in Germany. Living in Amsterdam since 1999, he continued his contacts with Berlin and co-operation with fernkopie. Presently he is partner at Neon, office for graphic design in Amsterdam.
Wim Westerveld designed the FF Sheriff and FF Letter Gothic specimens in collaboration with Joost van Swieten

Brigitte Willinger has been working as an editor and project manager for Design Austria, the national professional association of designers in Austria, since 1990. She is in charge of the association's publications, such as its newsletter, magazine, catalogues, and special periodicals, including a series on Austrian type designers. Moreover, she is responsible for the organization of design competitions. Apart from her affiliation with Design Austria, she works as a freelance translator specialized in the fields of art and design.
Brigitte Willinger wrote the article on FF Danubia

Ian Wright is an illustrator who lives and works in London. He studied graphic design at the London College of Printing. He is particularly well known for his portraits of musicians which have been used extensively in music packaging and editorial. Ian's work is primarily about responding to different materials and processes. He enjoys working with unexpected materials not readily associated with art and design. He is currently making large wall pieces for Milliken Carpet and Issey Miyake. In addition to his freelance practice Ian also teaches illustration at the University of Brighton.
Ian Wright designed the FF Beadmap page

xplicit ffm, founded in 1994, designs for the printed as well as the 'virtual' world.
With ca. twenty members in Frankfurt and Berlin as well as the media production company xplicit works, the studio covers a wide spectrum of design skills. Its fields of special interest are Corporate Design, type design, exhibition and catalogue design.
xplicit collectively designed the FF Meta specimen

© 2006

FontFont and all font names
in this index are trademarks of
FSI Fontshop International.
All other font names are trademarks
of their respective owners.